Summary of Contents

Funded by
MISSION COLLEGE
Carl D. Perkins Vocational and Technical Education Act Grant

BUILD YOUR OWN WEBSITE THE RIGHT WAY USING HTML & CSS

BY IAN LLOYD
3RD EDITION

Build Your Own Website The Right Way Using HTML & CSS

by Ian Lloyd

Copyright © 2011 SitePoint Pty. Ltd.

Program Director: Lisa Lang   **Editor**: Kelly Steele

Technical Editor: Tom Museth   **Indexer**: Angela Howard

Technical Director: Kevin Yank   **Cover Design**: Alex Walker

Printing History:

First Edition: April 2006

Second Edition: November 2008

Third Edition: July 2011

sitepoint

Published by SitePoint Pty. Ltd.

48 Cambridge Street
Collingwood VIC Australia 3066
Web: www.sitepoint.com
Email: business@sitepoint.com

ISBN 978-0-9870908-5-0 (print)

ISBN 978-0-9870908-8-1 (ebook)
Printed and bound in the United States of America

About Ian Lloyd

Ian Lloyd is a senior web designer/developer who works full time for a major financial services organization in the UK on their various websites. He is the author or co-author of a number of web development books, including SitePoint's *Ultimate HTML Reference*. He has also contributed articles to industry-leading sites such as *A List Apart, Think Vitamin*, and *.net* magazine. Ian has spoken at several high profile web conferences on the topic of web accessibility—including South By Southwest (SXSW) in Austin, Texas and @media in London—and founded one of the earliest online accessibility resources, Accessify (http://accessify.com/), in 2002.

Ian's on Twitter as @lloydi, or you can follow the book's Twitter account that he posts on (albeit less frequently, but on stuff more relevant to this book), which is @byowebsite.

About Tom Museth

Tom Museth first fell in love with code while creating scrolling adventure games in BASIC on his Commodore 64, and then usability testing them on reluctant family members. He then spent 16 years as a magazine writer, newspaper journalist, and production editor before deciding web development would be much more rewarding. He has a passion for jQuery, PHP, HTML5, and CSS3, is eagerly eyeing the world of mobile dev, and likes to de-stress via a book, a beach, and a fishing rod.

About SitePoint

SitePoint specializes in publishing fun, practical, and easy-to-understand content for web professionals. Visit http://www.sitepoint.com/ to access our books, newsletters, articles, and community forums.

For Manda, my "better half." This book would not have been possible without your continued support. All my love, Lloydi.

Table of Contents

Chapter 4   Shaping Up Using CSS 119

Chapter 5   Picture This! Using Images on Your Website

Chapter 9   Launching Your Website

Chapter 10   Enhancing the Site with HTML5 and CSS3

Chapter 11   Adding Interactivity with jQuery

Chapter 12   What to Do When Things Go Wrong

Preface

Congratulations on buying this book. Oh, wait a minute—perhaps you're yet to buy it. Perhaps you've just picked up this book in your local bookshop, and are trying to decide whether it's right for you. Why should this be the book that makes it into your shopping basket? The answer can be found in the title of the book. It's all about getting it right the first time and not learning bad habits—bad habits that you have to unlearn at a later date—for the purpose of a quick result.

Let's take a step back for a moment, and look at another skill that many people learn at some point in their lives: learning to drive. Apologies if that particular experience is also new to you, but stick with me. For many people, their first driving lessons can be very confusing; they have to figure out which pedals to press and in what order, and then drive off without hitting anything. Meanwhile, other more experienced people just jump into their cars, start the engine, and drive from A to B without really thinking about what they're doing. These drivers may have picked up a few bad habits along the way, but if they learned with a proper driving instructor, the chances are they were taught properly from the beginning—following a strict set of rules to ensure they stayed safe.

The driving instructor tells you to check your mirrors diligently, observe speed limits, and avoid cutting corners (literally as well as metaphorically!). Imagine, though, if the instructor told you to ignore the speed limit signs, to *put your foot down* because the road is clear, or that the one-way sign "wasn't important at that time of night." It'd be a miracle if you passed your driving test, and chances are those bad habits would stay with you (so long as you could manage to keep your license).

Learning to build web pages can be a bit like that.

I've been designing and building websites for over ten years now, but I can clearly remember the joy of creating my first site. Admittedly, in hindsight, it was quite a nasty-looking website, but it achieved the goal at the time—I had published a website, and I was able to create it with the bare minimum of tools. It gave me an enormous sense of achievement, and made me want to learn more and create even better websites.

At the time, there were a limited number of books available that provided what I wanted, but I lapped up everything I could find, learning some tricks from books, and gaining other ideas from visiting websites. But then I discovered that I'd been doing it all wrong. The books I'd learned from had given me what later turned out to be poor advice, while the websites I'd visited had been built by people learning from the same sources and hence, making use of similar, bad techniques. So, what had gone wrong?

In the early days of the Web, when people first started to properly embrace the technology—publishing home pages and developing online corporate presences for their companies—they all realized quickly that the medium was limited. Necessity is the mother of invention, though, so web developers began to coax tricks and displays out of their web pages that were never intended by the technologies they used. Browsers helped along the way, adding features that offered even more opportunities for this kind of behavior.

Numerous books have been written on the topics of web design and programming, as have many free tutorials that you can read on the Web. Many of them were written during those heady years, and were based on what seemed like best practices back then; however, their authors were constrained by browsers that often rendered the same well-designed pages in vastly different ways. This meant that the tutorials' authors needed to resort to *abusing* various features of these browsers, such as using data tables to lay out pages. This certainly encouraged many people to build their first web pages, but it ensured that bad habits were ingrained at an early stage, and many people are still using these bad practices years later.

Web developers the world over have learned bad habits (myself included) and must now try to unlearn them all. There's no longer a need for these practices—they often produce pages that are inflexible, slow to download, and difficult to maintain—but like the badly taught driver who insists on flouting the rules because it's worked for him so far, many developers find these outdated habits difficult to break.

I saw the light several years ago, and have tried to educate as many people as possible since. But for the eager beginner, those same old books are still peddling the same bad old ideas. This just *has* to stop. And it stops here and now.

You're not going to learn any bad habits in this book. Not one.

In this book, you'll learn the right way to build a website. If there's a wrong way to do things—a way that cuts corners to save time, but encourages bad techniques—I won't even tell you about it. Not even as a "by the way, you might try this ..." There's no need to avert your eyes—it will be taken care of for you!

What is a Browser?

If you use Microsoft Windows (Windows 7, Vista, or XP), you probably know the browser as the "little blue e on the desktop" (shown in Figure 1), commonly called Internet Explorer. A large number of people don't stray beyond using this program for the purposes of viewing web pages—for many, Internet Explorer *is* the Internet.

Internet Explorer
6 icon

Internet Explorer
7 & 8 icon

Internet Explorer
9 icon

Figure 1. Internet Explorer—the "little blue e on the desktop"

Internet Explorer (or **IE**, as we'll refer to it from now on) is the most commonly used browser, largely because Microsoft included it as part of the Windows operating system as far back as Windows 95. As it's the first browser that many people use, they tend to stick with it because it's familiar.

However, there are other browsers that you can use instead of IE. Still riding a wave of popularity is Firefox,[1] an alternative browser with a number of attractive features not available in IE (at the time of writing). It also handles the features of some web pages better than IE. Since the second edition of this book, another browser has been released and become very popular in a short space of time—Chrome, by some company called Google (of which you may have heard). Both Firefox and Chrome are available for Windows, Mac OS X, and Linux operating systems; IE, however, is only available for Windows operating systems.

---

[1] http://www.mozilla.com/en-US/firefox/new/

The screenshots you'll see in this book were taken using Firefox on Windows 7, unless stated otherwise. Because of the cross-platform nature of Firefox and the excellent standards support, I recommend that you download a copy of Firefox for the purposes of working through the exercises in this book.

You might like to try another browser, other than Firefox or Chrome, that supports web standards (a topic we'll cover very soon). For Windows users, Opera's web browser[2] offers excellent standards support and a unique set of features; it also has a very loyal following and, like Firefox, can be freely downloaded. Mac users can also use the Opera browser, or simply stick with the Apple browser that's installed by default, Safari[3], which again offers excellent support for web standards. A selection of Mac browser icons appears in Figure 2.

Figure 2. There are numerous browsers that you can try, as shown by the Mac dock

Happy with the browser you're currently using? If you're a Windows user and would prefer to stick with what you know, you can still use IE—as indeed the majority of people using the Web still do. In fact, you can be sure that almost everything you read in this book will work in all recent browsers, whatever your choice, without any real hiccups. Almost everything? I say *almost*, because there are still some differences in the way browsers handle the newer technologies; for example, CSS3. But even that's okay, as long as you know where to expect differences, and are happy that this doesn't adversely affect the end result. I'll be covering these differences in later chapters—no nasty surprises, I promise!

Who Should Read This Book

Does this sound like you?

- You're an absolute beginner—at least as far as creating web pages go.

---

[2] http://www.opera.com/download/

[3] http://apple.com/safari/

- You are confident with using a computer, but wouldn't necessarily call yourself a *power user*.
- You use the Web a lot, enjoy other people's websites, and would like to create your own for a hobby, or a community you belong to.
- You're quickly put off by the technobabble that computer people tend to speak when you try to discuss a technical problem.
- You're perhaps a little daunted about learning this new skill, but still keen to learn (with some friendly hand-holding).

If any of the above descriptions strike a chord with you, this is the book to put in your shopping cart. You'll be eased in gently, and building web pages like a pro in no time!

There's no need to worry if you feel that the terminology your 15-year-old nephew keeps spouting is beyond you when you ask him about building websites. I've assumed readers have no prior knowledge of any of these terms, and I'll be guiding you through the process of creating a website from scratch. By the end of this book, you'll know how to build the site, obtain some hosting, promote the site, and keep it running once it's live.

The best part is this: what you learn in this book, you'll never have to discard. You'll be learning how to build sites the right way from the get-go.

What You'll Learn from This Book

By the time you finish reading this book and trying out the exercises contained within, you'll be able to build a complete website—the right way—without incurring any costs for expensive software or web hosting.

Using an example website, I'll guide you through the process of developing web pages from scratch. From these humble beginnings, great things will evolve! By the end of the book, you'll be able to create a website that includes the following features:

- easy-to-use navigation
- a professional-looking site header
- a Contact Us page
- tables—the presentation of data in neatly organized grids
- attractive web page forms

- a simple image gallery
- a search engine that covers your site, as well as related sites
- simple statistics that you can use; for example, being able to see who's using your site, how they found your site, and so on

You'll also learn how to manage your website effectively, without it becoming a chore or too technical. I'll show you how you can:

- establish your own dot-com (or dot-net, dot-org, or the like) web address
- find a place to host your website
- upload your files to your website
- gain feedback from visitors while avoiding spam emails

We'll also look at how your site can fit in with and complement other existing social networking sites, by covering how to:

- create a Facebook page and embed site updates on your own site
- sign up for a Twitter account and display status updates on your site
- add Facebook **Like** and Twitter **Follow** buttons on your site

How You'll Learn to Build Your Website

This book will take you through each new topic using a step-by-step approach. It provides a mixture of examples and practical exercises that will soon have you feeling confident enough to try a little HTML for yourself.

HTML, Markup, CSS ... Welcome to Your First Bits of Jargon!

From here on in, you're going to see these terms more and more. But what do they mean?

HTML

HTML stands for Hypertext Markup Language. It's the primary language that's used to create web pages, so you'll come to know it very well through the course of this book. We'll be using HTML5, the latest version of the language. There are many ways that you can write HTML5 for it to be valid, ranging from lazy and—dare we say—sloppy ways, to strict and ordered. In this book, we'll use the more formal syntax in the example website, XHTML, and avoid demonstrating the "slipshod" way of writing code. This will encourage a better approach to writing markup and code, and foster a more logical way of thinking that's more likely to put you in better stead for future learning. The difference between HTML and XHTML is explained in the SitePoint HTML Reference.[4]

Markup

Imagine, if you will, that you're a newspaper editor. You've been given a news story, but the text—from the heading through to the conclusion—is all the same size, with the headings, paragraphs, quotes, and other textual features not clearly indicated. It's just one big block of text. For starters, you'd probably want to emphasize the headline, maybe by displaying it in bold or italic text (or in caps with an exclamation mark if you were working for a tabloid). As an editor, you'd probably grab a pen and start scribbling annotations on the printout: an *h* here to signify a heading, a *p* here, there, and everywhere to show where paragraphs start and end, and a *q* to denote quotations.

This is essentially what markup is—a set of simple tags that suggest the structure of a document: this section is a heading, this is a paragraph, and so on. We'll cover the various tags that HTML uses in detail a little later.

 Markup isn't Computer Code

Markup is not the same as *code*. Often, people incorrectly refer to markup as code, but code goes beyond the basic abilities of markup. With code, you can create programs and make your web page more dynamic, while markup simply deals with the page's structure. So, if you want to impress your friends and relatives, refer to it as markup rather than code. See, I told you I'd teach you good habits!

CSS

CSS stands for Cascading Style Sheets. We'll be using a combination of HTML and CSS to create websites. CSS is a language that lets you control how your web pages look, but we'll go over that in more detail later. For now, it's important that you know what the abbreviation stands for. You'll also learn that CSS, like HTML, evolves over time. As such, we'll be covering some of the new CSS3 properties in this book and explaining how they work across the various

---

[4] http://reference.sitepoint.com/html/html-vs-xhtml

browsers, while the bulk of it will be CSS2 (or CSS2.1, a minor update). Don't worry, you won't need to know the version numbers—there's no test at the end!

Web Standards

Web Standards advocate best practices for building websites. The term Web Standards may be used to describe a range of philosophies and specifications, but for our purposes, we're mostly referring to the recommendations published by the World Wide Web Consortium (**W3C**)—in their own words, "an international community where member organizations, full-time staff and the public work together ... to develop the Web to its maximum potential."

At a practical level, compliance (or adherence) to web standards refers to the development of web pages that validate according to the W3C recommendations, like those for HTML, XHTML, or CSS, or to the guidelines for accessibility.

Building the Example Site

All examples presented in this book are backed up with a sample of the markup you need to write and a screenshot that shows how the results should look.

Each example is complete. You'll see the picture build gradually, so you won't be left guessing how the example website evolved to a particular stage. The files we'll use in all the examples are provided in a separate code archive (described in more detail in a moment).

What you can expect from the example website:

- a fun website project that will be built up through the chapters
- a complete site that demonstrates all the features you're likely to need in your own website
- all the HTML and CSS used to build the site in a single download

You can pick up the project at any point, so mistakes you might have made in a previous chapter's exercises won't come back to haunt you!

What This Book Won't Tell You

While it might be tempting to cram everything into one book and claim that the reader will learn everything in a short time frame, the truth is that this isn't necessarily the right approach for everyone.

This book doesn't try to force-feed you everything there is to know about creating web pages; instead, it focuses on the most beneficial aspects that you'll find yourself using over and over again.

This book does *not* cover:

- JavaScript in any depth (we will very briefly cover some simple JavaScript effects using jQuery, before pointing you in the direction of further learning that's more in-depth)
- server-based programming/scripting languages; for example, ASP, PHP, or Ruby
- creating Flash-based content
- search engine optimization techniques

By the time you've finished this book and had a chance to tackle your own website, you might want to take the next steps to increasing your site-building knowledge. I'll make recommendations where appropriate throughout the book, and suggest other resources that you might like to check out.

So, this is where the introductory bits end and the learning process begins—learning how to build websites the *right* way. So step this way, ladies and gentlemen …

What's in This Book

Chapter 1: *Setting Up Shop*

In this chapter, we'll make sure that you have all the tools you're going to need to build your website. I'll explain where you can access the right tools—all of them for free! By the chapter's end, you'll be ready to get cracking on your first website.

Chapter 2: *Your First Web Pages*

Here, we'll learn what makes a web page. We'll explore HTML, understand the basic requirements of every web page, and investigate the common elements that you'll see on many web pages. Then, you'll start to create pages yourself. In fact, by the end of this chapter, you'll have the beginnings of your first website.

Chapter 3: *Adding Some Style*

Now we'll start to add a bit of polish to the web pages we created in Chapter 2. You'll learn what CSS is and why it's a good technology, before putting it into action for yourself. As the chapter progresses, you'll see the project website start to take shape as we apply background and foreground colors, change the appearance of text, and make web links look different according to whether they've been visited or not.

Chapter 4: *Shaping Up with CSS*

This chapter builds on Chapter 3's introduction to the color and text-styling abilities of CSS to reveal what CSS can do for border styles and page layouts in general. First, we'll review the full range of border effects that you can apply to elements such as headings and paragraphs. We'll experiment with dotted borders, and big, bold borders, as well as some more subtle effects. In the second half of the chapter, we'll learn how it's possible to use CSS to position the elements of a web page—including blocks of navigation—anywhere on the screen.

Chapter 5: *Picture This! Using Images on Your Website*

As the chapter title suggests, this one's all about images. We'll discover the difference between inline images and background images, and look into the issue of making images accessible for blind or visually impaired web surfers. We'll also learn how to adjust pictures to suit your website using the software that we downloaded in Chapter 1. Then, we'll put all this knowledge together in a practical sense to create a photo gallery for the project site.

Chapter 6: *Tables: Tools for Organizing Data*

Here, we'll learn when tables should be used and, perhaps more importantly, when they should *not* be used. Once the basics are out of the way, I'll show how you can breathe life into an otherwise dull-looking table—again, using CSS—to make it more visually appealing.

Chapter 7: *Forms: Interacting with Your Audience*

In Chapter 7, we learn all about forms—what they're used for, what's required to build a form, and what you can do with the data you collect through your form. I'll teach you what the different form elements—text inputs, checkboxes, and so on—do, and show you how to use CSS to make a form look more attractive. Finally, I'll show you how you can use a free web service to have the data that's entered into your form emailed to you.

Chapter 8: *Interacting with Social Media*

With the website almost built, it's time to start thinking about other websites and services out there that you can use to your advantage. As (seemingly) everyone is on Facebook or Twitter these days, it would be remiss of us not to look at the opportunities that those sites and their services can offer. We'll look at how you can embed your Facebook and Twitter updates on your site simply and easily and show how to add "Like" and "Follow" links.

Chapter 9: *Launching Your Website*

It's all well and good to build a website for fun, but you need a way for people to see it—that's what this chapter is all about. We'll learn about hosting plans, discuss the pros and cons of using free services, and look at the tools you'll need in order to transfer your files from your computer to a web server for the world to see.

Chapter 10: *Enhancing the Site with HTML5 and CSS3*

You will have already been using HTML5 up to this point, though not features that are new to HTML5. Likewise, you'll have a good grounding of CSS by this stage, but there are some new CSS3 features that you'll really love. In this chapter, we'll give the project site an HTML5 and CSS3 makeover, showing how you can enhance the site, but also pointing out some of the pitfalls and quirks to be aware of with these newer features.

Chapter 11: *Adding Interactivity with jQuery*

The days of static websites are well and truly over. You want to present a dynamic, interactive site that gives users a sense of ownership and inclusion—not to mention some seriously impressive effects. How do you add that all-important layer of "behavior" to your site? That's where jQuery—a downloadable JavaScript library brimming with functionality—comes in.

Chapter 12: *What to Do When Things Go Wrong*

In the previous chapters, you were guided through all the steps needed to build your website, but once you go off and do your own thing, you'll almost certainly encounter some problems. In this chapter, we'll look at some tools you can use in your browser to diagnose problems, find out the problem's source, and then rectify it.

Chapter 13: *Pimp My Site: Cool Stuff You Can Add for Free*

You've heard of the MTV reality program *Pimp My Ride*, right? No? Well, every week, these guys take an everyday car and transform it—with some well-placed and carefully executed cosmetic touches—into a real head-turner of a vehicle.

And that's the aim of this chapter for your website! You'll discover that there are all kinds of tools, plugins, and add-ons that you can build into your website to make it even more useful to you and your visitors. Among the tools on offer are site search facilities, statistics programs, and online discussion forums.

Chapter 14: *Where to Now? What You Can Learn Next*

In the final chapter, we summarize the skills you've learned in this book, and then consider your options for expanding on these. I'll recommend websites that can take you to the next level, and books that really should be on your bookshelf—or rather, open on your desk next to your computer! We want to ensure you continue to learn the good stuff once you've put this book down.

Where to Find Help

SitePoint has a thriving community of web designers and developers ready and waiting to help you out if you run into trouble. We also maintain a list of known errata for the book, which you can consult for the latest updates.

The SitePoint Forums

The SitePoint Forums[5] are discussion forums where you can ask questions about anything related to web development. You may, of course, answer questions too. That's how a forum site works—some people ask, some people answer, and most people do a bit of both. Sharing your knowledge benefits others and strengthens the community. A lot of interesting and experienced web designers and developers hang out there. It's a good way to learn new stuff, have questions answered in a hurry, and generally have a blast.

The Book's Website

Located at http://www.sitepoint.com/books/html3/, the website supporting this book will give you access to the following facilities:

The Code Archive

As you progress through this book, you'll note a number of references to the code archive. This is a downloadable ZIP archive that contains complete every line of example source code printed in this book. If you want to cheat (or save yourself

---

[5] http://www.sitepoint.com/forums/

from carpal tunnel syndrome), go ahead and download the archive[6]. It also includes a copy of the Bubble Under website, which we use as an example throughout the book.

Updates and Errata

No book is perfect, and I expect that watchful readers will be able to spot at least one or two mistakes before the end of this one. The Errata page[7] on the book's website, will always have the latest information about known typographical and code errors, as well as necessary updates for new browser releases and versions of web standards.

In addition to the official site hosted and maintained by SitePoint, I have also put together some resources at http://beginningwebdesign.com. Here, you'll be able to find links to a Twitter account for the book, a Facebook page, and more.

The SitePoint Newsletters

In addition to books like this one, SitePoint publishes free email newsletters, such as the SitePoint *Tech Times*, SitePoint *Tribune*, and SitePoint *Design View*. In them, you'll read about the latest news, product releases, trends, tips, and techniques for all aspects of web development. Browse the archives or sign up to any of SitePoint's free newsletters on our website.[8]

The SitePoint Podcast

You can also join the SitePoint Podcast[9] team for news, interviews, opinion, and fresh thinking for web developers and designers. We discuss the latest web industry topics, present guest speakers, and interview some of the best minds in the industry. You can catch up on all previous podcasts on our website, or subscribe via iTunes.

Your Feedback

If you're unable to find an answer through the forums, or you wish to contact Site-Point for any other reason, the best place to write is `books@sitepoint.com`. We have

---

[6] http://www.sitepoint.com/books/html3/code.php

[7] http://www.sitepoint.com/books/html3/errata.php

[8] http://www.sitepoint.com/newsletter/

[9] http://www.sitepoint.com/podcast/

a well-staffed email support system set up to track your inquiries, and if our support team members are unable to answer your question, they'll send it straight to us. Suggestions for improvements, as well as any mistakes you may find, are especially welcome. Finally, you can get in touch with me via my Facebook page if needed (although word of warning: I don't "do Facebook" all that often!).

Acknowledgements

While writing a book sometimes seems like a solitary process, the truth is that there are a lot of people who guide the hands that type the words on these pages. None of this would have been possible had I not been pointed in the direction of websites like webmonkey.com,[10] whose CSS tutorial first made me see the light, and individuals such as Jeffrey Zeldman, Molly Holzschlag, and Eric Meyer, whose pioneering work has benefited me (and many others) greatly. However, if I were to list the names of all the people who have inspired me in the last few years, this section would end up looking more like an index! You folks know who you are, keep up the good work!

I would like to acknowledge the work undertaken by the Web Standards Project[11] (of which I was once a member), in particular the InterAct team on the Web Standards Curriculum. I'd also like to give a little shout-out to my fellow *Britpackers*—wear those Union Jack pants with pride, folks!

Thanks to all those at SitePoint who have helped me craft each edition of this book over the years: Simon Mackie, Marc Garrett, Matthew Magain, Andrew Tetlaw, Georgina Laidlaw, Julian Carroll, Kelly Steele, Alex Walker, Lisa Lang, and Tom Museth.

Finally, thanks to Manda for putting up with me when deadlines loomed and I all but shut myself off from civilization to have the chapters in on time. Social life? Oh that! I remember … At those times it seemed like it would never end, but finally we can both see the fruits of my labor.

---

[10] http://www.webmonkey.com/
[11] http://interact.webstandards.org/

Conventions Used in This Book

You'll notice that we've used certain typographic and layout styles throughout the book to signify different types of information. Look out for the following items:

Markup Samples

Any markup—be that HTML or CSS—will be displayed using a fixed-width font, like so:

webpage.html (excerpt)

```html
<h1>A perfect summer's day</h1>
<p>It was a lovely day for a walk in the park. The birds were
    singing and the kids were all back at school.</p>
```

If the code is to be found in the book's code archive, the name of the file will appear at the top of the program listing, like this:

example.css

```css
.footer {
  background-color: #CCC;
  border-top: 1px solid #333;
}
```

If only part of the file is displayed, this is indicated by the word *excerpt*:

example.css (excerpt)

```css
  border-top: 1px solid #333;
```

If additional code is to be inserted into an existing example, the new code will be displayed in bold:

```css
.footer {
  background-color: #CCC;
  border-top: 1px solid #333;
  padding: 5px;
}
```

Where existing code is required for context, rather than repeat all the code, a vertical ellipsis [⋮] will be displayed:

```
.footer {
    ⋮
    margin: 5px;
}
```

Some lines of code are intended to be entered on one line, but we've had to wrap them because of page constraints. A ➥ indicates a line break that exists for formatting purposes only, and should be ignored:

```
URL.open("http://www.sitepoint.com/blogs/2007/05/28/user-style-she
➥ets-come-of-age/");
```

Tips, Notes, and Warnings

Hey, You!

Tips will give you helpful little pointers.

Ahem, Excuse Me ...

Notes are useful asides that are related—but not critical—to the topic at hand. Think of them as extra tidbits of information.

Make Sure You Always ...

... pay attention to these important points.

Watch Out!

Warnings will highlight any gotchas that are likely to trip you up along the way.

Chapter 1

Setting Up Shop

Before you dive in and start to build your website, we need to set your computer up so that it's ready for the work that lies ahead. This is what this chapter is all about: ensuring that you have all the tools you need installed and are ready to go.

If you were to look at the hundreds of computing books for sale in your local bookstore, you'd be forgiven for thinking that you need to invest in a lot of different programs to build a website. However, the reality is that most of the tools required are probably sitting there on your computer, tucked away where you wouldn't think to look for them. And if ever you don't have the tool for the job, there's almost certain to be one or more free programs available that can handle the task.

I've assumed that you already have an internet connection, most likely broadband (or similar). There's no need to worry if you have a slower connection, though: it won't affect any of the tasks we'll undertake in this book. It will, however, mean that some of the suggested downloads or uploads may take longer to complete, but you probably knew that already.

Planning, Schmanning

At this point, it might be tempting to look at your motives for building a website. Do you have a project plan? What objectives do you have for the site?

While you probably have some objectives, and some idea of how long you want to spend creating your site, we're going to gloss over the nitty-gritty of project planning to some extent. Project planning is still an important aspect to consider, but because you've picked up a book entitled *Build Your Own Website The Right Way*, I'll assume you probably want to get right into the building part.

As this is your first website, it will be a fairly simple one, so we can overlook some of the more detailed aspects of site planning. Later, once you've learned—and moved beyond—the basics of building a site, you may feel ready to tackle a larger, more technically challenging site. When that time comes, proper planning will be a far more important aspect of the job. But now, let's gear up to build our first simple site.

The Basic Tools You Need

As I mentioned, many of the tools you'll need to build your first website are already on your computer. So, what tools *do* you need?

- The primary—and most basic—tool required is a **text editor**, which is a program that allows you to edit plain text files. You'll use this to write your web pages.

- Once you've written a web page, you can see how it looks in a **web browser**—that's the application you use to view websites.

- Finally, when you're happy with your new web page, you can put it on the Internet using an **FTP client**; this is a utility that allows you to transfer files across the Internet using the File Transfer Protocol. Using FTP may seem a little complicated at first but, thankfully, you won't need to do it too often. We'll discuss FTP clients in detail in Chapter 9.

You already have most of these programs on your computer, so let's go and find them.

Windows Basic Tools

In the following section—and indeed the rest of the book—where we refer to the Windows operating system, that's a shorthand way of saying Windows 7 (in all its confusing varieties), Microsoft's latest incarnation of its operating system. Any instructions and screenshots will be with Windows 7 in mind. However, we'll also cater for people using older versions of Windows. There are still many people out there who use XP or Vista, so where instructions provided for Windows 7 differ from earlier versions, we'll explain these for you.

Your Text Editor: Notepad

The first tool we'll consider is the text editor. Windows comes with a very simple text editor called Notepad. Many professional web designers using complicated software packages first started out years ago using Notepad; indeed, many professionals using expensive pieces of software aimed to save time still resort to using Notepad for many tasks. Why? Well, because it's so simple, little can go wrong. It also loads much more quickly than full-featured web development programs. Bells and whistles are definitely not featured.

You can find Notepad in the **Start** menu under **All Programs > Accessories**.

 Shortcut to Notepad

To save yourself navigating to this location each time you want to open Notepad, create a shortcut on your desktop. With the **Start** menu open to display Notepad's location, hold down the **Ctrl** key, and then click and hold down the mouse button. Now drag the Notepad icon to your desktop. When you release the mouse button, a shortcut to the application will appear on your desktop, as in Figure 1.1. The same goes for any other application you may find yourself using frequently in Windows.

Figure 1.1. Creating a shortcut to Notepad

Notepad is the most basic of applications, as you can see from Figure 1.2.

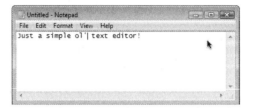

Figure 1.2. Notepad: a contender for the world's plainest program

Your Web Browser: Internet Explorer

Once you've created a web page using Notepad, you'll need a way to view the results of your handiwork. You'll remember that in the preface to this book, Internet Explorer (IE) was mentioned. Well, that's your viewer. As Figure 1.3 shows, Internet Explorer is in the **Programs** folder (accessed via **All Programs** from the **Start** menu, near the Windows logo), but a shortcut may also lurk on your desktop.

Figure 1.3. Internet Explorer: Microsoft's browser of choice

Mac OS X Basic Tools

Like Windows, the Mac operating system (specifically OS X; we won't be looking at previous versions of the Mac OS) has a number of tools that you can use straight out of the box. These tools are practically the equivalent to the Windows programs mentioned above.

Your Text Editor: TextEdit

While Windows has Notepad, the Mac has TextEdit, which can be found in the **Applications** folder, as Figure 1.4 illustrates.

Figure 1.4. TextEdit comes as part of Mac OS X's default installation

Unlike Notepad, TextEdit works as a rich text editor by default, which means we can work with fonts, make text bold and italic, and so on. However, we want to work with TextEdit as a plain text editor, so you'll need to adjust some of TextEdit's preferences. Start TextEdit, and then select **TextEdit > Preferences** from the menu to bring up the **Preferences** screen. Select **Plain text** within **New Document Attributes**; then close the **Preferences** screen. The next time you create a new file in TextEdit, it will be a plain text document.

Your Web Browser: Safari

The default browser for Mac users is Safari. You can usually find Safari in the **dock** (being the bar of icons at the bottom of your screen), but you can also access it through the **Applications** folder, as Figure 1.5 illustrates.

Figure 1.5. Safari is available via Mac's **Applications** folder

Stick It in the Dock

Just as you can drag shortcuts to programs onto the Windows desktop, you can add programs to the dock in Mac OS X. To add a program to the dock, just drag its icon from the **Applications** folder onto the dock, and *presto*! The application is now easily accessible whenever you need it.

If you're using a slightly older Mac, you may also have a copy of Internet Explorer installed. My advice on Internet Explorer for Mac? Send it to the Trash. The Mac version of IE was abandoned by Microsoft many years ago, so it is considerably outdated and rarely supported or used in the wider world. None of the newer Macs come with this application installed, and it bears no real resemblance to its Windows counterpart, for those more comfortable using IE.

Beyond the Basic Tools

You can certainly make a good start using the tools mentioned above. However, once you're dealing with a handful of web pages and other resources, you may want to go beyond the basics. We'll cover using some slightly more advanced applications later in the book.

Countless other text editors and web browsers are available for download, and many of them are free. Obviously, we don't have time to describe each and every one of them, so I've settled on a few options that have worked for me in the past that you might like to download and have at your disposal. And remember, they're all free!

Windows Tools

NoteTab

NoteTab's tabbed interface lets you have many different files open simultaneously without cluttering up your screen, as Figure 1.6 illustrates. Files that you've opened are remembered even after you close the program and open it again later, which is very useful when you're working on a batch of files over many days. You can download the free NoteTab, or its Light version, from http://www.notetab.com/.

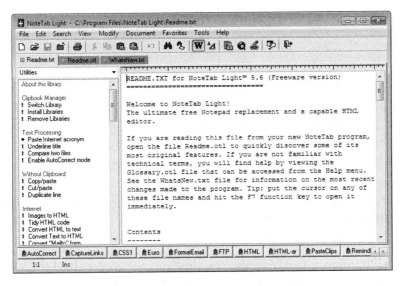

Figure 1.6. NoteTab Light's tabbed interface

Firefox

As mentioned in the preface, Firefox is a popular alternative to Internet Explorer and, as we proceed through this book, will be our browser of choice for a number of reasons. As with NoteTab, Firefox offers a tabbed interface that helps keep your computer free from window clutter. You can download Firefox from http://www.mozilla.com/firefox/; the browser is depicted in Figure 1.7.

Figure 1.7. Firefox—this creature is worth hunting down

Mac OS X Tools

It is true that there are fewer free programs available for the Mac operating system than there are for Windows. However, there are a few programs that you might like to consider as you move beyond the basics.

TextWrangler

TextWrangler is a free, simple text editor made by BareBones Software. As with NoteTab for Windows, TextWrangler can tidy up your workspace by allowing several text files to be open for editing at the same time (the documents are listed in a pull-out *drawer* to one side of the interface, rather than in tabs). You can download

TextWrangler—shown in Figure 1.8—from the BareBones Software website,[1] or from the Mac App store.

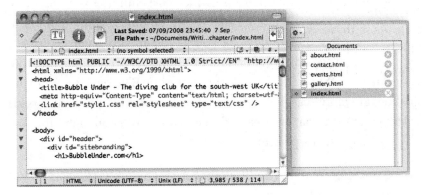

Figure 1.8. TextWrangler, a free text editor from BareBones Software

Firefox

Firefox is also popular with Mac users, many of whom prefer to use it instead of Safari (often because of the extra features—known as **add-ons**—that can be bolted on to the browser). A web page viewed in Firefox should display the same, regardless of whether the browser is installed on a PC running Windows, on a Mac running OS X, or on Linux, a free, open source operating system (generally favored by highly technical people who like to tinker with their computers a lot). The predictability of Firefox is a welcome change from the bad old days of endless browser competition, and is one very good reason why we'll mainly use Firefox in the examples included in this book.

Not Just Text, Text, Text

You can build an entire website using just the tools mentioned above, but it won't be the sexiest site on the Web. What's missing are images. So far, the programs we've mentioned are used to manipulate plain text or view web pages. If your website is going to be visually appealing, you'll need to create and manipulate images, either from scratch using photos you've taken, or by using images that you have the legal right to use on your website.

---

[1] http://www.barebones.com/products/textwrangler/

Unfortunately, when it comes to image-editing software, that old saying, "You get what you pay for" applies. A professional image-editing program that you install on your machine, like Photoshop or Fireworks, costs hundreds of dollars. While these programs offer some excellent capabilities, I'd only recommend that you buy them if you're sure that they're right for you. If you already have a copy of one of these, or a similar image-editing program, by all means use it and experiment with it. Programs like PaintShop Photo Pro X3 or Photoshop Elements (a cut-down version of Photoshop) are more reasonably priced; however, for the purposes of this book, we'll only look at tools that are free to download and offer enough functionality to give you an idea of what's possible.

Keep an eye open for free image editors that are included (usually as downloads, sometimes on disks) with internet, computing, and design magazines. Software vendors often give away older versions of their software in the hope that users might upgrade to a new version at a later date. Look out for PaintShop Photo Pro X3 (with a cheesy name like that, it's hard to miss!), or any image editor that supports **layers**—a way to construct an image by stacking two or more layers, one on top of the other. We'll keep our image editing fairly simple throughout this book, but it's certainly worth keeping an eye open for free (and full-featured) image-editing software, as such offers will not always be available.

 ### Taking the Big Boys for a Spin

The most commonly used image-editing packages are available for trial download. They are large downloads (hundreds of megabytes), and may need to be left to download overnight, even on a broadband connection.

These trial versions are typically available for 30 days' use; after that time, you can decide whether you want to buy the full software or stop using the program. Those 30 days, however, might provide just enough time for you to use the software while you work through this book.

| **Adobe Photoshop** | A trial of Photoshop's latest version is available for download.[2] If you'd rather try the lighter Photoshop Elements, trial versions are available for Windows[3] and Mac.[4] |

---

[2] http://www.adobe.com/products/photoshop/
[3] http://www.adobe.com/products/photoshopelwin/
[4] http://www.adobe.com/products/photoshopelmac/

Adobe Fireworks	You can download a trial version of Fireworks from the Adobe website.[5]
PaintShop Photo Pro X3	PaintShop Photo Pro X3 is available for Windows only. To download a trial version, visit Corel's website[6] and click the **Free Trials** link in the navigation bar.

Windows Tools

The standard Windows install hasn't always been blessed with image-editing software. Certainly this was the case with Windows XP, although, if you bought the computer as a bundle with PC, scanner, and digital camera, you might be lucky and find image-editing software included in the deal. (Scout around in your **Start > All Programs** menu to see what you can uncover).

In Windows Vista, the Photo Gallery application saw some big improvements over its previous XP incarnation and included some basic, but still useful, image manipulation tools, including cropping, color, and contrast adjustment. The Photo Gallery application can be found directly in the **Start** menu.

In Windows 7, however, those image adjustments were taken away again, at least from the default installation. You can choose to open the image from Photo Gallery into Paint, where you gain some *very* basic editing tools (cropping, rotating), as seen in Figure 1.9. Or, you could install these extra photo adjustment tools by grabbing the free Windows Live Photo Gallery.[7]

---

[5] http://www.adobe.com/products/fireworks/

[6] http://www.corel.com/servlet/Satellite/au/en/Content/1150905725000

[7] http://explore.live.com/windows-live-photo-gallery?os=mac

Figure 1.9. Windows' Photo Gallery application, which lets you open the image in Paint

Picasa

Whether you're using Windows 7, Vista, or XP, you may find the image-editing possibilities offered by the installed programs restrictive. With that in mind, you might like to try out an excellent image-management tool that Google offers for free download. The program is called Picasa (it's also available for Mac users), and it's well-equipped to handle most tasks that you're likely to encounter as you manage imagery for your website. Download a copy from the Picasa website,[8] and soon enough you'll be using this program to crop, rotate, add special effects, and catalog the images stored on your computer. Figure 1.10 gives you an idea of the program's interface.

Figure 1.10. Picasa: Google's full-featured image-management tool

Mac OS X Tools

The Mac has a reputation for being favored by designers and creative types, and the platform makes many tools available to the budding artist; however, they usually come at a price, one that's higher than the Windows equivalents. So, what free software can we use on the Mac, assuming that we want a more permanent tool than a 30-day trial version of Photoshop or Fireworks?

Preview

Preinstalled on every Mac that you buy these days, Preview handles a raft of simple image amendments such as cropping and rotating, though you probably know it best as "the app that opens when I view a PDF." We'll be explaining how to use it for some image changes in Chapter 5.

---

[8] http://picasa.google.com/mac/

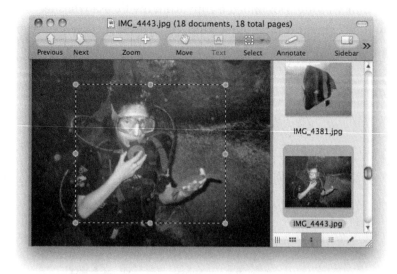

Figure 1.11. Preview handles the basics of image editing

iPhoto

Also included with Mac OS X is a program that probably needs no introduction to the experienced Mac user: iPhoto. This excellent program is not intended to be a fully featured image editor; it's really designed for managing and viewing large numbers of photos stored on a computer. It's great for organizing photo albums, but iPhoto also has some very useful editing facilities that take it beyond a mere cataloging tool.

Images can be rotated by arbitrary angles (using the Straighten tool in edit mode), and a whole range of color adjustments are possible, as seen in Figure 1.12. iPhoto can be found in the **Applications** folder, or in the dock.

Figure 1.12. Using the image-adjustment tools in iPhoto

Online Tools

I've focused on programs that you can download and install on your computer for the purposes of image editing, but there is another way that avoids this entirely. You can do a surprisingly large amount of editing online for free using Adobe's Photoshop Express[9]. The editor is accessed in the navigation menu under **Online Tools** and, once you've uploaded the image you want to tinker with, you'll discover a wide range of options. Removing red-eye, smoothing out blemishes, blurring or sharpening parts of the image: all of these are possible online. Then, when you're happy with your changes, you can save it back to your computer's hard drive.

Figure 1.13. Where to find Photoshop Express Editor

---

[9] http://www.photoshop.com/tools?wf=editor

Figure 1.14. Using Photoshop Express to crop an image

Creating a Spot for Your Website

So far, we've covered some of the tools you'll need to create your website. We've looked at programs that are readily available, and where you can find them on your computer. And when the free tools that came with your computer are not up to the job, I've suggested other programs that you can download and use. Our next task on the to-do list is to create a space for your website on the hard drive.

Windows

The best place to keep your website files is in a dedicated folder that's easy to find within the Documents library (in Vista and XP, just **Documents** or **My Documents**, respectively). The **Documents** library can easily be found by clicking on the Windows Explorer icon that sits in the Taskbar (the icon looks like a tabbed folder you might find in a letter tray). In Windows Vista, you'll find the **Documents** folder inside **C:\Users\yourusername**; in XP it's under **C:\Documents and Settings\yourusername**.

Now create a new folder here called "Web" by selecting **File > New > Folder**.

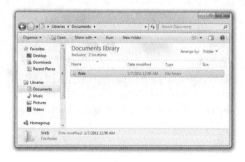

Figure 1.15. The Documents library in Windows 7 containing our new "Web" folder

Displaying the User Folder/My Documents Folder

Can't find your user folder on your Windows 7 or Vista desktop? Missing your **My Documents** folder in XP? You may have removed the icon by accident—it's easily done—or it may have never been set up in the first place. This is how you can place or return the folder to your desktop:

1. From the **Start Menu**, select **Control Panel**.

2. Select **Appearance and Personalization** (or **Appearance and Themes** in XP).

3. Windows 7 and Vista users: choose **Personalization**, and at top left is a list of options, including **Change Desktop Icons**. A new dialog box will appear, so check the **User's Files** option in the **Desktop Icons** section, and press **OK**. Close the **Appearance and Personalization** window. You can also access this feature by right-clicking on the desktop and choosing it from the pop-up menu, as seen in Figure 1.16

4. XP users: select **Change the desktop background** from the list of options, and click the **Customize Desktop...** button at the bottom. Check the **My Documents** option in the dialog box that appears and click **OK**. Close the **Appearance and Themes** window by pressing **OK**.

5. Your user folder/**My Documents** folder should now be on the desktop, as shown in Figure 1.17.

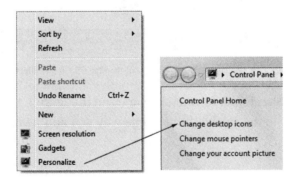

Figure 1.16. Getting to the Personalize options in Windows 7 is also possible by right-clicking on the desktop

Figure 1.17. The user folder displayed on the desktop in Windows 7, which contains **My Documents** folder

Mac OS X

In Mac OS X, there's already a handy place for you to store your website files: the **Sites** folder, shown in Figure 1.18. Open your home directory (from **Finder**, select **Go > Home**), and there it is.

Figure 1.18. Displaying the **Sites** folder in the Mac OS X home directory

It's easy to add the **Sites** folder to your sidebar (seen in Figure 1.19) for quick access: just drag the folder to the sidebar in the same way you add items to the dock.

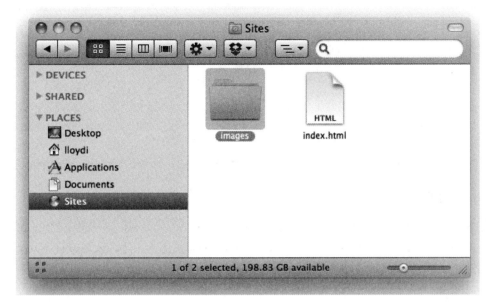

Figure 1.19. The **Sites** folder now placed in the sidebar

Summary

Believe it or not, we now have everything we need to build our own website—and all without spending a cent! Not only do we have the basic tools—our text editor (Notepad or TextEdit) and our web browser (Internet Explorer or Safari)—but we also know the alternatives that exist.

We've reviewed some simple and freely available image-editing programs that can help us spruce up our sites: Picasa for Windows, and Preview and iPhoto for Mac. Finally, we mentioned some more capable—and more expensive—options, such as Photoshop and PaintShop Pro X3.

Now we have the tools, let's learn how to use them!

Your First Web Pages

A wise man once said that a journey of a thousand miles begins with a single step.[1] In this chapter, you'll take that first metaphorical step on your journey towards website enlightenment, and create your first web page. By the end of the chapter, you'll have duplicated that first page to form the beginnings of a multipage website.

Nice to Meet You, HTML

We've already touched briefly on what HTML is. In this chapter, we'll learn the basics of HTML, periodically reviewing our progress in a browser, and steadily building up our knowledge of various HTML **elements**—the basic building blocks of HTML. Elements tell the web browser what each item in the page is: a paragraph, a heading, a quotation, and so on. These elements contain all the information that the browser requires, as we'll soon see.

Anatomy of a Web Page

In the preface, we said that learning HTML was like taking a driving lesson. To take that analogy further, imagine a web page as being the car in which you're learning

---

[1] http://www.quotationspage.com/quote/24004.html

to drive. Some aspects are essential to the process of driving, while others are mere fashion accessories.

To drive the car, you need to have wheels (including the steering wheel), and a place to sit. An engine is required to power the car, as is bodywork to which your (nonessential, but spiffy) trim can be attached. The car must also have a chassis to which the bodywork can be bolted. Anything less, and all you have is a collection of attractive—but useless—spare parts.

Like the car, your web page also needs some form of chassis: a basic structure upon which everything else can be built. But what does this hypothetical chassis look like? The best way to find out is to roll up our sleeves, figuratively speaking, and take a closer look at what's going on underneath the cosmetic features.

Viewing the Source

One of the great things about learning to build web pages is that we all have the ability to view the source code of other people's web pages. You can learn a lot by simply taking a peek at how another person's web page was built ... but how do you do that?

Although every browser uses slightly different terminology, the variations in how browsers let us view web page code are so small that the process doesn't need to be spelled out for every browser. Here's the technique you'd use to view a web page's source in IE:

- Bring up a page in your browser; for example, the Web Standards Project's home page.[2] The Web Standards Project (WaSP) is a group that promotes the benefits of building your website correctly, so you can be fairly confident that they've got it right.

- Position your cursor on the page other than over an image, and right-click (or **Ctrl**-click if you're on a Mac). You should be presented with a context menu similar to those shown in Figure 2.1.

---

[2] http://webstandards.org/

Figure 2.1. Selecting the View Source command in Internet Explorer and Firefox, respectively

■ Select **View Source** (**View Page Source** for Firefox), and a new window displays the page's underlying markup.

At this point, we'll skip analyzing the markup, but this is one of those tricks that's really useful to know from the beginning.

 Careful Who You Trust!

Most web pages don't use best-practice techniques, so avoid looking at a page's source unless the website in question is mentioned in this book as being a good example.

Basic Requirements of a Web Page

As we've already discussed, there are some basic must-have items in any web page. You would have seen all of these if you scanned through the markup that appeared when you tried to view the source a moment ago:

- a doctype
- an `<html>` tag
- a `<head>` tag
- a `<title>` tag
- a `<body>` tag

These requirements make up the basic skeleton of a web page. It's the chassis of your car with some unpainted bodywork, but no wheels or seats. A car enthusiast would call it a *project*—a solid foundation needing some work to turn it into something usable. The same goes for a web page. Here's what these requirements look like when they're combined in a basic web page:

```
<!DOCTYPE html>
<html lang="en">
  <head>
    <title>Untitled Document</title>
    <meta charset="utf-8"/>
  </head>
  <body>
  </body>
</html>
```

Those of you with eagle eyes may have also spotted the `<meta>` tag in the markup above. I know I'm yet to mention this, but we'll get to it soon enough. For now, be content with the knowledge that, although the `<meta>` tag is not part of the skeletal requirements of a web page, it serves many a useful purpose, especially supporting information about the web page.

The markup above is the most basic web page you'll see here. It contains practically no content of any value (at least, as far as a user who looks at it in a browser is concerned), but it's crucial that you understand what this markup means. Let's delve a little deeper.

The Doctype

```
<!DOCTYPE html>
```

This is known as the **doctype,**[3] which is short for Document Type Definition. It *must* be the first item on a web page, appearing even before any spacing or carriage returns. In earlier versions of this book, the doctype we used was to declare the page as XHTML 1.1 strict. It is, to be honest, quite nasty to glance at, given that this is your first exposure to the world of HTML. How nasty? Well, this is what we *used* to specify:

```
<!DOCTYPE html PUBLIC "-//W3C//DTD XHTML 1.0 Strict//EN"
"http://www.w3.org/TR/xhtml1/DTD/xhtml1-strict.dtd">
```

Try memorizing that if your life depended on it!

Thankfully, we can use the much simpler HTML5 doctype, and everything works smoothly. But what is this doctype?

Have you ever taken a document you wrote in Microsoft Word 2007 on one computer, and tried to open it on another that only had Word 2000 on it? Frustratingly, without some preemptive massaging when the file is first saved, this fails to work as expected. It fails because Word 2007 includes features that Bill Gates and his team had yet to dream up in 2000, so Microsoft needed to create a new version of its file format to cater for these new features.

Just as Microsoft has many different versions of Word, there have also been different versions of HTML over time, for example HTML 3.2, HTML 4, XHTML 1.1 and now HTML5. Mercifully, the different versions of HTML were designed so that there's no suffering the same kind of incompatibility gremlins as Word. If you throw some HTML5 at an older browser that fails to understand what it's been given, it will generally render it as plain text, which may be absolutely fine. Conversely, newer browsers will cope with old markup defined in earlier versions of HTML, even HTML elements that have since been dropped (or deprecated, to use the official language). The doctype's job is to specify which version of HTML the browser is about to be given. The browser then uses this information to decide how it should render items on the screen. There are a lot of doctypes that you could use but, trust me, you're best just sticking with the simple one that HTML5 gives us. And yes, eagle-eyes, you're right—this doctype doesn't actually state an HTML version at all, unlike previous doctypes. We'll avoid opening that particular can of worms, as it's

---

[3] http://reference.sitepoint.com/html/doctypes/

a big can; just take pleasure in the fact that you can easily remember this one, even without your life depending on it.

The html Element

So, the doctype has told the browser to expect a certain flavor of HTML. What comes next? Some HTML!

An HTML document is built using elements. Remember, elements are the bricks that create the structures that hold a web page together. But what exactly *is* an element? What does an element look like, and what is its purpose?

- An HTML element starts and ends with **tags**—the **opening tag** and the **closing tag**.[4]

- A tag consists of an opening angled bracket (<), some text, and a closing bracket (>).

- Inside a tag, there is a **tag name**; there may also be one or more **attributes**.

Let's take a look at the first element in the page: the html element.[5] Figure 2.2 shows what we have.

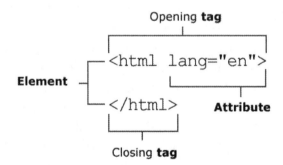

Figure 2.2. Components of a typical HTML element

It depicts the opening tag, which marks the start of the element:

---

[4] Like any good rule, there are exceptions: empty elements, such as meta, use special empty tags. We'll take a look at empty tags soon.

[5] http://reference.sitepoint.com/html/html/

```
<html lang="en">
```

Below this we see the closing tag, marking its end (and occurring right at the end of the document):

```
</html>
```

Here's that line again, with the tag name in bold:

```
<html lang="en">
```

And there is one **attribute** in the opening tag:

```
<html lang="en">
```

What's an Attribute?

HTML elements can have a range of attributes, depending on which element you're dealing with. Each attribute is made up of a **name** and a **value**, and these are always written as `name="value"`. In the example above, we can see the `lang` attribute, used to set the document's language—in this case `en` for English.

Some attributes are optional while others are compulsory, but together they give the browser important information that the element wouldn't otherwise offer. For example, the image element (which we will learn about soon) has a compulsory "image source" attribute, the value of which gives the filename of the image. Attributes appear only in the opening tag of any given element. We will see more attributes crop up as we work our way through this project, and, at least initially, I'll be making sure to point them out so that you're familiar with them.

Back to the purpose of the `html` element. This is the outermost "container" of our web page; everything else (apart from the `doctype`) is kept within that container. Let's peel off that outer layer and take a peek at the contents inside.

There are two major sections inside the `html` element: the `head` and the `body`.

The **head** Element

The head[6] element contains information *about* the page, but no information that will be displayed on the page itself. For example, it contains the `title`[7] element, which tells the browser what to display in its **title bar** (the title bar is the very top part of the browser window—the part with the minimize, maximize, and close buttons):

```
<head>
  <title>Untitled document</title>
  <meta charset="utf-8"/>
</head>
```

The **title** Element

The opening `<title>` and closing `</title>` tags are wrapped around the words "Untitled document" in the markup above. Note that the `<title>` signifies the start, while the closing `</title>` signifies the end of the title. That's how closing tags work: they have forward slashes just after the first < angle bracket.

The "Untitled document" title is typical of what HTML authoring software provides as a starting point when you create a new web page; it's up to you to change those words. As Figure 2.3 shows, it does pay to have a meaningful title, and not just for the sake of those people who visit our web page.

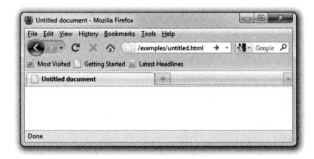

Figure 2.3. "Untitled document"—not a helpful title

---

[6] http://reference.sitepoint.com/html/head/
[7] http://reference.sitepoint.com/html/title/

The content of the `title` element is also used for other purposes:

■ It's the name that appears in the **Windows Taskbar**—that strip along the bottom of your Windows desktop that shows all the currently open windows—for any open document, as shown in Figure 2.4. It also appears in the dock on a Mac, as Figure 2.5 illustrates. When you have a few windows open, you'll appreciate any effort that's been made to enter a descriptive `title`!

Figure 2.4. The `title` appearing in the Windows Taskbar

Figure 2.5. The `title` displaying in the Mac dock

■ If users decide to add the page to their bookmarks (or favorites), the `title` will be used to name the bookmark, as Figure 2.6 illustrates.

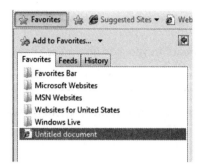

Figure 2.6. An "Untitled document" saved to IE's favorites

▨ Your title element is used heavily by search engines to work out what your page contains, and what information should be displayed in the search results.

meta Elements

Inside the head element in our simple example, we can see a meta element, shown in bold below:

```
<head>
  <title>Untitled Document</title>
  <meta charset="utf-8"/>
</head>
```

A meta element can be used in a web page for different reasons. Some are used to provide additional information that's not displayed onscreen to the browser or search engines; for instance, the name of the page's author or a copyright notice might be included in meta elements. In the example above, the meta tag tells the browser which **character set** to use—specifically, UTF-8, which includes the characters needed for web pages in just about any written language.

The Importance of UTF-8

If you neglect to select UTF-8 when saving your files, you're likely not to notice much of a difference. However, when another user whose language is different from yours tries to view your website, they'll probably end up with a screen of gobbledygook. Why? Because their computer is set up to display text in their native character set, while yours is set up to create English text. UTF-8 can handle just about any language there is (including some obscure ones), and most computers can read it, so UTF-8 is always a safer bet.

There are many uses for `meta` elements, but most of them will make no discernible difference to the way your page looks, and as such, will be of little interest to you—at least at this stage.

Self-closing Elements

The `meta` element is an example of a **self-closing element** (or an **empty element**). Unlike `title`, the `meta` element needn't contain anything between its opening and closing tags, so we could write it as follows:

```
<meta charset="utf-8"></meta>
```

HTML contains a number of empty elements. The boffins who put HTML together decided that writing all those closing tags would get annoying fairly quickly, so they decided to use self-closing tags: tags that end with `/>`. Hence, our `meta` example becomes:

```
<meta charset="utf-8"/>
```

The Memory Game: Remembering Difficult Markup

If you're thinking that `meta` elements are hard to remember, and wondering how on earth people commit them to memory—they don't. Even hardened and world-weary coders would have trouble remembering these elements exactly; instead, most of them copy from a source they know to be correct, most likely from their last project or piece of work. You'll probably do the same as you work with project files for this book.

Full-fledged web development programs, such as Dreamweaver, will normally take care of these tricky parts of coding. But if you're using a humble text editor and require some help, you need only remember that there's a completely searchable HTML reference on SitePoint's website.[8]

---

[8] http://reference.sitepoint.com/html/

Other head Elements

Other items, such as CSS markup and JavaScript code, can appear in the head element. We'll discuss these as we need them.

The body Element

Finally, we reach the place where it all happens. The page's body[9] element contains almost everything that you see on the screen: headings, paragraphs, images, any navigation that's required, and footers that sit at the bottom of the web page:

```
<!DOCTYPE html>
<html lang="en">
  <head>
    <title>Untitled Document</title>
    <meta charset="utf-8"/>
  </head>
  <body>
  </body>
</html>
```

The Most Basic Web Page in the World

Actually, that heading's a bit of a misnomer: we've already shown you the most basic page—the one without any content. However, to start to appreciate how everything fits together, you really need to see a page with some actual content on it. Let's have a go at it, shall we?

Open your text editor and type the following into a new, empty document (or grab the file from the code archive if you don't feel like typing it out):

```
                                          chapter2/examples/01_basic_web_page/basic.html
<!DOCTYPE html>
<html lang="en">
  <head>
    <title>The Most Basic Web Page in the World</title>
    <meta charset="utf-8"/>
  </head>
  <body>
```

---

[9] http://reference.sitepoint.com/html/body/

```
    <h1>The Most Basic Web Page in the World</h1>
    <p>This is a very simple web page to get you started.
        Hopefully you will get to see how the markup that drives
        the page relates to the end result that you can see on
        screen.</p>
    <p>This is another paragraph, by the way. Just to show how it
        works.</p>
  </body>
</html>
```

Once you've typed it out, save it as **basic.html**.

If you're using Notepad on Windows:

1. Select **File** > **Save As...** from the menu and find the **Web** folder you created inside your **Documents** folder.

2. Enter the filename as `basic.html`.

3. Select **UTF-8** from the **Encoding** drop-down list.

4. Click **Save**.

If you're using TextEdit on a Mac, first make sure that you're in plain text mode, and then:

1. Select **File** > **Save As...** from the menu.

2. Find the **Sites** folder, and enter the filename as `basic.html`.

3. Select **Unicode (UTF-8)** from the **Plain Text Encoding** drop-down list.

4. Click **Save**.

5. TextEdit will warn you that you're saving a plain text file with an extension other than .txt, and offer to append .txt to the end of your filename. We want to save this file with an .html extension, so click the **Don't Append** button, and your file will be saved.

Next, using Windows Explorer or Finder, locate the file that you just saved, and double-click to open it in your browser. Figure 2.7 shows how the page displays.

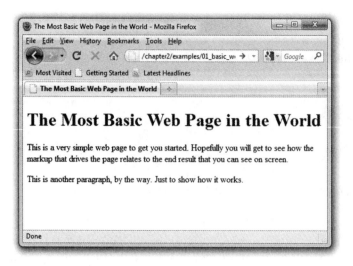

Figure 2.7. Displaying a basic page

Analyzing the Web Page

We've introduced two new elements to our simple page: a heading element, and a couple of paragraph elements, denoted by the <h1>[10] tag and <p>[11] tags, respectively. Do you see how the markup you've typed out relates to what you can see in the browser? Figure 2.8 shows a direct comparison of the document displays.

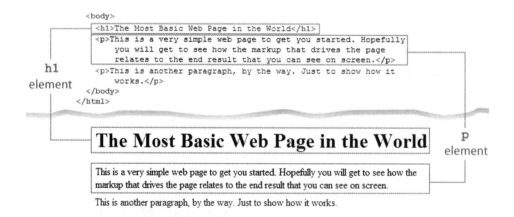

Figure 2.8. Comparing the source markup with the view presented in the browser

---

[10] http://reference.sitepoint.com/html/h1/
[11] http://reference.sitepoint.com/html/p/

The opening <h1> and closing </h1> tags are wrapped around the words "The Most Basic Web Page in the World," making that the main heading for the page. In the same way, the p elements contain the text in the two paragraphs.

A Case of Keeping Low

The tags are all lowercase, and our attribute names will be in lowercase, too. When using the HTML5 doctype, you may be quite sloppy with the markup style (for example, mixing upper case and lower case, not placing quotes around attributes, and much more). The key word here is *may*. It's generally considered good practice to follow the stricter XHTML markup rules, even if you're not using an XHTML doctype, as it fosters an ordered, logical style of markup. Therefore, throughout this book, we'll use an HTML5 doctype while following the rules for the more fussy XHTML syntax. You can find out more about the differences in SitePoint's HTML Reference page on HTML and XHTML Syntax.[12]

Headings and Document Hierarchy

In the example above, we use an h1 element to show a major heading. If we wanted to include a subheading beneath this heading, we'd use the h2 element. A subheading under an h2 would use an h3 element, and so on, until we hit h6. The lower the heading level, the lesser its importance and the smaller the font size (unless you've restyled the headings with CSS, but more of that in Chapter 3).

With headings, an important and commonsense practice is to ensure that they appear in sequence. In other words, you should start from level one, and work your way down the levels in numerical order. You can jump back up from a lower-level heading to a higher one, provided that content under the higher-level heading does not refer to concepts addressed under the lower-level heading. It may be useful to visualize your headings as a list:

- First Major Heading
  - First Subheading
  - Second Subheading
    - A Sub-subheading
- Another Major Heading
  - Another Subheading

---

[12] http://reference.sitepoint.com/html/html-xhtml-syntax

Here's the HTML view of the example shown above:

```
<h1>First Major Heading</h1>
<h2>First Subheading</h2>
<h2>Second Subheading</h2>
<h3>A Sub-subheading</h3>
<h1>Another Major Heading</h1>
<h2>Another Subheading</h2>
```

Paragraphs

Of course, no one wants to read a document that contains only headings, so you need to put some text in there. The element we use to deal with blocks of text is the p element. It's easy to remember as p is for paragraph. That's just as well, because you'll almost certainly find yourself using this element more than any other. And that's the beauty of HTML: most elements that you use frequently are either very obvious, or easy to remember once you're introduced to them.

For People Who Love Lists

Let's imagine that you want a list on your web page. To include an **ordered list** (the HTML term for a numbered list) of items, we use the ol element. An **unordered list**—known as bullet points to the average person—makes use of the ul element. In both types of list, individual points or list items are specified using the li element. So we use ol for an ordered list, ul for an unordered list, and li for a list item. Simple.

To see this markup in action, type the following into a new text document, save it as **lists.html**, and view it in the browser by double-clicking on the saved file's icon:

chapter2/examples/02_lists/lists.html

```
<!DOCTYPE html>
<html lang="en">
  <head>
    <title>Lists - an introduction</title>
    <meta charset="utf-8"/>
  </head>
  <body>
    <h1>Lists - an introduction </h1>
    <p>Here's a paragraph. A lovely, concise little paragraph.</p>
```

```
    <p>Here comes another one, followed by a subheading.</p>
    <h2>A subheading here</h2>
    <p>And now for a list or two:</p>
    <ul>
      <li>This is a bulleted list</li>
      <li>No order applied</li>
      <li>Just a bunch of points we want to make</li>
    </ul>
    <p>And here's an ordered list:</p>
    <ol>
      <li>This is the first item</li>
      <li>Followed by this one</li>
      <li>And one more for luck</li>
    </ol>
  </body>
</html>
```

How does it look to you? Did you type it all out? Remember, if it seems like a hassle to type out the examples, you can find all the markup in the code archive. Bear in mind, however, that copying and pasting markup, and then saving and running it, doesn't really give you a feel for creating your own website; it really pays to learn by doing. Even if you make mistakes, it's still a better way to learn (and you'll be pleased when you can spot and fix your own errors yourself). When displayed in a browser, the above markup should look like the page shown in Figure 2.9.

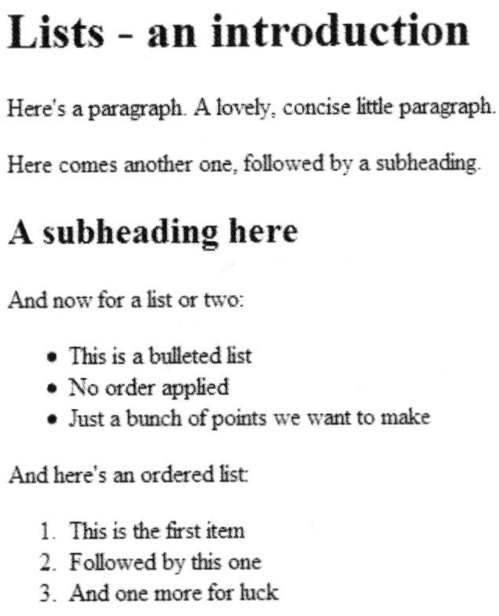

Lists - an introduction

Here's a paragraph. A lovely, concise little paragraph.

Here comes another one, followed by a subheading.

A subheading here

And now for a list or two:

- This is a bulleted list
- No order applied
- Just a bunch of points we want to make

And here's an ordered list:

1. This is the first item
2. Followed by this one
3. And one more for luck

Figure 2.9. Using unordered and ordered lists to organize information

There are a multitude of elements that you can use on your web page, and we'll learn more of them as our website development progresses. As well as the more obvious elements that exist, some are not immediately clear-cut; for example, what would you use div, span, or a elements for? Any guesses? All will be revealed in good time.

Commenting Your HTML

Back in the garage, you're doing a little work on your project car and, as you prepare to replace the existing tires with a new set, you notice that your hubcaps aren't bolted on; you'd stuck them to the car with nothing more than superglue. There must have been a good reason for doing that, but you're unable to recall what it was. The trouble is, if there was a reason to attach the hubcaps that way before, surely you should do it the same way again. Wouldn't it be great if you'd left yourself a note when you first did it, explaining why you used super glue instead of bolts? Then again, your car would look a bit untidy with notes stuck all over it. What a dilemma!

When you're creating a website, you may find yourself in a similar situation. You might build a site, and not touch it again for six months. Then when you revisit the work, you might find yourself doing the all-too-familiar head-scratching routine. Fortunately, there *is* a solution.

HTML, like most programming languages, allows you to use **comments.**[13] Comments are perfect for making notes on work you've done and, although they're included within your code, they won't affect the onscreen display. Here's an example of a comment:

```
                              chapter2/examples/03_comments/comments.html
<!DOCTYPE html>
<html lang="en">
  <head>
    <title>Comment example</title>
    <meta charset="utf-8"/>
  </head>
  <body>
    <p>I really, <em>really</em> like this HTML stuff.</p>
```

[13] http://reference.sitepoint.com/html/html-xhtml-syntax#html-xhtml-syntax__sect-comments

```
    <!-- Added emphasis using the em element. Handy one, that. -->
  </body>
</html>
```

Figure 2.10 shows the page viewed on the screen.

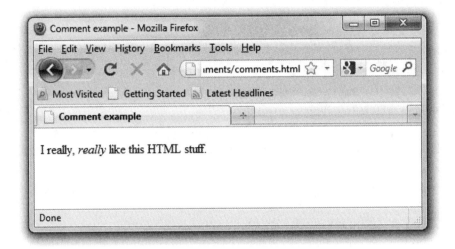

Figure 2.10. The comment remains hidden in the onscreen display

Comments must start with `<!--`, after which you're free to type whatever you like as a "note to self." Well, you're free to type *almost* anything ... except double dashes. Why not? Because that's a signal that the comment is about to end—the `-->` part.

Oh, and did you spot how we snuck in another new element? The emphasis element, denoted with the `<em>` and `</em>` tags, is used wherever ... well, do I *really* need to tell you? Actually, that last question was to illustrate this point. Did you notice that the word "really" appeared in italics? Read that part to yourself now, and listen to the way it sounds in your head. Now you know when to use the `em` element. We'll discuss `em` in more detail towards the end of this chapter.

Using Comments to Hide Markup from Browsers Temporarily

There's no limit to the amount of information you can put into a comment, and this is why comments are often used to hide a page section temporarily. Commenting may be preferable to deleting content, particularly if you want to put that information back into the web page at a later date; if it's in a comment, you won't have to retype it. This is often called **commenting out** markup. Here's an example:

chapter2/examples/04_commenting_out_markup/commentout.html

```
<!DOCTYPE html>
<html lang="en">
  <head>
    <title>Commenting out XHTML</title>
    <meta charset="utf-8"/>
  </head>
  <body>
    <h1>Current Stock</h1>
    <p>The following items are available for order:</p>
    <ul>
      <li>Dark Smoke Window Tinting</li>
      <li>Bronze Window Tinting</li>
      <!-- <li>Spray mount</li>
      <li>Craft knife (pack of 5)</li> -->
    </ul>
  </body>
</html>
```

Figure 2.11 shows how the page displays in Firefox.

Figure 2.11. The final commented list items are not displayed

Remember, you write a comment like this: `<!--Your comment here followed by the comment closer, two dashes and a right-angled bracket-->`.

Symbols

Occasionally, you may need to include the greater-than (>) or less-than (<) symbols in the text of your web pages. This is a problem because these symbols are also used to denote tags in HTML. So, what can we do? Thankfully, we can use code-like **entities** in our text instead of these symbols. The entity for the greater-than symbol is `&gt;`—which we substitute for the greater-than symbol in our text, as shown in the following simple example. The result of this markup is shown in Figure 2.12.

chapter2/examples/05_symbols/entity.html

```
<!DOCTYPE html>
<html lang="en">
  <head>
    <title>Stock Note</title>
    <meta charset="utf-8"/>
  </head>
  <body>
    <p>Our current stock of craft knives &gt;
    OUT OF STOCK (more due in 3 days)</p>
  </body>
</html>
```

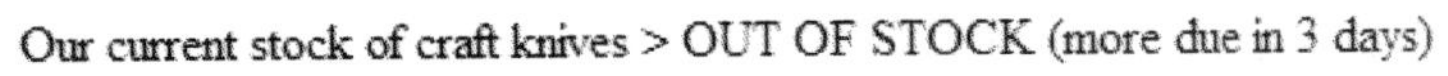

Our current stock of craft knives > OUT OF STOCK (more due in 3 days)

Figure 2.12. The `&gt;` entity is displayed as > in the browser

Many different entities are available for a wide range of symbols, most of which don't appear on your keyboard. They all start with an ampersand (&) and end with a semicolon. Some of the most common are shown in Table 2.1.

Table 2.1. Some common entities

Entity (used in markup)	Symbol (displayed on screen)
&gt;	>
&lt;	<
&amp;	&
&pound;	£
&copy;	©
&trade;	™

Diving into Our Website

So far, we've looked at some very basic web pages as a way to ease you into the process of writing your own HTML markup. Maybe you've typed them up and tried them out, or maybe you've pulled the pages from the code archive and run them in your browser. Perhaps you've even tried experimenting for yourself—it's good to have a play around. None of the examples shown so far are worth keeping, though. Those pages won't be needed again as you progress through the book, but you will be using the ideas introduced in them. We'll develop a fictitious project that will be completed over the course of this book: a website for a local diving club.

The diving club comprises a group of local enthusiasts, and the website will enable club members to:

- share photos from previous dive trips
- stay informed about upcoming dive trips
- provide information about ad hoc meetups
- read other members' dive reports and write-ups
- announce club news

The site also has the following goals:

- attract new members
- provide links to other diving-related websites
- offer a convenient way to search for general diving-related information

The site's audience may be smallish, but regular visitors and club members are keen to be involved. It's a fun site that people will want to come back to again and again, and it's a good project to work on. But it's yet to exist. You're going to commence building it right now, so let's start with our first page: the site's home page.

The Home Page: the Starting Point for All Websites

At the beginning of this chapter, we looked at a basic web page with nothing on it (the car chassis with no bodywork or interior). You saved the file as **basic.html**. Open that file in your text editor now, and strip out the following:

- the text contained within the opening `<title>` and closing `</title>` tags
- all the content between the opening `<body>` and closing `</body>` tags

Save the file as **index.html**.

Here's the markup you should have in front of you now:

```
chapter2/website_files/01_skeleton/index.html

<!DOCTYPE html>
<html lang="en">
  <head>
    <title></title>
    <meta charset="utf-8"/>
  </head>
  <body>
  </body>
</html>
```

Let's start building this website, shall we?

Setting a Title

Remembering what we've learned so far, let's make a few changes to this document. Have a go at the following:

- Change the title of the page to read "Bubble Under—The diving club for the south-west UK."

- Add a heading to the page—a level one heading—that reads "BubbleUnder.com."

■ Immediately after the heading, add a paragraph that reads, "Diving club for the south-west UK—let's make a splash!" (This is your basic marketing-type tagline, folks.)

Once you make these changes, your markup should look like this (the changes are shown in bold):

chapter2/website_files/02_setting_a_title/index.html

```html
<!DOCTYPE html>
<html lang="en">
  <head>
    <title>Bubble Under—The diving club for the south-west
       UK</title>
    <meta charset="utf-8"/>
  </head>
  <body>
    <h1>BubbleUnder.com</h1>
    <p>Diving club for the south-west UK—let's make a
       splash!</p>
  </body>
</html>
```

Save the page, and then double-click on the file to open it in your chosen browser. Figure 2.13 shows what it should look like.

BubbleUnder.com

Diving club for the south-west UK - let's make a splash!

Figure 2.13. Displaying our work on the home page

Welcoming New Visitors

Now, let's expand upon our tagline a little. We'll add a welcoming subheading—a second level heading—to the page, along with an introductory paragraph:

```
chapter2/website_files/03_welcoming_new_visitors/index.html (excerpt)

<body>
  <h1>BubbleUnder.com</h1>
  <p>Diving club for the south-west UK - let's make a splash!</p>
  <h2>Welcome to our super-dooper Scuba site</h2>
  <p>Glad you could drop in and share some air with us! You've
     passed your underwater navigation skills and successfully
     found your way to the start point - or in this case, our
     home page.</p>
</body>
```

Apologies for the diving terminology puns, they're truly cringe-worthy!

Hey! Where'd It All Go?

In an effort to save on space (and trees, if you've bought the hard copy version of this book), I'll avoid repeating markup all the time, instead focusing on the parts that have changed or been added to. And remember: if you think you've missed something, don't worry. You can find all the examples in the book's code archive.

Once you've added the subheading and the paragraph that follows it, save your page once more, and take another look at it in your browser. (You can either hit the refresh/reload button in your browser, or double-click on the file icon in the location where you saved it.) You should be looking at something like the display shown below in Figure 2.14.

BubbleUnder.com

Diving club for the south-west UK - let's make a splash!

Welcome to our super-dooper Scuba site

Glad you could drop in and share some air with us! You've passed your underwater navigation skills and successfully found your way to the start point - or in this case, our home page.

Figure 2.14. The home page taking shape

So, the home page reads a lot like many other home pages at this stage: it has some basic introductory text to welcome visitors, but not much more. What exactly is the site about, or, to be more precise, what will it be about once it's built?

What's It All About?

Notice that, despite our inclusion of a couple of headings and paragraphs, there's little to suggest what this site is about. All visitors know so far is that the site's about diving. Let's add some more explanatory text to the page, along with some contact information:

1. Beneath the current content on the page, add another heading. This time, make it a level three heading that reads "About Us" (remember to include both the opening and closing tags for the heading element).

2. Next, add the following text:

   Bubble Under is a group of diving enthusiasts based in the south-west UK who meet up for diving trips in the summer months when the weather is good and the bacon rolls are flowing. We arrange weekends away as small groups to cut the costs of accommodation and travel, and to ensure that everyone gets a trustworthy dive buddy.

   Although we're based in the south-west, we don't stay on our own turf: past diving weekends have included trips up to Scapa Flow in Scotland and to Malta's numerous wreck sites.

   When we're not diving, we often meet up in a local pub to talk about our recent adventures (any excuse, eh?).

3. Now add a "Contact Us" section, signified by a level three heading.

4. Finally, add some simple contact details as follows:

   To find out more, contact Club Secretary Bob Dobalina on 01793 641207 or email bob@bubbleunder.com.

Save Yourself Some Trouble

If you don't feel like typing out all this content, you can paraphrase, or copy it from the code archive. I've deliberately chosen to put a realistic amount of content on the page, so that you can see the effect of several paragraphs on our display.

Just to recap, various heading levels signify the importance of the different sections and paragraphs within your document. With this in mind, the markup in the body of your document should be similar to this:

chapter2/website_files/04_whats_it_all_about/index.html *(excerpt)*

```
<h1>BubbleUnder.com</h1>
<p>Diving club for the south-west UK - let's make a splash!</p>
<h2>Welcome to our super-dooper Scuba site</h2>
<p>Glad you could drop in and share some air with us! You've
    passed your underwater navigation skills and successfully
    found your way to the start point - or in this case, our home
    page.</p>
<h3>About Us</h3>
<p>Bubble Under is a group of diving enthusiasts based in the
    south-west UK who meet up for diving trips in the summer
    months when the weather is good and the bacon rolls are
    flowing. We arrange weekends away as small groups to cut the
    costs of accommodation and travel and to ensure that everyone
    gets a trustworthy dive buddy.</p>
<p>Although we're based in the south-west, we don't stay on our
    own turf: past diving weekends away have included trips up to
    Scapa Flow in Scotland and to Malta's numerous wreck
    sites.</p>
<p>When we're not diving, we often meet up in a local pub
    to talk about our recent adventures (any excuse, eh?).</p>
<h3>Contact Us</h3>
<p>To find out more, contact Club Secretary Bob Dobalina on
    01793 641207 or email bob@bubbleunder.com.</p>
```

You can see how our home page is shaping up in Figure 2.15.

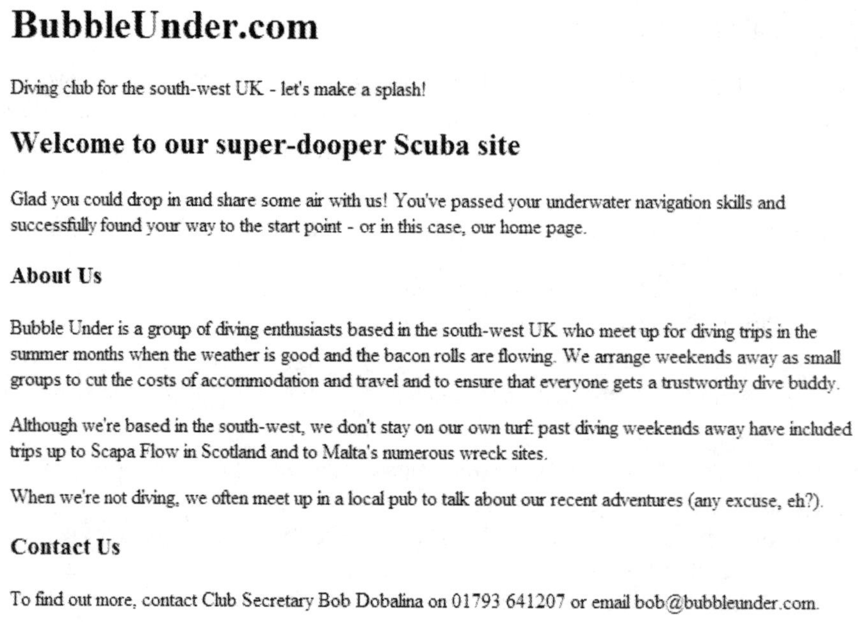

BubbleUnder.com

Diving club for the south-west UK - let's make a splash!

Welcome to our super-dooper Scuba site

Glad you could drop in and share some air with us! You've passed your underwater navigation skills and successfully found your way to the start point - or in this case, our home page.

About Us

Bubble Under is a group of diving enthusiasts based in the south-west UK who meet up for diving trips in the summer months when the weather is good and the bacon rolls are flowing. We arrange weekends away as small groups to cut the costs of accommodation and travel and to ensure that everyone gets a trustworthy dive buddy.

Although we're based in the south-west, we don't stay on our own turf: past diving weekends away have included trips up to Scapa Flow in Scotland and to Malta's numerous wreck sites.

When we're not diving, we often meet up in a local pub to talk about our recent adventures (any excuse, eh?).

Contact Us

To find out more, contact Club Secretary Bob Dobalina on 01793 641207 or email bob@bubbleunder.com.

Figure 2.15. Viewing **index.html**

It's still not very exciting, is it? Trust me, we'll get there. What's important to focus on at this stage is your site's content, and how it might be structured. We're yet to go into great detail about document structure, other than to discuss the use of heading levels, but we'll look at this in more detail later in the chapter. In Chapter 3, we'll see how you can begin to **style** your document—that is, change the font, color, letter spacing, and more—but for now, let's concentrate on the content and structure.

Clickable Email Links

It's all well and good to put an email address on the page, but it's hardly perfect. To use this address, a site visitor would need to copy and paste it into an email message. Surely there's a simpler way? There certainly is:

```
<p>To find out more, contact Club Secretary Bob Dobalina
    on 01793 641207 or <a
    href="mailto:bob@bubbleunder.com">email
    bob@bubbleunder.com</a>.</p>
```

This clickable email link uses the `a` element, which is used to create links on web pages (and will be explained later in this chapter). The `mailto:` prefix tells the browser that the link needs to be treated as an email address (that is, the email program should be opened for this link). The content that follows the `mailto:` section should be a valid email address in the format *username@domain*.

Add this to the web page now, save it, and refresh the view in your browser. Try clicking on the underlined text; it should open your email program automatically with the **To:** address already completed.

So far, the page seems a little boring, doesn't it? Let's sharpen it up a little. We can only keep looking at a page of black and white for so long—let's insert an image into the document. Here's how the `img` element is applied within the context of the page's markup:

chapter2/website_files/05_clickable_email_and_image/index.html (excerpt)

```
<h2>Welcome to our super-dooper Scuba site</h2>
<p><img src="divers-circle.jpg" width="200" height="162"
    alt="A circle of divers practice their skills"/></p>
<p>Glad you could drop in and share some air with us! You've
    passed your underwater navigation skills and successfully
    found your way to the start point - or in this case, our home
    page.</p>
```

The `img` element is used to insert an image into our web page, and the attributes `src`, `alt`, `width`, and `height` describe the image that we're inserting. `src` (short for "source") is just the name of the image file. In this case, it's **divers-circle.jpg**, which you can grab from the code archive. `alt` is some alternative text that can be displayed in place of the image if, for some reason, it's unable to be displayed. This is useful for blind visitors to your site, search engines, and users of slow internet connections. width and height should be obvious, giving the width and height of the image measured in pixels. We'll cover pixels when we look into images in more detail later.

Go and grab **divers-circle.jpg** from the code archive, and put it into your website's folder. The image is shown in Figure 2.16.

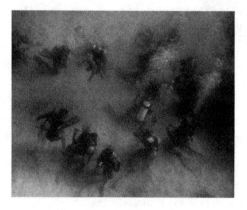

Figure 2.16. Divers pausing in a circle

Open **index.html** in your text editor and add the following markup just after the level two heading (h2):

chapter2/website_files/05_clickable_email_and_image/index.html *(excerpt)*

```
<p><img src="divers-circle.jpg" width="200" height="162"
    alt="A circle of divers practice their skills"/></p>
```

Save the changes, and view the home page in your browser. It should look like the display shown in Figure 2.17.

BubbleUnder.com

Diving club for the south-west UK - let's make a splash!

Welcome to our super-dooper Scuba site

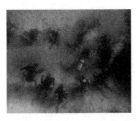

Glad you could drop in and share some air with us! You've passed your underwater navigation skills and successfully found your way to the start point - or in this case, our home page.

About Us

Bubble Under is a group of diving enthusiasts based in the south-west UK who meet up for diving trips in the summer months when the weather is good and the bacon rolls are flowing. We arrange weekends away as

Figure 2.17. Displaying an image on the home page

Adding Structure

Paragraphs? No problem. Headings? Well and truly under your belt. In fact, you're now familiar with the basic structure of a web page. The small selection of tags that we have discussed so far are easy enough to remember, each purpose being quite obvious (remember: p = paragraph). But what on earth is a div?

A div is used to *divide* up a web page (note the abbreviation) and, in doing so, provide a definite structure that can be used to great effect when combined with CSS.

When you place content inside a div, it has no effect on the styling of the text it contains, except that it adds a break before and after the contained text. Unlike a p element, the div adds no margins or padding. Compare the following:

```
<p>This is a paragraph.</p>
<p>This is another paragraph.</p>
<p>This is yet another paragraph.</p>
<p>And just one more paragraph.</p>

<div>This is a div.</div>
```

```
<div>The content of each div appears on a new line.</div>
<div>But unlike paragraphs, there is no additional padding.</div>
<div>A div is a generic block-level container.</div>
```

The difference can be seen in Figure 2.18.

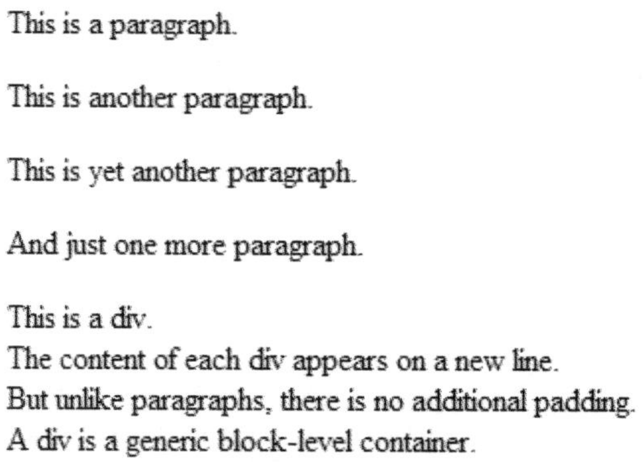

This is a paragraph.

This is another paragraph.

This is yet another paragraph.

And just one more paragraph.

This is a div.
The content of each div appears on a new line.
But unlike paragraphs, there is no additional padding.
A div is a generic block-level container.

Figure 2.18. Paragraphs have additional spacing above and below, unlike div elements

As stated, the purpose of a div is to divide up a web page into distinct sections—a basic structural framework with no styling—whereas p should be used to create a paragraph of text.

 Use Elements as Intended

Never use an HTML element for a purpose for which it was not intended. This really is a golden rule.

Rather than leaving the paragraph tags as they are, you might decide to have this:

```
<div>
  <p>This is a paragraph inside a div.</p>
  <p>So is this.</p>
</div>
```

You can have as many paragraphs as you like inside that `div` element, but note that you cannot place `div` elements inside paragraphs. Think of a `div` as a container that's used to group related items together, and you can't go wrong.

If we look at our home page in the browser, it's possible to identify areas that have a certain purpose. These are listed below, and depicted in Figure 2.19. We have:

- a header area that contains:
    - the site name
    - a tagline
- an area of body content

Figure 2.19 shows how content segments can be carved up into distinct areas based on their purpose.

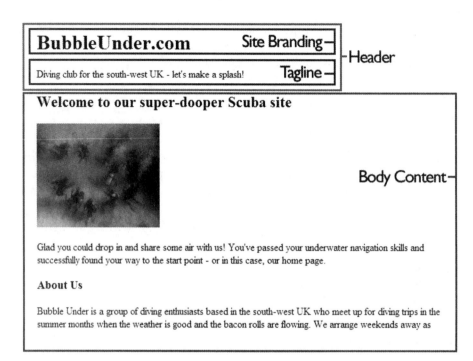

Figure 2.19. Distinct sections in a basic web page

Take the home page we've been working on (**index.html**) and, in your text editor of choice, add <div> and </div> tags around the sections suggested in Figure 2.19. While you're adding those divs, add an id attribute to each, appropriately allocating the names header, sitebranding, tagline, and bodycontent. Remember that attribute names should be written in lowercase, and their values should be contained within double quotation marks.

No Sharing ids

id attributes are used in HTML to uniquely identify elements, so no two elements should share the same id value. You can use these ids later, when you're dealing with elements via CSS or JavaScript.

h1, header, and head

An id attribute set to header should not be confused with headings on the page (h1, h2, and so on); nor is it the same as the head of your HTML page. The id= attribute could just as easily have been named topstuff or pageheader. It doesn't matter, so long as the attribute name describes the *purpose* of that page section to a fellow human being (or to yourself 12 months after you devised it, and have forgotten what you were thinking at the time!).

 A Heads Up on Headers

New in HTML5 is a `header` element, which we'll see in a later chapter. In fact, the introduction of `header` is really an acknowledgement that so many people were marking up their documents in this way, using `id="header"`, that it's become standardized. While it might seem sensible to use it now in our examples, some of the new HTML5 elements can present their own problems. To err on the side of caution, we'll learn all the absolutely safe elements that we can use first, and then give the completed site an HTML5 makeover at the end. It'll help you to understand how HTML has changed over time, while avoiding any difficulties at an early stage of your learning. Because no one wants that, right?

To get you started, I've done a little work on the first part of the page. In the snippet below, that section has been changed to a `div` with an `id` attribute:

chapter2/website_files/06_adding_structure_with_divs/index.html *(excerpt)*

```
<div id="header">
  <h1>BubbleUnder.com</h1>
  <p>Diving club for the south-west UK - let's make a splash!</p>
</div> <!-- end of header div -->
```

Now, try doing the same: apply `div`s to the parts of the content that we've identified as "site branding" and "tagline."

Nesting Explained

We already know that `div`s can contain paragraphs, but a `div` can also contain a number of other `div`s. This is called **nesting**. It's just a matter of putting one `div` inside the other, and making sure your closing tags are right. Nesting elements can help to logically group sections of a web page together, just like how in the real world, you might place a selection of small boxes containing similar items inside a larger box.

Take the following code as an example; see how we've nested `divs` and `ps` inside another `div` with the `id` of `outer`? The indenting should help you identify the hierarchy of elements.

```html
<div id="outer">
  <div id="nested1">
    <p>A paragraph inside the first nested div.</p>
  </div>
  <div id="nested2">
    <p>A paragraph inside the second nested div.</p>
  </div>
</div>
```

As Figure 2.19 shows, some nesting is taking place: the "site branding" and "tagline" divs are nested inside the "header" div.

The Sectioned Page: All Divided Up

All being well, your HTML should now look like this:

chapter2/website_files/06_adding_structure_with_divs/index.html

```html
<!DOCTYPE html>
<html lang="en">
  <head>
    <title>Bubble Under - The diving club for the south-west
      UK</title>
    <meta charset="utf-8"/>
  </head>
  <body>
    <div id="header">
      <div id="sitebranding">
        <h1>BubbleUnder.com</h1>
      </div>
      <div id="tagline">
        <p>Diving club for the south-west UK - let's make
          a splash!</p>
      </div>
    </div> <!-- end of header div -->
    <div id="bodycontent">
      <h2>Welcome to our super-dooper Scuba site</h2>
      <p><img src="divers-circle.jpg" width="200" height="162"
        alt="A circle of divers practice their skills"/></p>
      <p>Glad you could drop in and share some air with us! You've
```

```
          passed your underwater navigation skills and
          successfully found your way to the start point - or in
          this case, our home page.</p>
        <h3>About Us</h3>
        <p>Bubble Under is a group of diving enthusiasts based in
          the south-west UK who meet up for diving trips in the
          summer months when the weather is good and the bacon
          rolls are flowing. We arrange weekends away as small
          groups to cut the costs of accommodation and travel and
          to ensure that everyone gets a trustworthy dive
          buddy.</p>
        <p>Although we're based in the south-west, we don't stay on
          our own turf: past diving weekends away have included
          trips up to Scapa Flow in Scotland and to Malta's
          numerous wreck sites.</p>
        <p>When we're not diving, we often meet up in a local pub
          to talk about our recent adventures (any excuse,
          eh?).</p>
        <h3>Contact Us</h3>
        <p>To find out more, contact Club Secretary Bob Dobalina on
          01793 641207 or
          <a href="mailto:bob@bubbleunder.com">email
          bob@bubbleunder.com</a>.</p>
      </div> <!-- end of bodycontent div -->
    </body>
</html>
```

 Indenting Your Markup

It's a good idea to indent your markup when nesting elements on a web page, as demonstrated with the items inside the div section above. Indenting your code can help resolve problems later, as it's clearer which items sit inside other items. Note that indenting is only really useful for the person—perhaps just you—who's looking at the source markup. It has no effect on how the browser interprets or displays the web page.[14]

Notice that, in the markup above, comments appear after some of the closing div tags. These comments are optional but, again, commenting is a good habit to get

---

[14] The one exception is the `pre` element. Pre is short for preformatted, and any text marked up with this element appears onscreen exactly as it appears in the source; hence, carriage returns, spaces, and any tabs that you've included will be evident. The `pre` element is chiefly used to show code examples.

into as it helps you fix problems later. Often, it's not possible to view your opening and closing `<div>` tags in the same window at the same time, as they're wrapped around large blocks of HTML. If you have several nested `<div>` tags, you might see this at the end of your markup:

```
    </div>
  </div>
</div>
```

In such cases, it might be difficult to work out which div is being closed off at each point. It's probably yet to be apparent to you why this is important or useful, but once we start using CSS to style our pages, errors in the HTML can have an impact. Adding some comments here and there can really help you debug later:

```
    </div> <!-- end of inner div -->
  </div> <!-- end of nested div -->
</div> <!-- end of outer div -->
```

Formatting Made Simple

If you're using an HTML editing program, rather than just a simple text editor, you may be able to automatically format your markup and fix any indenting errors. For example, in Dreamweaver, you can choose **Commands > Apply Source Formatting**. I think it's magic! Just look at the "before and after" scenarios in Figure 2.20.

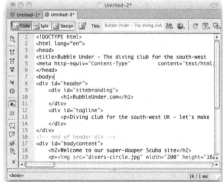

Figure 2.20. HTML in Dreamweaver before (left) and after (right) source formatting

How does the web page look? I've skipped using a screenshot this time, because adding those div elements should make no visual difference at all. The changes we just made are structural, and we'll build on them later.

 Show a Little Restraint

Avoid going overboard when adding divs. Some people can get carried away as they section off the page, with <div> tags appearing all over the place. Overly enthusiastic use of the div can result in a condition now known as "div-itis." So be careful not to litter your markup with superfluous <div> tags just because you can.

Splitting Up the Page

We've been making good progress on our fictitious site, but is a website really a website when it contains only one page? Just as a sentence can comprise one word, so too can there be one-page websites. But you didn't buy this book to learn how to create a one-page website, did you?

Let's take a look at how we can split the page we've been working on into separate entities, and how these pages relate to each other.

First, let's ensure that your page is in good shape before we go forward. The page should reflect the markup shown in the last large block in the previous section (after we added the <div> tags). If not, go to the code archive and grab the version that contains the divs (**/chapter2/website_files/06_adding_structure_with_divs/index.html**). Save it as **index.html** in your website's folder (if you see a prompt that asks whether you want to overwrite the existing file, click **Yes**).

Got that file ready? Let's break it into three pages. First, make two copies of the file:

- Click on the **index.html** icon in Windows Explorer or Finder.
- To copy the file, select **Edit > Copy.**
- To paste a copy in the same location, select **Edit > Paste.**
- Repeat the process once more.

You should now have three HTML files in the folder that holds your website files. The **index.html** file should stay as it is for the time being, but take a moment to rename the other two (in lowercase only). Select each file in turn, choosing **File > Rename**, if you're using Windows. Mac users need simply select the file by clicking on it, and then hitting **Return** to edit the filename.

- Rename one file as **contact.html**.
- Rename the other as **about.html**.

 Where's my file extension?

If your filename appears as just **index** in Windows Explorer, it means that your system is currently set up to hide extensions for files that Windows recognizes. To make the extensions visible, follow these simple steps:

1. Launch Windows Explorer.

2. Windows 7 and Vista users, select **Organize > Folder and Search Options...**; XP users, select **Tools > Folder Options...**.

3. Select the **View** tab.

4. In the **Advanced Settings** group, make sure that **Hide extensions for known file types** is unticked.

We have three identical copies of our HTML page. Now, we need to edit the content so that each page includes only the information relevant to that page.

To open an existing file in Notepad, select **File > Open...**, and in the window that appears, change **Files of type** to **All Files**. Now, when you go to your **Web** folder, you'll see that all the files in that folder are available for opening.

Opening a file in TextEdit is a similar process. Select **File > Open...** to open a file, but make sure that **Ignore rich text command** is checked.

In your text editor, open each page in turn and edit them as follows (remembering to save your changes to each before you open the next file):

index.html   Delete the "About Us" and "Contact Us" sections (both the headings and the paragraphs that follow them), ensuring that the rest of the markup remains untouched. Be careful not to delete the `<div>` and `</div>` tags that enclose the body content.

about.html	Delete the introductory spiel (the level two heading and associated paragraphs, including the image) and remove the "Contact Us" section (including the heading and paragraphs).
contact.html	You should have the hang of this now. This time, we're removing the introductory spiel and the "About Us" section. (If you are unsure whether you've got it right, keep reading: we'll show the altered markup in a moment.)

Now each of the three files contains the content that suits its respective filename, but a further change is required for the two newly created files. Open **about.html** in your text editor and make the following amendments:

- Change the contents of the `title` element to read "About BubbleUnder.com: who we are and what this site is for."

- Change the level three heading `<h3>About Us</h3>` to a level two heading. In the process of editing our original home page, we lost one of our heading levels. Previously, the "About Us" and "Contact Us" headings were marked up as level three headings that sat under the level-two "Welcome" heading. It's not good practice to skip heading levels; that is, an `h2` following `h1` is preferable to an `h3` following an `h1`.

Next, open **contact.html** in your text editor and make the following changes:

- Amend the contents of the `title` element to read "Contact Us at Bubble Under."
- Change the level three heading to a level two heading, as you did for **about.html**.

If everything has gone to plan, you should have three files named **index.html**, **about.html**, and **contact.html**.

The markup for each should be as follows:

```
                                                        index.html

<!DOCTYPE html>
<html lang="en">
  <head>
    <title>Bubble Under - The diving club for the south-west
        UK</title>
    <meta charset="utf-8"/>
  </head>
  <body>
    <div id="header">
      <div id="sitebranding">
        <h1>BubbleUnder.com</h1>
      </div>
      <div id="tagline">
        <p>Diving club for the south-west UK - let's make a
            splash!</p>
      </div>
    </div> <!-- end of header div -->
    <div id="bodycontent">
      <h2>Welcome to our super-dooper Scuba site</h2>
      <p><img src="divers-circle.jpg"
          alt="A circle of divers practice their skills"
          width="200" height="162"/></p>
      <p>Glad you could drop in and share some air with us! You've
          passed your underwater navigation skills and
          successfully found your way to the start point - or in
          this case, our home page.</p>
    </div> <!-- end of bodycontent div -->
  </body>
</html>
```

```
                                                        about.html

<!DOCTYPE html>
<html lang="en">
  <head>
    <title>About Bubble Under: who we are and what this site is
        for</title>
    <meta charset="utf-8"/>
  </head>
  <body>
    <div id="header">
```

```
      <div id="sitebranding">
        <h1>BubbleUnder.com</h1>
      </div>
      <div id="tagline">
        <p>Diving club for the south-west UK - let's make a
           splash!</p>
      </div>
    </div> <!-- end of header div -->
    <div id="bodycontent">
      <h2>About Us</h2>
      <p>Bubble Under is a group of diving enthusiasts based in
         the south-west UK who meet up for diving trips in the
         summer months when the weather is good and the bacon
         rolls are flowing. We arrange weekends away as small
         groups to cut the costs of accommodation and travel and
         to ensure that everyone gets a trustworthy dive
         buddy.</p>
      <p>Although we're based in the south-west, we don't stay on
         our own turf: past diving weekends away have included
         trips up to Scapa Flow in Scotland and to Malta's
         numerous wreck sites.</p>
      <p>When we're not diving, we often meet up in a local pub
         to talk about our recent adventures (any excuse,
         eh?).</p>
    </div> <!-- end of bodycontent div -->
  </body>
</html>
```

```
                                                    contact.html
<!DOCTYPE html>
<html lang="en">
  <head>
    <title>Contact Us at Bubble Under</title>
    <meta charset="utf-8"/>
  </head>
  <body>
    <div id="header">
      <div id="sitebranding">
        <h1>BubbleUnder.com</h1>
      </div>
      <div id="tagline">
        <p>Diving club for the south-west UK - let's make a
           splash!</p>
      </div>
```

```
    </div> <!-- end of header div -->
    <div id="bodycontent">
      <h2>Contact Us</h2>
      <p>To find out more, contact Club Secretary Bob Dobalina on
          01793 641207 or <a
          href="mailto:bob@bubbleunder.com">email
          bob@bubbleunder.com</a>.</p>
    </div> <!-- end of bodycontent div -->
  </body>
</html>
```

Linking Between Our New Pages

We've successfully created a three-page website, but there's a small problem: there are no links between the pages. Try for yourself. Open **index.html** in a web browser and take a look at the display. How will you go from one page to another?

To enable site visitors to move around, we need to add navigation. Navigation relies on **anchors**, more commonly referred to as links. The HTML for an anchor, or link, is as follows:

```
<a href="filename.html">Link text here</a>
```

The a element (where a is for anchor) might be less intuitive than using p for paragraph or li for list item, but you'll come to know this one quickly—after all, it's what the Web is built on.

▨ The a element contains the **link text** that will be clicked (by default, it appears on the screen as blue underlined text).

▨ The href attribute refers to the page that you're linking to (be that a file stored locally on your computer, or a page on a live website). Unfortunately, again, href is not immediately memorable (it stands for "hypertext reference"), but you'll use it so often that you'll soon remember it.

 Don't Click Here!

The link text—the words inside the anchor element that appear underlined on the screen—should be a neat summary of that link's purpose (for example, email bob@bubbleunder.com). All too often, you'll see links asking you to "Click here to submit an image," or "Click here to notify us of your change of address" when "Submit an image," or "Notify us of your change of address" more than suffices. Never use "Click here" links—it really is bad linking practice, and is discouraged for usability and accessibility reasons.[15]

Let's create a simple navigation menu that you can drop into your pages. Our navigation is just a list (an unordered list using ul and li elements) of three links. Here's the markup:

```
<ul>
  <li><a href="index.html">Home</a></li>
  <li><a href="about.html">About Us</a></li>
  <li><a href="contact.html">Contact Us</a></li>
</ul>
```

We'll place all this inside a div, so that we can easily see what this block of HTML represents:

```
<div id="navigation">
  <ul>
    <li><a href="index.html">Home</a></li>
    <li><a href="about.html">About Us</a></li>
    <li><a href="contact.html">Contact Us</a></li>
  </ul>
</div> <!-- end of navigation div -->
```

Now, we paste this markup into an appropriate place on each of our pages. A good position would be just after the header, before the main body content starts.

---

[15] Jukka Korpela's article provides greater detail if you're interested: "Why 'Click here' is bad linking practice" [http://www.cs.tut.fi/~jkorpela/www/click.html].

In the code below, the navigation block appears in position on the home page:

```
                    chapter2/website_files/07_linking_between_pages/index.html
<!DOCTYPE html>
<html lang="en">
  <head>
    <title>Bubble Under - The diving club for the south-west
        UK</title>
    <meta charset="utf-8"/>
  </head>
  <body>
    <div id="header">
      <div id="sitebranding">
        <h1>BubbleUnder.com</h1>
      </div>
      <div id="tagline">
        <p>Diving club for the south-west UK - let's make a
            splash!</p>
      </div>
    </div> <!-- end of header div -->
    <div id="navigation">
      <ul>
        <li><a href="index.html">Home</a></li>
        <li><a href="about.html">About Us</a></li>
        <li><a href="contact.html">Contact Us</a></li>
      </ul>
    </div> <!-- end of navigation div -->
    <div id="bodycontent">
      <h2>Welcome to our super-dooper Scuba site</h2>
      <p><img src="divers-circle.jpg" width="200" height="162"
          alt="A circle of divers practice their skills"/></p>
      <p>Glad you could drop in and share some air with us!
          You've passed your underwater navigation skills and
          successfully found your way to the start point - or in
          this case, our home page.</p>
    </div> <!-- end of bodycontent div -->
  </body>
</html>
```

You should now be looking at a page like the one shown in Figure 2.21.

BubbleUnder.com

Diving club for the south-west UK - let's make a splash!

- Home
- About Us
- Contact Us

Welcome to our super-dooper Scuba site

Glad you could drop in and share some air with us! You've passed your underwater navigation skills and successfully found your way to the start point - or in this case, our home page.

Figure 2.21. Displaying simple navigation on the page

Add the block of links to **contact.html** and **about.html**, and try clicking on the links that you've just added. It should be possible to flick between all three pages, as shown in Figure 2.22.

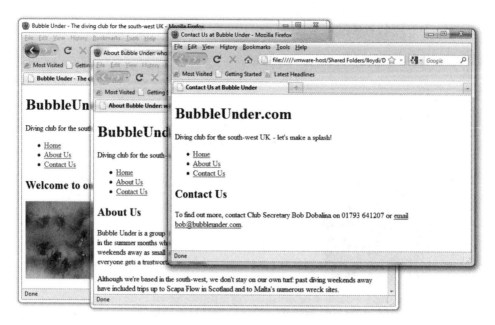

Figure 2.22. Navigable web pages

This is a landmark. You're now the creator of a working, navigable website. Let's discuss a few more HTML elements that you can add to your pages.

The `blockquote` (Who said that?)

We're going to add a sound bite—well, a written quote, to be precise—to the About Us page. Here are the lines:

> "Happiness is a dip in the ocean followed by a pint or two of Old Speckled Hen. You can quote me on that!"

We'll add the quote after the final paragraph in **about.html** using a `blockquote`[16] element; here's the markup you'll need:

chapter2/website_files/08_blockquote/about.html *(excerpt)*

```
<blockquote>
  <p>"Happiness is a dip in the ocean followed by a pint or two of
     Old Speckled Hen. You can quote me on that!"</p>
</blockquote>
```

---

[16] http://reference.sitepoint.com/html/blockquote/

Or is it? Who's doing the talking? Well, it's our dear (fictional) Club Secretary, Bob Dobalina:

chapter2/website_files/08_blockquote/about.html *(excerpt)*

```html
<p>Or as our man Bob Dobalina would put it:</p>
<blockquote>
  <p>"Happiness is a dip in the ocean followed by a pint or two of
      Old Speckled Hen. You can quote me on that!"</p>
</blockquote>
```

The quotation can contain as many paragraphs as you like, as long as each one starts and ends with the correct tags, and the opening `<blockquote>` tag is closed off properly.

Figure 2.23 shows how the `blockquote` above will appear on the page.

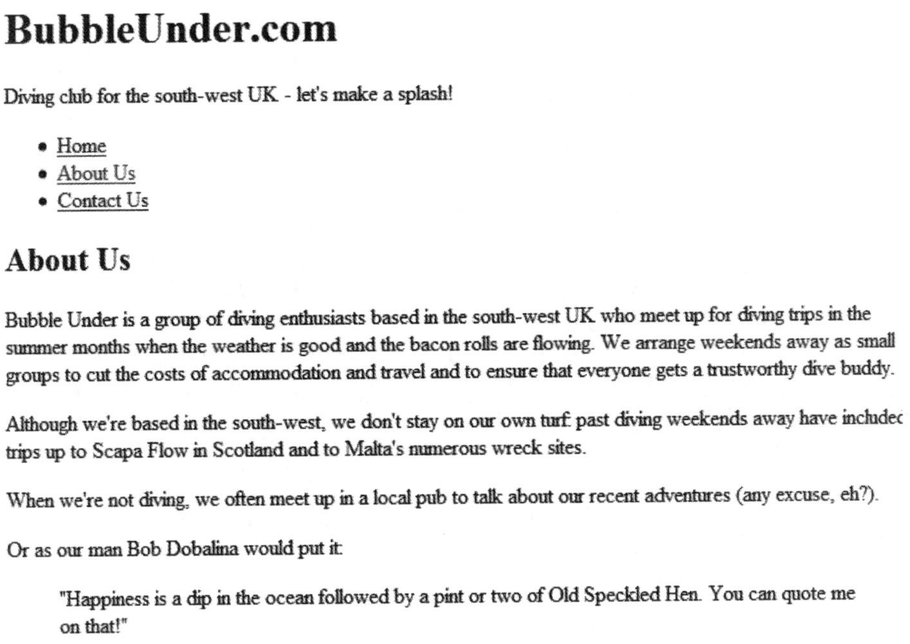

BubbleUnder.com

Diving club for the south-west UK - let's make a splash!

- Home
- About Us
- Contact Us

About Us

Bubble Under is a group of diving enthusiasts based in the south-west UK who meet up for diving trips in the summer months when the weather is good and the bacon rolls are flowing. We arrange weekends away as small groups to cut the costs of accommodation and travel and to ensure that everyone gets a trustworthy dive buddy.

Although we're based in the south-west, we don't stay on our own turf: past diving weekends away have included trips up to Scapa Flow in Scotland and to Malta's numerous wreck sites.

When we're not diving, we often meet up in a local pub to talk about our recent adventures (any excuse, eh?).

Or as our man Bob Dobalina would put it:

> "Happiness is a dip in the ocean followed by a pint or two of Old Speckled Hen. You can quote me on that!"

Figure 2.23. Displaying a quotation on the page

Displaying blockquotes

In most browsers, your use of `blockquote` will indent the quoted text in the page display. This effect can be overridden if it's not to your taste, but we'll cover that in a later chapter. On the flip side, you should *never* use the `blockquote` element for the purposes of indenting text; that would be very poor form. Only use `blockquote` for its intended purpose: to present a quotation. There are other, better ways to create visual indentations, namely CSS.

The `cite` Element

If the quote to which you've referred is written elsewhere—in a magazine, for instance, or a book, or even your own website—you can add some information to communicate the quote's source. One way is to use the `cite` element. A citation, by default, will style the text in italics. Here's how the markup would look for a citation:

```
<p>I remember reading <cite>Salem's Lot</cite> by Stephen King as
    a child, and being very scared of the dark for days after.</p>
```

So what do we do if text is both a quotation *and* a citation? The `blockquote` element has a `cite` attribute for this very purpose:

```
<blockquote cite="http://www.petermoore.net/sftb/chapter1.htm">
    <p>It didn't take long for a daily routine to form: when they
        left for work in the morning I'd still be in bed. And when
        they came home they'd find me sitting on the sofa, drinking
        beer and watching TV soaps.</p>
</blockquote>
```

We're not using the `cite` element (or the `cite` attribute) in the diving website, but you may find them useful in your own website projects.

strong and em

We mentioned the `em` element earlier in this chapter; it's a fairly straightforward element to remember. If you can imagine yourself adding some kind of inflection as you say a word, then emphasis is probably what you need. If you're looking to strike a more forceful tone, you should consider going in `strong`.

By default, using em will style text in italics, while using strong makes the text bold. You can combine the two if you want, but usually one will suffice. The example below should help you understand what these elements are used for. Figure 2.24 shows how they appear in the browser.

```
<p>Although Jimmy was told to <strong>never</strong> put his hands
    on the exhaust pipe, he <em>still</em> couldn't help
    himself.</p>
```

Although Jimmy was told to **never** put his hands on the exhaust pipe, he *still* couldn't help himself.

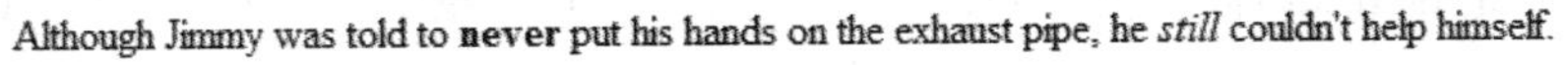

Figure 2.24. Displaying different emphasis styles in the browser

Taking a Break

The chapter's almost at an end, so why take a break? Well, this is just an excuse for a headline pun. We have one more element to look at: the break element.

The break element (br)[17] basically replicates what happens when you hit the carriage return on an old typewriter; to create a paragraph, you'd hit **Enter** twice to give the necessary spacing. In HTML, the fact that you're marking up a paragraph with <p> and </p> tags means that the spacing is worked out for you automatically by the browser. However, if you just want to signify the start of a new line, rather than a new paragraph, the element you need is br, as demonstrated in this limerick:[18]

```
<p>The limerick packs laughs anatomical,<br/>
Into space that is quite economical.<br/>
But the good ones I've seen,<br/>
So seldom are clean,<br/>
And the clean ones so seldom are comical.</p>
```

---

[17] http://reference.sitepoint.com/html/br/

[18] http://en.wikipedia.org/wiki/Limerick_(poetry)

Avoid Multiple Breaks

It's all too easy to resort to using multiple breaks in a web page to achieve a visual effect. If you find yourself doing this, you almost certainly need to look for a more suitable technique (we'll look at how this visual effect should be achieved later). This element is particularly hard to control or style—sometimes impossible. In my recent experience, it's generally only used for verse, as above, or for creating a new line in a postal address. So, be careful and restrained in your use of br.

Note that br is an empty element, just like meta and img, so in HTML it's written as <br/>.

Summary

Wow, what a great start we've made. In this chapter, you've created three linked pages from a single web page. You've become familiar with the most commonly used HTML tags, as well as some of the less common types that you can apply to your web pages. But somehow, despite all your efforts, the web pages are looking a little on the bland side. Fear not, it's only Chapter 2—we're going to fix that very soon. In the next chapter, we'll be adding some splashes of color, so that our pages look more like a fun diving site, and less like a boring old Word document.

Chapter 3

Adding Some Style

In Chapter 1 and Chapter 2, we stepped through the process of setting up your computer so that we could develop websites, and pulled together the beginnings of a website with which you could impress your friends and family. The trouble is, when you came to show off your fledgling site to your nearest and dearest, they weren't *that* impressed. What have you done wrong?

The answer is nothing. It's true that your website may look a little bland at present, but the underlying structure on which it's built is rock-solid. To return to our automotive analogy, you now have the perfect chassis and some decent bodywork, and, while your car's yet to turn heads, it's only a matter of time. Just let them see what you can do with this rolling shell!

In this chapter, we'll begin the process of adding that lick of paint to your site. The tool for the job is **Cascading Style Sheets—CSS** to those in the know (or with limited typing abilities). Let's take a look at what CSS can do for you.

What is CSS?

As this chapter revolves almost exclusively around CSS, it's a good idea to begin with a basic discussion of what CSS is, and why you should use it. As we've already mentioned, CSS stands for Cascading Style Sheets, but that's too much of a mouthful for most people—we'll stick with the abbreviation. We also won't concern ourselves too much with which version of CSS for now. There are slight differences between CSS2 and CSS2.1 that you'll only really care about once you become a super-nerd in this topic. Most of the book's examples will be CSS2 or 2.1; we'll only start to become particular with version numbers in Chapter 10, where browser support for CSS3, and its extra functionality, needs more attention.

CSS is a language that allows you to change the appearance of elements on the page: the size, style, and color of text; background colors; border styles and colors; even the position of elements on the page. Let's take a look at some CSS in action; we'll start by learning about **inline styles**.

Inline Styles

If you're familiar with Microsoft Word (or a similar word processing package), you may well have created your fair share of flyers, advertisements, or personal news-letters (as well as the more mundane letters to the local authorities and so on). In doing so, you've probably used text formatting options to color certain parts of your text. It's as simple as highlighting the words you want to change, and then clicking on a color in a drop-down palette. The same effect can be achieved in HTML using a little bit of inline CSS. This is what it looks like:

```
<p style="color: red;">The quick brown fox jumps over
    the lazy dog.</p>
```

In the example above, we use a `style` attribute inside the opening `<p>` tag. Applying a style to a specific HTML element in this way is known as using an inline style.

 But wait a minute—inline styles?

If you have dabbled with CSS before, you may be thinking, "But this isn't the right way to do it," to which I say, "Just wait a short while—all will be explained soon."

We just need to run through these basics first before approaching the best way of doing this.

The `style` attribute can contain one or more **declarations** between its quotation marks. A declaration is made up of two parts: a **property**, and a **value** for that property. In the example above, the declaration is `color: red` (`color` being the property and `red` being its value).

If you wanted to, you could add another declaration to the example above. For instance, as well as having the text display in red, you might want it to appear in a bold typeface. The property that controls this effect is `font-weight`; it can have a range of different values, but mostly you'll use `normal` or `bold`. As you might expect, you'd use the following markup to make the paragraph red and bold:

```
<p style="color: red; font-weight: bold;">The quick brown fox
    jumps over the lazy dog.</p>
```

Notice that a semicolon separates the two declarations. You could carry on adding styles in this way, but beware, this approach can be messy. There are cleverer ways to apply styling, as we'll see very soon.

Adding Inline Styles

Open **about.html** in your text editor, and add an inline style. We want to make the text in the first paragraph after the "About Us" heading bold and blue. Refer to the previous example as you create the style.

Does the markup for your paragraph look like this?

```
<p style="color: blue; font-weight: bold;">Bubble Under is a group
    of diving enthusiasts based in the south-west UK who meet up
    for diving trips in the summer months when the weather is good
    and the bacon rolls are flowing. We arrange weekends away as
    small groups to cut the costs of accommodation and travel and
    to ensure that everyone gets a trustworthy dive buddy.</p>
```

If your markup looks like that shown here, save **about.html** and take a look at it in your browser. It should appear like the page shown in Figure 3.1.

BubbleUnder.com

Diving club for the south-west UK - let's make a splash!

- Home
- About Us
- Contact Us

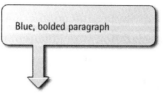

Blue, bolded paragraph

About Us

Bubble Under is a group of diving enthusiasts based in the south-west UK who meet up for diving trips in the summer months when the weather is good and the bacon rolls are flowing. We arrange weekends away as small groups to cut the costs of accommodation and travel and to ensure that everyone gets a trustworthy dive buddy.

Although we're based in the south-west, we don't stay on our own turf: past diving weekends away have included trips up to Scapa Flow in Scotland and to Malta's numerous wreck sites.

When we're not diving, we often meet up in a local pub to talk about our recent adventures (*any* excuse, eh?).

Figure 3.1. Content displayed using blue and bold styles

The span Element

You can easily color a whole paragraph like this, but more often than not, you'll want to pick out just specific words to highlight within a paragraph. You can do this using a span element, which can be wrapped around any content you like. Unlike p, which means paragraph, or blockquote, which signifies a quotation, span has no meaning. A span is little more than a tool for highlighting the start and end of a section to which you want to apply a style.[1] Instead of making that whole paragraph blue, we might want just the first two words—Bubble Under—to be blue and bold. Here's how we can use the span element to achieve this:

```
<p><span style="color: blue; font-weight: bold;">Bubble
Under</span> is a group of diving enthusiasts based in the
south-west UK who meet up for diving trips in the summer
months when the weather is good and the bacon rolls are
flowing. We arrange weekends away as small groups to cut the
costs of accommodation and travel and to ensure that everyone
gets a trustworthy dive buddy.</p>
```

When we view that markup in a browser, we see the display shown in Figure 3.2.

---

[1] Applying a span also enables you to do some other clever stuff to your web page using JavaScript; for our purposes, though, its scope is limited to what it allows you to do using CSS.

BubbleUnder.com

Diving club for the south-west UK - let's make a splash!

- Home
- About Us
- Contact Us

> Blue, bolded text

About Us

Bubble Under is a group of diving enthusiasts based in the south-west UK who meet up for diving trips in the summer months when the weather is good and the bacon rolls are flowing. We arrange weekends away as small groups to cut the costs of accommodation and travel and to ensure that everyone gets a trustworthy dive buddy.

Although we're based in the south-west, we don't stay on our own turf: past diving weekends away have included trips up to Scapa Flow in Scotland and to Malta's numerous wreck sites.

When we're not diving, we often meet up in a local pub to talk about our recent adventures (*any* excuse, eh?).

Figure 3.2. Using the span element to pick out specific words for styling

Let's take a quick look at other ways to apply inline styles (this is separate to our project site, so feel free to experiment).

```
<p style="font-style: italic">The quick brown fox jumps over the
    lazy dog.</p>
```

Not surprisingly, that CSS declaration will italicize all the text in the paragraph. Here's another example, in which span is used to highlight specific words:

```
<p>The quick brown fox <span style="font-style: italic;
    font-weight: bold">jumps</span> over the lazy dog.</p>
```

Embedded Styles

Inline styles offer a simple and quick method to apply some CSS effects to specific sections of a document, but there are better ways to style a page. After all, it would be more ideal if you could set styles in just one place, rather than having to type them out every time you wanted to use them, surely?

Embedded stylesheets are the logical next step. An **embedded stylesheet** is a section you add to the start of a web page that sets out all the styles that will be used on that page. To do this, you need to use the style[2] element inside the head:

```
<head>
  <title>Bubble Under - The diving club for the south-west
      UK</title>
  <meta charset="utf-8"/>
  <style type="text/css">
    p {
      font-weight: bold;
    }
  </style>
</head>
```

In the markup shown above, we've moved the inline style into an embedded stylesheet. The embedded stylesheet starts with a `<style type="text/css">` tag and, predictably, ends with a `</style>` tag. The actual style declarations are enclosed in a set of **curly braces**: { and }. The `p` that appears before the first curly brace tells the browser what elements the style rules are for; in this case, we're making the text inside every `p` element bold. The `p` is called the **selector**, and it's a great tool for quickly and easily changing the appearance of lots of elements on your page. The selector instructs the browser to apply all the declarations between the curly braces to certain elements. The selector, curly braces, and declarations combine to form what's called a **rule**.

In this case, our stylesheet contains one rule: "Style all the paragraphs on this page so that the text appears in a bold font."

We could add more declarations to our rule. For instance, if we wanted to make the text bold and blue, we'd add the declaration `color: blue` to our rule:

---

[2] http://reference.sitepoint.com/html/style/

```
<style type="text/css">
  p {
    font-weight: bold;
    color: blue;
  }
</style>
```

Jargon Break

Okay, okay, there's been an awful lot of jargon so far. Let's recap: Figure 3.3 brings the theory into focus.

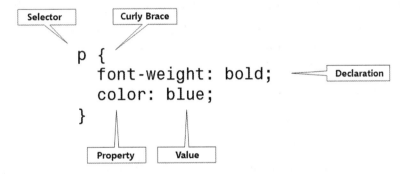

Figure 3.3. The anatomy of a rule

Why Embedded Styles Are Better Than Inline Styles

In the example provided in Figure 3.3, text in all paragraphs will display in bold, blue type. This saves you from typing `<p style="font-weight: bold; color: blue">` every time you start a new paragraph—a clear benefit over inline styles.

If you wanted to change the color of all paragraph text to red, you need only change it in the stylesheet at the top of the page:

```
<style type="text/css">
  p {
    font-weight: bold;
    color: red;
  }
</style>
```

That's efficiency for you. For this reason, an embedded stylesheet is a marked improvement over inline styles. But what if you have a website comprising many pages? If you want to make your changes across the whole site, embedded stylesheets used in the way I demonstrated still falls short of the perfect solution. Why? Because, to make a site-wide change, you'd have to edit the embedded stylesheet on *every single page* of that site. That's why the best solution is to use an external stylesheet.

External stylesheets

Why External Stylesheets Are Better Than Embedded Styles

An **external stylesheet** provides a location where you can place styles to be applied on all your web pages. This is where the true power of CSS lies, and it's for this reason why we've spent minimal time applying inline or embedded styles to our diving club project site.

The Bad Old Days

In the past, or The Bad Old Days as we'll call them, people would create websites on a page-by-page basis, and style them on a page-by-page basis using all manner of nasty elements of which I daren't even speak! Sometimes, these sites grew beyond the webmaster's wildest imagination. "Fantastic," thought Mr. or Ms. Webmaster. "My website now has over 200 pages. Soon I'll be bigger than Microsoft!" A few months later, the webmaster would decide to redesign the website and realize, with considerable horror, that each and every single web page would need to be altered to redesign the site in a consistent manner. Every page needed 20 or more different tweaks, and each tweak had to be applied consistently to every page of the site. Inevitably, some pages were missed and eventually the redesign plan was dropped unceremoniously. In short, the ugly website remained ugly for a lot longer, before dying a nasty death through sheer negligence (indeed, there are many such legacy documents littered throughout the Web today). This needn't be the case, though.

Happy Days! CSS Support Is Here

The large majority of web browsers in use today offer excellent support for CSS. This wasn't always the case, which is why some people were slow to adopt CSS-based design in the past. Some browsers choke on a few of the more advanced CSS techniques, causing odd effects on the page, while others simply ignore your advanced styles (the latter is definitely preferable!). By and large, though, you can style your web pages using CSS and be confident that what you see on your screen is the same as what 99.5% of your intended audience sees.

CSS gives you the power to set styling rules in one place. When you want to make changes to your website, you make changes in that one place, and your whole website changes automatically to reflect those new styles.

Creating an External CSS File

If you're to make use of all the benefits of an external stylesheet, you'll first need to create a CSS file that can be shared among the pages of your website. Open your text editor and enter the following in a new document:

chapter3/website_files/04_style_sheet_link/style1.css

```
/*
CSS for Bubble Under site
*/

p {
   font-weight: bold;
   color: blue;
}
```

Save the file in the same folder as your HTML files, naming it **style1.css**; you can save a CSS file in the same way you saved your HTML files.

Note that the first few lines we typed into our CSS file won't actually do anything. Like HTML, CSS allows you to add comments. It's a shame that the tags for HTML comments differ from those for CSS comments, but they perform exactly the same function: they allow you to make notes about your work without affecting the on-screen display. In CSS, a comment starts with a /* and ends with a */; the browser ignores anything in between. Above, we used the comment simply to make a note about the purpose of the file, namely that it's the CSS for the Bubble Under site. We've also added a rule so that all the type in our paragraphs is now bold and blue.

Linking CSS to a Web Page

Before your CSS can have any effect, you need to link it to the web pages to which you want the styles to apply. To do this, you need to add a `link`[3] element to the `head` of each and every web page that will be styled using CSS. Our site contains just three pages at the moment, so this will be nice and easy. The `link` element simply links a file to the page on which the element appears; in this case, the linked file is a stylesheet.

Below, the new line appears in the context of the home page:

chapter3/website_files/04_style_sheet_link/index.html *(excerpt)*

```
<head>
  <title>Bubble Under - The diving club for the south-west
      UK</title>
  <meta charset="utf-8"/>
  <link href="style1.css" rel="stylesheet" type="text/css"/>
</head>
```

Let's take a look at what the markup means.

The `href` attribute tells the web browser where the stylesheet file (**style1.css**) can be found, in the same way that the `href` attribute is used in an anchor to point to the destination file (for example, `<a href="home.htm">Home</a>`).

The `rel="stylesheet"` and `type="text/css"` parts of the link tag tell the browser what kind of file is being linked to, and how the browser should handle the content. You should always include these important attributes when linking to a **.css** file.

Empty Element Alert!

The `link` element is another one of those empty elements we covered in Chapter 2, without separate start and end tags. `link` is a complete element in its own right, and ends using the space and forward slash (following XHTML syntax rules).

Now that we know how to link our pages to our CSS file, let's try it out on our project site:

---

[3] http://reference.sitepoint.com/html/link/

- Open each of your web pages—**index.html**, **about.html**, and **contact.html**—in your text editor. Add the following line just before the closing `</head>` tag in each of those files:

```
<link href="style1.css" rel="stylesheet" type="text/css"/>
```

- Be sure to save each page. Then, try opening each one in your web browser.

All your paragraphs should now display in bold, blue text. If so, congratulations —you've now linked one stylesheet to three separate pages. If you change the color specified in your **.css** file from blue to red, you should see that change reflected across your pages the next time you open them. Go ahead, give it a try.

Now, using bold, blue text might be a good way to make sure your stylesheets are correctly linked, but it's not the design effect we want to use. Remove the p rule, but leave the comment, and we'll start building our stylesheet for real.

Starting to Build Our Stylesheet

The stylesheet is ready to be used. It's saved in the right location, and your web pages (all three—count 'em) are linked to it correctly. It's time to set some styles.

One of the first changes that people often make to a website's default styling is to the font (or typeface) that's used. On Windows, most browsers use Times New Roman as the default—it's the font that has been used in all the screenshots we've seen so far. For many people, though, it's a bit dull, probably because it's used more than any other. It's very easy to change fonts using CSS's font-family property.

The best place to use this is within the body element, as shown below:

chapter3/website_files/04_body_verdana/style1.css

```
/*
CSS for Bubble Under site
*/

body {
  font-family: Verdana;
}
```

Here, I've chosen to use the Verdana font. It's applied to the body element because body contains every element that you will see on the web page. The nature of how CSS is applied means that every element contained in the body element will take on the same font (unless another font is specified for a given element or elements within body—but more on that a little later).

Great, Verdana it is! But what if some people who view your site don't have Verdana installed on their computers? Hmm, that's a tricky one. The short answer is that the browser will make its best guess on which font it should use instead, but the browser need not do *all* the guesswork. The font-family property allows us to enter multiple fonts in the order in which we'd prefer them used if a particular font is missing on a user's computer. So, we could type the following:

```
body {
    font-family: Verdana, Helvetica, Arial, sans-serif;
}
```

To translate: "Style everything in the body of my web page so that the text appears as Verdana. Failing that, use Helvetica and, failing that, Arial. If none of the above are installed, just use whichever sans-serif font is available."

This is known as a **font stack**, and there are various combinations that you might like to try later on. Check out what Michael Tuck has to say in "8 Definitive Web Font Stacks"[4] if you can't wait to have a play around with the fonts available to you.

We'll use this selection of three fonts (and the sans-serif fallback) in our diving site, so let's open the stylesheet file and play around with some CSS.

1. Type the above CSS into **style1.css**.
2. Save the file, and then open the home page (**index.html**) in your browser.

If everything went to plan, your web page (all three of them, actually) should display slightly differently to how they did before. Figure 3.4 shows how our newly styled home page appears.

---

[4] http://www.sitepoint.com/eight-definitive-font-stacks/

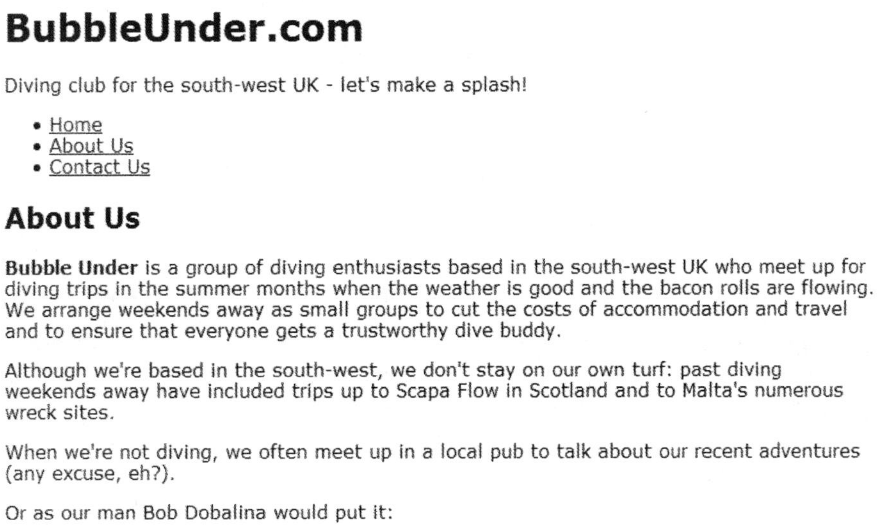

BubbleUnder.com

Diving club for the south-west UK - let's make a splash!

- Home
- About Us
- Contact Us

About Us

Bubble Under is a group of diving enthusiasts based in the south-west UK who meet up for diving trips in the summer months when the weather is good and the bacon rolls are flowing. We arrange weekends away as small groups to cut the costs of accommodation and travel and to ensure that everyone gets a trustworthy dive buddy.

Although we're based in the south-west, we don't stay on our own turf: past diving weekends away have included trips up to Scapa Flow in Scotland and to Malta's numerous wreck sites.

When we're not diving, we often meet up in a local pub to talk about our recent adventures (any excuse, eh?).

Or as our man Bob Dobalina would put it:

Figure 3.4. A font change in the stylesheet affects the body of our web pages

Sans-serif Fonts: Better for Onscreen Viewing

A serif font is defined as such for the little flourishes evident at the ends of each letter. These flourishes, shown in Figure 3.5, are known as **serifs**. They're great for printed material, as they give a little shape to the words, making them easier to read.

However, on the screen, serif fonts can be a little messy, especially when they're used for smaller type—most screens lack the pixels to do these flourishes justice. For this reason, many websites use **sans-serif** fonts (from French, translating as "without serif") when the size is set quite small.

Note that when you refer to a sans-serif font in CSS, you must hyphenate the two words, i.e. `sans-serif`.

Figure 3.5. Highlighting the serifs in the Georgia font

 Exploring the Font Universe

In case you're thinking, "This is all well and good, but there's a really cool font I'd prefer to use," you may just be in luck. There are ways of providing browsers with nonstandard fonts, but it's an involved process due to the different ways that browsers support them. There are also a number of services on the Web (free ones too!) that help to make this process easier for you. We'll take a look at what's involved when providing more fancy-pants fonts in Chapter 10.

Stylish Headings

The first element that we'll style is the level one heading, denoted by the h1 element. Let's add some rules to our CSS file to see what's possible when it comes to those headings. In your text editor, add the following to **style1.css**:

```
h1 {
  font-family: "Trebuchet MS", Arial, Helvetica, sans-serif;
}
```

Save the CSS file and refresh your view of the home page in your browser. Can you see what's changed? All the first-level headings now display in the Trebuchet MS font, while everything else displays in Verdana.

We've chosen another sans-serif font, but it's different enough to provide plenty of contrast with the paragraphs, as Figure 3.6 illustrates.

Some Font Names Deserve Quotes

In the code example above, "Trebuchet MS" appears in quotation marks. You don't need to wrap quote marks around font names unless the font comprises several words, such as "Courier New" or "Times New Roman." A single-word font name, such as Arial or Verdana, does not need to be wrapped inside quotes.

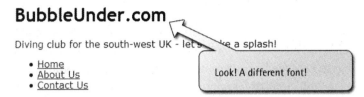

Figure 3.6. h1 headings displayed in one sans-serif font (Trebuchet MS) while paragraph text displayed in another (Verdana)

Have a quick look around your fledgling website, and you'll see that the new styles have been applied to all your web pages. Let's now go a step (or two) further.

What's going on? Nothing's Changed!

If you try refreshing your browser's view of a page and nothing appears to be different, check that you saved the changes you made to the CSS file. If you did, check that you typed the CSS exactly as described. If there's no problems there, you may be experiencing a caching problem with your browser.

Web browsers cache some content. **Caching** is when your browser accesses files previously saved to the hard drive when you visit a given web page, rather than downloading new files each time. For example, you enter the URL, and the browser pulls the page—or resources required for the page such as images—that's stored in its cache. This speeds up the process of displaying a web page that has been previously loaded. Unfortunately, your cache can soon become out-of-date, and when that happens, the page you visit might not display the most recent data.

This happens most frequently with images, but it can also occur using CSS files. The good news is that you have control over your browser's cache settings. Therefore, the amount of space the cache takes up on your hard disk before cached content is replaced with newer data can be adjusted. You can poke around your browser's settings for terms like "Cache" or "Temporary Internet Files" to change these settings; however, most users opt to leave their caches to the default settings.

If you're positive that you've made the necessary changes to your CSS file (and saved them) correctly, you may need to force-reload the CSS file in your browser. To force the browser to retrieve the most up-to-date version of your CSS file, simply hold down the **Shift** key (**Ctrl** for Internet Explorer) and click on the **Refresh** (or **Reload**) icon on your browser's toolbar.

A Mixture of New Styles

Let's make some more changes to the look of the site—we'll add more styles to the body, and alter the appearance of the navigation. Copy the CSS below into your **style1.css** file (or copy it from the book's code archive):

```
chapter3/website_files/07_blue_background/style1.css

/*
CSS for Bubble Under site
*/

body {
  font-family: Verdana, Helvetica, Arial, sans-serif;
  background-color: #e2edff;
  line-height: 125%;
  padding: 15px;
}

h1 {
  font-family: "Trebuchet MS", Helvetica, Arial, sans-serif;
  font-size: x-large;
}

li {
  font-size: small;
}
```

```
h2 {
  color: blue;
  font-size: medium;
  font-weight: normal;
}

p {
  font-size: small;
  color: navy;
}
```

Save the CSS file, and then click **Reload** (or **Refresh**) in your browser. With some luck, you'll be looking at a page like the one shown in Figure 3.7.

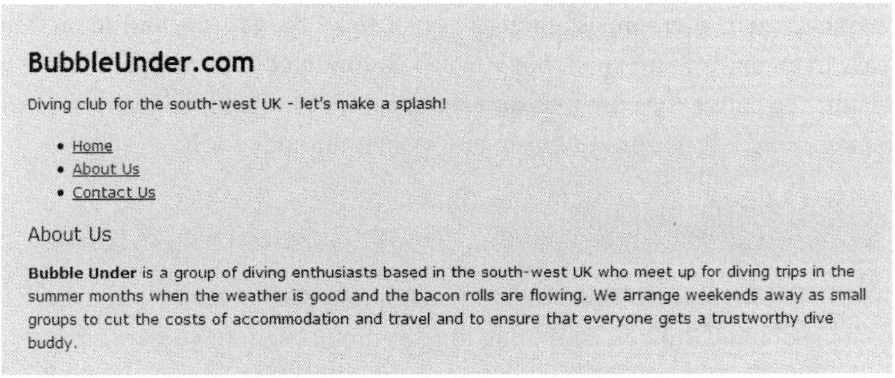

BubbleUnder.com

Diving club for the south-west UK - let's make a splash!

- Home
- About Us
- Contact Us

About Us

Bubble Under is a group of diving enthusiasts based in the south-west UK who meet up for diving trips in the summer months when the weather is good and the bacon rolls are flowing. We arrange weekends away as small groups to cut the costs of accommodation and travel and to ensure that everyone gets a trustworthy dive buddy.

Figure 3.7. Applying subtle changes to the CSS to affect the font's display

A New Look in a Flash!

We've introduced quite a few style declarations here. Let's examine them in the order in which they appear in the CSS file:

```
body {
    font-family: Verdana, Helvetica, Arial, sans-serif;
    background-color: #e2edff;
    line-height: 125%;
    padding: 15px;
}
```

The background-color property can be applied to most elements on a web page, and there are many different ways in which you can specify the color itself. One is to use recognized color names[5] such as navy, blue, red, yellow, and so on. These are easy to remember and spell, but you can be limited by the range. Another way of referencing colors is to use a **hexadecimal** color specification. Yes, you're right, that *does* sound a little scary. I mean, just look at the code for it:

```
background-color: #e2edff;
```

It's hardly intuitive, is it? This obscure-looking reference (#e2edff) translates to a light shade of blue. But you could not, as a beginner, begin to guess what the color was. Thankfully, there are numerous tools on the Web that let you choose a color from a chart (often called a **color picker**), and then give you the code to match. Take a look at some of these tools, and you'll soon be able to find the hexadecimal numbers you need to create your ideal color schemes.[6]

---

[5] http://reference.sitepoint.com/html/color-names
[6] A good selection of links to color scheme tools is available at http://www.clagnut.com/blog/260/.

What the Heck's Hex?

Colors in HTML can be written as a hexadecimal color specification. Hexadecimal is that weird counting system that goes up to 16 instead of 10. That's right: when you count in hexadecimal, there are not ten, but **16 digits**. The hexadecimal sequence looks like this:

0, 1, 2, 3, 4, 5, 6, 7, 8, 9, A, B, C, D, E, F, 10, 11, 12 …

After we reach 9, we go through A, B, C, D, E, and F before we hit 10. That gives us six extra digits to use when we count. Sound confusing? Well, as it so happens, computers can count in hexadecimal far better than humans can!

The key is that all those numbers that we know and love in the decimal system, like 2,748, 15,000,000, and 42, can be represented in hexadecimal. And Table 3.1 proves it!

Table 3.1. Decimal to Hexadecimal Conversion

Decimal	Hexadecimal
7	7
15	F
2,748	ABC
15,000,000	E4E1C0
42	2A

When a color is expressed as a hexadecimal number, such as ff0000, that number actually comprises three values joined together. The values represent the proportions of red (the ff part), green (the first two zeros), and blue (the second two zeros) that are mixed to create the specified color. Those three primary colors can be combined to display any color on the screen, similar to the way a television set uses different amounts of red, green, and blue to create a single dot on its screen.[7] In this example, ff is the value for red, while the green and blue values are zero. It may not surprise you, then, to learn that #ff0000 will give you the color red.

---

[7] If you thought the primary colors were red, blue, and yellow, you're not wrong! Head over to http://en.wikipedia.org/wiki/Primary_color to learn all about the additive and subtractive methods of color mixing.

The line-height property is an interesting one. By increasing that value (we used 125% in our example), you can increase the space between lines of text—which can greatly increase legibility. Try tweaking this value, saving your CSS file, and seeing how the new value affects the text on your web page.

The padding property is used to provide space between the outside edge of the element in question and the content that sits inside it. Because we're referring to the body element, you can think of the outside edge as being the top, bottom, and sides of the browser's **viewport**—the part of the browser where the web page is viewable, excluding the browser's tool bars, menus, or scroll bars. We'll take a look at padding in more detail in Chapter 4.

The value we've given to this property specifies how much space should exist between the edge of the viewport and the content. In this case, we've specified 15px, or 15 pixels. We mentioned pixels before, when we specified the size of an image, but what is a **pixel**? Basically, one pixel is one of the tiny dots that make up what you see on the computer screen. The screen itself is made up of hundreds of thousands of these pixels, so a 15-pixel border will barely take up much space on your screen!

Now, to the paragraph styles:

chapter3/website_files/07_blue_background/style1.css *(excerpt)*

```
p {
  font-size: small;
  color: navy;
}
```

We've already seen that it's possible to change the color of text in a paragraph; now, we'll settle on the appropriate color of navy.

Let's see what's changed with the list-item style:

chapter3/website_files/07_blue_background/style1.css *(excerpt)*

```
li {
  font-size: small;
}
```

The size of each list item has changed ever so slightly through our application of the `font-size` property. Here, we've decided to set the font size using the `small` keyword, but we could just as easily have used the percentage or pixel methods. As we've already seen, there are many ways to alter the look of your pages using CSS! Font-size keywords range from `xx-small` to `xx-large`, and offer a quick way to style text. Unfortunately, each browser implements font-size keywords slightly differently, so there's no guarantee that an `xx-large` font will render at the same size in all browsers. Still, unless you're extremely worried about precise sizing, these keywords make a good starting point.[8]

We've also introduced a new rule for the `h1` element (the main heading on our web pages that displays the site name) and, once again, used a `font-size` property to specify the size of the text (extra large!):

chapter3/website_files/07_blue_background/style1.css (excerpt)

```
h1 {
  font-family: "Trebuchet MS", Helvetica, Arial, sans-serif;
  font-size: x-large;
}
```

The `h2` element also receives a minor makeover:

chapter3/website_files/07_blue_background/style1.css (excerpt)

```
h2 {
  color: blue;
  font-size: medium;
  font-weight: normal;
}
```

Browsers usually display headings in bold type, but we can have them display in standard type by giving the `font-weight` property a value of `normal`.

---

[8] For more reasons than we have space to discuss, text sizing in CSS is a topic that causes heated debate in some circles. As you become familiar with CSS, you may want to learn more about the other text-sizing techniques that it offers. A good place to start is at SitePoint's CSS discussion forum at http://www.sitepoint.com/launch/cssforum/.

A Beginner's Palette of Styling Options

We've looked at some examples of styles that can be applied to your web pages through CSS, but they've been a mixed bag, and deliberately so. There are so many more from which you can pick and choose—too many possibilities, in fact, to list them all here. Still, this section lists some of the basic properties and values with which you might like to experiment. Feel free to try any of these in your CSS file. Note that we'll add to this list in subsequent chapters; it's by no means exhaustive!

`color`
`background-color`
As we've seen, both these properties can take color keywords, such as `red`, `blue`, or `green`, or can take hexadecimal color specifications, such as `#ff0000`.

`font-family`
This property takes a list of fonts that you choose in order of preference. Be sure to provide options that users are likely to have on their computers (for example, Arial, Verdana). This list should end using one of the generic CSS fonts, such as `serif` or `sans-serif`, that any browser that supports CSS will recognize.

`font-size`
This property can be any one of the following:

font size keywords
- `xx-small`
- `x-small`
- `small`
- `medium`
- `large`
- `x-large`
- `xx-large`

relative font sizes
- a percentage (for example, `140%`)
- em units (for example, `1.2em`; `1em` is equal to the height of the M font character)

fixed font sizes
- pixels (for example, `20px`)
- points (for example, `12pt`)

Fixed font sizes used to be more problematic, as they couldn't be scaled up or down to suit the reader's needs in Internet Explorer 6; if you stated a font size of 10 pixels, it didn't matter if the user chose maximum font size, it would stubbornly stay at 10 pixels! Fortunately, subsequent versions of IE fixed this problem. For most browsers, the default behavior when scaling a page is to zoom the whole page proportionally. So, just bear it in mind if you know that your audience is still using IE6.[9]

`font-weight`	`bold` or `normal`
`font-style`	`normal` or `italic`
`text-decoration`	`none`, `underline`, `overline`, or `line-through`

 Backing It Up!

Before you experiment using the CSS properties above, it might be an idea to make a backup of your CSS file, in case you run into difficulties. Remember, you can download the examples used in this chapter from the code archive if you accidentally mangle your CSS file. If this happens, don't worry! It's all part of the learning process, and you can be sure that no animals will be harmed in the process.

Recap: the Style Story so Far

Let's allow ourselves a moment to reflect. Our site now boasts a CSS file using a selection of attractive styles. We're in the enviable position of being able to change the site at whim by altering just that one CSS file. Now we'll try styling some more elements on our web pages.

Changing the Emphasis

1. Open **about.html** in your text editor.

---

[9] You'll inevitably hear horror stories from battle-weary web developers who still have to support this ageing, problematic, and often excruciating browser. Oh yeah, I've been there and have the scars to prove it!

2. Find the paragraph about meeting up in a local pub, and add an emphasis element as shown here:

chapter3/website_files/08_emphasis_italics/about.html *(excerpt)*

```
<p>And when we're not diving, we often meet up in a local pub
    to talk about our recent adventures (<em>any</em> excuse,
    eh?).</p>
```

3. Save the page, and then view it in your web browser; it should appear as shown in Figure 3.8. As you can see, emphasis elements appear in italics by default. We're going to use CSS to change that default style.

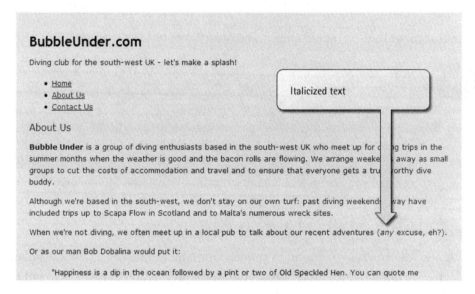

Figure 3.8. Using emphasis to set type to italics by default

4. Open **style1.css** (if you haven't already opened it for editing) and add the following rule below the others:

chapter3/website_files/09_emphasis_capitals/style1.css *(excerpt)*

```
em {
  font-style: normal;
  text-transform: uppercase;
}
```

5. Save the CSS file, and refresh your browser's view of the About Us page. Does your page look like Figure 3.9?

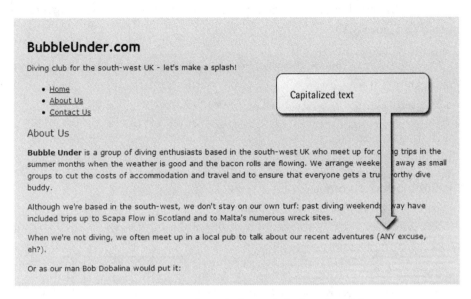

Figure 3.9. Changing the emphasis to capitalized text from italics

Now, whenever you add an **em** element to any web page of your site (assuming that page is linked to **style1.css**), the emphasized text will appear in capital letters, not italics. But this raises an interesting point: when should you override a browser's default style for one of your own choosing? Presumably, the default styles that browsers use were selected carefully; how can you be sure that redefining the styles is a good idea? Surely italics are a suitable style for emphasis? They probably are. As they say in the Spider-Man film, "With great power comes great responsibility," so be sure to exercise caution. Just because you *can* change a default style, doesn't always mean you should.

Perhaps a compromise is in order. Let's change the emphasis so that it's still italic, but also appears in uppercase letters. All we need to do is remove the `font-style` declaration; the `em` element will then revert to its default italicized appearance, as depicted in Figure 3.10:

chapter3/website_files/10_emphasis_capitals_italics/style1.css *(excerpt)*

```
em {
  text-transform: uppercase;
}
```

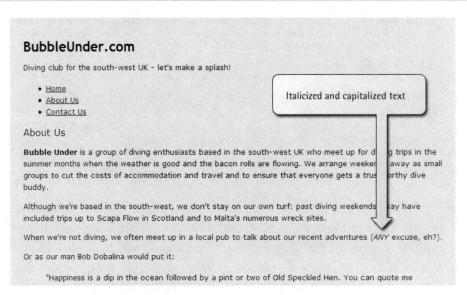

Figure 3.10. Emphasis displayed as uppercase italics

Emphasis or Italics? Strong or Bold?

You might well be asking yourself, "If I want an italic font, can't I use an italic element?" In fact, HTML provides an `i` element for just this purpose, but its use isn't perhaps obvious to a newcomer. Why not? Well, marking text as `i` says nothing about its meaning; `i` only communicates how it should be presented on the screen, not its emphasis in tone. According to the spec, it "represents a span of text in an alternate voice or mood, or otherwise offset from the normal prose." So you should use `<em></em>` for emphasis, but you'd be better off using `<i></i>` for a technical term, an idiomatic phrase, or the name of a boat:

```
<p>We went for a jolly on the <i>QE2</i>, hurrah!</p>
<p>I bet that had a certain <i>je ne sais quoi</i>, eh?</p>
```

Likewise, the b element (for bold), another old HTML element, shouldn't be used for stressing importance. The correct element to use for that is strong or, if you just want to display headings in bold, proper heading elements (h1, h2, and so on), and style them as you choose with CSS. (It's an all-too-common fault whereby people bold a paragraph to make it appear like a heading—so please don't.) You would use the b element where you need to differentiate a word or phrase from its surrounding text, for example:

```
<p>Each of the barrels were stamped <b>FRAGILE</b> and were ready
   to ship.</p>
```

Why is it important to know the difference between i/em and b/strong? It might seem like no big deal as you look at the italicized text in your web browser. Imagine, though, if you were blind, and you used software that read web pages aloud to you, instead of displaying them on the screen. This program (called a **screen reader**) might read text marked up with an em element using slight emphasis, and text marked up with strong in a more powerful voice (though this, of course, depends on the screen reader being used). But what would it do with text marked up with i or b? Because these elements indicate nothing about the significance of the text, screen readers wouldn't treat them in any special way—thus potentially losing the meaning that you were trying to convey. A search engine (for example, Google, Yahoo) *may* also place more importance on a user's search terms that appear within a strong element than a b element (though the search engine companies never give anything solid away about how their search algorithms work!).

Another presentational tag that you might see others use, but should *never* copy, is the u element. Wrap this around some text, and needless underlining occurs that only serves to baffle users. This is because in web pages underlined text normally signifies a link—which the u element most definitely isn't!

Looking at Elements in Context

Here's a riddle for you: which of these items is bigger? A pen or a sheep? Well, the answer is either, depending on the context. If you were a farmer, you'd swear that the pen is bigger. After all, you spend many hours a week rounding up herds of sheep into a big, solid pen. If, however, you're an office worker, you'd opt for the sheep being the larger of the two—after all, it's a lot easier to pick up a pen and flip it around your fingers.

Context can change a situation quite drastically, and we can use context to our advantage in CSS. We can style an element in a number of ways, depending on its position. With that in mind, let's head back to our example site for another lesson. Don't be sheepish, now!

Currently, we've styled paragraphs so that they appear in a navy sans-serif font (Verdana, specifically), as does almost everything else on the page:

chapter3/website_files/10_emphasis_capitals_italics/style1.css *(excerpt)*

```
body {
  font-family: Verdana, Helvetica, Arial, sans-serif;
}

p {
  font-size: small;
  color: navy;
}
```

This is all well and good, but there's one paragraph on our site that differs from the others in terms of its purpose. Can you spot which one it is? It's our first paragraph, the one in the tagline. Here's the HTML for that section:

index.html *(excerpt)*

```
<div id="tagline">
  <p>Diving club for the south-west UK - let's make a splash!</p>
</div>
```

It's distinct from the actual document content, so it might benefit from some alternate styling. That this particular paragraph is contained within a specific div element —with an id attribute of tagline—can be useful. Because it's within its own div, we can set a rule for this paragraph and this paragraph only.

1. Open the CSS file for editing, and add the following after the first paragraph rule:

```
                    chapter3/website_files/11_styled_tagline/style1.css (excerpt)
#tagline p {
  font-style: italic;
  font-family: Georgia, Times, serif;
}
```

2. Save the file, and refresh the About Us page (or any of the three, for that matter) in your browser. Your page should look similar to the one in Figure 3.11.

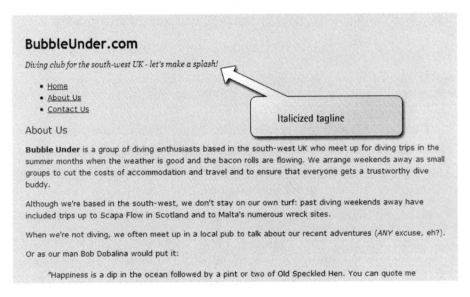

Figure 3.11. Putting the tagline in italics

What's happening here? Perhaps a translation is required. This CSS rule means, "For any paragraph element that occurs inside an element that has an id of tagline, set the text to italics and the font to Georgia, Times, or another serif font if you don't have either of those."

 ## Getting a Positive ID

The # notation in the CSS refers to an element with a specific id attribute—in this case, tagline. We'll learn more about selecting ids and manipulating them in subsequent chapters.

Contextual Selectors

`#tagline p` is known as a **contextual selector**. Here are some other examples:

```
#navigation a {
    text-decoration: none;
}
```

Translation: for any link found inside the navigation area—an element with an id of `navigation`—remove any decoration on that text; in other words, remove the underline (any other links on the page will remain underlined).

```
#footer p {
    line-height: 150%;
}
```

Translation: set the vertical height between lines of text contained in paragraphs inside the footer area (for example, a `div` element with an id of `footer`) to 150%. This would override the browser default of 100%, or other line-height values that might be set, such as for the body text.

```
h1 b {
    color: red;
}
```

Translation: for any text inside a level one heading that's marked up as `b`, set the color to red (any other instance of `strong` on the page won't be set to red).

```
h2 a {
    text-decoration: none;
}
```

Translation: don't underline the text of any link inside a level two heading (the default setting underlines all links, so other links on the page will remain underlined).

Grouping Styles

If you want to apply the same style to different elements on a web page, there's no need to repeat yourself. For example, let's say that you want to set heading levels one through three in yellow text with a black background. Perhaps you'd do this:

```
h1 {
  color: yellow;
  background-color: black;
}

h2 {
  color: yellow;
  background-color: black;
}

h3 {
  color: yellow;
  background-color: black;
}
```

That's very repetitive. Plus, once you have a lot of styles on the page, it's even more difficult to maintain. Wouldn't it be great if you could reduce some of that work? Well, you can! Here's how:

```
h1, h2, h3 {
  color: yellow;
  background-color: black;
}
```

Translation: if the element is a level one heading, a level two heading, or a level three heading, set the text to yellow and the background to black.

 Comma = "Or"

You can think of the commas in CSS selectors (like the one above) as the word "or."

Let's try grouping some styles in our project site. We're yet to have any h3 headings, but we will soon.

1. Edit your CSS file (**style1.css**) by adding the following to the bottom of it:

chapter3/website_files/12_grouped_headings/style1.css *(excerpt)*

```
h1, h2, h3 {
    font-family: "Trebuchet MS", Helvetica, Arial, sans-serif;
    background-color: navy;
    color: white;
}
```

2. Save the file, and refresh the About Us page in your browser. You should see a page like the one shown in Figure 3.12.

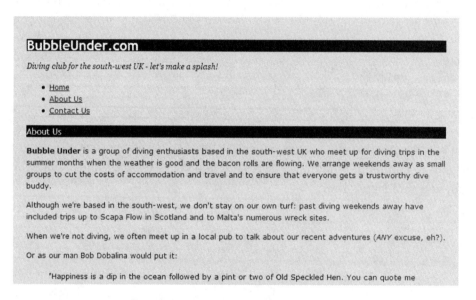

Figure 3.12. Displaying the changed heading styles

That CSS really does kill several birds with one stone (figuratively speaking, of course; I did say no animals would be harmed!). As well as styling many pages from one central location (your CSS file), you have the added convenience of being able to style many elements in one go. Your CSS file becomes easier to manage and—a nice side-benefit—smaller, and therefore quicker to download.

Filenames for Your Stylesheets

Although we've been working with **style1.css** for some time, you may be wondering why we named the file this way. The name is deliberate. You might want to add another style to your website at a later date, and numbering is a basic way to keep track of the styles you can apply to a site.

So, why not name it **marine.css**—after all, it uses marine colors, references to sea animals, and so on? That's a fair question, but it's important to remember with CSS is that you can always change the styles later, and your naming convention might, at a later date, bear no relevance to the styles a file contains. For example, you can edit **marine.css** such that all the colors in your website are changed to ochres, browns, and sandy yellows. This ability to change the website's design in one action is the whole point of CSS! With the new design, your website could have an earthy, desert feel to it, yet you might still have 200 or more pages referring to a stylesheet called **marine.css**. It's not quite right, is it? This is why I've chosen an abstract name for the CSS file, and I recommend that you do the same for the websites you develop.

But something interesting is happening in our CSS file: it appears that we may have a conflict in our rules. Or have we?

Which Rule Wins?

When we added the grouped declaration for the headings, we changed some styles that we'd set previously. A look at the source shows that the level two heading, h2, has been set to be blue *and* white in different places on our stylesheet:

chapter3/website_files/12_grouped_headings/style1.css *(excerpt)*

```
h2 {
  color: blue;
  font-size: medium;
  font-weight: normal;
}
⋮
h1, h2, h3 {
  font-family: "Trebuchet MS", Helvetica, Arial, sans-serif;
  background-color: navy;
  color: white;
}
```

Because the declaration specifying that the h2 should be white comes later, it has overridden the earlier blue specification. It doesn't matter if you've defined an h2 to be blue 100 times throughout your stylesheet; if the last definition says it should be white, then white it will be!

Recapping Our Progress

Time for another breather. What have we learned? Well, we've discovered some more styles that you can apply in CSS, we've seen how you can style certain elements depending on their context, and more recently, we've discussed how you can group elements that need to be styled in the same way. But there is one feature that we have only briefly touched on that really demands more attention, because it's so fundamental to the way the Web functions. That topic is links.

Styling Links

Links are everywhere on the Web: they truly are the basis of everything you see online. Nowadays, we're used to seeing highly decorative web pages adorned by a wealth of images and features. Take a step back in time, though, and you'll find that the World Wide Web was little more than a collection of linked documents. Go back to the earliest browsers and you will see that those links were underlined, which remains the case today. By default, most browsers use the following color scheme for links:

blue   an unvisited link

purple   a link to a web page that you've previously visited

red   an active link (one you're clicking on; you may have noticed links flash red momentarily when you initially click on them)

This color scheme isn't to everyone's taste, but it's what we're stuck with for now. At least, it's what we *would* be stuck with if we were unable to use CSS to redefine those colors.

At its most basic, a CSS style for links might look like this:

```
a {
  font-weight: bold;
  color: black;
}
```

Now, instead of being blue and having a normal font weight, your links appear in bold, black type. Try adding that to your **style1.css** file, saving it, and seeing how it affects your web pages—Figure 3.13 illustrates this.

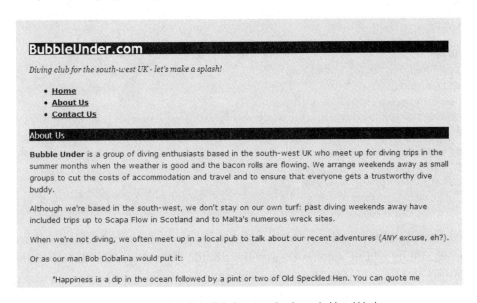

Figure 3.13. Styling all the links in our navigation to bold and black

Link States

As I mentioned previously, there are various types of links (unvisited, visited, active) that you'll come across on a web page. There's one other state that I'm yet to mention, but it's one with which you're probably familiar: the **hover** state, which occurs when you pass your cursor over the link. In CSS, you can change the styling of all these link states using **pseudo-classes**, which sounds complicated but really is straightforward. You can think of a pseudo-class as being like an internal class the browser automatically applies to the link while it's in a certain state. Here is some CSS that shows the color/style scheme for the different link states:

```
a {
  font-weight: bold;
}

a:link {
  color: black;
}

a:visited {
  color: gray;
}

a:hover {
  text-decoration: none;
  color: white;
  background-color: navy;
}

a:active {
  color: aqua;
  background-color: navy;
}
```

The different states are addressed within the CSS through the use of the a element selector, and by adding a colon (:) and the pseudo-classes link, visited, hover, or active. Adding pseudo-classes to your stylesheet means the browser will apply the rule when the element is in the state specified by the pseudo-class.

Getting Your Link States in Order

Browsers usually aren't fussy about the order in which you specify rules in your CSS file, but links should always be specified in the order shown above: link, visited, hover, and active. Try to remember the letters LVHA. More cynical users might find it easier to remember this mnemonic with the phrase, "Love? Ha!" We can thank Jeffrey Zeldman for that little gem.[10]

---

[10] *Designing With Web Standards* (Berkeley: New Riders, 2003)

Let's change the styles for different link states in our project site:

1. Open the project site's CSS file (**style1.css**), and add the preceding CSS at the bottom of the file.

2. Save the CSS file.

3. Open any of the three web pages in your browser (or hit **Reload**) to see how the styled links display.

Figure 3.14 shows the three link states: the home link is unvisited, the link to the About Us page shows that it has been visited previously (shown in a lighter gray), and the link to the Contact Us page is being hovered over by the user's cursor.

Feel free to experiment in the CSS file with different foreground and background colors, as well as other text formatting styles that were detailed in the table earlier in this chapter.

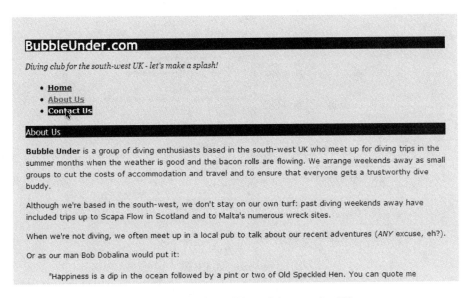

Figure 3.14. Styling three different link states using CSS

Clearing Your History

Your browser automatically stores a certain amount of your browsing history, and uses this information to decide whether a link has been visited or not (and, hence, how the link should be displayed). If you're building a site and testing links, you might want to check how an unvisited link looks but, because of your browsing history, they may all show as having been visited. This is almost certainly the case with our three-page project site—the links in your navigation list are probably all gray. To reset this, you can clear your browser's history.

In IE, select **Tools > Internet Options**. You'll see a button under **Browsing History** that reads **Delete**. Click on this and it will bring up a **Delete Browsing History** dialog with more options, as shown in Figure 3.15; make sure that the **History** checkbox has been ticked, then click the **Delete** button on that dialog. Afterwards, reload the web page. Any links you may have visited will now appear as unvisited. The process for clearing history in older versions is a little easier—just look for the button on the **Internet Options** dialogue that says **Clear History**.

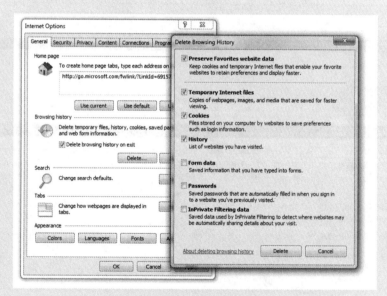

Figure 3.15. Clearing the history in IE displays unvisited link styles again

Other browsers have similar options, which may be found in locations such as **Tools > Options** or **Preferences > Privacy**. I won't list all the methods for deleting your history from various browsers here, but if you rummage around, you should be able to manage it without too much difficulty.

Class Selectors

To date, we've discussed the ways in which we can style various elements, such as paragraphs and headings; we've also seen how we can style elements in specific areas of the page using the id attribute. However, implementing broad-brush styles, such as coloring the text in all p elements navy, is very much a blanket approach to design. What if you want some of those paragraphs (or any elements, for that matter) to look different from the rest? **Class selectors** are the answer.

A class selector lets you define a style that can be used over and over again to style many different elements. So, for example, let's say you wanted to make some parts of your text stand out—to make them look more appealing or fun than other parts of the document.

You could do so in your CSS like this:

```
.fun {
   color: #339999;
   font-family: Georgia, Times, serif;
   letter-spacing: 0.05em;
}
```

Here, we've created a style rule for a class called "fun." The fact that it is a class selector is denoted by the period at the beginning of the class name. We've slipped another property into this rule: letter-spacing defines the space between each of the letters. We've set a spacing of 0.05em here. 1em is the height of the M character in any font, so 0.05em is 5% of that height. It doesn't sound like much of a difference, but when it comes to typography, subtle changes are usually more effective than extreme modifications. (By all means, you could try a larger figure just to see what it does.)

In order to make use of the style once it has been added to your stylesheet, add the class="fun" attribute to an element:

```
<p class="fun">A man walks into a bar; you would've thought he'd
   see it coming!</p>
```

Let's apply some classes to our project site. First, we'll need to add the style rule shown above to the stylesheet we're working on:

1. Open **style1.css** and add the CSS from the previous block to the bottom of that file.
2. Save **style1.css**, and then open **about.html**.
3. Find the paragraph that's contained inside the `blockquote` element.
4. Add the `class="fun"` attribute to the paragraph's opening tag.

This is how your markup should look right now:

```
                    chapter3/website_files/15_fun_blockquote/about.html (excerpt)

<blockquote>
  <p class="fun">"Happiness is a dip in the ocean followed by a
     pint or two of Old Speckled Hen. You can quote me on
     that!"</p>
</blockquote>
```

Note that the `class` attribute was applied at the paragraph level. If there were a few paragraphs in our man Bob's quotation, it could look like this:

```
<blockquote>
  <p class="fun">"Happiness is a dip in the ocean followed by a
     pint or two of Old Speckled Hen. You can quote me
     on that!</p>
  <p class="fun">"Join us for a weekend away at some of our
     favorite dive spots and you'll soon be making new
     friends.</p>
  <p class="fun">"Anyway, about time I got on with some
     <em>proper</em> work!"</p>
</blockquote>
```

There's a lot of repetition in there. Surely there's a tidier way to apply this style? There sure is:

```
<blockquote class="fun">
  <p>"Happiness is a dip in the ocean followed by a pint or two of
     Old Speckled Hen. You can quote me on that!</p>
  <p>"Join us for a weekend away at some of our favorite dive
     spots and you'll soon be making new friends.</p>
  <p>"Anyway, about time I got on with some <em>proper</em>
     work!"</p>
</blockquote>
```

In this example, we apply that `class` of `fun` to the `blockquote` element, so that everything contained in that element inherits the style of the parent container. This saves us from having to apply these different classes all over our pages (an affliction that has become known as *class-itis*—a not-too-distant relation of *div-itis*, which we discussed in Chapter 2).

class vs id

So far, we've looked at both `class` selectors (which involve periods: ".") and `id` selectors (which involve pound or hash signs: "#"). Are you confused by them? It's true that these selectors are similar, but there is one important difference: *a specific id can only be applied to one HTML element.* So, for example, on any web page, there can only be one element with an `id` of `mainnavigation`, and only one with an `id` of `header`. A class, on the other hand, can appear as many times as required.

Limiting Classes to Specific Elements

Imagine you want to italicize any `blockquote` element that has a `class` attribute with the value `fun`, but not other elements with that class value. Think it sounds tricky? Not with CSS! Take a look:

```css
.fun {
    font-family: Georgia, Times, serif;
    color: #339999;
    letter-spacing: 0.05em;
}

blockquote.fun {
    font-style: italic;
}
```

Now, any text inside a pair of `<blockquote class="fun">` and `</blockquote>` tags will appear in italics.

By prefixing our normal class selector with an element name, we're telling the browser to apply the following declarations to that element-and-class combination only. It's as simple as *element*.*class*, but make sure you don't leave any spaces!

Specifically Speaking

Those with an eagle eye will have noticed that not all the `.fun` styles in the previous example are actually applied to the quotation. The `font-family` and `letter-spacing` declarations take effect, but the color change does not! This can be explained with the concept of **specificity**.

Specificity simply means that the rule that's the most specific is the one that is applied. Determining which rule is the most specific is a bit complex, but understandable. In our stylesheet, the specificity is easy to determine: the `.fun` rule is applied to the `blockquote` element, and properties are inherited by the `p` elements, but property values are only inherited in the absence of any other declaration. We have another color declaration in our project site—the one that we created at the start of the chapter that states that all paragraphs should be navy-colored:

```
p {
  color: navy;
}
```

The rule with the element selector `p` has a greater specificity for the `p` elements, because the selector specifically targets `p` elements, whereas the `.fun` rule does not. Imagine if, however, we added another rule like this:

```
.fun p {
  color: green;
}
```

The effect would be this: all paragraph text is navy, except for the paragraphs inside elements with the `class fun`, which would be green. This is because the `.fun p` selector is more specific for those paragraphs. Note that, unlike the conflicting rules we encountered in the section called "Which Rule Wins?", this battle between style rules has no relation to the order in which they appear in the stylesheet.

Specificity can be confusing, so don't lose too much sleep over it; for now, it's enough just to be aware of the concept, as this may be the reason why one of your styles fails to take effect when you're convinced it should. Specificity is covered in great depth in the SitePoint CSS Reference if you'd like to explore it further.[11]

---

[11] http://reference.sitepoint.com/css/specificity/

Styling Partial Text Using span

So, a class can be applied in many different places—perhaps to a specific paragraph, or to a block of several paragraphs contained in a blockquote, or to a div that holds many forms of content. But what would you do if you wanted to apply the style to a very small section of text—maybe just a couple of words, or even a couple of letters, within a paragraph? For this, once again, you can use the span element.

Earlier in this chapter, I showed how you could use the span element in conjunction with inline styles to pick out and style specific words within a paragraph. The exact same technique can be used with classes: we simply place an opening <span> tag at the point at which we want the styling to begin, and the closing </span> tag where we want it to end. The advantage of this technique over the inline style demonstrated earlier is that the style is defined in a single location, so you could potentially add the fun class to many different elements on many different pages with a minimum of hassle. When you decide that you want to have a different kind of fun (so to speak), you need only change your stylesheet (**style1.css**) for that new style to be reflected across your site:

```
<p><span class="fun">Bubble Under</span> is a group of diving
    enthusiasts based in the south-west UK who meet up for diving
    trips in the summer months when the weather is good and the
    bacon rolls are flowing. We arrange weekends away as small
    groups to cut the costs of accommodation and travel and to
    ensure that everyone gets a trustworthy dive buddy.</p>
```

Try applying the span element as suggested in the above HTML code to your About Us page. If you save the changes and check them in your browser (remember to hit **Reload**), your page should look like the one shown in Figure 3.16.

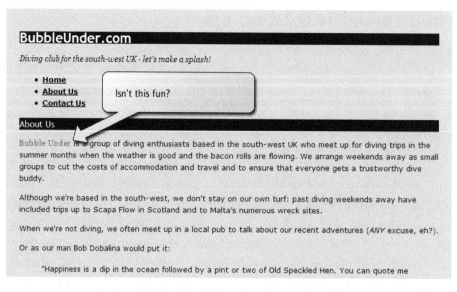

Figure 3.16. Applying the fun class to two specific words

Avoid Throwing (Needless) spans into the Works

The span element is mostly used with a class attribute. There are very few occasions when you'll want to apply a span element to your HTML on its own without a class or id of some kind.

Before you apply a span to any given element on your web page, take a moment to think about whether there's another element that's better suited to the task. For example, it's advisable not to do this:

```
<p>Do it <span class="shouty">now</span>!</p>
```

A more appropriate choice would be to use the strong element:

```
<p>Do it <strong>now</strong>!</p>
```

Think of the meaning of what you're writing, and aim for the HTML element that best suits the purpose. Other examples might be em, cite, and blockquote.

Summary

It's been another busy chapter, but my, how our site's blossoming! A chapter or two ago we hadn't even built a web page, but now we know how to apply a (virtual) lick of paint to any type of HTML element on a page, a specific section of a web page depending on its id, or arbitrary portions of a page—sometimes in several different places—using class selectors.

The website is starting to look a little more colorful, but the layout is still fairly basic. In the next chapter, we'll look at how it's possible to change the layout of elements on a page—their position, shape, size, and more—using CSS. Styling text? Been there, done that. Let's move to the next level!

Shaping Up Using CSS

For many years, web developers regarded CSS as a tool that could be used to style text on web pages, and add a splash of color here and there, but little more. And for a long time, that was all you could *realistically* use it for, because browser support for CSS was below par. Thankfully, progress has been made!

You've now reached a point at which many budding web designers stop experimenting with CSS. Not you! In this chapter, we're going to delve a little further into the capabilities of CSS as we use it to:

- alter the shape and size of specific areas of content
- change backgrounds and border styles
- position items anywhere on the web page

Let's begin, then, by seeing how we can use CSS to change the shape and size of items on a web page. However, before we can understand this technique, we need to grasp the difference between **block-level elements** and **inline elements**.

Block-level Elements versus Inline Elements

Any given web page comprises two basic types of elements: block-level elements and inline elements. It is important to appreciate the differences between these element types, particularly where CSS is concerned.

 The Basic Rules of Block-level and Inline Elements

When explaining the difference between these two types of elements, I like to use an analogy of stacking/nesting boxes. You know the kind you usually buy in a set of five, where they are packed one inside the other. You can take them out, stack them one on top of the other like a tower, or put them side by side—but you can't place the biggest box *inside* the smallest box; the laws of physics still apply!

Block-level elements are like these boxes. They can contain other block-level elements, possibly many levels deep, but there are rules about what kind of block-level elements can be kept inside the containing-level elements. Just as a big box won't go into a small box, we can't put a `div` element inside a `p` (paragraph) element; We can, however, put a `p` inside a `div`. You'll come to know the rules over time, and there are ways you can check to see if you have it right.

That's block-level elements. So what are inline elements? Think of these as the trinkets and whatnot that we usually keep inside such boxes. They can only ever go inside these boxes, or fit down the gaps between the nested boxes, or taken out and left scattered next to the boxes. But they can never wrap around these large boxes—it's impossible. So, translating the analogy back, an inline element cannot be wrapped around a block-level element.

To summarize:

- A block-level element can contain other block-level elements, as well as inline elements.

- An inline element can only contain other inline elements.

Block-level Elements

As I just explained, a block-level element is any element that can contain other elements (block-level and inline). To identify a block-level element, look for any element that's:

- normally displayed *on its own line*, or across multiple lines (other elements probably appear above or below it, but not on either side—not by default, anyway)
- being used as a *container* for one or more elements

Here are a few examples of common block-level elements:

- h1, h2, h3, and so on, through to h6
- p
- div
- blockquote
- ul and ol
- form[1]

When you create a paragraph of text, there's no need to tell the browser to add a carriage return, start a new line, and add another carriage return at the end of the paragraph; the opening <p> and closing </p> tags do that for you. Consider the text that appears on our site's About Us page:

```
chapter4/website_files/01_block_level_elements/about.html (excerpt)
<h2>About Us</h2>
<p><span class="fun">Bubble Under</span> is a group of diving
    enthusiasts based in the south-west UK who meet up for diving
    trips in the summer months when the weather is good and the
    bacon rolls are flowing. We arrange weekends away as small
    groups to cut the costs of accommodation and travel and to
    ensure that everyone gets a trustworthy dive buddy.</p>
<p>Although we're based in the south-west, we don't stay on our
    own turf: past diving weekends away have included trips up to
    Scapa Flow in Scotland and to Malta's numerous wreck
    sites.</p>
<p>When we're not diving, we often meet up in a local pub to
    talk about our recent adventures (<em>any</em> excuse,
    eh?).</p>
<p>Or as our man Bob Dobalina would put it:</p>
<blockquote class="fun">
  <p>"Happiness is a dip in the ocean followed by a pint or two
      of Old Speckled Hen. You can quote me on that!"</p>
</blockquote>
```

---

[1] Forms will be discussed in detail in Chapter 7.

The heading (h2) and three paragraphs are all block-level elements. They represent blocks of content, where clearly defined breaks appear above and below each block. This is clear in Figure 4.1, where the block-level elements are outlined.

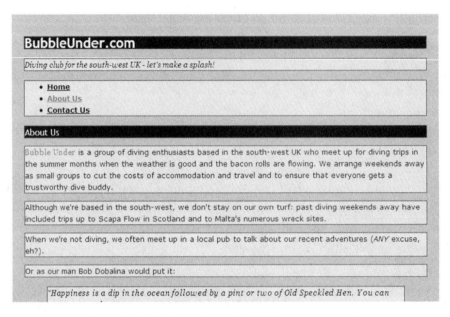

Figure 4.1. Blocks of content revealing HTML block-level elements

Inline Elements

An easy way to identify an *in*line element is to remember that it sits *in*side another element. As we established in my stacking/nesting boxes analogy, we can have a box of old photos, or a box containing just one photo, but we can't have a photo full of boxes—it's physically impossible! Similarly, it's against the specifications to use an inline element to contain a block-level element. A good example of an inline element is span (covered in Chapter 3), used to group words together in order to apply a style:

chapter4/website_files/01_block_level_elements/about.html *(excerpt)*

```
<p><span class="fun">Bubble Under</span> is a group of diving
    enthusiasts based in the south-west UK who meet up for diving
    trips in the summer months when the weather is good and the
    bacon rolls are flowing. We arrange weekends away as small
    groups to cut the costs of accommodation and travel and to
    ensure that everyone gets a trustworthy dive buddy.</p>
```

Other examples of inline elements include:

- em
- strong
- cite
- a

Looking at the example markup above, any one of those inline elements could be applied to the words "Bubble Under":

```
<p><em>Bubble Under</em> is a group of diving enthusiasts…</p>
<p><strong>Bubble Under</strong> is a group of diving
    enthusiasts…</p>
<p><cite>Bubble Under</cite> is a group of diving enthusiasts…</p>
<p><a href="http://www.bubbleunder.com/">Bubble Under</a> is a
    group of diving enthusiasts…</p>
```

In fact, even the image element, img, is inline, although we use it a little differently from the elements mentioned above. Instead, img doesn't provide any information to the browser about how text should be treated; an image is simply an image.

Inline Begets Inline

It's perfectly okay to nest one inline element inside another. Here's an example of an inline element that contains another inline element:

```
<p><span class="fun"><a href="http://www.bubbleunder.com/">Bubble
    Under</a></span> is a group of diving enthusiasts based in
    the south-west UK who meet up for diving trips in the summer
    months when the weather is good and the bacon rolls are
    flowing. We arrange weekends away as small groups to cut the
    costs of accommodation and travel and to ensure that everyone
    gets a trustworthy dive buddy.</p>
```

Actually, taking the individual examples just shown, even the markup below would constitute acceptable and valid HTML (although it may seem like overkill):

```
<p><strong><em><cite><a href="http://www.bubbleunder.com/">Bubble
    Under</a></cite></em></strong> is a group of diving
    enthusiasts…</p>
```

Watch Your Symmetry

One rule of XHTML syntax is that opening and closing tags should be symmetrical. If you open one tag, then another, those tags should be closed in reverse order. In the example above, the tags are correctly opened and closed as follows (indenting is for effect only):

```
<strong>
  <em>
    <cite>
      <a href="http://www.bubbleunder.com/">
        Bubble Under
      </a>
    </cite>
  </em>
</strong>
```

This rule of symmetry applies to *any* kind of element—block-level or inline—and can be checked using online validators (covered in Chapter 9).

Inline Elements Can Never Contain Block-level Elements

The previous example showed perfectly acceptable usage of an inline element containing other inline elements. Now, I'm going to turn that on its head and show you what you should *never* do:

```
<span class="fun"><p>Bubble Under is a group of diving enthusiasts
    based in the south-west UK who meet up for diving trips in the
    summer months when the weather is good and the bacon rolls are
    flowing. We arrange weekends away as small groups to cut the
    costs of accommodation and travel and to ensure that everyone
    gets a trustworthy dive buddy.</p></span>
```

Why is this wrong? Well, what we have here is an inline element, span, wrapped around a block-level element, p, so this markup is invalid. Bad, naughty markup! As mentioned, we'll discuss validity in the section called "Validating Your Web Pages" in Chapter 9. For now, just remember: block-level elements can only be contained within other block-level elements.

Well, *almost* only … There is an exception to this rule, introduced in HTML5. You can now wrap a link around multiple items,so if you specify anything other than the HTML5 doctype, the following wouldn't be allowed:

```
<a href="monkey.htm"> <h1>The Monkey House</h1>
<div>Purveyors of fine simian products</div> </a>
```

Stick with the HTML5 doctype `<!DOCYPE html>`, however, and it's perfectly okay to do this.

If you think I have belabored the point of difference between these two types of elements, please accept my apology. It's just that often people fail to appreciate the differences between block-level and inline elements. And it's a very important point, because these two element types have very different capabilities where CSS is concerned. Let's look at this in detail now.

Styling Inline and Block-level Elements

Inline elements allow for a limited range of styling options, as outlined below (this is a simplified recap of the discussion from Chapter 3):

- colors (text and background)

- font properties (size, font family, and other decorative transformations such as underlining, and so on)

This is all fairly superficial, cosmetic stuff, to be honest. However, with block-level elements, you have a much wider range of CSS tools at your disposal, such as being able to:

- give a block of text a fixed width or height

- create padding effects to prevent text from pushing right up against the edge of the block in which it's contained

- move a block to any location on the web page, regardless of the position in which it appears in the markup

In this chapter, we'll see examples of all these techniques, for which the markup is available for download from the code archive. Then, we'll apply the techniques to our project site. Let's begin by looking at how you can shape and size blocks of content.

Sizing Up the Blocks

By default, a block-level element will take up 100% of the available width—whatever the size of its parent container, be that another `div` element, or even the document's body—and whatever height it needs. So far, the paragraphs we've created have fit this description but, if you wish, you can change these defaults.

Setting a Width

Let's imagine that you have a document comprising many paragraphs, and you'd like to draw attention to one of them in some way other than changing the font. For starters, you could try altering the paragraph width. Here's the CSS that does just that (as well as making the font bold):

```
.attentiongrab {
    width: 50%;
    font-weight: bold;
}
```

I've used a class selector here; do you remember it from the last chapter? It will let us apply this particular style as many times as we like. Here's some HTML to go with the above CSS:

```
<p>We've stayed in quite a few caravan parks and camp sites over
    the last couple of months, and I've started to notice a few
    things that seem to suggest that there are some unwritten
    rules of staying at these places. Unwritten until now, that
    is.</p>
<p>Everyone else on site will be better prepared and better
    equipped than you. It's a fact. No matter what extras you
    might carry, someone a couple of plots down will still have
    more. Utensil envy is rife.</p>
<p class="attentiongrab">When you first park, the distance
    between the power supply and your van's power socket will be
    precisely 2 inches longer than the inadequate power lead that
    you own.</p>
<p>On the hottest evenings, you will be parked next to someone
```

```
with a very flashy van that's equipped with an air-con unit.
It will be facing you, blowing out hot air and taunting you
with its efficient hum.</p>
```

Figure 4.2 shows how the text appears on the screen.

We've stayed in quite a few caravan parks and camp sites over the last couple of months, and I've started to notice a few things that seem to suggest that there are some unwritten rules for staying at these places. Unwritten until now, that is.

Everyone else on site will be better prepared and better equipped than you. It's a fact. No matter what extras you might carry, someone a couple of plots down will still have have more. Utensil envy is rife.

When you first park, the distance between the power supply and your van's power socket will be precisely 2 inches longer than the inadequate power lead that you own.

On the hottest evenings, you will be parked next to someone with a very flashy van that's equipped with an air-con unit. It will be facing you, blowing out hot air and taunting you with its efficient hum.

Figure 4.2. Reducing a paragraph's width to 50% of neighboring paragraphs

Setting a Height

The process for setting the height of a block of content is as simple as setting the width—although you'll probably have less use for styling the height of paragraph text than styling the width. A case where you may want to set a specific height is in a navigation area, as long as the number of navigation items in the list doesn't vary dramatically between pages.

Consider this HTML:

```
<div id="mainnavigation">
  <h3>Site Navigation</h3>
  <ul>
    <li><a href="home.html">Home</a></li>
    <li><a href="recent.html">Recent Work</a></li>
    <li><a href="portfolio.html">Portfolio</a></li>
    <li><a href="testimonials.html">Testimonials</a></li>
    <li><a href="contact.html">Contact</a></li>
  </ul>
</div>
```

As with our project site, the navigation area is in a div that has an id attribute
(mainnavigation). We saw at the beginning of this chapter that a div is a block-
level element, so we can play around with it. Let's specify a height and width for
it in CSS:

```
#mainnavigation {
  background-color: #ffcc33;
  color: navy;
  font-weight: bold;
  width: 200px;
  height: 400px;
}
```

Note that I've also added a splash of background color (#ffcc33) to make the resized
block easier to see.

In the CSS, I've used the width *and* height properties, applying pixel values to
achieve a rectangular shape. Figure 4.3 shows how the page looks in the browser.

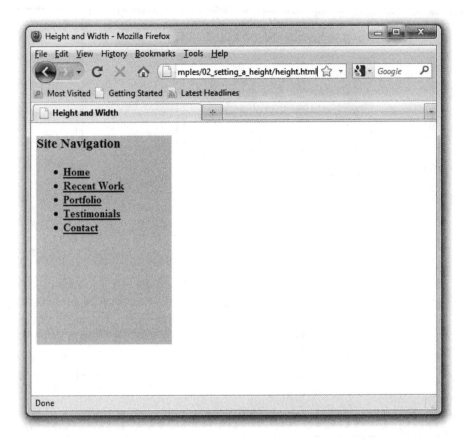

Figure 4.3. Displaying the `div` set to 200 pixels wide and 400 pixels high

What if the navigation area becomes too big?

I mentioned that we could set the navigation block height this way, as long as the number of navigation items didn't vary dramatically between pages. So what would happen if the navigation *did* grow too big for the space we'd allowed for it? The answer to this question depends on the browser, actually.

- In Firefox, and IE7 and above, the height attribute is honored and the list items overflow out of the bottom of that `div`, beyond the yellow background.

- In older versions of IE (version 6 and below), the yellow background area expands vertically as the navigation grows.

These differences are depicted in Figure 4.4.

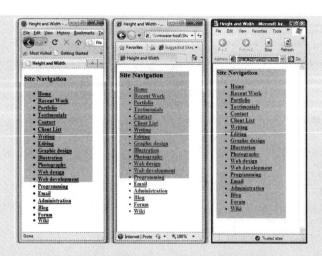

Figure 4.4. Firefox 3 and IE8 behave differently to IE6, as content outgrows its allotted area

Arguably, IE6's behavior of ignoring the height and stretching the background to fit is the preferable reaction, but it's a poor implementation of CSS standards. So, if you can, be aware of setting a height in situations like the above when it's likely the content will outgrow its container. That said, if you *do* set a height and run out of room later, the beauty of CSS is that you can simply make a change in that one place to give your navigation a little more breathing space site-wide.[2]

Adding Borders to Block-level Elements

You can use block-level elements to apply a range of border effects, including different border thicknesses, various border styles (solid lines, dotted lines, and more) and a range of border colors. The CSS properties we can use to achieve these effects are: `border-width`, `border-style`, and `border-color`.

Example Borders

Let's see some examples in action.

Simple Black Border

Figure 4.5 depicts a basic entry-level border: a solid black line, five pixels thick.

---

[2] There is a CSS property that you can use to control the behavior of content that overflows a fixed area. This is best used on sections of a web page where the amount of content is likely to vary a lot. See "overflow" on SitePoint's CSS Reference [http://reference.sitepoint.com/css/overflow/] for more information.

> When you first park, the distance between the power supply and your van's power socket will be precisely 2 inches longer than the inadequate power lead that you own.

Figure 4.5. A simple black border

The CSS for this effect is as follows:

```
.highlight {
  border-width: 5px;
  border-style: solid;
  border-color: black;
}
```

Naming Your Classes

You'll notice that I've used the class name `highlight`. I've used that name because I'm imagining a hypothetical situation where I wanted to highlight a particular paragraph within a page of content. This is good practice. The basic rule is to use names that describe the purpose or meaning of the content to which the class names are applied.

It may be tempting, however, to name your classes according to how they appear visually. For instance, I could've used the class name `blackborder` for the above example. There's a very simple reason why I avoided that path: what if, one day, I decided to use a red border to emphasize a section? By using the class name `highlight`, I can change the way paragraphs are highlighted in the future easily, without being confused by the labeling, or having to adopt a new class name every time it appeared in the HTML.

Inset Border

If a solid line doesn't do it for you, you could try an `inset` border, which gives the effect shown in Figure 4.6.

> When you first park, the distance between the power supply and your van's power socket will be precisely 2 inches longer than the inadequate power lead that you own.

Figure 4.6. An inset border

The color applied in this example is a shade of gray, shown here as a hexadecimal code:

```
.highlight {
  border-width: 10px;
  border-style: inset;
  border-color: #999999;
}
```

Colored Ridge Border

You can apply some color in combination with a border style to create a two-tone effect. In Figure 4.7, a ridged effect works nicely with the red border color. (Again, you don't have to take my word for it regarding the color—check out the file in the code archive for yourself.)

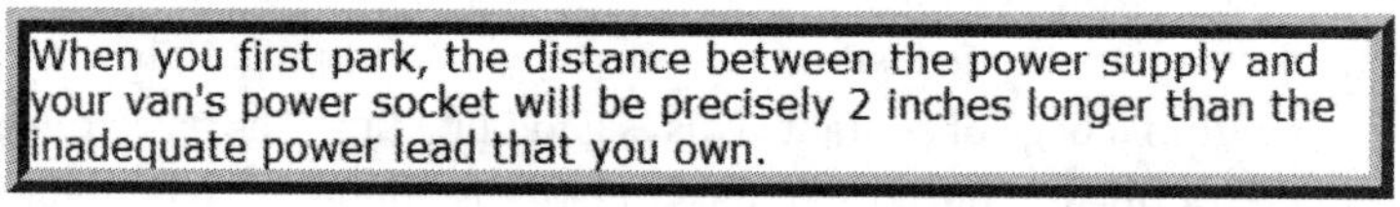

Figure 4.7. A colored ridge border

The code that creates this effect is shown below:

```
.highlight {
  border-width: 10px;
  border-style: ridge;
  border-color: red;
}
```

Bold Border Effects

You're not limited to using solid lines for the border, though. The examples depicted in Figure 4.8 and Figure 4.9 show `dotted` and `dashed` effects respectively; both borders are set to purple with a ten-pixel thickness.

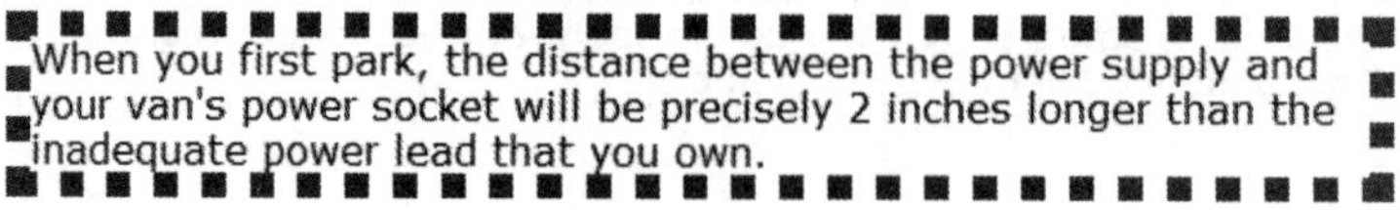

Figure 4.8. A bold, dotted border

```
.highlight {
  border-width: 10px;
  border-style: dotted;
  border-color: purple;
}
```

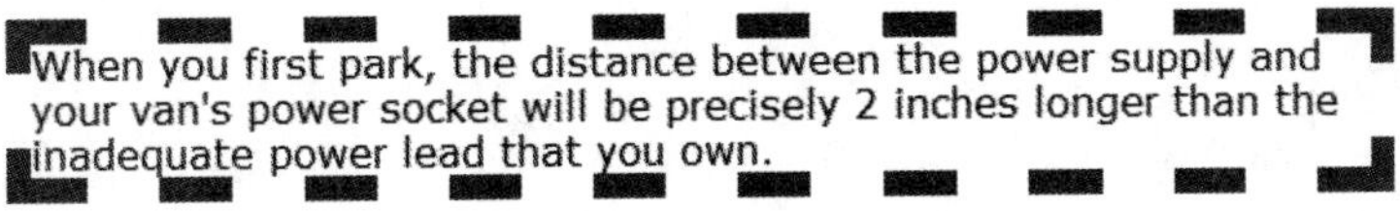

When you first park, the distance between the power supply and your van's power socket will be precisely 2 inches longer than the inadequate power lead that you own.

Figure 4.9. A bold, dashed border

```
.highlight {
  border-width: 10px;
  border-style: dashed;
  border-color: purple;
}
```

All the border styles above are a bit intense. Let's have a look at some more refined examples.

Simple Gray Border

The example depicted in Figure 4.10 uses a simple gray single-pixel border.

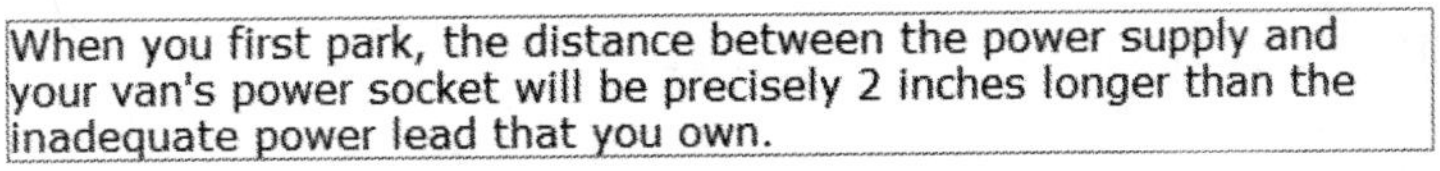

When you first park, the distance between the power supply and your van's power socket will be precisely 2 inches longer than the inadequate power lead that you own.

Figure 4.10. A simple gray border

Here's the CSS that achieves this effect:

```
.highlight {
  border-width: 1px;
  border-style: solid;
  border-color: gray;
}
```

Simple Gray Border (Version 2!)

In Figure 4.11, the border has been thickened slightly (to two pixels), but because we've altered the color to a lighter shade (silver), it doesn't appear too bold.

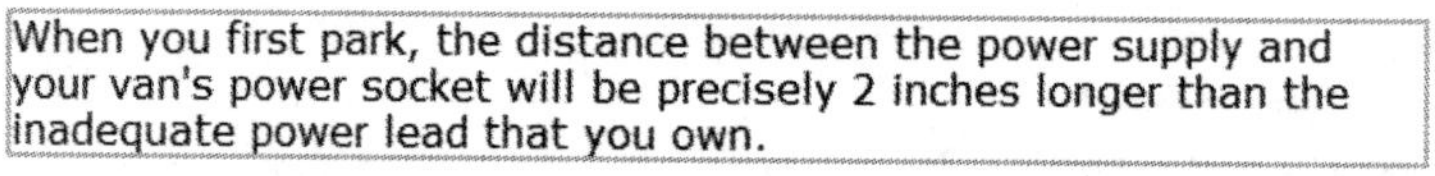

When you first park, the distance between the power supply and your van's power socket will be precisely 2 inches longer than the inadequate power lead that you own.

Figure 4.11. Simple gray border (V2)

And the CSS for it:

```
.highlight {
  border-width: 2px;
  border-style: solid;
  border-color: silver;
}
```

Dotted, Red Border

The red border in Figure 4.12 isn't too severe because it's only one pixel wide; its dotted appearance lightens the effect even more.

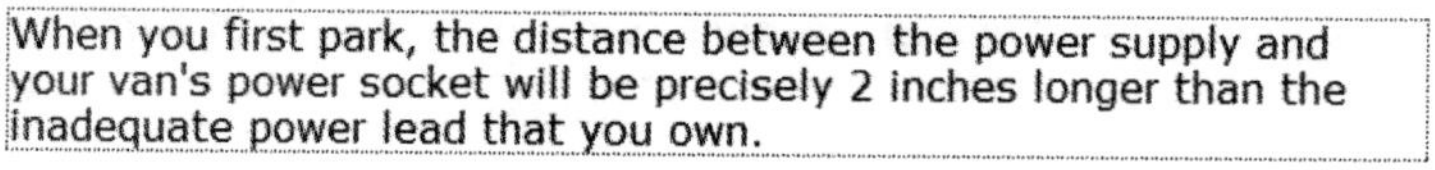

When you first park, the distance between the power supply and your van's power socket will be precisely 2 inches longer than the inadequate power lead that you own.

Figure 4.12. A dotted, red border

Here's the CSS for this border:

```
.highlight {
  border-width: 1px;
  border-style: dotted;
  border-color: red;
}
```

Dashed, Gray Border

The dashed version in Figure 4.13 is less subtle than the dotted single-pixel border, but you'll certainly find uses for this style.

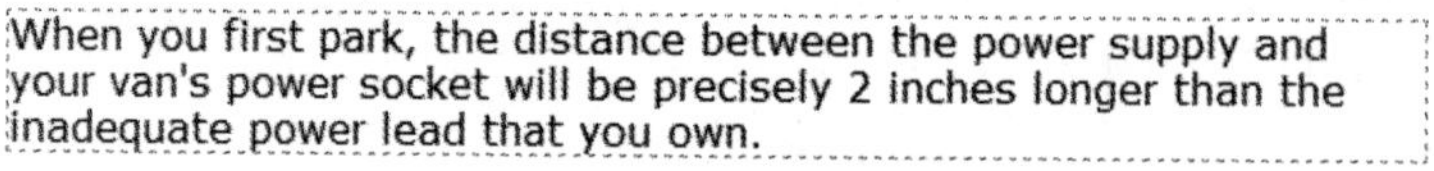

When you first park, the distance between the power supply and your van's power socket will be precisely 2 inches longer than the inadequate power lead that you own.

Figure 4.13. A dashed, gray border

```
.highlight {
  border-width: 1px;
  border-style: dashed;
  border-color: gray;
}
```

Double Borders

You can set a double border on block-level elements, as Figure 4.14 shows.

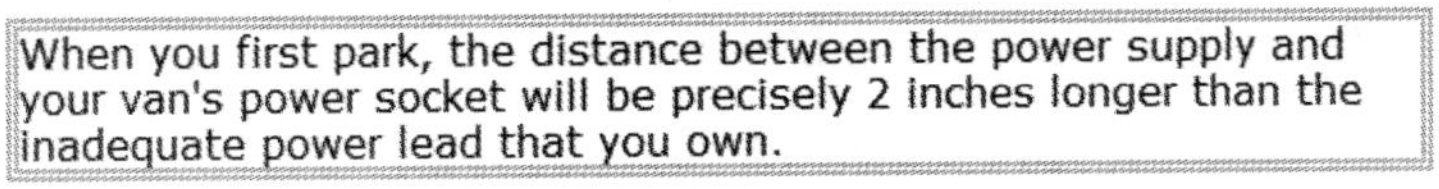

When you first park, the distance between the power supply and your van's power socket will be precisely 2 inches longer than the inadequate power lead that you own.

Figure 4.14. Double border

The markup that creates this effect appears below:

```
.highlight {
  border-width: 5px;
  border-style: double;
  border-color: silver;
}
```

Styling Individual Sides of an Element

In addition to applying borders to all sides of a block-level element, you can style individual edges of the element using `border-top`, `border-bottom`, `border-left`, and `border-right`. Here's an example of a block that has different styles applied to each of its sides:

```
.highlight {
  border-top-width: 1px;
  border-top-style: solid;
  border-top-color: red;
  border-bottom-width: 3px;
  border-bottom-style: dotted;
  border-bottom-color: blue;
  border-left-width: 5px;
  border-left-style: dashed;
  border-left-color: yellow;
  border-right-width: 7px;
```

```
    border-right-style: double;
    border-right-color: fuchsia;
}
```

Let's be honest: as Figure 4.15 shows all too clearly, this looks ugly! However, you can use any of those CSS properties on its own. For example, border-bottom is often used by itself effectively to create dividing lines between sections of page content.

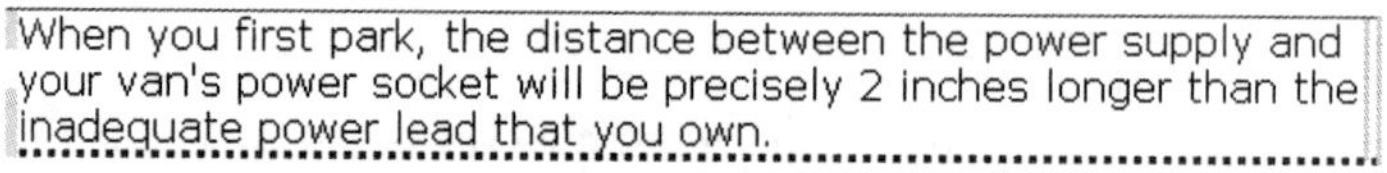

When you first park, the distance between the power supply and your van's power socket will be precisely 2 inches longer than the inadequate power lead that you own.

Figure 4.15. Displaying a different border for each side of the element

Shorthand Border Styles

As we saw in the previous example, there's a large number of CSS declarations. Wouldn't it be nice if you could set up a border using just one declaration instead of three? Good news—you can:

```
.highlight {
  border: 5px solid black;
}
```

This is a shorthand method for styling borders, and browser support for this style of CSS notation is excellent. Given that it saves you some typing, as well as file download sizes (albeit by a pinch), I'd recommend this method for styling borders. You can even use border-top, border-bottom, border-left, and border-right to style individual sides using this shorthand notation.

Border Styles You Can Use

The examples above demonstrated most of the styles that you can use. Below is a list of all the different options available; feel free to experiment with whatever combinations you like.

border thickness

This can be specified using pixels (px), points (pt), or ems.

Alternatively, you could just use one of the border thickness keywords: thin, medium, or thick.

border style

A border can take any of the following styles:

- `solid` (the default value)
- `double`
- `dotted`
- `dashed`
- `groove`
- `ridge`
- `inset`
- `outset`

border color

Border color is specified in the same way as the colors of other elements—either as a hexadecimal code, or as one of the color keywords.

Until now, I've been using generic examples to explain the possibilities that are available. Now, we're going to apply some of these styles to our project site, using only a smattering here and there. Be aware that overusing borders can make a website look very blocky and, possibly, quite ugly.

Shaping and Sizing Our Diving Site

Let's make some minor changes to the project site, beginning with the body element. Open up **style1.css** and find the rule for the body element (it should be the first item that occurs after the comment). Add a declaration to style the whole page with a border, like so:

chapter4/website_files/01_block_level_elements/style1.css (excerpt)

```
body {
    font-family: Verdana, Helvetica, Arial, sans-serif;
    background-color: #e2edff;
    padding: 15px;
    line-height: 125%;
    border: 4px solid navy;
}
```

Take a look at any of the pages in your browser, and they should be similar to the display depicted in Figure 4.16.

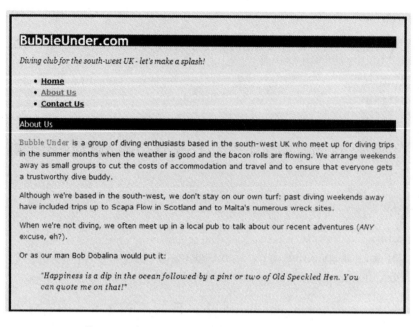

Figure 4.16. Surrounding the entire web page with a border

Next, let's make some changes to the navigation area. Back in Chapter 2, I suggested adding id attributes to key sections of the web pages. We'll make use of those attributes in this procedure.

In **style1.css**, add a new rule for the navigation id. Set the area's width to 180 pixels, and add a dotted navy border that's one pixel wide. Your CSS should look like this:

```
                    chapter4/website_files/03_navigation_border/style1.css (excerpt)
#navigation {
  width: 180px;
  border: 1px dotted navy;
}
```

Save **style1.css**, and then take a look at your website in a browser. Figure 4.17 shows what you should see.

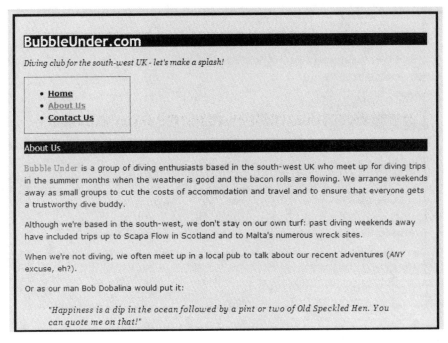

Figure 4.17. The navigation displaying definite dimensions

We'll make another tweak to the navigation and change the background color:

```
                         chapter4/website_files/04_navigation_bgcolor/style1.css (excerpt)

#navigation {
  width: 180px;
  border: 1px dotted navy;
  background-color: #7da5d8;
}
```

I've chosen another shade of blue (remember from Chapter 3 that a range of color picker tools are available to help you find the hexadecimal codes for different colors). The result of this work is shown in Figure 4.18.

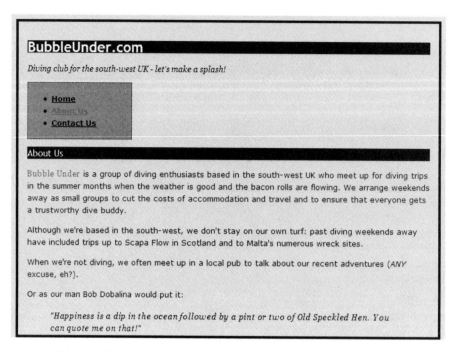

Figure 4.18. The navigation displaying as a distinct, functional area of the web page

That looks better, but the background color we've chosen makes the visited link text a bit difficult to read. Let's fix that by choosing a darker color for the visited link. Find the rule for visited links and change it to the following:

```
a:visited {
  color: navy;
}
```

That's much better! Next, let's style the tagline a little more by applying a background color and border effect to set it off nicely. In your stylesheet, find the markup that styles the tagline, and add the declaration shown in bold below:

chapter4/website_files/05_tagline_border/style1.css (excerpt)

```
#tagline p {
  font-style: italic;
  font-family: Georgia, Times, serif;
  background-color: #bed8f3;
  border-top: 3px solid #7da5d8;
  border-bottom: 3px solid #7da5d8;
}
```

Figure 4.19 shows how this markup displays in the browser.

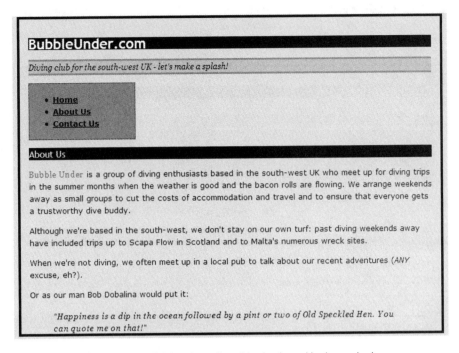

Figure 4.19. Highlighting the tagline with a border and background color

Finally, let's change the styling of the h2 headings so that they look a bit different from the h1s (it *is* possible to go overboard with that dark background effect). Now is also a good time to rearrange some of our rules that, if you've just been adding to the bottom of the file, may be jumbled all over the place, rather than appearing in a logical order. Cut and paste all the heading rules so that they appear together, to make them easier to locate later on:

```
h1, h2, h3 {
  font-family: "Trebuchet MS", Helvetica, Arial, sans-serif;
}

h1 {
  font-size: x-large;
  background-color: navy;
  color: white;
}

h2 {
  color: navy;
```

```
  font-size: 130%;
  font-weight: normal;
}
```

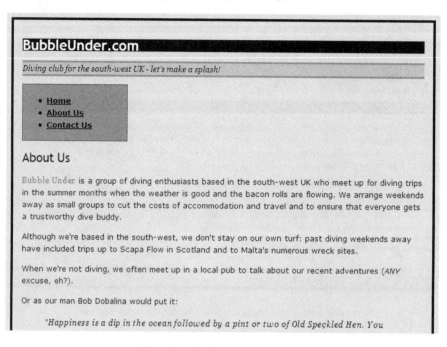

Figure 4.20. Varying the heading styles

We've chosen a new height of 130% for our h2 headings, which (in most browsers) is a bit bigger than large, but slightly smaller than x-large. The page now displays like the one shown in Figure 4.20.

Adding Padding

If you take a look at the headings on the project site, and at the borders that I demonstrated earlier in this chapter, you'll notice that the text sits right next to the border; it looks a little uncomfortable, don't you think? To remedy this, let's add some padding—extra buffer space between the border and the text. Not surprisingly, the CSS property for this extra space is padding.

Here are three different ways we can apply padding to a block-level element: using pixels, ems, or percentage values:

```
.pixelpadding {
  padding: 30px;
  border: 1px dashed gray;
}
.empadding {
  padding: 2em;
  border: 1px dashed gray;
}
.percentagepadding {
  padding: 5%;
  border: 1px dashed gray;
}
```

Figure 4.21 shows how these CSS styles render on the screen.

This paragraph has been styled with padding measured in pixels.

This paragraph has been styled with padding measured in ems.

This paragraph has been styled with padding measured as a percentage.

Figure 4.21. Three methods of padding, all achieving the same result on the screen

Which unit of measurement is best?

Which method of measurement should you use for your padding: pixels, ems, or percentages? If each of the examples above create the same effect on the web page, what difference does your choice make? The answer is: it depends on how you want your design to behave.

If you intend your design to change with the browser window, percentages is the way to go. Any value that's set using percentages will change as the size of the browser window changes; the bigger the browser window, the bigger your padding will become.

If you want your design to scale well with different font sizes, including (and this is a critical point) IE6, you should use ems, because the measurements will be based on how your users set the font size in their browsers. If you use pixels (px) or points (pt), most browsers will let you scale the font up and down from your chosen size; only IE6 ignores this, hence the need to use ems.

If you're after a precise design with graphical elements that line up exactly, regardless of the font setting or browser window size, pixels is the most predictable method of all. A pixel will *nearly* always represent a single dot on the user's screen. Why nearly? Because most browsers have a page zoom facility that magnifies everything in proportion, over which you have little control.

Note that page zooming differs from font resizing, so it's good to understand the subtle distinction. Page zoom scales everything proportionally, while text resizing only affects the text inside the various containers; this can often result in some odd effects, as you'll see later in the chapter.

Introducing Padding to the Project Site

Adding a bit of breathing space to your layout sure can improve it. Let's now address an issue on the project site—namely, the first-level headings.

Find the section in **style1.css** in which you set the color and size of your h1, and add padding as shown below:

chapter4/website_files/07_heading_padding/style1.css *(excerpt)*

```
h1 {
    font-size: x-large;
    background-color: navy;
    color: white;
    padding-top: 2em;
    padding-bottom: .2em;
    padding-left: .4em;
}
```

Next, let's give our headings a bit of head room:

chapter4/website_files/07_heading_padding/style1.css *(excerpt)*

```
h2 {
    color: navy;
    font-size: 130%;
```

```
   font-weight: normal;
   padding-top: 15px;
}
```

Finally, find the tagline and give that some padding, too. Use the values below:

chapter4/website_files/07_heading_padding/style1.css (excerpt)

```
#tagline p {
   font-style: italic;
   font-family: Georgia, Times, serif;
   background-color: #bed8f3;
   border-top: 3px solid #7da5d8;
   border-bottom: 3px solid #7da5d8;
   padding-top: .2em;
   padding-bottom: .2em;
   padding-left: .8em;
}
```

Refresh the view in your browser, and you'll see the clear improvement shown in Figure 4.22.

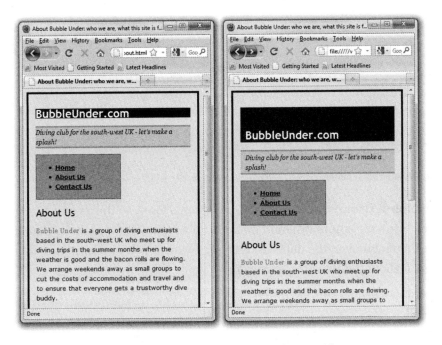

Figure 4.22. Before and after: the benefits of extra padding

Margins

So, you've learned that you can size a block-level element, give it a border of your choosing, and apply padding so that its content avoids bumping right up against its edges. Let's take a look at another very useful CSS property: the margin property.

The margin property allows us to specify how much space should exist *outside* an element's border. The only difference between the CSS for the two paragraphs shown in Figure 4.23 is that the declaration margin: 30px has been added to the second one.

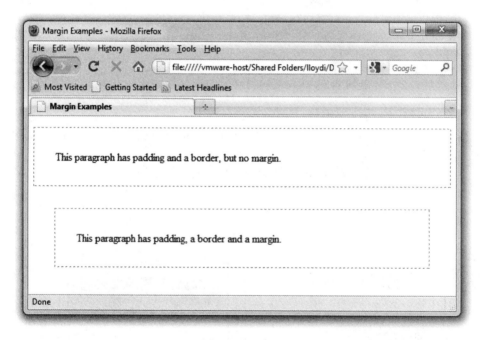

Figure 4.23. The difference between padding and margin is clearer when a border is present

We're going to change the margin of two elements for now: the ul and h2 elements. Different browsers apply different default top margin values to these elements. Rather than relying on the defaults, let's set a value of 15 pixels, so that there's no confusion about the size of this margin:

chapter4/website_files/07_heading_padding/style1.css *(excerpt)*

```
h2, ul {
  margin-top: 15px;
}
```

The Box Model

What we've been looking at in this chapter is the **box model**. A block-level element can be manipulated using a combination of margin, border, padding, height, and width values. These properties can be seen together in Figure 4.24.

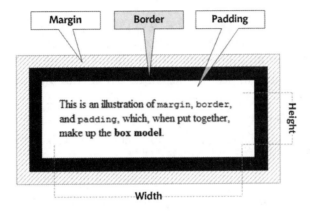

Figure 4.24. The box model explained

 The Broken Box Model

If you're using IE version 6 or later (check in **Help** > **About Internet Explorer** and look for **Version**), you should have little problem sizing and manipulating block-level elements as I've described here, as long as you've included a doctype at the beginning of your web page. Without a doctype, IE reverts to **quirks mode**.

In quirks mode, IE calculates widths and heights using a different—and incorrect—method. This problem arises because IE versions 4 and 5, which were among the first browsers to support CSS, got some of the details wrong (such as the box model). Microsoft fixed those problems in IE6, but in the interim many sites on the Web had been written to use Microsoft's incorrect interpretation of the CSS rules. Microsoft was in a prickly situation: professional web developers demanded that Microsoft fix the bugs but, if it complied, users would be left to battle with most web pages not displaying as intended, sometimes with horrible results.

Microsoft's answer was to use a technique called **doctype switching**. If developers included a doctype, their pages would be displayed according to the correct rules. Pages without a doctype (most pages on the Internet at that time) would be displayed in quirks mode—the same way they appeared in IE5.

If you stick to advice given in this book and use the markup provided, you should avoid any problems relating to quirks mode. However, if you do see noticeable differences between web pages viewed in IE and in other browsers, you may be experiencing the "broken box model" problem. If you think this is the case, your best course of action would be to head over to SitePoint's CSS Forum and ask your questions.[3]

Positioning Elements Anywhere You Like!

Without any intervention, a web browser will simply display the items on the page in the same order as they appear in the source. So, if your markup contains a heading followed by navigation, a second heading, three paragraphs of text, and a quotation—that's precisely what you'll see on the screen, in that exact order. And until now, this has been the way we've approached our project site, adding content in the order in which we've wanted it to appear on the page. But in this section, I'm going to show you some of the really powerful effects that CSS can achieve: you're going to learn how to position certain sections of the site in specific areas on the screen.

With regards to CSS layouts, there are many, many different ways that you can approach this task. Ultimately, I cannot possibly teach you every available method. If you want to investigate the topic further, I'd recommend that you pick up a copy of another SitePoint book: *HTML Utopia: Designing Without Tables Using CSS*.[4]

Showing the Structure

Let's remind ourselves of the specific sections in our website:

---

[3] http://www.sitepoint.com/launch/cssforum/
[4] http://www.sitepoint.com/books/css2/

contact.html

```
<!DOCTYPE html>
<html lang="en">
  <head>
    <title>Contact Us at Bubble Under</title>
    <meta charset="utf-8"/>
    <link href="style1.css" rel="stylesheet" type="text/css"/>
  </head>
  <body>
    <div id="header">
      <div id="sitebranding">
        <h1>BubbleUnder.com</h1>
      </div>
      <div id="tagline">
        <p>Diving club for the south-west UK - let's make a
           splash!</p>
      </div>
    </div> <!-- end of header div -->
    <div id="navigation">
      <ul>
        <li><a href="index.html">Home</a></li>
        <li><a href="about.html">About Us</a></li>
        <li><a href="contact.html">Contact Us </a></li>
      </ul>
    </div>
    <div id="bodycontent">
      <h2>Contact Us</h2>
      <p>To find out more, contact Club Secretary Bob Dobalina on
         01793 641207 or email
         <a href="bob@bubbleunder.com">bob@bubbleunder.com</a>.
         </p>
    </div> <!-- end of bodycontent div -->
  </body>
</html>
```

 Border control

When you're about to lay out your web page using CSS, remember this useful tip: temporarily add a border to each section you're planning to move. Borders make it much easier to see the effects of your markup, and afterwards you simply remove that temporary style.

Let's add a new (but temporary) rule to our stylesheet (**style1.css**) applying a border to each of the elements. Insert this rule at the end of the stylesheet, so that it overrides any border styles you might have set earlier:

chapter4/website_files/08_page_structure/style1.css *(excerpt)*

```
#header, #sitebranding, #tagline, #navigation, #bodycontent {
    border: 1px solid red;
    padding: 2px;
    margin-bottom: 2px;
}
```

Here, I've applied some padding, as well as a bottom margin, to make it easier for us to see the items that are nested (the `sitebranding` and `tagline` sections are inside the `header` section). Let's see what that CSS has done to our web pages; Figure 4.25 shows the document displayed in the browser.

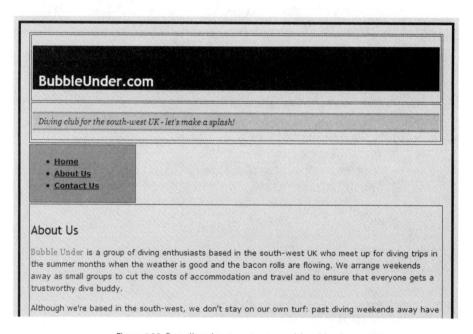

Figure 4.25. Revealing the page structure with red borders

It looks a bit ugly, doesn't it? It's going to get even uglier—for a short while—as we move the text about. You know how it is when you move furniture around in your house: while you're halfway through the job, it can seem a little chaotic, but it will all work out in the end. That's exactly what's going to happen with our project site.

Now, let's start moving these boxes around!

Absolute Positioning

Perhaps the easiest method for positioning items using CSS is **absolute positioning**. Using absolute positioning, we specify top and left positions (or coordinates) for the item in question. Imagine directing a store owner to retrieve some jewelry for you from the shop window with the words, "Can I have the watch that's five along and three down?"

Using absolute positioning is as simple as adding a `position: absolute` declaration to your CSS rule, and then specifying where you'd like that element positioned. In the following example, we use `top` and `left` to position a `div` 200 pixels from the top of the browser viewport, and 200 pixels from its left edge:

```
<!DOCTYPE html>
<html lang="en">
  <head>
    <title>Absolute Positioning</title>
    <meta charset="utf-8"/>
    <style type="text/css">
      #redblock {
        position: absolute;
        top: 200px;
        left: 200px;
        color: white;
        background-color: red;
        width: 90px;
        height: 90px;
        padding: 5px;
      }
    </style>
  </head>
  <body>
    <h1>Absolute Positioning</h1>
    <div id="redblock">This is the red block.</div>
    <p>The red block is positioned 200 pixels from the top and 200
        pixels from the left.</p>
  </body>
</html>
```

Figure 4.26 shows the resulting display.

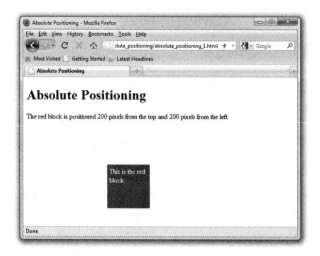

Figure 4.26. Absolute positioning in action

Getting Ready to Move into Position

We're now going to position every element on our page using fixed coordinates relative to the browser window's top and left sides. Because of this, it's worth taking the time to undo some stylistic changes that can complicate matters. We'll now undo the `padding` and `border` properties that we set on the `body` element earlier.

1. Open **style1.css** and remove the `padding` and `border` declarations on the `body` element.

2. In their place, add two new declarations to set both `padding` and `margin` to zero.

The `body` element rule in your stylesheet should now look like this:

```
chapter4/website_files/09_body_no_padding_or_margin/style1.css (excerpt)

body {
  background-color: #e2edff;
  font-family: Verdana, Helvetica, Arial, sans-serif;
  line-height: 125%;
  padding: 0;
  margin: 0;
}
```

Nothing Is Always Nothing

What's the difference between zero feet, zero meters, and zero furlongs? There's no difference—they're all measuring a zero distance, so the unit is unimportant.

This principle applies in the above CSS—hence why there's no qualifying unit of measurement for the `padding` and `margin` properties. If we want a value of nothing, there's no need to specify a unit of measurement, because whatever the unit might be, it amounts to nothing!

Refresh the view in your browser, and you should see a page like the one shown in Figure 4.27.

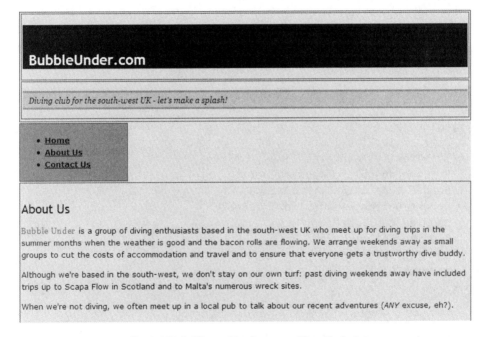

Figure 4.27. Padding and border removed from the body

The headings in the page—BubbleUnder.com (h1) and About Us (h2)—are surrounded by margins, which the browser inserts by default if we don't specify margins of our own. It's a good idea to remove them—we're aiming to "trim the fat," trying to have each heading as close as possible to the top-left of its containing `div`. This will make the headings easier to position, and ensure that the page looks the same across browsers.

1. In **style1.css**, scroll down the page to find the h1 rule.

2. Add a declaration to set the margin to zero:

```
chapter4/website_files/10_headings_no_margin/style1.css (excerpt)

h1 {
    font-size: x-large;
    background-color: navy;
    color: white;
    padding-top: 2em;
    padding-bottom: .2em;
    padding-left: .4em;
    margin: 0;
}
```

3. Locate the #tagline p rule and remove its margins, too:

```
chapter4/website_files/10_headings_no_margin/style1.css (excerpt)

#tagline p {
    font-style: italic;
    font-family: Georgia, Times, serif;
    background-color: #bed8f3;
    border-top: 3px solid #7da5d8;
    border-bottom: 3px solid #7da5d8;
    padding-top: .2em;
    padding-bottom: .2em;
    padding-left: .8em;
    margin: 0;
}
```

4. Refresh the page in your browser. The gaps that previously appeared above and below the headings should have disappeared, as shown in Figure 4.28.

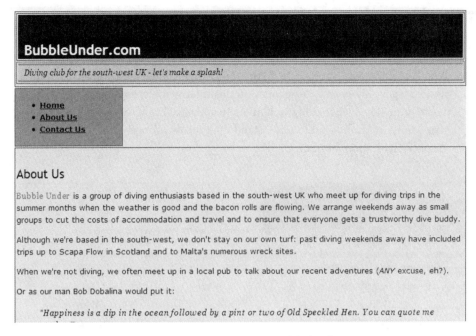

Figure 4.28. Eliminating space around the headings

Now, hold your breath—this is where it *can* get really ugly! But trust me, I'll guide you through this quickly and painlessly (and you'll appreciate why I've suggested adding the red borders to the page elements while their positions are shifting).

1. Add the following to the end of your CSS file:

chapter4/website_files/11_absolute_mess/style1.css *(excerpt)*

```
#navigation, #bodycontent, #header {
  position: absolute;
}
```

2. Save the stylesheet.

3. Refresh the view in your browser.

4. Enter a state of shock when you see how bad the page looks!

Your page should look like it's been picked up, thrown in the air, and fallen back to Earth with all the page parts landing in a pile, as in Figure 4.29. Don't worry, this is normal!

Avoiding the Messy Part

In case you're wondering why the layout is deliberately being messed up, and whether you're going to have to do this every time you create a website in future, don't despair. Many web designers skip this intermediate step, and go straight to positioning items where they want them to appear. This ability comes with practice. I think it's important to understand the process properly first, before we dispense with these basics.

Figure 4.29. Absolute positioning makes the page a mess

So, what's happened here? Well, the three sections of the page now sit on top of one another, all absolutely positioned at the top-left corner of the page. Why? Because that's what we've told the browser to do with them. All it knows is to position them *absolutely*; it doesn't know *where* to position them. They just sit there in a pile: the `header` area first, the `navigation` on top of that, and finally, the `bodycontent`, king of the heap!

Let's begin to fix the site by moving the navigation and main content area to appear below the header area. In **style1.css**, add the following rule:

chapter4/website_files/12_header_visible/style1.css *(excerpt)*

```
#navigation, #bodycontent {
  top: 120px;
}
```

This will move the blocks down so that the header is no longer obscured. Figure 4.30 shows how the markup displays.

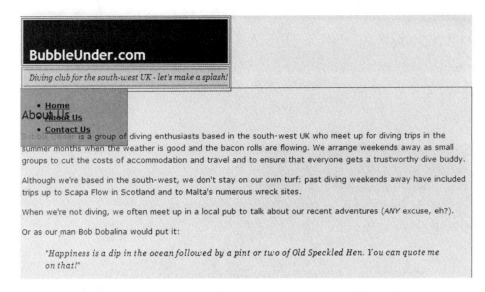

Figure 4.30. Pushing navigation and content down 120 pixels to reveal the header area

What we've done here is tell the browser to move both the `navigation` and `bodycontent` areas to an absolute position that's 120 pixels from the top of the web page—no questions asked! The browser has honored that request. Now we're going to throw it another request: move the `bodycontent` area to the right, so that it no longer obscures the `navigation`. As the navigation was previously set to a `width` of 180 pixels, let's try moving the `bodycontent` section to the right by 200 pixels; that should easily move it clear (and leave some space between it and the navigation).

Here's what you need to add to **style1.css**. I've included all the CSS relating to positioning that we added in the previous few steps, so you can check that everything's okay with your stylesheet:

chapter4/website_files/13_body_content_positioned/style1.css *(excerpt)*

```
#navigation, #bodycontent, #header {
  position: absolute;
}


#navigation, #bodycontent {
  top: 120px;
}
```

```
#bodycontent {
    left: 200px;
}
```

Let's see how that markup looks in the browser. Your page should display as shown in Figure 4.31.

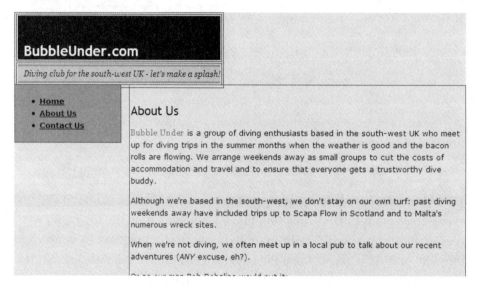

Figure 4.31. Using positioning to distinguish navigation from content

We still need to address a few maintenance issues before this looks like a finished page:

▨ The header area and tagline aren't stretching to fill the width of the web page.

▨ There is some unnecessary space around the h1 element and tagline.

▨ The red borders and padding between block elements need to be removed (they've served their purpose admirably).

▨ A comment or two should be added to the CSS to explain what we've done.

We're going to complete all these tasks in one go. By now, you should be feeling confident enough to have a go at it yourself. As always, don't worry if you get stuck—the solution awaits you on the other side of this guidance. Let's make this website look completely shipshape!

1. Position the navigation and body content 107 pixels from the top instead of 120 pixels—this will allow for a snugger fit when we remove the red borders.

2. Next, tell the browser that the `header` `div` and the tagline should fill the available width (that is, they need to take up 100% of the width).

3. The red borders that were applied to the various `divs` earlier (for the purposes of seeing the layout more clearly) need to be removed. Delete the entire rule.

4. Finally, it would be a good idea to add a comment above all the positioning code to note what you've been doing. This will allow you to easily identify this section's job, and note that it controls positioning, rather than cosmetic effects.

How did you go? Here's the stylesheet again, at least the part that we've been concentrating on for positioning purposes. The most recent changes are shown in bold:

chapter4/website_files/14_almost_done/style1.css *(excerpt)*

```css
/*
This section deals with the position of items on the screen.
It uses absolute positioning - fixed x and y coordinates measured
from the top-left corner of the browser's content display.
*/

#navigation, #bodycontent, #header {
  position: absolute;
}

#navigation, #bodycontent {
  top: 107px;
}

#bodycontent {
  left: 200px;
}

#header {
  width: 100%;
}
```

So, the big question is, what's this markup done to our website? Let's take a look. Does your display resemble Figure 4.32?

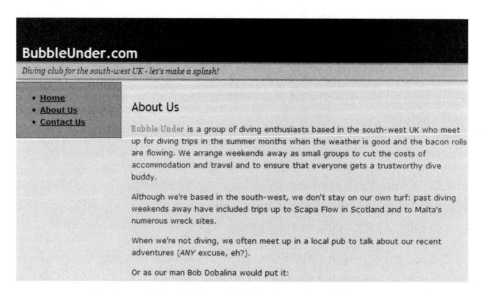

Figure 4.32. A conventional web page layout

I'm almost happy with it. How about you? The header and tagline might complement each other better if they had matching borders. Give the header a top border of three pixels, using the same shade of blue that we used for the tagline. And let's remove the dotted border around the navigation box—it's a bit out of place with our new design:

chapter4/website_files/15_final_layout/style1.css *(excerpt)*

```
#navigation {
  width: 180px;
  background-color: #7da5d8;
}

#header {
  border-top: 3px solid #7da5d8;
}
```

Save the changes in **style1.css**, refresh the view in your browser, and see how it looks—like Figure 4.33, I hope!

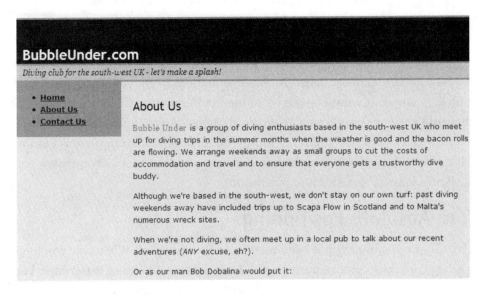

Figure 4.33. The completed web page layout

Finally, the page is set out as intended, with the navigation on the left—where you'd expect it to be—the content on the right, and a header (and tagline) that stretches all the way along the top. We've achieved a full CSS layout, which will truly help us out in the future should we want to redesign the look of the site, and it applies to all pages on the site.

Did you notice that throughout this whole chapter we didn't touch the page content once, nor the actual HTML? Everything has been changed through the CSS. We've seen how the content can be manipulated using a combination of borders, padding, widths, sizes, and positioning in CSS. Now visualize what this project website will look like a couple of years from now, with many pages of content. Just think how easy it will be to redesign!

Want the navigation to sit on the right-hand side? No problem. Just change the co-ordinates for the navigation in the CSS, move the content to the left as if you're moving a piece in a slide puzzle, and before you know it, the whole site will have changed. This is the true power of using CSS to build sites (but then you've never known any other way, you lucky soul!).

Other Layout Options

As I mentioned earlier, there are many ways to approach a CSS layout. In this book, I've opted for the simplest, most trouble-free method to get you up to speed with the idea; however, it would be remiss of me not to mention the other positioning techniques you can use. No need to worry, though—I'm not going to ask you to redo the website all over again! Instead, I'll provide some general examples, as I did with the border styles earlier in this chapter. But first, let's take a look at one more aspect you should know about absolute positioning.

More Absolute Positioning

So far, all our positioning has been relative to the viewport. Whenever you have positioned anything, you've positioned it from the top-left corner of the page. When you start to play around with absolutely positioned elements, and you start putting them inside each other, a different approach is required.

To illustrate, let's take our red box example from before, and add a yellow box:

```
<!DOCTYPE html>
<html lang="en">
  <head>
    <title>Absolute Positioning</title>
    <meta charset="utf-8"/>
    <style type="text/css">
      #redblock {
        position: absolute;
        top: 200px;
        left: 200px;
        background-color: red;
        width: 100px;
        height: 100px;
      }
      #yellowblock {
        position: absolute;
        top: 20px;
        left: 20px;
        background-color: yellow;
        color: red;
        width: 50px;
        height: 50px;
        padding: 5px;
```

```
      }
    </style>
  </head>
  <body>
    <h1>Absolute Positioning</h1>
    <div id="redblock">
      <div id="yellowblock">Yellow!</div>
    </div>
    <p>The red block is positioned absolutely using coordinates of
        200 pixels from the top, and 200 pixels from the left.</p>
    <p>The yellow block inside is positioned 20 pixels from the
        top of its parent element, and 20 pixels to the left.</p>
  </body>
</html>
```

Here, we've put a `div` with the `id` `yellowblock` inside our `redblock` `div`, and then positioned it absolutely—20 pixels from the top and 20 pixels from the left. Where do you think the yellow block is going to appear? The display is illustrated in Figure 4.34.

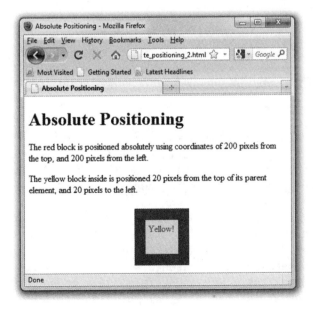

Figure 4.34. The yellow block appears inside the red block

How did it end up there? Well, whenever you absolutely position an element, (such as the red box), everything inside that element (the yellow box) is positioned in relation to that containing element. Fear not if this sounds a bit confusing—it may seem like an advanced concept at this stage, but we won't be using it in our project site. I wanted to mention it, though, so that you're aware of it when you start to play around with positioning on your own sites.

Relative Positioning

With absolute positioning, items are positioned from a specific starting point: the top-left corner of the viewport, or the top-left corner of a containing element. With **relative positioning**, any value that you apply will be implemented *relative to the item's original location before this positioning rule was applied*. Here is some example CSS. Notice the rule that is applied to elements with the nudged class:

```
p {
  background-color: #ccc;
}

.nudged {
  position: relative;
  top: 10px;
  left: 10px;
}
```

Here's some HTML in which the class name nudged is applied to the middle paragraph:

```
<p>Next came a massage that I was not expecting. It started with a
   bit of manipulation of the temples, followed by the barber's
   attempt to drag the top half of my face down towards my chin
   (and vice-versa) with his big burly hands. I'm sure it's good
   for you. I wasn't sure it was good for me, though. He then
   made his way down to my shoulders and managed to pull me
   around in such a way that I squealed like a girl. This was not
   relaxing -- this was painful! Evidently I was knotted up. I
   must have needed it, I reasoned.</p>
<p class="nudged">There was an audible crack as he grabbed my head
   and twisted it to the right, all of it quite unexpected. To
   the left, no cracking sound. And we weren't quite done
   yet...</p>
<p>To finish off, the barber got a pair of tongs. He took a ball
   of cotton wool and wrapped it tightly around the tip of the
   tongs, so that it looked like a large cotton bud. He then
```

```
doused the cotton wool in what must have been pure alcohol,
set it on fire, and began to fling it at my face. Using one
hand to cover the top of my ear and my hair, he flashed it
against my ear, singeing the small hairs in and around the
ear.</p>
```

The class could have been applied to any paragraph (or, for that matter, any other block-level element). Figure 4.35 shows the text with the original position of the paragraph, and the effect after the class name has been added to the p element.

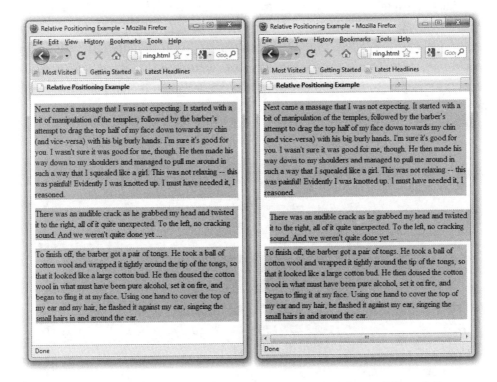

Figure 4.35. The middle paragraph positioned relative to the previous element—before and after

Notice how the markup has moved our paragraph across and down by ten pixels, so that neither the left-hand nor right-hand sides of that paragraph line up with the others? It really has been *nudged*, rather than indented from the left-hand side.

In case you're wondering, the text in this example is describing the "joys" of a traditional Turkish shave. It's fun … if you like that kind of thing!

Benefits of Relative Positioning

Relative positioning might be an improvement over the absolute positioning technique that I proposed when discussing our project site. I say *might* because it really depends on the layout of your page, as well as which browser you're using. There's no hard-and-fast rule. If text sizes are increased in the browser, the document can more easily **reflow**—that is, adjust the layout to suit the new text size—if relative positioning is used. (In IE, you would use **View** > **Text Size** > **Larger** or **Largest**.) With the fixed header area (a space of 107 pixels), a large increase in text sizes could potentially cause text to exceed the allotted space and intrude onto the content or navigation area, as shown in Figure 4.36. However, as mentioned earlier in this chapter, most browsers now zoom the whole page proportionally rather than just the text parts; if you want to scale only the text, you'll need to dig a little deeper in the browser menus to find that option. What this tells you is that people viewing your site will also need to search around a bit just to scale the text, so this is a problem that is diminishing over time.

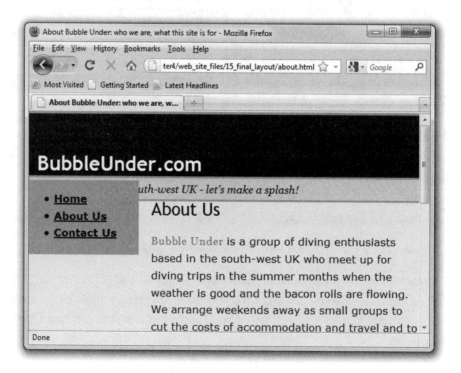

Figure 4.36. Sometimes, very large font sizes and fixed position layouts don't mix

So, why did we use the absolute positioning method instead of relative positioning on our project site? Using relative positioning for a CSS layout can be tricky to accomplish; you might even be put off at an early stage in your CSS career if you were to get it wrong. In practice, a well-seasoned web developer will use a mixture of absolute, relative, and **floated positioning** schemes. It really is a job of judging each site or page build on a case-by-case basis; with experience, you'll know just by looking at the design which scheme will be best.

 Stretching Your Wings with Elastic Design

There is an approach to building web pages called **elastic** web design, where all measurements are specified using ems—borders, margins, padding, everything. Yet, it certainly falls into the realm of advanced web design, and outside of this book's scope. As an indication of what's possible, though, try making this small change to our project's stylesheet:

Locate the line that positions our navigation and body content areas 107 pixels from the top of the viewport, and replace it with the following:

chapter4/website_files/16_em_based_positioning/style1.css *(excerpt)*

```
#navigation, #bodycontent {
    top: 6.54em;
}
```

Save the file and refresh your browser. There should be no noticeable difference—until you change the font size. Because the div elements are positioned using ems, the design holds together much better, even for large font sizes. The number 6.54 might seem random; I determined it by trial and error to be the distance from the top of the viewport to the bottom of the tagline, regardless of the font size in use.

Earlier in this chapter, we discussed the choices available for units of measurement, and this is one case when a definite advantage is gained by using ems. Read more in Patrick Griffith's article on elastic design.[5]

---

[5] http://www.alistapart.com/articles/elastic/

Floated Positioning

A technique favored by many web developers is to use **CSS floats**—making use of the CSS `float` property to lay out a page. Put simply, when you float an area of content, you move it to one side, allowing other content to flow around it. With careful planning, you can float several items on a page, creating effects similar to the multicolumn layouts we see in newspapers. Let's take a look at a simple example of a float:

```
#nav {
  float: right;
  width: 300px;
  background-color: yellow;
}
```

This will move a block with an `id` of `nav` to the right of the web page, setting it to just 300 pixels wide. The text that follows it moves up the page to fill the space that's been vacated by the floated element. Here's the HTML that achieves this effect:

```
<div id="nav">
  <ul>
    <li><a href="index.html">This is an area of navigation
        items</a></li>
    <li><a href="index.html">which is floated on the
        right.</a></li>
    <li><a href="turkish.html">Turkish Shaving Stories.</a></li>
    <li><a href="http://www.bubbleunder.com/">Diving
        Stories.</a></li>
  </ul>
</div> <!-- end of nav div -->
<h1>Turkish Shaving Stories</h1>
<p>Next came a massage that I was not expecting. It started with a
    bit of manipulation of the temples, followed by the barber's
    attempt to drag the top half of my face down towards my chin
    (and vice-versa) with his big burly hands. I'm sure it's good
    for you. I wasn't sure it was good for me, though. He then
    made his way down to my shoulders and managed to pull me
    around in such a way that I squealed like a girl. This was not
    relaxing -- this was painful! Evidently I was knotted up. I
    must have needed it, I reasoned.</p>
<p>There was an audible crack as he grabbed my head and twisted it
    to the right, all of it quite unexpected. To the left, no
```

```
cracking sound. And we weren't quite done yet ...</p>
<p>To finish off, the barber got a pair of tongs. He took a ball
   of cotton wool and wrapped it tightly around the tip of the
   tongs, so that it looked like a large cotton bud. He then
   doused the cotton wool in what must have been pure alcohol,
   set it on fire, and began to fling it at my face. Using one
   hand to cover the top of my ear and my hair, he flashed it
   against my ear, singeing the small hairs in and around the
   ear.</p>
```

Figure 4.37 shows the effect as it displays in the browser.

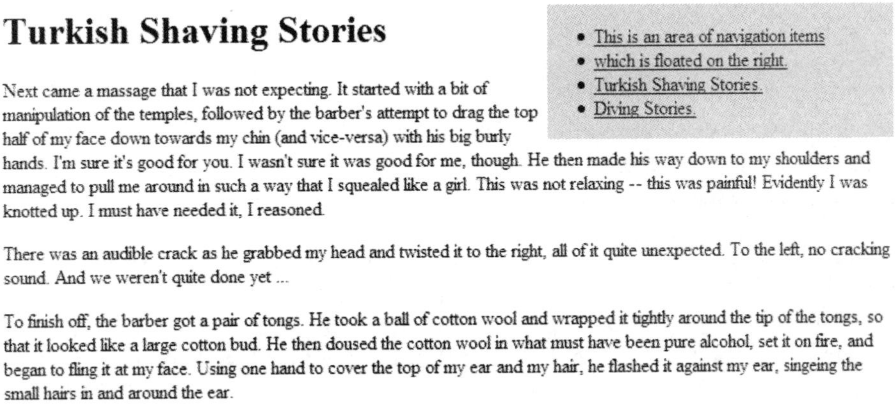

Turkish Shaving Stories

- This is an area of navigation items
- which is floated on the right.
- Turkish Shaving Stories.
- Diving Stories.

Next came a massage that I was not expecting. It started with a bit of manipulation of the temples, followed by the barber's attempt to drag the top half of my face down towards my chin (and vice-versa) with his big burly hands. I'm sure it's good for you. I wasn't sure it was good for me, though. He then made his way down to my shoulders and managed to pull me around in such a way that I squealed like a girl. This was not relaxing -- this was painful! Evidently I was knotted up. I must have needed it, I reasoned.

There was an audible crack as he grabbed my head and twisted it to the right, all of it quite unexpected. To the left, no cracking sound. And we weren't quite done yet ...

To finish off, the barber got a pair of tongs. He took a ball of cotton wool and wrapped it tightly around the tip of the tongs, so that it looked like a large cotton bud. He then doused the cotton wool in what must have been pure alcohol, set it on fire, and began to fling it at my face. Using one hand to cover the top of my ear and my hair, he flashed it against my ear, singeing the small hairs in and around the ear.

Figure 4.37. A simple CSS float at work

If you want to avoid having the text form an L shape when it wraps around the item, apply the CSS `padding` property to the content area. In the example above, the navigation is set to display 300 pixels wide, so if we add a padding value of 310 pixels on the right of the content area, this should do the trick. Here's an updated version of the file:

```
#nav {
  float: right;
  width: 300px;
  background-color: yellow;
}
```

```
.contentconstrained {
  padding-right: 310px;
}
```

The class attribute value `contentconstrained` should be applied to a `div` that surrounds all the paragraphs that it needs to affect, like so:

```
<div id="nav">
  <ul>
    <li><a href="index.html">This is an area of navigation
        items</a></li>
    <li><a href="index.html">which is floated on the
        right.</a></li>
    <li><a href="turkish.html">Turkish Shaving Stories.</a></li>
    <li><a href="http://www.bubbleunder.com/">Diving
        Stories.</a></li>
  </ul>
</div> <!-- end of nav div -->
<div class="contentconstrained">
<h1>Turkish Shaving Stories</h1>
<p>Next came a massage that I was not expecting. It started with a
    bit of manipulation of the temples, followed by the barber's
    attempt to drag the top half of my face down towards my chin
    (and vice-versa) with his big burly hands. I'm sure it's good
    for you. I wasn't sure it was good for me, though. He then
    made his way down to my shoulders and managed to pull me
    around in such a way that I squealed like a girl. This was not
    relaxing -- this was painful! Evidently I was knotted up. I
    must have needed it, I reasoned.</p>
<p>There was an audible crack as he grabbed my head and twisted it
    to the right, all of it quite unexpected. To the left, no
    cracking sound. And we weren't quite done yet ...</p>
<p>To finish off, the barber got a pair of tongs. He took a ball
    of cotton wool and wrapped it tightly around the tip of the
    tongs, so that it looked like a large cotton bud. He then
    doused the cotton wool in what must have been pure alcohol,
    set it on fire, and began to fling it at my face. Using one
    hand to cover the top of my ear and my hair, he flashed it
    against my ear, singeing the small hairs in and around the
    ear.</p>
</div> <!-- end of contentconstrained div -->
```

Figure 4.38 shows the outcome.

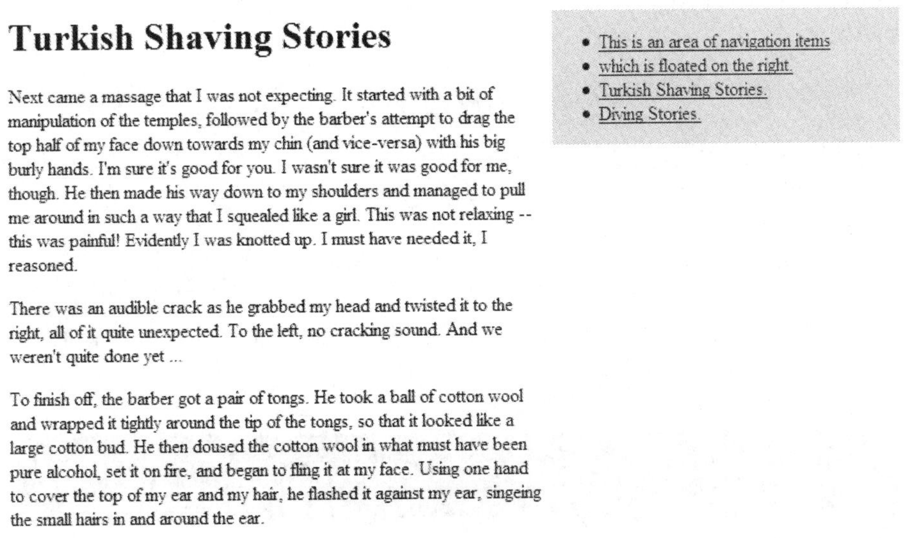

Turkish Shaving Stories

Next came a massage that I was not expecting. It started with a bit of manipulation of the temples, followed by the barber's attempt to drag the top half of my face down towards my chin (and vice-versa) with his big burly hands. I'm sure it's good for you. I wasn't sure it was good for me, though. He then made his way down to my shoulders and managed to pull me around in such a way that I squealed like a girl. This was not relaxing -- this was painful! Evidently I was knotted up. I must have needed it, I reasoned.

There was an audible crack as he grabbed my head and twisted it to the right, all of it quite unexpected. To the left, no cracking sound. And we weren't quite done yet ...

To finish off, the barber got a pair of tongs. He took a ball of cotton wool and wrapped it tightly around the tip of the tongs, so that it looked like a large cotton bud. He then doused the cotton wool in what must have been pure alcohol, set it on fire, and began to fling it at my face. Using one hand to cover the top of my ear and my hair, he flashed it against my ear, singeing the small hairs in and around the ear.

- This is an area of navigation items
- which is floated on the right.
- Turkish Shaving Stories.
- Diving Stories.

Figure 4.38. A tidier use of floats

We won't use floats much on our project site, but we will float the image featuring a circle of divers (remember them from Chapter 2?) on the front page. However, because we don't want to float every image on the site, we can't just apply our CSS to every img element. Instead, we'll refer to this image as our feature image, and name the img element accordingly, using a class selector. We'll also give it some margins, so that it sits nicely next to our welcome message.

Edit your home page (**index.html**), and make the following change to your markup:

```
chapter4/website_files/17_floated_image/index.html (excerpt)
```

```html
<div id="bodycontent">
  <h2>Welcome to our super-dooper Scuba site</h2>
  <p><img src="divers-circle.jpg" class="feature" width="200"
      height="162" alt="A circle of divers practice their
      skills"/></p>
  <p>Glad you could drop in and share some air with us! You've
      passed your underwater navigation skills and successfully
      found your way to the start point - or in this case, our
      home page.</p>
</div> <!-- end of bodycontent div -->
```

Now add the following to our stylesheet to float our image to the right of the body content:

```
chapter4/website_files/17_floated_image/style1.css (excerpt)
.feature {
  float: right;
  margin: 10px;
}
```

Save your changes and refresh your browser to see the result (depicted in Figure 4.39).

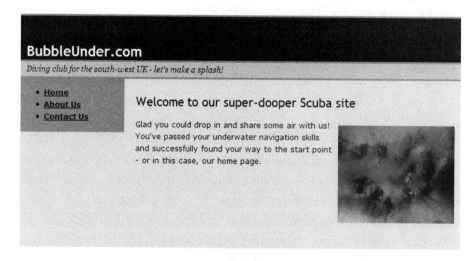

Figure 4.39. A circle of divers learning how to float

This is as far as I'm going to take you with floats. They have a habit of becoming complex and difficult to get right once you have a few floats on the page. If you want to learn more about using floats to create flexible and exciting layouts, I can recommend two other SitePoint books that go into more detail, namely *The CSS Anthology: 101 Essential Tips, Tricks & Hacks*[6] and, in particular, *HTML Utopia: Designing Without Tables Using CSS*.[7]

---

[6] http://www.sitepoint.com/books/cssant2/
[7] http://www.sitepoint.com/books/css2/

Styling Lists

Our standard navigation list can benefit from a little more styling. By default, the bullet points are small black blobs, but you can change these easily to different predefined shapes. Let's head back to our project's stylesheet to see how this works.

1. In **style1.css**, find the `li` element selector.

2. Add the following declaration (new addition shown in bold):

style1.css (excerpt)

```
li {
   font-size: small;
   list-style-type: circle;
}
```

3. Save the CSS file and refresh the view in your browser.

4. Change the value of `list-style-type` to `disc`, `square`, and `none`, saving the CSS file after each change, and checking each page display in the browser. We'll stick with the `none` option on our project site, which should look like Figure 4.40.

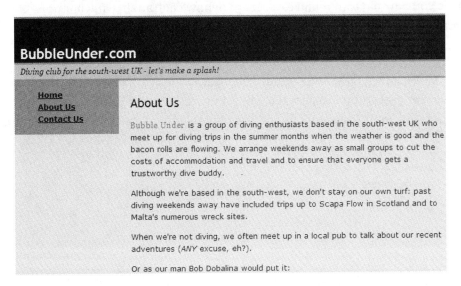

Figure 4.40. Applying different list-bullet styles in CSS—even none

It's possible to use CSS to style lists to a greater extent, including:

- making the links appear as buttons by utilizing the CSS `border` and `padding` properties
- creating a larger clickable area for the link (rather than just the text itself)
- setting list items out in a horizontal line

These more advanced techniques are discussed and explained thoroughly in *The CSS Anthology: 101 Essential Tips, Tricks & Hacks*[8] by Rachel Andrew. The book devotes almost a whole chapter to styling navigation, and presents many styles that you can try out. I strongly advise you to grab a copy if you want to learn some really cool CSS tricks (once the basics are under your belt, of course!).

Summary

This has been another very productive chapter. We began by learning about the difference between inline and block-level elements. Next, we looked at the various ways in which we can style block-level elements, such as adding a `border`, `padding`, and sizing. The theory was then put into practice as we applied some of these styles to the project website. Finally, we learned how the entire structure of the web pages could be rejigged—site-wide—using CSS positioning, and we touched on the styling of list elements.

I hope you now have firsthand experience of how centralizing all your presentation rules—colors, fonts, or layout schemes—can be such a bonus. In a later chapter, I'll show how you can make use of this technique quickly and easily.

In the next chapter, I'm going to guide you through the use of images on your website. We'll cover background images that are set using CSS, and inline images that you can drop into your web pages as content (like the divers image from Chapter 2).

---

[8] http://www.sitepoint.com/books/cssant2/

Chapter 5

Picture This! Using Images on Your Website

Back in Chapter 2, we made a simple concession so that the website wouldn't look so bland: we added the image of divers (using the img[1] element). This really needed to be done. First and foremost, the Web is a visual medium, and while great writing may keep a particular audience captivated, the saying "a picture tells a thousand words" is as true as it ever was. Unfortunately, we glossed over a discussion of all the different actions you can perform using images in our haste to have that first visual element on the page.

In this chapter, we're going to pick up where we left our discussion on images. We'll see how you can use them to enhance a site's content, and apply them as decorative backgrounds. I'll also explain some simple techniques for managing and adjusting images, using some of the software that I suggested you download in the section called "Not Just Text, Text, Text" in Chapter 1.

Let's begin by taking a look at **inline images**.

---

[1] http://reference.sitepoint.com/html/img/

Inline Images

Let's take a brief moment to remind ourselves what the HTML for an inline image looks like:

```
<img src="divers-circle.jpg" width="200" height="162"
    alt="A circle of divers practice their skills"/>
```

You've probably seen this line several times since Chapter 2, yet paid it scant attention. A refresher of its constituent parts is in order.

Anatomy of the Image Element

- The element name is `img`. Note that this is an empty element, without a separate closing tag.[2] The final forward slash is there to satisfy XHTML syntax, and indicates that the element is "self-closing." With an HTML5 doctype (which we're using), you could omit this trailing slash and it would have no effect on the display of the image in any way, nor would it make your markup invalid.

- The `src` attribute defines the source of the image: the location and filename that the browser needs to display the image. In our example, the filename is `divers-circle.jpg`.

- The `alt` attribute is an important attribute that I'll explain in detail below.

- The `height` and `width` attributes tell the browser the dimensions at which the image should be displayed. This is particularly useful if the user's web connection speed is a little slow; the browser can then reserve the appropriate space for the image before it has downloaded. If you've ever browsed a slow-loading page and had to wait while the page realigns itself as new images load in, you'll understand how annoying it can be when heights and widths are omitted.

Both the `height` and `width` attributes are extremely handy, yet, unlike the `src` and `alt` attributes, they're not essential to the image element. However, because of their usefulness, most people choose to leave them in.

---

[2] If you look at the source of other websites, you may spot `img` tags without a trailing forward slash. In earlier versions of HTML (such as version 4.01), it was unnecessary to close the tag in this way.

The `alt` Attribute: Making Images Useful to Everyone

In our diving site example, the `img` element has an `alt` attribute with the value A circle of divers practice their skills. What's this for? Well, the `alt` attribute provides an *alt*ernative text version of the image that most people see on the screen. I say most, because some people are unable to see this image. Here are a few scenarios to consider:

- The person browsing your site is blind (see the section called "Screen Readers: Hearing the Web").
- The user is accessing your website on a slow connection and has temporarily disabled images to speed the process up.
- The user is on a *very* slow connection—so slow, in fact, that images simply take too long to load.

In all these examples, the `alt` attribute provides an alternative for these users to receive the information they need. Figure 5.1 shows what the users in the second and third scenarios will see.

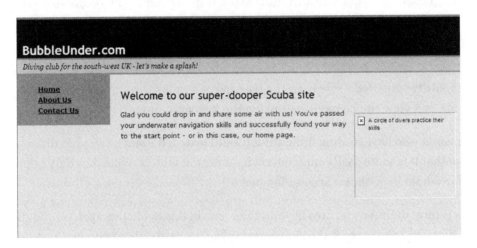

Figure 5.1. When a slow connection delays the image download

If users browse the site over a very slow connection and are presented with the screen shown in Figure 5.1, they could read the text alternative and, based on that description, decide whether to wait until the image downloaded completely, or click on a link to go elsewhere. The `alt` attribute delivers a similar benefit to users who browse the site with images disabled. If the description seems interesting, the user might choose to switch on images (in IE go to the **Tools** menu, select **Internet**

Options, go to the **Advanced** tab, and under **Multimedia** tick the box labeled **Show Pictures**). For a blind user, though, this so-called alternative is actually an *essential* feature of the image upon which they rely.

Web Accessibility

The practice of making sure that images have appropriate `alt` attributes comes under the general banner of **web accessibility**. This is an area of web design and programming that some people choose to specialize in (as it can be quite tricky at times), but you'll gain a great introduction to it simply by following the advice in this book. A truly accessible website is one that can be accessed and used by everyone— including those who have disabilities.

Here are some example scenarios, and the issues they may present:

- people who have poor eyesight (Are your font sizes too small? Can they be scaled up?)

- blind users (Do your `alt` attributes explain the visual elements on your page?)

- deaf users (If you use any sounds on the site—for example, an audio interview —do you have an alternative text version?)

- mobility-impaired users (Can the user move a mouse around easily, if at all? If not, can your site be navigated using the keyboard alone?)

- people who have reading difficulties (Could text on the site be worded differently, so that it is more easily understood by a person who is dyslexic, or by people for whom English is a second language?)

This is most definitely an area beyond the scope of this book. I've avoided providing any detailed solutions for the above examples; it's really about encouraging you to think about the issues. However, it's generally agreed that if you're making the effort to ensure your `alt` attributes are right, you're already helping to make your site more accessible.

If you'd like to learn more about web accessibility, a great free—and reliable— resource can be found at Dive Into Accessibility.[3]

---

[3] http://diveintoaccessibility.org/

Screen Readers: Hearing the Web

Once upon a time, blind users had to rely on Braille alternatives to printed content, or ask a friend to read content aloud to them. By using electronic media such as web pages, blind users now have a genuine alternative: the **screen reader**. A screen reader is a type of software that provides a sound-based replication of a web page—it reads aloud the text that appears on screen. Some screen readers are used only to access websites, while others provide audible feedback for the entire operating system and many other applications, including office productivity and email programs.

For the sake of these users, it's especially important that you take care with your `alt` attributes; the screen reader will read these aloud when it comes across images on your web pages. As Figure 5.2 shows, an image without a description, or one that fails to provide any insight (with just the word "IMAGE") is quite unhelpful.

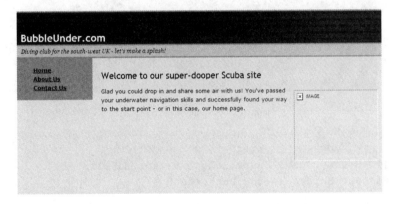

Figure 5.2. An `alt` attribute that leaves everyone in the dark

If you'd like to learn more about the way screen readers work and, in particular, how they handle images on your web pages, you could try the WebAIM screen reader simulation.[4] If you want to try a screen reader on your own website, download a trial version of JAWS (for Windows).[5]

What Makes a Good `alt`?

I could write a lot about the topic of `alt` attributes, as it's quite a subjective field. What one person believes is an appropriate description of an image may not be seen

---

[4] http://www.webaim.org/simulations/screenreader/
[5] http://www.freedomscientific.com/products/fs/jaws-product-page.asp

that way by others. Fortunately, there are a few simple rules that you can use as guidelines:

- If the image conveys useful information, describe the image as briefly but accurately as possible. For example, check out Figure 5.3 and the code that follows:

Figure 5.3. Describing the image you see

```
<img src="sydney.jpg" width="500" height="354"
    alt="Sydney Opera House, night-time shot with the
    Harbour Bridge in the background"/>
```

- If the image is purely decorative, and provides no practical information, use an empty `alt` attribute (`alt=""`). This informs screen readers that the image is irrelevant, and that there's no need to read it out. Note that this is *not* the same as omitting the `alt` attribute—that's a real no-no!

- If the image is being used as a link, do not describe the image as it appears; instead, describe the *function* of the image. So, if you're using an image of the Sydney Harbour Bridge as a call to action, the `alt` attribute should reflect just that. See the `alt` text below Figure 5.4 that's used to describe its function:

Figure 5.4. Using an image as a link

```
<a href="win-holiday.html"><img src="win-a-trip.jpg"
    width="500" height="354" alt="Win a trip to
    Sydney!"/></a>
```

There are many other aspects to web accessibility, and you might like to learn more about these in due course. For our purposes, though, taking care of the alt attributes used with images will be of great benefit.

JPEG versus GIF versus PNG

You may have wondered why some images have a **.gif** file extension while others use **.jpg** or **.png**. I'm now going to explain the difference, because it's extremely important.

JPEG, GIF, and PNG are the most commonly used image formats on the Web. Each has its advantages, but here's a summary of how they can be best used:

- **JPEG** images, or JPEGs, are great for photographic images. JPEG images achieve small file sizes by using "lossy compression," which means that there is a loss of detail from the original image during the compression process. In photographs, the effect of lossy compression is minimal, but in images comprising clear, crisp lines (such as illustrations or logos), this compression can make the image appear blurred.

■ **GIF** images, on the other hand, are great for illustrations and logos, as well as images that have large areas of a single color. They're poor for photographs, though, because GIFs can only show 256 colors. This might sound like a lot, but a colorful photograph can contain millions of different colors. GIFs also offer transparency, the ability to make part of the image see-through (we'll cover transparency very soon).

■ The **PNG** format combines the best aspects of both these image formats (millions of colors, transparency), even adding more. There is one (admittedly decreasing) problem: IE6 lacks full support for the PNG format. Given that IE9 is the current version, this is a smaller issue than it once was, but there are still people out there using IE6 who will receive a slightly degraded view of some PNG images.

Transparency

When you save an image, it will most likely be rectangular and fill the entire space. But imagine that you have an image that's an irregular shape—for instance, an oval-shaped company logo. The straight edges of image files don't really lend themselves to placing that image on a background. The GIF format, however, allows you to specify the transparent portions of an image. Of the 256 colors that make up a GIF, only one can be set to transparent, as illustrated in Figure 5.5.

A JPG does not support transparency

A GIF with a transparent background

Figure 5.5. The differences between JPEG and GIF support for transparency

While the GIF offers some transparency, it's a little flawed; the image may have a "matte" effect around the transparent area. Because only one of those 256 colors can be set as transparent, when a GIF image sits on a background with different colors, it will only match up well in certain places. If you check the top image (it's in the code archive in **chapter 5 > examples > 04_transparency**), you'll see the effect around the bottom half of the image where the matte color blue clashes with the yellowish background. If only there were a better image type you could use, hmm?

PNG: King of Transparency

Undoubtedly, the best image format for using transparent images is PNG, because it's capable of handling **alpha channel** transparency. This means that PNG can handle different levels of transparency—it doesn't just turn transparency on or off the way a GIF does.

A good example is demonstrated on a website I recently worked on, along with the designer Jon Hicks. In the header of the page is an old VW split-screen ambulance with a nice transparent effect, including a soft shadow underneath it. All current browsers handle this PNG image perfectly well, but cranky old IE6 fails to get the transparency right at all, instead leaving a large pale blue mask. Yet, at the time the site was built, we checked the statistics of another well-visited VW site, and discovered that IE6 usage was down to under 1%; hence, it was acceptable to provide a better experience for 99% of IE users while leaving the remaining 1% with a functional site.

Figure 5.6. IE6 with poor PNG transparency (right) while Firefox 3.6 renders correctly (left)

Adding an Image Gallery to the Site

One of the great joys of diving is being amongst all the beautiful creatures that live in the sea. You can try to explain the wonder of all this to a non-diver but, usually, they're unable to comprehend it. Our website provides a great opportunity to show people how beautiful these underwater sights can be.

It's time to grow the project site a little by adding a new page: a simple image gallery. Before we start looking at the images themselves, we need to tweak the existing website files slightly to accommodate the new page.

Updating the Navigation

1. Open **index.html** in your text editor.

2. Find the navigation section and add another link to your list of links, like so:

chapter5/website_files/01_link_in_nav/index.html *(excerpt)*

```
<div id="navigation">
  <ul>
    <li><a href="index.html">Home</a></li>
```

```
    <li><a href="about.html">About Us</a></li>
    <li><a href="contact.html">Contact Us</a></li>
    <li><a href="gallery.html">Image Gallery</a></li>
  </ul>
</div> <!-- end of navigation div -->
```

3. Save the file, and then look at it in the browser to make sure the link appears appropriately.

4. Repeat the steps above for **about.html** and **contact.html**.

The navigation in all your pages should look like that shown in Figure 5.7.

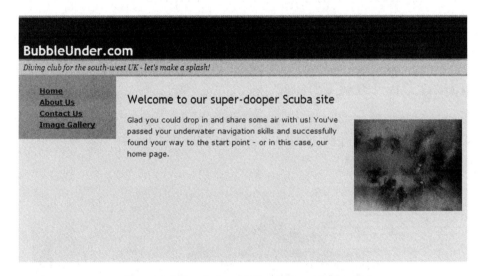

Figure 5.7. Adding the Image Gallery to the navigation list

There's just one small problem: the gallery page is yet to exist! Let's rectify that now.

Adding the New Gallery Page

1. Create a copy of **contact.html** and rename it **gallery.html**, just as we did back in Chapter 2.

2. Open the newly created gallery page in your text editor, and change the level 2 heading (h2) content to "Image Gallery."

3. Remove the single paragraph that appears below that heading, and replace it using the following:

```
chapter5/website_files/01_link_in_nav/gallery.html (excerpt)

<p>Below are some of the great views that club members have
    captured on film (or digital memory) on various dive
    trips.</p>
<p>Please do drop me a line (that's Bob) if you would like to
    <a href="mailto:bob@bubbleunder.com">submit an image</a> to
    this gallery.</p>
```

4. Change the `title` content to: Image Gallery—Underwater Photography from Bubble Under's members.

5. Finally, save the amendments and check the page in your browser.

Adding the First Image

Now, we're ready to add the first picture to our gallery, a picture of a turtle. But this is one tough turtle; it appears that a local shark has taken quite a chomp out of his side, as Figure 5.8 reveals.

Figure 5.8. Ouch! That must have hurt!

I made a point of commenting on that image—after all, it's quite a sight, isn't it? Clearly the image deserves a descriptive `alt` attribute, better than `A picture of a turtle`, which falls well short of the full story. Here's the markup we'll use instead for this image:

```
<p><img src="gallery/turtle-bite.jpg" width="400" height="258"
    alt="A turtle swims comfortably among the coral, despite its
    old injury - a large shark bite on one side"/></p>
```

 Get the Picture

You'll find this image—and all the others that we'll use in this chapter—in the code archive.

Note that the value of this `src` attribute is a little different from the others we've seen so far. That forward slash tells the browser that the image is inside a folder. In this case, `gallery/turtle-bite.jpg` informs the browser that the image file (**turtle-bite.jpg**) is inside a folder named **gallery**. So, before you add this image to the gallery, create the **gallery** folder inside your website's folder. (We learned how to create a folder back in Chapter 1. In Windows, select **File > New > Folder**; on a Mac, select **File > New Folder**.) Then place the image inside it.

When you've saved the image inside the folder, add the previous markup to **gallery.html**, like so:

chapter5/website_files/01_link_in_nav/gallery.html (excerpt)

```
<div id="bodycontent">
  <h2>Image Gallery</h2>
  <p>Below are some of the great views that club members have
      captured on film (or digital memory) on various dive
      trips.</p>
  <p>Please do drop me (that's Bob) a line if you would like to
      <a href="mailto:bob@bubbleunder.com">submit an image</a> to
      this gallery.</p>
  <p><img src="gallery/turtle-bite.jpg" width="400" height="258"
      alt="A turtle swims comfortably among the coral, despite its
      old injury - a large shark bite on one side"/></p>
</div> <!-- end of bodycontent div -->
```

Save the page and ensure it appears as expected in your browser—like Figure 5.9.

The size of the photo is sensible: at a width of 400 pixels, it fits quite well on the page without any further adjustment. Soon, I'll show you how to resize larger photos, as most photos you take on a digital camera will be far too large for the gallery page.

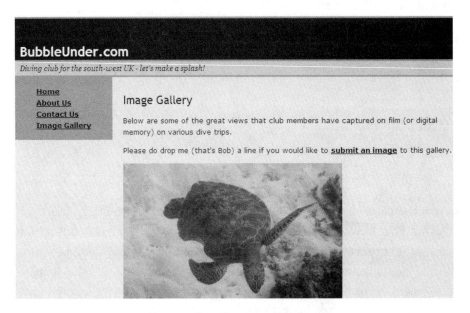

Figure 5.9. The gallery page taking shape

Formatting the Picture Using CSS

When building image galleries, a common mistake that many people make is to use a graphics program to create borders around their images. As we saw in Chapter 3, we can use CSS for border effects; let's use this technique now. How about a reasonably thick, white border, reminiscent of Polaroid snaps?

1. Open **style1.css** and add a new rule for the img element, like so:

chapter5/website_files/03_polaroid_effect/style1.css *(excerpt)*

```
img {
    border: 15px solid white;
}
```

2. Save the CSS file, and go back to your web page (**gallery.html**) and refresh it. You should be looking at a view like the one shown in Figure 5.10.

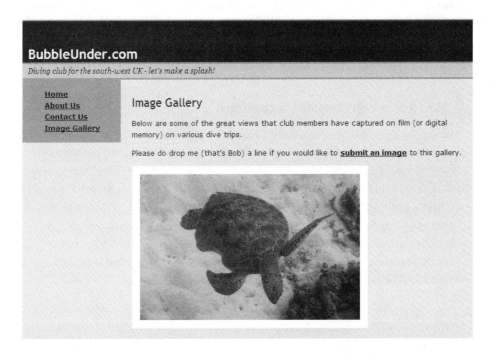

Figure 5.10. The white border gives the photo a Polaroid-like effect

Of course, you're free to try out any effect you like. Perhaps you'll experiment using some of the effects we discussed in Chapter 4. For the purpose of this project site, I'm going to maintain the white borders. I know it's a little conservative, but you *can* overdo it if you're not careful.

Beware of the Knock-on Effects

If you go to the home page now, the divers image will also have a thick, white border around it. Well, we did ask for *all* images to have a white border—the browser's just following orders! If you'd rather keep the white borders to just the images on the gallery page, you'll have to be more specific with your selector, so that the rule will only take effect on that page. Don't worry about it right now—but don't forget it, because we'll deal with the issue in the section called "Basic Image Editing".

Captioning the Picture

Pick up any newspaper, flick through the pages, and you'll notice that photos are accompanied by captions. It's standard practice, so I'm going to show you how we can implement image captions here. First, let's think about what information might appear beneath this photo. You'll probably want a description of the photo, perhaps including a location, and almost certainly crediting the photographer. All these items could be styled the same way, but I'm going to use two new styles.

 When is a `caption` not a caption?

Strangely, a *picture* caption element hasn't always existed in HTML. This may seem like an oversight, but there *is* a `caption` element. However, rather than captioning photos, that element is instead used for captioning tables, which we'll be looking at in Chapter 6. Two new elements were introduced in HTML5, namely `figure` and `figcaption`. These would be perfect for the job, if it weren't for pesky old Internet Explorer. We need to provide some additional guidance, so we'll revisit this in Chapter 10 with our HTML5 makeover. For now, we'll use techniques that work in all browsers, and please trust me, these use perfectly acceptable and valid HTML.

1. In **gallery.html**, remove the opening and closing paragraph tags that surround the picture of the turtle, and replace them using `<div class="galleryphoto">` and `</div>` tags instead:

chapter5/website_files/04_unstyled_caption/gallery.html *(excerpt)*

```
<div class="galleryphoto">
  <img src="gallery/turtle-bite.jpg" width="400"
      height="258" alt="A turtle swims comfortably among the
      coral, despite its old injury - a large shark bite on
      one side"/>
</div>
```

2. Next, add a paragraph after the image (but inside the containing div), like so:

chapter5/website_files/04_unstyled_caption/gallery.html *(excerpt)*

```
<div class="galleryphoto">
  <img src="gallery/turtle-bite.jpg" width="400"
      height="258" alt="A turtle swims comfortably among the
      coral, despite its old injury - a large shark bite on
      one side"/>
  <p>This turtle was spotted swimming around the Great Barrier
      Reef (Queensland, Australia) quite gracefully, despite
      having had a large chunk taken out of its right side,
      presumably in a shark attack. [Photographer: Ian
      Lloyd]</p>
</div>
```

3. Finally, let's add a span element around the photo credit part of the caption, so that we can style it differently:

chapter5/website_files/04_unstyled_caption/gallery.html *(excerpt)*

```
<p>This turtle was spotted swimming around the Great Barrier
    Reef (Queensland, Australia) quite gracefully, despite
    having had a large chunk taken out of its right side,
    presumably in a shark attack. <span
    class="photocredit">[Photographer: Ian Lloyd]</span></p>
```

4. Save **gallery.html** and take a look at the page in your browser. It should resemble Figure 5.11. You won't see any real stylistic changes, but it's important to look at the page first, so that you can understand why I suggest the changes I'm about to recommend.

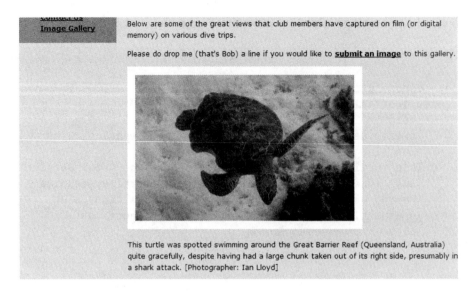

Figure 5.11. The picture now has a caption, yet to be styled

It's common for a picture caption to be displayed in a different font to that of the document's main body text; this can apply to the font's weight and size, too. That's the first aspect we'll change. Secondly, the gap between the text and the photo is a little too big, so I will show you how we can fix that using the `margin` property. Finally, I'm going to add a stylistic touch beneath the caption that will help us once we add more photos to the gallery.

1. Open **style1.css** and add the following CSS:

```
                              chapter5/website_files/05_styled_caption/style1.css (excerpt)

.galleryphoto p {
  font-size: 65%;
  font-weight: bold;
  margin-top: 0;
  width: 430px;
  line-height: 1.4em;
}
```

This markup makes the necessary changes to the font, reduces the width of the caption to make it easier to read, removes the spacing immediately above the paragraph that describes the photo, and decreases the space between the lines so that it's more suitable.

2. Next, add a new rule for the `photocredit` class:

> *chapter5/website_files/05_styled_caption/style1.css (excerpt)*
>
> ```css
> .photocredit {
>   font-weight: normal;
>   color: gray;
> }
> ```

This will affect the text contained in the `span` element only.

 An Alternative Approach

> Incidentally, you could use some selector wizardry to achieve the same effect without having to use the `photocredit` class at all. It would look like this:
>
> ```css
> .galleryphoto p span {
>   font-weight: normal;
>   color: gray;
> }
> ```
>
> This contextual selector translates as "for every `span` inside a `p` that's inside an element using a class of `galleryphoto`, make it normal font and gray". If you opted for this approach, you could remove the `class` attribute from the `span` element. I've suggested using a class selector in this instance for future-proofing purposes, as you might want to use a photo credit elsewhere in the site, outside the context of the photo gallery.

3. Save the CSS file, refresh the web page once more, and review your work. It should look like the page shown in Figure 5.12.

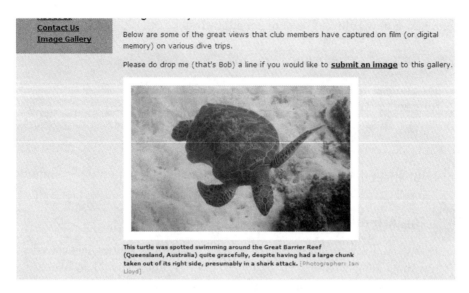

Figure 5.12. The caption—now using style rules

Now, remember previously how our nice white gallery photo borders were being applied to all the images on the website? We now have a very simple way to deal with this issue. The `<img>` tag for the gallery photo now resides within a `div` element, with the `class galleryphoto`. Therefore, we can use that class name in the selector of the rule that applies the border, like so:

chapter5/website_files/05_styled_caption/style1.css *(excerpt)*

```
.galleryphoto img {
  border: 15px solid white;
}
```

If you make the above change to the site stylesheet, only the gallery photos will have the white border. Problem solved! Isn't CSS great?

Lastly, we're going to add some style declarations to the `.galleryphoto` rule, in order to apply some layout adjustments to the `div` that contains the image and associated text. This class will be used to help separate the many different photos that will eventually display on this page.

1. Add the following to **style1.css**:

chapter5/website_files/07_custom_divider/style1.css *(excerpt)*

```css
.galleryphoto {
  padding-bottom: 20px;
  border-bottom: 1px solid navy;
  margin-bottom: 10px;
}
```

2. Save the CSS file, and refresh the view in your browser once more. It should look similar to Figure 5.13.

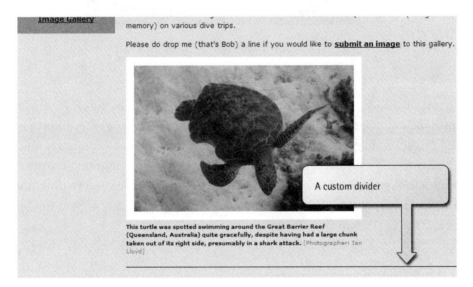

Figure 5.13. A custom divider provides a clean separation between our photos

Basic Image Editing

Image Cropping

When preparing images for display on web pages, it's easy to make the mistake of *resizing* the image to fit the available space without *cropping* it in some way first. It's all too easy to end up using small images that try to pack in far too much detail—detail that, ultimately, is lost. It's much better to crop first, then resize (the latter we'll cover shortly). In the image shown in Figure 5.14, the blue water around the fish is unnecessary. We can make the image smaller—but keep the fish the same size—by cropping it.

Figure 5.14. Uncropped fish image

Picasa

In Chapter 1, I suggested that Windows users may want to download Picasa[6] for the purposes of managing photos (be they your own happy snaps, or photos used on the project site). Among other features, Picasa offers a range of special effects that you can apply at the touch of a button. Imagine that another two images have been added to our **gallery** folder—trebling the gallery size! Once you've downloaded Picasa, any image that is added to this folder will automatically appear in Picasa's library, just like the two shown in Figure 5.15.

---

[6] http://picasa.google.com/

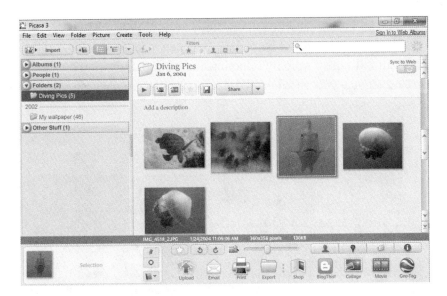

Figure 5.15. Picasa—booming with gallery images

If you double-click on one of the images, a range of new tools will appear on the left-hand side, as illustrated in Figure 5.16.

Figure 5.16. The range of basic photo fixes offered by Picasa

Perhaps the most important tool you will use here is **Crop**: you can remove any extraneous clutter, and focus on the most important part of the image.

Just press the **Crop** button, and drag a rectangle around the area to which you want to crop the image, as shown in Figure 5.17. You can also choose to crop the image to a predetermined aspect ratio by selecting any of the dimension buttons: **10×15**, **13×18**, or **20×25**. Once you've selected the size, click the **Apply** button to crop the picture.

Figure 5.17. A fishy pic receives a good solid cropping!

Preview

We mentioned a handy little program for Mac users back in Chapter 1 called Preview. This is the program that automatically opens on the Mac when opening PDF documents, but it also has a surprisingly decent set of image-editing tools built in. My preferred way of working with Preview for simple image edits is to always have Preview in the dock. I then simply select the images in **Finder** that I want to edit and drag that whole selection onto the Preview icon. They'll open in Preview—small thumbnail images to the right and the selected image in the left pane. To crop, I click and drag a box over the area I want and press **Command + K** (or choose **Tools > Crop**). Preview then does the crop but—and this is important—it has not yet saved this change. You may either commit that change to the image straight away by choosing **File > Save** or, if you have a lot of images to crop, you can do the following:

1. Go through each image, applying the cropping as you choose.

2. Once all crops are done, choose **File** > **Save All**. If you accidentally quit Preview, you will be relieved to know you haven't lost your changes; Preview helpfully reminds you that you've made numerous modifications, and asks if you'd like to save or discard them. This has saved my skin many times, I can tell you!

To crop an image, open it and choose the **Selection** tool from the toolbox to the right of your image. Click and drag your mouse to mark where you wish to crop; then choose the **Edit** > **Trim Selection** option from the menu bar, as shown in Figure 5.18. *Voila!*

Figure 5.18. Cropping images using Preview

Special Effects

Programs like Photoshop offer a wide range of special effects, and whole books are devoted to explaining the various techniques you can use. Needless to say, there's no room in this tome for such discussions, but the photo editing programs we've looked at do have some nifty tools you should explore.

Picasa

Figure 5.19 shows a screenshot featuring our recently cropped picture of a fish on the right-hand side; under the **Effects** tab to its left are a number of available effects, such as black and white, sepia tone, and soft focus.

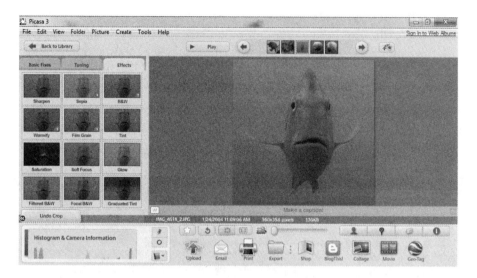

Figure 5.19. Selecting special effects in Picasa

I'm going to leave this image just as it is—but now that you know where to find the effects, why not go and experiment for yourself?

Preview

Preview has never sold itself as a graphics program. Even if you don't have iPhoto at your disposal, Preview should be lurking in the **Applications** folder waiting to be used. Although it's not a full graphics or photo-editing program, there are a number of useful features that you should investigate:

- Preview is quite the workhorse when it comes to converting image types. I often open images in Preview then choose **Save As**; for example, open a BMP and save as PDF. If you have an image in a format that is not web-friendly, Preview may be just the tool to convert it to a GIF, JPG, or PNG.

- As well as cropping, Preview will let you rotate images, flip them (mirror) vertically or horizontally, and adjust colors too (with the latter being quite powerful).

■ You can annotate images with Preview. Although the tools are rather crude, they'll let you place text over images in a range of fonts and colors, as well as other basic shapes. Nothing too spectacular, but with a bit of care you can achieve some good results, and save them in an image format of your choice.

Resizing Large Images

It's highly unlikely that everyone will submit the right-sized images for our gallery. Let's take an image from this book's code archive (I know it's not really code, but let's not split hairs!) and resize it. The image you want is **jellyfish.jpg**. It's a giant image—1,359 pixels in width—so it needs some serious knocking down in size! Here's how you can do the job using a couple of different programs.

Picasa

If you already have images somewhere on your hard drive, they'll automatically appear in the Picasa library. An easy way to use Picasa to create a web-page-friendly image from a larger photo is as follows:

1. In the Picasa gallery, find the image you want to use and click on it.

2. Select **File > Export Picture to Folder** from the menu.

3. You'll be presented with the dialog pictured in Figure 5.20, which allows you to choose from a series of preset widths. You can only choose widths of 320, 480, 640, 800, and 1,024 pixels using the slider control—but these are all sensible sizes for web pages. Instead of using the slider, enter a value of 400 in the pixels text field. You can also select the amount of JPEG compression you want to use from the **Image Quality** control (the lower the number, the smaller the file size … and the worse the photograph will look).

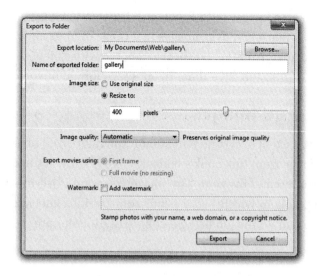

Figure 5.20. Exporting a large image for the Web using Picasa

4. Click the **Browse...** button and select your **Web** folder inside **Documents**. (Don't select the **gallery** folder; if you do, Picasa will create another folder named **gallery** inside your **gallery** folder!)

5. Enter the name of the folder to which you'd like the resized image saved in **Name of exported folder:**. In this case, enter `gallery`.

6. Click **OK** and the resized picture will be saved.

Preview

1. From the menu, select **Tools > Adjust Size**.

2. A new dialog appears, and may have the sizes set to cms or similar. As we're working with images for the Web—and therefore for viewing onscreen—we'll need to select pixels as the unit of measurement.

3. Enter a width of **400** (the height will adjust accordingly). Click **OK**.

4. Save the file by selecting **File > Save**.

Other Software

The instructions above cover Picasa (Windows) and Preview (Mac) only, but most graphics applications will perform similar functions. If you're unable to find the equivalent process in your image editor, try the built-in help files, or search the Web for tutorials (for example, resizing images in Photoshop).

 Tutorial Search

A quick search on Google found these tutorials:

■ Photoshop Tutorial: How to Resize an Image, a YouTube video
(http://www.youtube.com/watch?v=qu5adJfxuhw)

■ How to Resize an Image in PaintShop Pro Photo
(http://www.ehow.com/how_2322677_resize-image-paint-shop-pro.html)

■ Apple's excellent iPhoto Tutorial
(http://www.apple.com/support/iphoto/tutorial/)

Filling up the Gallery

With the wave of a magic wand—not to mention the techniques we've been using (HTML, CSS, and image editing)—we can easily finish off our gallery. You can see the results below in Figure 5.21. Of course, if you prefer you can retrieve this from the code archive:

chapter5/website_files/08_complete_gallery/gallery.html *(excerpt)*

```html
<div class="galleryphoto">
  <img src="gallery/turtle-bite.jpg" width="400" height="258"
      alt="A turtle swims comfortably among the coral, despite
      its old injury - a large shark bite on one side"/>
  <p>This turtle was spotted swimming around the Great Barrier
      Reef (Queensland, Australia) quite gracefully, despite
      having had a large chunk taken out of its right side,
      presumably in a shark attack. <span
      class="photocredit">[Photographer: Ian Lloyd]</span></p>
</div>
<div class="galleryphoto">
  <img src="gallery/jellyfish.jpg" width="400" height="300"
      alt="A jellyfish flanked by smaller fish"/>
  <p>Jill was just snorkelling when she took this picture - the
      jellyfish was only a couple of feet under the surface,
      hence the light is excellent. Jill assures us that the
      jellyfish had no "nasty, stingy, dangly bits"!
      <span class="photocredit">[Photographer: Jill
      Smith]</span></p>
</div>
<div class="galleryphoto">
  <img src="gallery/turtle-face.jpg" width="400" height="300"
      alt="A close-up, straight-on shot of a turtle feeding on the
      coral"/>
  <p>"I was right next to him as he bit chunks of coral off for
      dinner - what a sound!" So describes club member Paul who
      took this shot in Fiji. <span
      class="photocredit">[Photographer: Paul Spencer]</span></p>
</div>
<div class="galleryphoto">
  <img src="gallery/what-a-star.jpg" width="400" height="318"
      alt="Black and white patterned starfish"/>
  <p>You're a star - and don't let anyone tell you any different!
      <span class="photocredit">[Photographer: Helen
      Cranfield]</span></p>
</div>
<div class="galleryphoto">
  <img src="gallery/reef2.jpg" width="400" height="285"
      alt="Another beautiful example of the Great Barrier Reef"/>
  <p>Another cracking shot of the reef from Mark.
      <span class="photocredit">[Photographer: Mark
      Willams]</span></p>
</div>
```

Figure 5.21. The complete gallery

Moving Beyond a Simple Gallery

This is a simple example of an image gallery. As you add more images, the page will take longer and longer to download. For this reason, most people opt for a two-step design: a page containing full-sized versions of the images, and a page comprising **thumbnails**, small, thumbnail-sized copies of the image (well, approximately) that link to the bigger versions. However, if you think that your site's image gallery has the potential to grow beyond all manageability, you might want to look into an automated system of some kind; many are available, and plenty just happen to be free!

Search for "free thumbnail gallery generator," or similar, to attract lots of results.[78]. Mac users, if you have iPhoto, can make use of the **Export** facility (**Share** in later versions) to create a thumbnail gallery.

---

[7] http://freewarehome.com/Graphics/Graphic_Manipulation/

[8] A good collection is listed at http://freewarehome.com/Graphics/Graphic_Manipulation/.

For a simple walk-through of the steps to create a thumbnail-based gallery, take a look at http://www.youtube.com/watch?v=RqZTXj0Mudw, a short video by Luis Estrada on YouTube.[9]

Sourcing Images for Your Website

The creation of an online gallery is all well and good if you have a large collection of suitable photos at your disposal, but what if you need an image that isn't in your collection? There are numerous websites that allow you to download and use images **royalty-free**, such as iStockphoto[10] and Fotosearch.[11] Royalty-free means that the image, once purchased, is free of royalty charges—ongoing payments to the owner based on sales or downloads made; these are usually a percentage of the sales price. It does not mean that the image itself is free to use. But once you've paid the one-off fee, you probably won't be all that worried about spending a dollar or two if it's a great image.

Another potential source of images is Flickr,[12] where you can search images based on what keywords have been assigned, better known as *tags*. For example, you could search for all photos tagged with the word "scuba"[13] and look for a suitable image in the search results.

 Using Images from Flickr

Flickr is a photo-sharing service, not a professional photo stock library, and every Flickr photographer has a different policy on how the photos can be used. The licensing details are clearly listed on each photo's page. Even if the photo is marked "All Rights Reserved," you could try dropping the photographer a line—many people will quite happily let you use one of their photos if it's not for personal financial gain (indeed, many people will be quite flattered to have been asked).

---

[10] http://www.istockphoto.com/
[11] http://www.fotosearch.com/
[12] http://www.flickr.com/
[13] http://www.flickr.com/photos/tags/scuba/

Background Images in CSS

So far, we've used purely inline images. Inline images constitute an integral part of page content, but there's another way that you might use images in a website: as decorative backgrounds.

In the last chapter, we learned how to specify background colors for any block element. We can assign background images in a similar way. In practice, we can do both: provide a background image for browsers using a fast web connection, and an alternative background color for those using a slower one. In fact, this background color can be displayed for the first group of users while the background image is loading. Let's take a look at a simple example.

Repeated Patterns

In your CSS file, you can add a `background-image` property and value:

```css
#repeatedclouds {
  border: 1px solid black;
  padding: 20px;
  background-color: #aebbdb;
  background-image: url(clouds.jpg);
}
```

Here's the HTML that refers to this CSS:

```html
<div id="repeatedclouds">
  <p>Content of some kind goes here.</p>
  <p>Some more content goes here.</p>
</div>
```

Using the CSS code above, the browser will simply repeat the selected background image, filling the available space; I've added a `border` and `padding`, in order to make it easier to see the shape of the box and the white-page background peeking through around the edges. Figure 5.22 shows how the effect displays on the screen. (Remember that you can obtain this example from the code archive).

Figure 5.22. A background image of a cloud pattern, repeated to fill the space

Notice that this rule also includes a background color. Whenever you choose a background image, you should also choose a suitable color alternative, in case images fail to download with your page. If the browser finds the image you've referred to, it will use it; if not, it will display the specified background color—like the page shown in Figure 5.23. This is an important point. Imagine that, in one section of your page, you had a dark background image with white text displayed on it. If the user disables images, or the background image doesn't download for some reason, you'll need a dark background color in place. Otherwise, the user may get white text on a white background, rendering that section of the page unreadable.

Figure 5.23. Displaying a plain-colored background in place of an image

Horizontal Repeats

It is possible to set a background so that it repeats only in one direction—for example, from left to right. You may remember the process of plotting graphs along the x-axis (the horizontal axis) or the y-axis (the vertical axis) in math class from your school days. We use the same x and y notations to specify direction in CSS. For example, the following code repeats an image along the horizontal axis:

```
#verticalfade {
  border: 1px solid black;
  padding: 20px;
  padding-top: 300px;
  background-color: #e3e3e3;
  background-image: url(vert-fade.gif);
  background-repeat: repeat-x;
}
```

The effect is depicted in Figure 5.24.

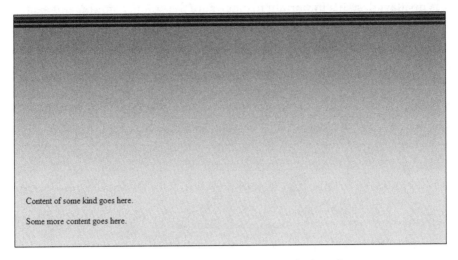

Figure 5.24. Repeating a background image horizontally

Ironically, an image that you want to repeat horizontally will usually be taller than it is wide. Such images provide an efficient way to create interesting effects using what are, generally, small image sizes (in terms of download size). The image used to create the effect we saw in Figure 5.24 is shown in Figure 5.25.

Figure 5.25. The vertical image used for the horizontal repeat

When background images are repeated in one direction only, setting the background color becomes even more important. For instance, consider what would happen if we removed the background color from the previous example—Figure 5.26 reveals the result. If no background color is set, the browser's default background color will be used instead. Usually this is white, but it can be changed by the user in their browser settings. As you can see, once the background image ends, the background color is displayed, so it's important to make sure the colors complement each other.

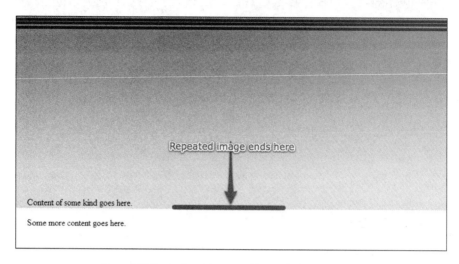

Figure 5.26. The horizontal repeat without a background color

Vertical Repeats

And it's just as easy to create the same repeat effect vertically:

```
#horizontalfade {
  border: 1px solid black;
  background-color: white;
  background-image: url(hori-fade.gif);
  background-repeat: repeat-y;
  padding: 20px;
  padding-left: 180px;
}
```

Figure 5.27 displays the result.

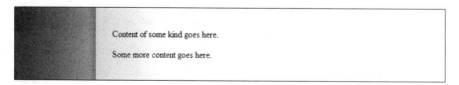

Figure 5.27. Repeating a background image vertically

Nonrepeating Images

You may simply want to display a background image once, and once only; for example, dropping a company logo in behind text, like a watermark effect. Whatever your plans, the CSS that displays a background image once is simple and very similar to the previous examples. In such cases, you need to use no-repeat to tell the browser not to repeat the image at all, and specify the location where the image should appear.

Here's the CSS to use:

```
#palmtree {
  border: 1px solid black;
  background-color: white;
  background-image: url(palm-trees.jpg);
  background-repeat: no-repeat;
  background-position: right top;
  padding: 60px;
  padding-right: 210px;
}
```

Figure 5.28 shows the effect.

Figure 5.28. Palm trees as a nonrepeating background image

The background-position property requires two values: the horizontal position (left, center, or right) and the vertical position (top, center, or bottom). If you use no-repeat without a background-position, the browser defaults to placing the image in the top-left corner.

Shorthand Backgrounds

In the same way that we can set the color, style, and thickness of a border using the `border` shorthand property, we can set a background image and color using the `background` shorthand property:

```css
#repeatedclouds {
  border: 1px solid black;
  padding: 20px;
  background: #aebbdb url(clouds.jpg);
}

#palmtree {
  border: 1px solid black;
  background: white url(palm-trees.jpg) no-repeat right top;
  padding: 60px;
  padding-right: 210px;
}
```

Fixed Heights and Widths

One final example remains before we start applying some of these visual techniques to our project site: artistic effects using fixed dimensions. In Chapter 4, we saw how we can fix a block-level element to a certain size. Here, I'll show how you can achieve the same end using a background image rather than a solid background color. When this is combined using a contrasting text color, you can create an interesting and artistic text overlay effect. (Note that in this example, I've used padding to move the line of text away from the top of the containing `div` element). Here's the CSS:

```css
.sunset {
  border: 1px solid black;
  color: white;
  font-weight: bold;
  font-size: 300%;
  background: black url(sunset.jpg);
  width: 650px;
  height: 125px;
  padding-left: 50px;
  padding-top: 400px;
}
```

The HTML for this effect couldn't be simpler:

```
<div class="sunset">Sunsets are a gift of nature.</div>
```

The effect of the HTML and CSS working in harmony produces the display shown in Figure 5.29.

Figure 5.29. A sized `div` using a background image

The effect looks good, though, I have to agree that the sunset is rather spectacular, too.

I think we're done exploring the theory here. Let's roll up our sleeves and integrate these techniques into the project site!

Setting a Background for Our Navigation

The evolution of our site continues apace! Firstly, what I'd like to make look a little prettier is the navigation area. The image I want to use is shown in Figure 5.30 (and is available from the code archive, of course).

Figure 5.30. Decorative background for the navigation

I know what you're thinking: this image is the correct width, but it's far too tall for our current navigation area. However, the size of the navigation area can easily be set within the CSS to match the height of our new background image. Here's the modified markup:

```
#navigation {
  width: 180px;
  height: 484px;
  background: #7da5d8 url(backgrounds/nav-bg.jpg) no-repeat;

}
```

Figure 5.31 shows the effect in context.

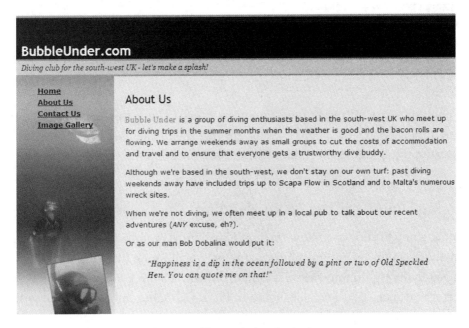

Figure 5.31. The new-look navigation bar

Applying a Fade to the Tagline

The tagline under the main heading performs its task efficiently, but is a little basic, and too blocky. One way to reduce this chunky look is to apply a background image using a smoothing effect. Let's use a graduated fade, as in Figure 5.32.

Figure 5.32. The tagline background image

For the effect we're after, the image should be locked to the right-hand edge of the tagline paragraph. This can be achieved easily using CSS:

style1.css *(excerpt)*

```css
#tagline p {
  font-style: italic;
  font-family: Georgia, Times, serif;
  border-top: 3px solid #7da5d8;
  border-bottom: 3px solid #7da5d8;
  padding-top: .2em;
  padding-bottom: .2em;
  padding-left: .8em;
```

```
  margin: 0;
  background: #bed8f3 url(backgrounds/tagline-fade.jpg) repeat-y
    right;
}
```

The position keyword `right` is all you need to use to keep the image hugging the tagline's right-hand side; `repeat-y` ensures that the image will repeat downwards (vertically) if the font size is increased, thereby boosting the size of the tagline overall.

A Lick of Paint for the Main Heading

I'm now going to show you how the main header (`h1`) can be livened up a little, using the previous technique. Once again, I've opted for an image that's going to be attached to the right-hand side. This time, though, it's not a fade, and it can't be repeated. Instead, it's the image shown in Figure 5.33, but only a part of it will be visible in the header.

Figure 5.33. The background image for our main heading

The image is tonally dark (ensuring that the BubbleUnder.com white text will be legible on top), and the left edge fades out nicely to match the navy background color that the `h1` headings use. We discussed this technique when we applied the graduated fade to the tagline—and the best way to appreciate the technique is to try it out. Type the example out or extract it from the code archive. I'd recommend resizing your browser window, so that you can see the effect such changes have on the background image.

We've used an image that's taller than the main page heading; this ensures that the page displays well if users resize their fonts, causing the height of the container to grow. Yes, you *do* need to think about these possible scenarios!

Let's look at the CSS for this effect. Make sure that the code below appears after the grouped h1, h2, h3 rule; we want to redefine the simple blue background that was applied in Chapter 4 using this more stylish version:

chapter5/website_files/11_heading_background/style1.css *(excerpt)*

```css
h1 {
  font-size: x-large;
  color: white;
  padding-top: 2em;
  padding-bottom: .2em;
  padding-left: .4em;
  margin: 0;
  background: navy url(backgrounds/header-bg.jpg) repeat-y right;
}
```

The effect is shown in Figure 5.34.

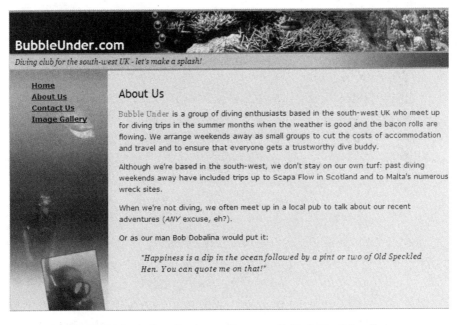

Figure 5.34. A selection of background images applied to finish off the effect

Summary

In this chapter, we've seen how you can source free images from the Web, or use your own photos, to compile an image gallery for your site. We've discussed the processes of resizing images to suit your site's specific needs and how to apply various effects. I've also explained how you can use CSS to add creative effects to your images (for instance, defining colored borders in a stylesheet, rather than producing them in image-editing software), as well as how you can apply images as decorative backgrounds that can be used once on a page or repeated.

It's amazing how much a website can be improved by a liberal sprinkling of imagery. Just a couple of chapters back, our project site was a fairly dull-looking collection of documents; now it's starting to look more like a proper website—one that we could very easily restyle by making a few changes in our CSS file.

In Chapter 6, we'll learn all about **tables**, as I show you how you can use these to display data in a clean, easy-to-understand format.

Tables: Tools for Organizing Data

The title of this book is Build Your Own Website *The Right Way*. It's important to emphasize this point as we begin this chapter because in the "Bad Old Days," the content of this chapter—tables—would have been right up near the front of the book as the author taught you how to use tables to create exciting page layouts! This approach has since been recognized as bad, bad, *bad*! But, you know what? There are still books that teach you to use tables for layout. Thankfully, you didn't pick up one of those books—bonus points to you!

As the name suggests, tables are designed to present *tabular data*, such as:

- a calendar of events
- a bank statement
- a contacts list

And many more uses beyond. In fact, there are many circumstances in which tables are a sensible choice—but laying out an entire web page is definitely not among them.

What is a Table?

Several times in the preceding chapters, I compared web techniques to tools that you might use in Microsoft Word, and in the case of tables, there's another direct correlation. If you've used the Microsoft Office program, you've probably inserted a table before, using the toolbar icon shown in Figure 6.1.

Figure 6.1. The **Insert Table** icon in Microsoft Word

You can use this tool to create a table like the one in Table 6.1 very easily.

Table 6.1. An example of a table

Name	Contact (Home)	Contact (Work)	Location
Jane Bradley	02380 123123	02380 577566	Southampton
Fred Bradley	01273 177166	01273 946376	Brighton
Lionel Rundel	01793 641207	01793 626696	Swindon

A table is the most sensible, tidy way to organize this kind of data. You can easily scan down a column, or along a row, and see what's what. The exact same effect can be achieved on a web page.

Before we embark on table creation, though, let's make a couple of essential changes to our project site; that way, we have an appropriate place to use tables. What sort of data would warrant the use of tables on a diving website? How about a table of forthcoming club events? That'll do nicely!

1. First, we need to add some links to *all* the website's files. We need to make one addition to the navigation on the left of the page. I think this new navigation item should appear between the About Us and Contact Us page navigation links. Be sure to add it to all the files in the website, as shown here:

```
<div id="navigation">
  <ul>
    <li><a href="index.html">Home</a></li>
    <li><a href="about.html">About Us</a></li>
    <li><a href="events.html">Club Events</a></li>
    <li><a href="contact.html">Contact Us</a></li>
    <li><a href="gallery.html">Image Gallery</a></li>
  </ul>
</div> <!-- end of navigation div -->
```

2. Next, take a copy of **index.html**, and rename it in Windows Explorer (or Finder, if you're using a Mac) to **events.html**.

Open **events.html** and make the following changes:

▨ Change the content between the opening `<title>` and closing `</title>` tags to read "Forthcoming club diving events and trips with Bubble Under."

▨ Change the page heading (the `h2` element) to read "Forthcoming Club Events."

▨ Delete everything except the heading inside the `div` whose `id` is `bodycontent`.

▨ Beneath that heading, add a new paragraph that reads:

> Bubble Under members love meeting up for dive trips around the country. Below are all the dive trips that we currently have planned. For more information about any of them, please get in contact with that event's organizer.

If you've completed all those steps, your code should look like this:

```html
<!DOCTYPE html>
<html lang="en">
  <head>
    <title>Forthcoming club diving events and trips with Bubble
        Under</title>
    <meta charset="utf-8"/>
    <link href="style1.css" rel="stylesheet" type="text/css"/>
  </head>
  <body>
    <div id="header">
      <div id="sitebranding">
        <h1>BubbleUnder.com</h1>
      </div>
      <div id="tagline">
        <p>Diving club for the south-west UK - let's make a
            splash!</p>
      </div>
    </div> <!-- end of header div -->
    <div id="navigation">
      <ul>
        <li><a href="index.html">Home</a></li>
        <li><a href="about.html">About Us</a></li>
        <li><a href="events.html">Club Events</a></li>
        <li><a href="contact.html">Contact Us</a></li>
        <li><a href="gallery.html">Image Gallery</a></li>
      </ul>
    </div>
    <div id="bodycontent">
      <h2>Forthcoming Club Events</h2>
      <p>Bubble Under members love meeting up for dive trips
          around the country. Below are all the dive trips that we
          currently have planned. For more information about any
          of them, please get in contact with that event's
          organizer.</p>
    </div> <!-- end of bodycontent div -->
  </body>
</html>
```

Why Tables Are Bad and CSS Rocks

It's time for a very short history lesson.

The reason why web designers used to use tables for layout was simple: in the early days of web development, tables were the only way to achieve a layout that resembled a magazine- or newspaper-like grid. Designers wanted to have a heading at the top of the page, a column on the left for navigation, a column in the middle for content, and a third column on the right for more links. The problem was that using tables to achieve such effects was an abuse of the markup—known as a **hack**—but it worked at the time, and people saw nothing wrong with it.

Today, CSS is so well-supported that there's really no excuse for using tables for layout, and CSS is definitely the better tool for the job. Nevertheless, many websites still use table-based layouts. This doesn't mean that this approach is right: it's simply an old habit that refuses to die quietly in the corner as it should—although you can play your part to help redress the situation. But just what are the advantages of using CSS instead of tables? Here are a few for you to consider:

Design and redesign flexibility

A CSS-based layout ensures that you place all your styles (from cosmetic touches such as font styling, to the major structural rules) in one location. Change the layout rules you set in that stylesheet, and you affect every page that refers to it. Using a table-based layout locks your page design in at page-level, so changing a layout becomes a major problem—one that's unable to be resolved simply by changing the stylesheet.

Better accessibility

A table is supposed to be used for tabular data only. For this reason, some **assistive devices** (such as screen readers, which we discussed in the section called "Screen Readers: Hearing the Web" in Chapter 5) are a bit confused when the content is not presented as expected. In other words, these kinds of devices expect to access tabular data inside a table; if the table is being used for a purpose for which it was never intended, all bets are off, and accessibility may be the first casualty. If you use a table for the purposes of layout, content that may appear to be located logically on the screen might be illogical when read out by a screen reader. This is a phenomenon known as table linearization, which we'll explore in detail shortly.

Quicker downloads (or perception of download)

A table-based page layout often renders more slowly than an equivalent CSS-based layout; this is especially true of pages that have a lot of content. There are a couple of reasons for this. The first is that a table-based layout will generally require much more markup to hold the page together—acting like a scaffold, so to speak. Using a table-based layout, it's more than a matter of marking up sections of the page with `div` elements. This extra markup adds to the page file size, and therefore, the amount of time it takes to download the file.

The second reason relates to the user's *perception* of download speed. Browsers don't download entire web pages in one go; when they ask for a web page, they receive it as a trickle of information, and try to render that information as it arrives. In the case of our site, the browser would render the header, then the navigation, and finally the body content. If the trickle of information is so slow that there's a pause halfway through the body content, the browser is still able to display the first half of the body content without any trouble. It's a different scenario altogether when using table-based layouts. In a table-based layout, the browser needs to have downloaded *all* the content in the table before it knows how to accurately render that information on the screen. As such, a CSS-based page layout will usually appear on the screen faster than a table-based layout.

If there's one point to remember from this chapter, it's this: despite what anyone tells you, using tables is fine. They should not be used for page layout (that's where they gain their bad reputation from), but it's *perfectly okay to use tables for their originally intended purpose*—the presentation of data in a grid.

Anatomy of a Table

Before we start adding the table to our Events page, let's take a step back and look at the example we saw in Table 6.1: the simple table of telephone contact details. At a glance, we can identify some specific areas of the table, namely the headers, rows, columns, and table data cells. Figure 6.2 explains this diagrammatically.

Although I mentioned columns, there's no need to indicate these in the HTML. At its most basic level, a table is put together using commands that tell the browser where to start a new row, or a new cell within any given row; as the columns are a natural by-product of this approach, it's unnecessary to declare each new column.

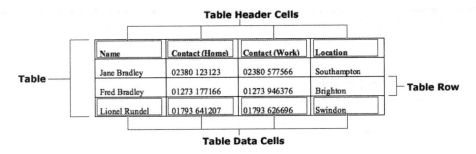

Figure 6.2. The anatomy of a table

The areas marked in Figure 6.2 have the following direct equivalents in HTML:

table[1]   contains the entire table

tr[2]   contains an entire row of a table (hence table row)

th[3]   signifies a table header cell

td[4]   a general table data cell

Let's see how the example table looks in HTML:

```
<table>
  <tr>
    <th>Name</th>
    <th>Contact (Home)</th>
    <th>Contact (Work)</th>
    <th>Location</th>
  </tr>
  <tr>
    <td>Jane Bradley</td>
    <td>02380 123123</td>
    <td>02380 577566</td>
    <td>Southampton</td>
  </tr>
  <tr>
    <td>Fred Bradley</td>
    <td>01273 177166</td>
```

[1] http://reference.sitepoint.com/html/table/
[2] http://reference.sitepoint.com/html/tr/
[3] http://reference.sitepoint.com/html/th/
[4] http://reference.sitepoint.com/html/td/

```
    <td>01273 946376</td>
    <td>Brighton</td>
  </tr>
  <tr>
    <td>Lionel Rundel</td>
    <td>01793 641207</td>
    <td>01793 626696</td>
    <td>Swindon</td>
  </tr>
</table>
```

Can you see how the two marry up? The elements that make up a table can seem a little daunting when you first encounter them, but like so many HTML elements, their names are quite easy to remember.

Styling the Table

The table element is fairly simple: it's the element that contains all the data that makes up the table, though, as Figure 6.3 shows, it *is* quite ugly.

Name	Contact (Home)	Contact (Work)	Location
Jane Bradley	02380 123123	02380 577566	Southampton
Fred Bradley	01273 177166	01273 946376	Brighton
Lionel Rundel	01793 641207	01793 626696	Swindon

Figure 6.3. The uninspiring default appearance of a table

How can we jazz this up? If you're thinking CSS, give yourself a pat on the back—CSS is definitely the way to go!

Borders, Spacing, and Alignment

Let's start by putting some borders around these cells. Figure 6.4 shows the impact of the following CSS code:

```
td {
  border: 1px solid black;
}
```

Name	Contact (Home)	Contact (Work)	Location
Jane Bradley	02380 123123	02380 577566	Southampton
Fred Bradley	01273 177166	01273 946376	Brighton
Lionel Rundel	01793 641207	01793 626696	Swindon

Figure 6.4. One-pixel borders placed around each cell

Perhaps this isn't quite what you expected. That space between each of the cell's borders is called **cell spacing**; it can be turned off by applying the border-collapse: collapse; declaration to the table element.

Let's turn off the cell spacing, and add a little more decoration to our table. We will also set the table headings to align to the left of the cell. By default, the content inside table headings (th) is aligned to the center, which can be confusing (and almost *always* looks wrong when the other table cells are left-aligned). Figure 6.5 shows the results of the suggested changes (and a few other enhancements too):

```
table {
  border-collapse: collapse;
  border: 1px solid black;
}

th {
  text-align: left;
  background: gray;
  color: white;
  padding: 0.2em;
}

td {
  border: 1px solid black;
  padding: 0.2em;
}
```

Name	Contact (Home)	Contact (Work)	Location
Jane Bradley	02380 123123	02380 577566	Southampton
Fred Bradley	01273 177166	01273 946376	Brighton
Lionel Rundel	01793 641207	01793 626696	Swindon

Figure 6.5. Style rules applied to the table

It's looking a lot sharper now.

class-ifying Your Tables

Tables can be used for a variety of purposes, and each type of table may warrant a different look. For this reason, it's a good idea to use classes in your CSS selectors for tables.

For example, imagine your site includes the following types of tables:

- rates
- schedule
- events

You could set different style rules for each table type in your CSS:

```
table.rates {
  /* declarations for rates tables */
}

table.schedule {
  /* declarations for schedule tables */
}

table.events {
  /* declarations for events tables */
}
```

Then, when you added a table to your HTML, all you'd need to do is give it the appropriate class attribute:

```
<table class="rates">
```

A little forethought goes a long way!

Making Your Tables Accessible

I introduced the idea of web accessibility in the section called "Web Accessibility" in Chapter 5 to emphasize the importance of the img element's alt attribute. It's vital to consider accessibility when it comes to tables, too. The question that all web designers ask themselves at some point in their careers is, "How on earth does a screen reader read out a table?"

Linearization

In reading out the content of a table, a screen reader **linearizes** that content. Linearization simply means that the screen reader reads the content in the order in which it appears in the table's markup. As an example, consider Table 6.2, which displays TV listings. Visually, it's easy to associate a time slot with the associated program.

Table 6.2. An example of TV listings set out in a table

9:30 p.m.–10:00 p.m.	10:00 p.m.–11:00 p.m.	11:00 p.m.–11:45 p.m.
Regional News	*Glee*	*Mad Men*

We can quickly and easily see when each program starts and ends. Let's take a look at the markup:

```
<table>
  <tr>
    <td>9:30 p.m.-10:00 p.m.</td>
    <td>10:00 p.m.-11:00 p.m.</td>
    <td>11:00 p.m.-11:45 p.m.</td>
  </tr>
  <tr>
    <td>Regional News</td>
    <td>Glee</td>
    <td>Mad Men</td>
  </tr>
</table>
```

The linearized interpretation of this would be: "9:30 p.m.–10:00 p.m., 10:00 p.m. –11:00 p.m., 11:00 p.m.–11:45 p.m., *Regional News*, *Glee*, *Mad Men*." That's relatively incomprehensible as far as content goes! We could fix this problem by changing the orientation of the table; that is, making the program names run down the left column and the time slots run down the right. Or we could mark up the cells that contain the names of the programs using th instead of td, and adding a scope[5] attribute to each of the th elements. We'll look into this second solution later in the chapter, when we discuss some advanced table concepts.

---

[5] http://reference.sitepoint.com/html/th/scope/

summary

No, I'm not about to summarize what we've just discussed in this chapter just yet! Instead, I'm going to introduce the table's summary[6] attribute. This is an invisible attribute—it won't render on the screen or, for that matter, when you print the web page—that can be used to provide extra information about the table to assistive devices. Here's an example of a summary:

```
<table summary="Area representatives, and their home and work
    telephone numbers">
```

When you add a summary, be brief but descriptive. This attribute should be used like the alt attribute is for images: be brief, but not to the point of inviting questions.

Captioning Your Table

If you think the summary attribute seems like a bit of a wasted opportunity because it's hidden from the table's onscreen display, don't worry. You can use the caption[7] element for this purpose. The caption element is contained inside the table element. You can use CSS to style it, too, just as you can style headings. Here's how the markup looks:

```
<table summary="Area representatives, and their home and work
    telephone numbers">
  <caption>Contact details</caption>
  <tr>
    <th>Name</th>
    <th>Contact (Home)</th>
    <th>Contact (Work)</th>
    <th>Location</th>
  </tr>
```

One note of caution: while caption is the proper way of providing a table heading, it can be tricky to style with CSS consistently across all browsers. This may only pose a small problem—after all, it's fine if there's some difference in rendering across web browsers. That said, some designs sit poorly with the caption element, so the developer might choose, instead, to omit it entirely and use a heading, for

[6] http://reference.sitepoint.com/html/table/summary/
[7] http://reference.sitepoint.com/html/caption/

example an h2 or h3. This is still acceptable—proper headings give the page structure, help search engines understand the nature of the page, and aid accessibility. But if you *can* use caption and style it as you choose, it's the better option to go with.

So far, we've looked at some of the basics of tables, and discussed some examples that demonstrate the key concepts. I've shown you how to use CSS to style the table content, and how to make the table content accessible, but it's best to see this in practice. Let's move along to our project site and see how we can apply some of this knowledge.

Adding an Events Table

You've learned about the various elements that make up a table. Now, you're going to build one of your own:

1. Open up **events.html** in your text editor.
2. Type the following code beneath the paragraph you added earlier:

chapter6/website_files/02_events_table/events.html *(excerpt)*

```
<table class="events" summary="Details of upcoming club events and
    dive trips">
  <caption>Club events/dive trips for the next six
      months</caption>
  <tr>
    <th>Date</th>
    <th>Event Description</th>
    <th>Approximate Cost</th>
    <th>Contact</th>
  </tr>
  <tr>
    <td>12 July</td>
    <td>Committee meeting, deciding on next year's trips</td>
    <td>N/A</td>
    <td>Bob Dobalina</td>
  </tr>
  <tr>
    <td>19 July</td>
    <td>7-day trip to Hurghada (package deal) - limited
        spaces</td>
    <td>&pound;260 pp (all inclusive), departing Luton</td>
    <td>Bob Dobalina</td>
  </tr>
```

```
<tr>
  <td>5 August</td>
  <td>Ocean &amp; Sports Diver Theory Course</td>
  <td>Call for details</td>
  <td>Jeff Edgely</td>
</tr>
<tr>
  <td>12 August</td>
  <td>Murder Mystery Weekend, Cotswolds (no diving!)</td>
  <td>&pound;65 pp (accommodation included)</td>
  <td>Jill Smith</td>
</tr>
</table>
```

Remember that you don't *have* to type this out yourself—you can grab the markup from the code archive instead.

All the features that we've covered in the chapter are present here: the table summary attribute, the caption element, table headers (th), and the basic items of construction that you need for every table—the table, tr, and td elements. But, never mind the markup, how does it look in the browser? Figure 6.6 reveals all.

In my mind, this display can be summed up in one word: yuck! Like the unstyled table we saw earlier, this is very unattractive, and not easy to interpret. Fortunately, it's CSS to the rescue once again. Our first task should be to make our table more legible and add some borders to it.

Figure 6.6. The basic, unstyled table

Open **style1.css** and add a new rule for the th and td elements. Here's the CSS you need:

```
                    chapter6/website_files/03_events_table_borders/style1.css (excerpt)
table.events {
  border-collapse: collapse;
}

table.events th, table.events td {
  padding: 4px;
  border: 1px solid #000066;
}

table.events th {
  font-size: x-small;
}

table.events td {
  font-size: small;
}
```

We've created four rules.

The first affects all `table` elements that have a `class` attribute set to `events`. The rule uses the `border-collapse` property to turn off the cell spacing effect we saw earlier.

The second rule uses a selector that's slightly more complicated: `table.events th, table.events td` affects all `th` and `td` elements between the `<table class="events">` and `</table>` tags. Unfortunately, a simpler declaration, such as `table.events th, td`, affects the `th` elements inside our table and *all* `td` elements. We're killing a couple of birds with one stone here, those proverbial birds being the `border` and `padding` for each cell.

The last two rules take care of the `font-size` for our cells and headers.

Figure 6.7 shows the effect of the above CSS on our web page.

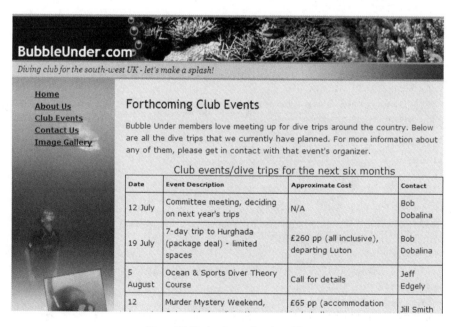

Figure 6.7. Borders improving the table

Next, we'll improve the alignment of the table header text. As I mentioned before, the default setting for `th` centers the header text, preventing most of your content from lining up with that header. It's crazy, I know. Let's fix it quickly and easily.

In **style1.css**, modify the declaration for the table header (`th`) element, like so:

chapter6/website_files/03_events_table_borders/style1.css *(excerpt)*

```
table.events th {
  font-size: x-small;
  text-align: left;
}
```

That should solve the problem, but let's go a little further to make the table header look more attractive.

1. Add some more declarations to the `table.events th` rule—one to change the foreground (or text) color to white, and one to add a background image, and a few padding rules:

chapter6/website_files/04_styled_table_header/style1.css *(excerpt)*

```
table.events th {
  font-size: x-small;
  text-align: left;
  background: #241374 url(backgrounds/header-bg.jpg);
  color: #ffffff;
  padding-top: 0;
  padding-bottom: 0;
  padding-left: 2px;
  padding-right: 2px;
}
```

2. While we're here, we might as well spruce up the table's caption:

chapter6/website_files/04_styled_table_header/style1.css *(excerpt)*

```
table.events caption {
  color: #000066;
  font-size: small;
  text-align: left;
  padding-bottom: 5px;
  font-weight: bold;
}
```

3. Save the stylesheet and refresh the browser to see how it looks. Compare your work with Figure 6.8.

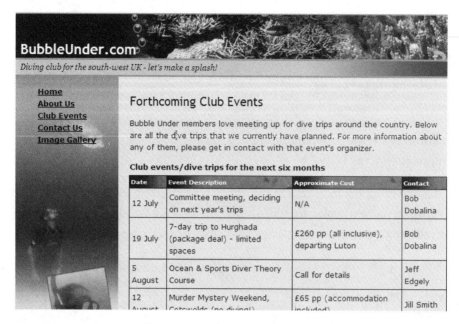

Figure 6.8. A much improved table header

I want to draw your attention to two points in that last addition. First, the background image is actually the same as the one we used in the page header (the large coral montage underneath the BubbleUnder.com text at the top), but it looks very different here. Why? In the page header, we positioned the image so that it hugs the bottom right-hand edges; in the th declaration, no positioning was specified, so the image starts at the top left, and that portion of the image is quite different. Utilizing an image that's already used elsewhere in the website can save ourselves a little download time, because the image will already have downloaded, and the computer doesn't have to request a different image file for this background.

The second point I want to make is about the text color. Here, I've specified a color of #ffffff. This is the hexadecimal color specification for white, and although it may be easier to remember the word "white" than an obscure hex value, it's important to be familiar with a handful of hex values so that you're comfortable with them the next time you see one. Another hex value that you'll come across often is #000000, which means black (the red, green, and blue values are 0, 0, and 0—in other words, there's no light at all—so #000000 represents black).

Stylish Table Cells

I have just one more suggestion for our Events table. While it looks fine now, I'd like to give it that extra bit of polish. Once again, I'm going to suggest using a background image for this effect: a subtle, faded background that will be positioned at the top of each table cell. Here's the markup:

chapter6/website_files/05_stylish_table_cells/style1.css *(excerpt)*

```
table.events td {
  font-size: small;
  background: #e2edff url(backgrounds/td.jpg) repeat-x top;
}
```

That background color—yet another obscure-looking hex value—is a very light blue that matches the blue that appears in the top of the image. The background image repeats horizontally (as demonstrated in Chapter 5), and is positioned along the top of the cell, giving our data table the sleek look depicted in Figure 6.9.

It's up to you to decide how far you want to take your table styling. You are limited only by your imagination—or, in my case, skill at using graphics applications!

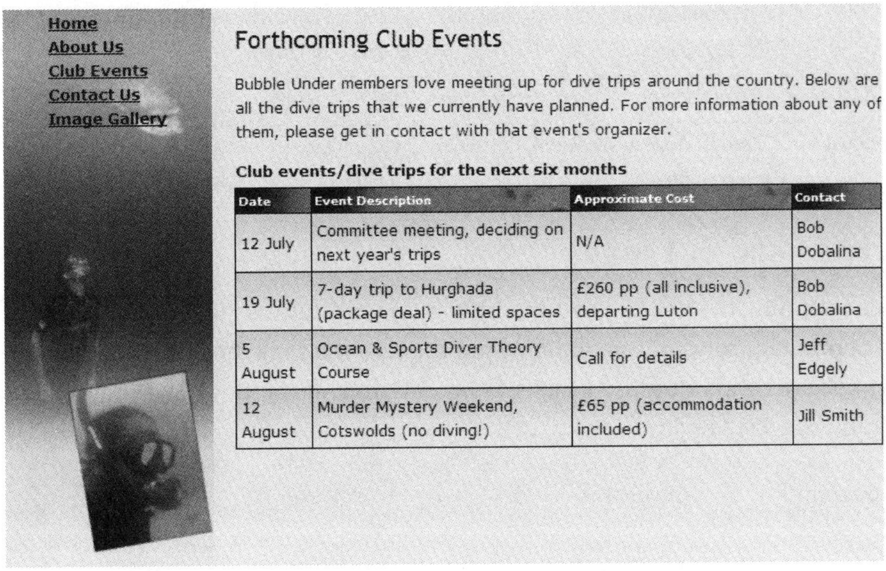

Figure 6.9. The final presentation of the data table

Advanced Tables

In the earlier examples we saw in this chapter, and with the table we've created in the project website, the tables' structures have been quite simple: we have straight columns and rows, and no complications. So what kinds of complications *could* we encounter?

Merging Table Cells

The complication that you're most likely to come across as you work with tables arises within merged table cells. Let's consider the table from the project site again, and imagine it has the slightly different layout shown in Table 6.3 (I've removed the formatting to make it a little clearer).

Table 6.3. A more complicated table construction

Date	Event Details		Contact
	Event Description	Approximate Cost	
12 July	Committee meeting to decide on next year's trips	N/A	Bob Dobalina
19 July	7-day trip to Hurghada (package deal), limited spaces	£260 pp (all inclusive), departing Luton	Bob Dobalina
5 August	Ocean and Sports Diver Theory Course	Call for details	Jeff Edgely
12 August	Murder Mystery Weekend, Cotswolds (no diving!)	£65 pp (accommodation included)	Jill Smith

rowspan and colspan

In this example, the headings of the first and last columns ("Date" and "Contact") span across two rows of the table. Along the top, the table header with the text "Event Details" takes up the space of two columns. To achieve this effect, we use the following HTML attributes:

- rowspan[8]
- colspan[9]

---

[8] http://reference.sitepoint.com/html/td/rowspan/
[9] http://reference.sitepoint.com/html/td/colspan/

It would be marked up as follows (the code is partly abbreviated):

```
<table>
  <tr>
    <th rowspan="2">Date</th>
    <th colspan="2">Event Details</th>
    <th rowspan="2">Contact</th>
  </tr>
  <tr>
    <th>Event Description</th>
    <th>Approximate Cost</th>
  </tr>
  <tr>
    <td>12 July</td>
    <td>Committee meeting, deciding on next year's trips</td>
    <td>N/A</td>
    <td>Bob Dobalina</td>
  </tr>
```

Note that the first row appears to have three cells (1 column + 2 columns + 1 column = 4); the second row has only two table headers, but because the left- and right-most cells in the previous row have been set with a `rowspan` of 2, everything adds up quite nicely.

Are you confused? If so, you're not the first person to find `rowspan` and `colspan` tricky; many a web designer has tripped over this in the past. If your `rowspan` and `colspan` mathematics are wrong, your table constructions can do some *very* weird (and not so wonderful) things! That's why I placed this exercise in the advanced section of this chapter. If you want to merge table cells, there are two ways that you can approach it:

- Use a dedicated web development tool that's capable of handling and creating tables visually (such as Dreamweaver).[10]

- Rough it out on paper! Start using a simple table that has no merges, and simply cross out the lines you don't need. As you do so, make a note of the increased numbers of rows or columns that these cells span. Only when you're finished with your paper layout should you start translating this back to HTML.

---

[10] http://www.adobe.com/products/dreamweaver/

Advanced Accessibility

Badly constructed tables cause some of the biggest accessibility headaches. While it's beyond the scope of this book to tell you everything about web accessibility, there is a feature you can add that improves access to tabular content for assistive technology such as screen readers.

The scope Attribute

When you look at a table of data on the screen, it's easy to glance at a header and then scan down the column and see the data that relates to that header. But for a blind user who relies on a screen reader to interpret and read back that table data, it can be tricky to associate data stored deep within a table with its appropriate header. The scope attribute can make this easier.

The scope[11] attribute is applied to a header and has two possible values: row and col. Essentially, the scope attribute says to the browser (and any other piece of technology that needs to make use of it), "Hey, see this header cell? Well, everything below it is related to this cell, and don't you forget it!" The code below puts this a little more formally:

```
<tr>
  <th scope="col">Date</th>
  <th scope="col">Event Description</th>
  <th scope="col">Approximate Cost</th>
  <th scope="col">Contact</th>
</tr>
```

The table we're using on our project website has headers at the top of the columns only, but you might use tables that have headers down the left-hand side as well, like the one shown in Figure 6.10.

Figure 6.10. Applying scope="row" and scope="col" to table headers

---

[11] http://reference.sitepoint.com/html/th/scope/

Here's the HTML for this example:

```html
<table>
  <caption>Train times and departures</caption>
  <tr>
    <td></td> <!-- empty cell in the top-left corner -->
    <th scope="col">Departure Time</th>
    <th scope="col">Platform</th>
    <th scope="col">Buffet Coach</th>
  </tr>
  <tr>
    <th scope="row">Southampton</th>
    <td>13:03</td>
    <td>12</td>
    <td>Yes</td>
  </tr>
  <tr>
    <th scope="row">Edinburgh</th>
    <td>14:47</td>
    <td>4</td>
    <td>Yes</td>
  </tr>
  <tr>
    <th scope="row">Newcastle</th>
    <td>15:55</td>
    <td>7</td>
    <td>No</td>
  </tr>
</table>
```

If you start to merge cells using `colspan` and `rowspan`, it becomes incredibly tricky to mark the table up in a way that ensures its accessibility. Tools are available to help, though—namely the `headers` and `id` attributes, which are explained in the article *Bring on the Tables*, by Roger Johansson.[12] At this point, I'll simply say that it's far better to keep your tables simple. When using complicated tables (with `rowspan`, `colspan`, `headers`, and `id` attributes), it's hard to ensure that it'll be understood by assistive technology such as screen readers. Even for those readers that *do* fully support complex tables, there's a high cognitive load on the user to recall the various methods and keystrokes required to access the information. This really is a topic that you can leave for now!

---

[12] http://www.456bereastreet.com/archive/200410/bring_on_the_tables/

Summary

When you need to present information in a tidy, organized fashion, tables are the right technique for the job, and using HTML, you have all the necessary tools at your disposal. In this chapter, we've seen how you can use combinations of simple HTML elements to provide necessary order, and employ CSS to style tables in such a way that they can be visually appealing. We've also covered some of the basic considerations to make tabular information accessible to a much wider audience.

Now that we've given tables their due attention, we can move on to another topic that's essential to grasp if you're going to have people interact with one another—not to mention your good self—on your website. That topic is forms. If you're done here, the next chapter will fill you in on the details!

Forms: Interacting with Your Audience

One of the great things about the Internet is the never-ending wealth of information it puts at your disposal. The term *web surfing* came about because, like real-world surfers, users never know where they'll end up; if a topic piques their interest, they'll head in that direction. But the process of simply reading, clicking on a link, and reading some more is passive. Users aren't directly involved; they're simply on the receiving end of all that information. At some point, users need to interact with the website, altering that one-way flow of information.

Imagine this scenario: you're looking to book a holiday—perhaps a surfing trip or a diving holiday—so you search for information about resorts, read other people's reviews, and look at some stunning pictures. You make a quick decision about which resort you'd like to visit; then you decide to find a site through which you can book a trip, arrange your flights, and so on. As you book the holiday, you need to enter details, such as your name and address. You may have to select travel dates from a drop-down list, or specify certain features that you want to include in your holiday using checkboxes. To make these kinds of selections, you use HTML forms.

In this chapter, you'll learn about the various elements that make up a form, the tasks for which those elements should (and should not) be used, and how to make sense of information submitted through forms. As part of the practical work of this chapter, we're going to add a simple form to the diving project site; it will allow users to notify the webmaster of forthcoming diving events. But, to begin with, let's investigate the different parts of a form.

Anatomy of a Form

It might not surprise you to learn that a form begins with an opening `<form>` tag and ends with a closing `</form>` tag. Inside that `form`[1] element, the browser can expect to find HTML elements that capture data in some way. Though the `form` element lacks any visual characteristics to speak of, it's a block-level element, so it will cause the browser to create breaks before and after its opening and closing tags.

Before we describe what a `form` does, it's a good idea to review an example of a `form` as we'd see it in the browser. Take a look at the example in Figure 7.1.

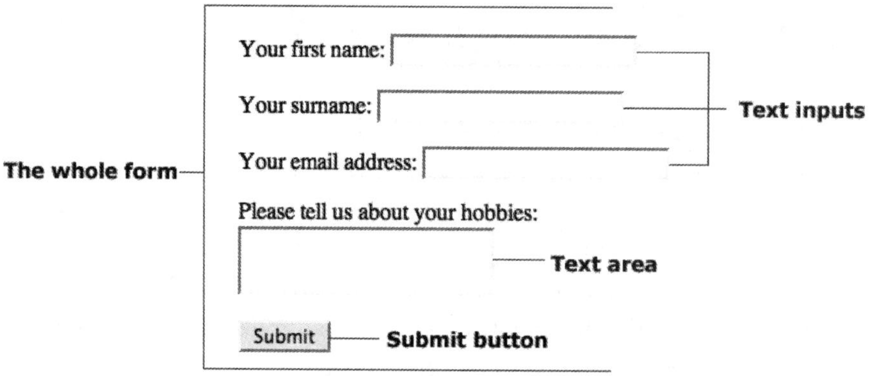

Figure 7.1. The basic anatomy of a form

The `form` element is a special kind of container. It holds a variety of HTML elements that can exist only inside the `form` element, including:

- `fieldset`
- `legend`
- `input`
- `textarea`
- `select`

---

[1] http://reference.sitepoint.com/html/form/

I'll explain all these elements through the course of this chapter, but let's begin with a simple form that you can build for yourself. Then, we'll discuss all the different elements we might want to use in our forms.

A Simple Form

Let's gain a feel for what a form does. Open your text editor and enter the following markup:

chapter7/examples/01_simple_form/simpleform.html

```
<!DOCTYPE html>
<html lang="en">
  <head>
    <title>A Simple Form</title>
    <meta charset="utf-8"/>
  </head>
  <body>
    <h1>A Simple Form</h1>
    <form method="get" action="simpleform.html">
      <p>
        <label for="yourname">Enter your name:</label>
        <input type="text" name="yourname" id="yourname"/>
      </p>
      <p><input type="submit"/></p>
    </form>
  </body>
</html>
```

Save the page as **simpleform.html**, and open it in your browser. You should see a basic example of a form, like the one shown in Figure 7.2, which has:

- one text input to enter your name
- a submit button that sends the details entered into the form

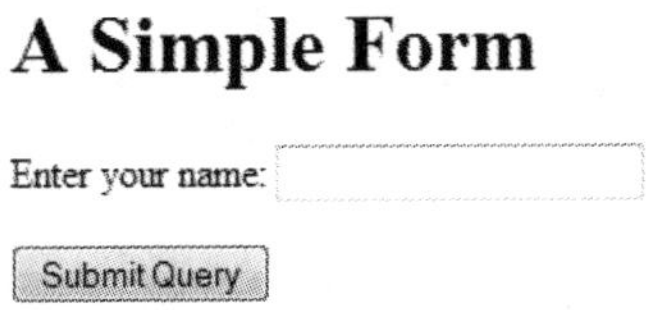

A Simple Form

Enter your name: [   ]

[Submit Query]

Figure 7.2. A form whittled down to the basics

Now enter your name in the text input and click on the submit button (it's usually labeled **Submit Query**, or just **Submit**). The page should reload, with your name disappearing from the text box, and if you look in the address bar, you'll see that the data you entered has been appended to the address for that page. It should look similar to this:

```
file:///C:/Documents%20and%20Settings/Bob%20Dobalina/My%20Document
s/Web/simpleform.html?yourname=Bob
```

We're yet to do anything with the data, but you can appreciate that even with this basic example, the entered data is there for the taking (and manipulating).

Let's look at the different elements you can place in a form, and their uses.

The Building Blocks of a Form

The `form` Element

As we've already seen, a form begins with the `form` element. You will see a few important attributes in an opening `<form>` tag, and these are:

`method`[2]

This tells the browser *how* to send the data in the form when the user clicks the submit button. The options are `get` and `post`. The option you use will depend on what you're doing with the data (see the "Get It or Post It?" tip following for more on this). For now, we'll use `get` for our simple examples.

`action`[3]

This attribute tells the browser *where* to send the data that was collected in the form. Normally, this will specify another web page that can read and interpret the data entered.

 Get It or Post It?

The decision about whether to use `get` or `post` in the `method` attribute of your `form` normally won't be yours if you want to avoid writing the form processing

---

[2] http://reference.sitepoint.com/html/form/method/
[3] http://reference.sitepoint.com/html/form/action/

code. As you'll see later, we'll use a third-party form processor to make our form useful, and that will dictate which method we use. However, it's useful to know a couple of points about these methods:

- If you specify a `get` method, your form data will appear in the address bar of the page to which you submit that form. This can be useful, so if you want to you can bookmark that page (or "Add to Favorites" if you use IE) with those pieces of information included. For example, because Google's search form includes `method="get"`, you can bookmark a search for "cake shops Southampton." Then, every time you call up that bookmark, Google will give you its up-to-date list of Southampton cake shops.

- Sometimes, you'll want stop users from being able to bookmark the results of their form usage, or ensure that the information in the form isn't visible to passersby. For instance, take the login form for an internet banking site. You'd want to make sure that only the actual bank account holder (not another family member, for example) can access the details for the account in question; you certainly would want to prohibit others from seeing the user's password, too. In cases like these, we use the `post` method.

Additionally, there's an upper limit to the amount of data that can be passed using `get`, particularly with older browsers. It's also worth noting that if you're sending a large amount of data, `post` is the preferred method.

As usual, there's more to this topic if you're interested. A good place to start is *Methods GET and POST in HTML Forms—What's the Difference?* by Jukka Korpela.[4] We won't be addressing any more on this in the chapter.

The `fieldset` and `legend` Elements

These two elements really do go hand in hand; `fieldset`[5] groups related elements within a form together (by drawing a box around them), while `legend`[6] lets you caption that group of elements appropriately. Here's the HTML for this dynamic duo:

```
<form method="get" action="simpleform.html">
  <fieldset>
    <legend>All About You</legend>
```

---

[4] http://www.cs.tut.fi/~jkorpela/forms/methods.html
[5] http://reference.sitepoint.com/html/fieldset/
[6] http://reference.sitepoint.com/html/legend/

```
    <p>
      <label for="yourname">Enter your name:</label>
      <input type="text" name="yourname" id="yourname"/>
    </p>
    <p><input type="submit"/></p>
  </fieldset>
</form>
```

Figure 7.3 shows how the form looks with these elements added.

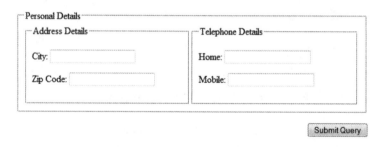

Figure 7.3. A form to which a `fieldset` and `legend` have been applied

Nesting `fieldsets`

You're not limited to using just one `fieldset` and `legend`. On more complex forms, you can nest these elements to provide more clarity within form sections, as Figure 7.4 shows.

Figure 7.4. Nested `fieldsets` help to organize form inputs

The `label` Element

Form **controls** (for example, text inputs) are the bits of the form the user interacts with to enter their data. The `label`[7] element tells the user what kind of data should be entered in each control.

---

[7] http://reference.sitepoint.com/html/label/

The `label` element is linked directly to the `input` to which it relates, using the `for`[8] attribute. The value of the `for` attribute should be the same as the `id` attribute of the `input` element.

The `label` element also enables the user to activate a `radio input` or `checkbox input`, or place the focus on a `text input` or `select` element.

The `input` Element

With the preamble out of the way, we can go to the nuts and bolts of the form: the section in which we actually capture data from users. The first element that you'll learn to use is the `input`[9] element; this inserts controls into the form that the user can interact with.

The `input` element is very versatile. Its appearance and behavior can be changed dramatically using the `type`[10] attribute. Some of the most common values of the `type` attribute are:

- `text`
- `password`
- `checkbox`
- `radio`
- `hidden`
- `submit`

Each of these values places a unique control on your page. Let's start by looking at the most commonly used one—the **text input** control.

Text Input

You've seen this control countless times on web pages. The text input, depicted in Figure 7.5, is the most basic type of form data users can enter.

Enter your name: [   ]

Figure 7.5. A simple text input

---

[8] http://reference.sitepoint.com/html/label/for
[9] http://reference.sitepoint.com/html/input/
[10] http://reference.sitepoint.com/html/input/type/

The HTML for this control is straightforward:

```
<p>
  <label for="yourname">Enter your name:</label>
  <input type="text" name="yourname" id="yourname"/>
</p>
```

Let's look at each component:

the label element

The label is used to label a control, so that users know what kind of data they should enter.

the type attribute

We can set the input element as a simple text input control by setting the type attribute to text.

the name[11] attribute

Remember in our very first form, the name we entered appeared at the end of the address bar when the form was submitted? The code is below:

```
file:///C:/Documents%20and%20Settings/Bob%20Dobalina/My%20Docum
ents/Web/simpleform.html?yourname=Bob
```

The yourname part came from the name attribute of the input element, which can be used to identify which piece of data came from a given control.

the id[12] attribute

At first glance, the id attribute seems identical to the name attribute, and for some types of controls, it is. However, as we'll see later, some controls can share the same name, and it's in these cases that the id is used to distinguish between controls on the page.

The id attribute is referred to by the label element's for attribute. It can be used for several purposes; you've already seen it used in this book to aid the styling of layouts created with CSS. However, in this example, its purpose is to give the label a referral point.

---

[11] http://reference.sitepoint.com/html/input/name/
[12] http://reference.sitepoint.com/html/core-attributes/id/

You might want to also add a couple of optional attributes to a text input:

size[13]

> tells the browser how many characters the text box should display (ideally, you should set a width with CSS)

maxlength[14]

> places an upper limit on how many characters the user can enter into the text box

Setting the Value of a Text Box

If you'd like to set the initial value of a text box, you can use the `value` attribute to do so. Load the following markup into a form, and a text box with the value "Bob" (without the quotation marks, of course) will be displayed:

```
<p>
  <label for="yourname">Enter your name:</label>
  <input type="text" name="yourname" id="yourname" value="Bob"/>
</p>
```

Password Input

The **password input** control is almost identical to the text input control, with one notable exception: the characters typed into the control aren't displayed on the screen. Instead, they're replaced by asterisks or dots, as shown in Figure 7.6:

```
<p>
  <label for="password">Your password:</label>
  <input type="password" id="password" name="password"/>
</p>
```

Figure 7.6. A password input control displays entered characters as asterisks

---

[13] http://reference.sitepoint.com/html/input/size/
[14] http://reference.sitepoint.com/html/input/maxlength/

A Password INPUT Does Not Make a Secure Form

Although the password input control stops potential scammers from identifying a user's password as they're typing it in, it stops short of making the form any more secure during the actual data submission. For that, you need to consider security more seriously. To ensure that form data is sent securely, you must use a protocol called HTTPS. You may be unaware of this, but HTTPS is used when you fill in a form on an ecommerce website such as Amazon or eBay—it's this that causes the little padlock icon to display in the status or address bar on your browser.

Hidden Inputs

As the name suggests, a **hidden** input doesn't appear in the page at all. Hidden fields are typically used to send additional data to the form processor; these have been input by the creator of the form (or through an automated application), rather than by the user. An automated application can insert the time and date into a hidden field (rather than ask the user what the current time is), but tricky scripting like this is beyond the scope of this book.

Later in the chapter, we'll use hidden fields to identify ourselves to a third-party form processor. For now, all you need to understand is that the following markup won't cause anything to appear on the screen:

```
<input type="hidden" name="peekaboo" value="hereiam"/>
```

However, it will be passed to the form processor (along with all the other data in-putted) when the user submits the form:

```
file:///C:/Documents%20and%20Settings/Bob%20Dobalina/My%20Document
s/Web/hidden.html?peekaboo=hereiam
```

Checkboxes

Checkboxes are an excellent tool for gathering answers to *yes* or *no* questions. A text input is completely free and open, but with a checkbox, the user has a direct choice of yes or no, as the example in Figure 7.7 demonstrates.

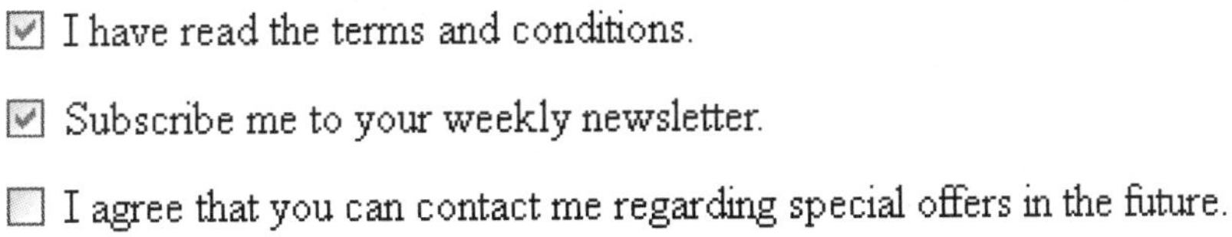

☑ I have read the terms and conditions.

☑ Subscribe me to your weekly newsletter.

☐ I agree that you can contact me regarding special offers in the future.

Figure 7.7. Using checkboxes in a form

Here's how you can achieve that effect in HTML:

```
<p>
  <input type="checkbox" name="terms" id="terms"/>
  <label for="terms">I have read the terms and conditions.</label>
</p>
<p>
  <input type="checkbox" name="newsletter" id="newsletter"/>
  <label for="newsletter">Subscribe me to your weekly newsletter.
    </label>
</p>
<p>
  <input type="checkbox" name="offers" id="offers"/>
  <label for="offers">I agree that you can contact me regarding
    special offers in the future.</label>
</p>
```

Preselecting Checkboxes

Often, when you're working with checkboxes, you might want them to be already checked (or selected) when the page loads; the onus is then on users to uncheck them as they see fit. To achieve this, we use the checked attribute. Oddly enough, the value you need to use for checked is checked (rather than checked="yes" or checked="true"):

```
<p>
  <input type="checkbox" name="terms" id="terms"/>
  <label for="terms">I have read the terms and conditions</label>
</p>
<p>
  <input type="checkbox" name="newsletter" id="newsletter"/>
  <label for="newsletter">Subscribe me to your weekly newsletter.
    </label>
</p>
<p>
```

```
  <input type="checkbox" name="offers" id="offers"
      checked="checked"/>
  <label for="offers">I agree that you can contact me regarding
      special offers in the future</label>
</p>
```

Radio Buttons

Checkboxes are handy when you require the respondent to tick more than one option. But what would you do if you wanted the user to select only one option? For this scenario, we use **radio buttons**, as shown in Figure 7.8.

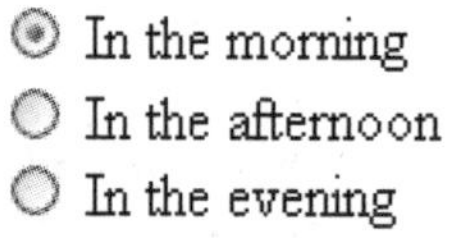

⦿ In the morning
○ In the afternoon
○ In the evening

Figure 7.8. Radio buttons as they may appear in a form

This code creates the radio buttons:

```
<p>
  <input type="radio" name="timeslot" id="morning"
      value="morning"/>
  <label for="morning">In the morning</label>
  <br/>
  <input type="radio" name="timeslot" id="afternoon"
      value="afternoon"/>
  <label for="afternoon">In the afternoon</label>
  <br/>
  <input type="radio" name="timeslot" id="evening"
      value="evening"/>
  <label for="evening ">In the evening</label>
</p>
```

The key difference between this and the checkbox example is that, in this case, we have three different options, *yet the* name *attribute is the same for all three inputs.* This is essential: it's having the same value in the name attribute that binds the three inputs together. They share the same name, but each input has a different value attribute. As a user selects an option and submits the form, the appropriate value is sent to the server.

It's also worth pointing out that each input has a different id. In fact, *any* id that's assigned to an element in the document *must* be unique, whether it's a form element, an image, or another HTML element. In this case, it also benefits the label elements, which must refer to unique identifiers.

"What have these so-called *buttons* got to do with radios anyway?"

Earlier radios featured push-buttons that listeners would use to select a station. You could only press one button in at a time, and when you did, the previously selected button would pop up again. This is where the radio button name originates. Younger readers will just have to take my word on the subject!

Preselecting Radio Buttons

The technique we use to preselect a given radio button is exactly the same as that used for checkboxes:

```
<p>
  <input type="radio" name="timeslot" id="morning" value="morning"
    checked="checked"/>
  <label for="morning">In the morning</label>
  <br/>
  <input type="radio" name="timeslot" id="afternoon"
    value="afternoon"/>
  <label for="afternoon">In the afternoon</label>
  <br/>
  <input type="radio" name="timeslot" id="evening"
    value="evening"/>
  <label for="evening ">In the evening</label>
</p>
```

The select Element

Radio buttons allow you to choose only one item from a range of options, which is useful ... up to a point. But what would happen if you had 20 or more options? Do you really want to display them all on the screen when only one will be selected? Probably not. A better option is to use the select[15] element. This control lets users choose from a range of items, but takes up less space on your web page; initially taking up a single line, users view the options by clicking on the drop-down arrow

---

[15] http://reference.sitepoint.com/html/select/

(using a mouse or keyboard). You've probably used this form control countless times, illustrated in Figure 7.9.

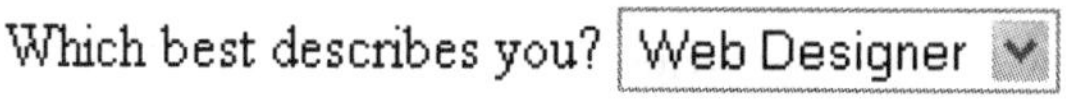

Which best describes you? | Web Designer ▾ |

Figure 7.9. The `select` element produces a drop-down list control for forms

The `select` element contains an array of `option` elements. Each `option` correlates to an option in the drop-down list. Here's the HTML for this type of form control:

```
<p>
  <label for="role">Which best describes you?</label>
  <select name="role" id="role">
    <option>Secretary</option>
    <option>Web Designer</option>
    <option>Manager</option>
    <option>Cleaner</option>
    <option>Other</option>
  </select>
</p>
```

Preselecting Options

Like checkboxes and radio buttons, it's possible to preselect one of the options in a drop-down menu. To do so, we need to use a `selected` attribute with a value of `selected`.

Here's the `select` element once again, this time with the "Web Designer" option preselected:

```
<p>
  <label for="role">Which best describes you?</label>
  <select name="role" id="role">
    <option>Secretary</option>
    <option selected="selected">Web Designer</option>
    <option>Manager</option>
    <option>Cleaner</option>
    <option>Other</option>
  </select>
</p>
```

Making Multiple Selections

It's actually possible to create a list that allows several items to be selected at the same time, but this technique is frowned upon by most usability experts. This is because it requires the user to hold down the **Ctrl** key and click on the items required—it's not exactly obvious, and awkward if the user is only using a keyboard, let alone has to scroll as well. In many cases, checkboxes are the better option over multiple `select` lists.

The `textarea` Element

A text input control is good for capturing short pieces of information, but ineffective for longer amounts of text. As the viewable area can only show minimal text, you've probably experienced these limitations firsthand when inputting chunks of text into a search engine, and the words start to disappear from view. The better choice for larger amounts of text is the `textarea`[16] element, shown in Figure 7.10.

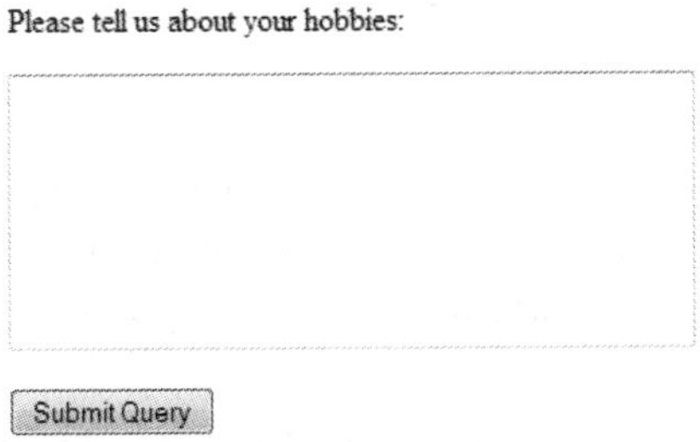

Please tell us about your hobbies:

Submit Query

Figure 7.10. Using a `textarea` element for collecting chunks of text

Here's some code that displays a `textarea`:

```
<p><label for="hobbies">Please tell us about your
    hobbies:</label></p>
<p><textarea name="hobbies" rows="7" cols="40"
    id="hobbies"></textarea></p>
```

---

[16] http://reference.sitepoint.com/html/textarea/

Submit Buttons

Users must click on the submit button to send the data they've entered into the form. Strangely, it's also a type of `input` element, even though it's impossible to put anything *into* it at all! All you can do is activate the button by clicking on it.

Although submit buttons use an `input` tag, I left this one until last—rather than grouping it with the text box, password, radio button, and checkbox controls. This is simply because the submit button will almost always be the last element in your form.

Inserting a submit button is easy. The code below produces the display shown in Figure 7.11:

```
<p><input type="submit"/></p>
```

Submit Query

Figure 7.11. The humble submit button

The wording on this button is a little bland, because we're yet to set a `value` attribute, so the browser uses its default. Adding in a `value` helps to make the button a little more friendly and intuitive, as Figure 7.12 illustrates:

```
<p><input type="submit" value="Send Your Feedback"/></p>
```

Send Your Feedback

Figure 7.12. A more friendly button

 No Mouse Required!

The most common way to submit a form is to use a mouse, but it's not the only way. Instead of clicking on the button, it's possible to fill in the form data, and then hit **Enter**.

The Default Control Appearance

It's worth noting that forms can vary in their appearance when displayed on different browsers and operating systems. Throughout this book, I have used Firefox for Windows for most screenshots, but it's vital that you're aware of how users of other systems will see your forms. Imagine that we combined each type of form element into one form; let's see how it looks across the browsers on offer.

Figure 7.13 shows a form displayed in Firefox on Windows.

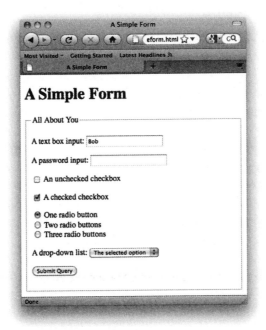

Figure 7.13. Firefox for Windows displays our combined form elements

This is similar to Internet Explorer. Subtle differences include a `fieldset` with rounded border corners and a slightly larger submit button. Figure 7.14 shows IE9 on Windows 7; however, it's worth mentioning that there's a variation between IE6, IE7, and IE8.

Firefox on Mac OS X resembles its Windows cousin, but inherits a bit more of a Mac OS X flavor. The selected checkboxes and radio buttons are blue, as Figure 7.15 illustrates.

Figure 7.14. IE9 has subtle differences with rounded corners and a larger submit button

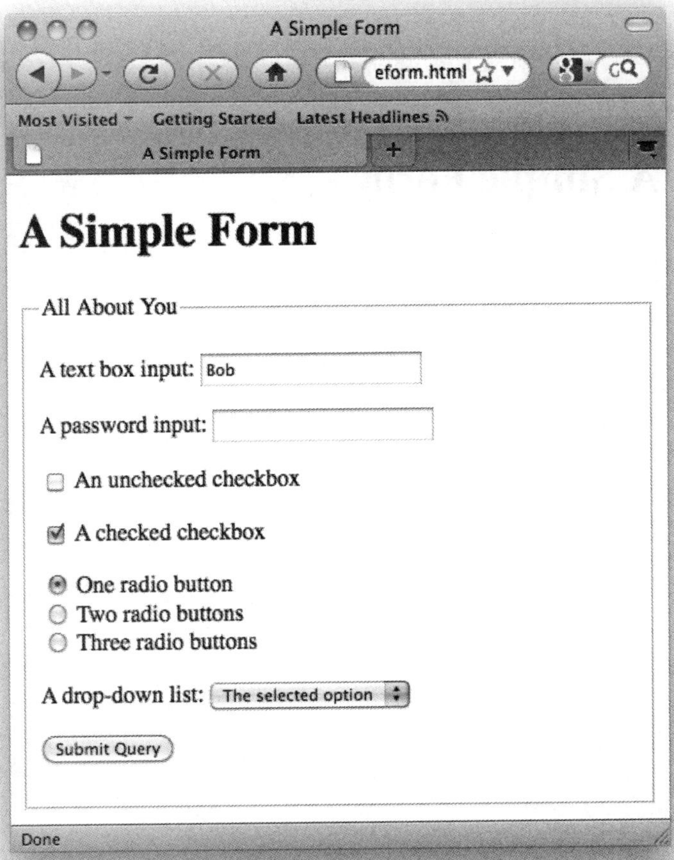

Figure 7.15. Firefox on Mac OS X—naturally with Mac OS X controls

Safari is almost identical to Firefox on Mac OS X. The drop-down has also changed to a Mac OS X-style list, and our submit button has nicely rounded ends, as shown in Figure 7.16.

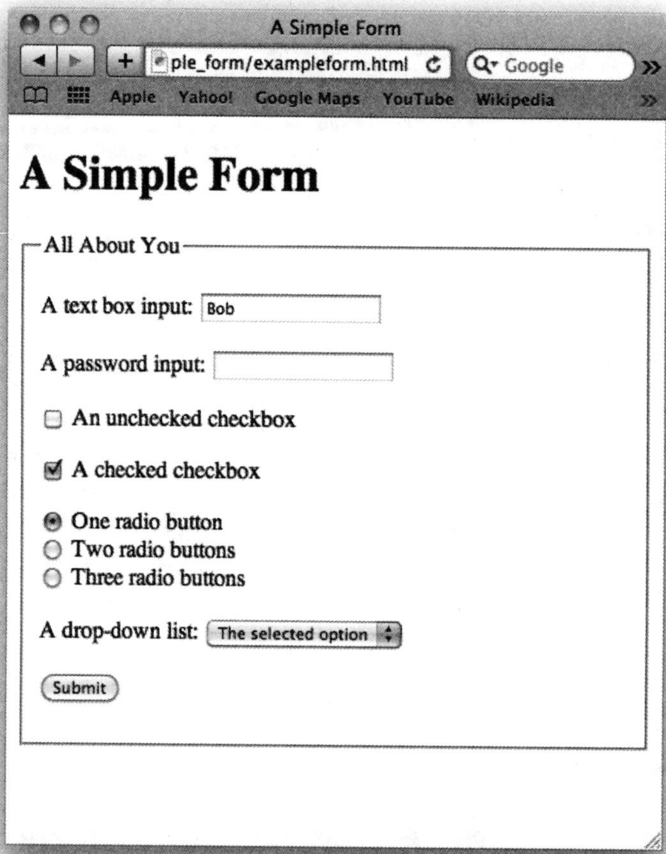

Figure 7.16. Safari is almost identical to Firefox on Mac OS X

As you can see, there's a subtle degree of variation in how the browsers display the controls. While we can customize the appearance of many of these with CSS, the appearance of radio buttons, checkboxes, and drop-down lists is largely determined by the user's operating system. This is one aspect of CSS that we need not be too precious about—forms are notoriously difficult to style identically across browsers, but that's okay too. *Vive la difference*, and all that.

Building a Contact Page

Let's apply some of our newfound knowledge by adding a contact form to the project site. In the process, I'll show you again how CSS can spruce up the plain default styling of these HTML elements. This time around, instead of adding new pages to the project site, we'll be expanding on the existing *Contact Us* page.

 Processing the Data: It's Coming!

In the past, a problem I've had with many web design and development books was the lack of explanation on how you might *use* the form data entered by the user. I would merrily build a form, click the submit button, and then ask, "Now what?"

Processing form data is a significant task. It requires programming know-how or, at the very least, web hosting with support resources that can explain to the beginner how to set up form handling. As you're reading an HTML beginners' book, chances are that your programming skills have yet to develop, but don't despair. By the end of the chapter, I will have demonstrated an easy method for receiving the form data submitted by your users. This form-building exercise will *not* be a purely cosmetic affair that leaves you wanting to know more about the black art of handling form data!

Editing the Contact Us Page

1. In your text editor, open **contact.html**.

2. We need to edit the wording in the body of the page. It's useful to have an email address or telephone number on the page, just in case the visitor prefers to contact you via those means. With this in mind, let's replace the page paragraph with the following:

chapter7/website_files/01_new_paragraph/contact.html (excerpt)

```
<p>To let us know about a forthcoming dive event, please use
    the form below.</p>
<p>If you need to get in touch urgently, please call Bob
    Dobalina on 01793 641207. For anything else, please <a
    href="mailto:bob@bubbleunder.com">drop us a line by
    email</a>.</p>
```

Adding a `form` and a `fieldset` Element

Now let us set up the basics for the form, using the `form`, `fieldset`, and `legend` elements.

1. In **contact.html**, add an opening `<form>` tag and a closing `</form>` tag in between the two paragraphs that you just added (previously) to the page.

2. In the opening `<form>` tag, add the following attributes:

   ▨ `action=""` (We'll be filling in the blanks later.)

   ▨ `method="post"` (We're using post because we intend to submit a fair amount of data through this form.)

   ▨ `class="contact"` (We'll use this when it comes to applying styles to our form.)

3. Next, add a `fieldset` and a `legend` element. Remember that the `fieldset` is contained inside the `form` element, and the `legend` immediately follows the opening `fieldset` tag.

4. For the `legend` element, use the phrase "Tell Us About a Dive Event."

Your HTML should look like this:

chapter7/website_files/02_form_and_fieldset/contact.html *(excerpt)*

```
<p>To let us know about a forthcoming dive event, please use the
    form below.</p>
<form action="" method="post" class="contact">
  <fieldset>
    <legend>Tell Us About a Dive Event</legend>
  </fieldset>
</form>
<p>If you need to get in touch urgently, please call Bob Dobalina
    on 01793 641207. For anything else, please <a
    href="mailto:bob@bubbleunder.com">drop us a line by
    email</a>.</p>
```

If so, save **contact.html**, and take a look at it in the browser. It should appear similar to Figure 7.17.

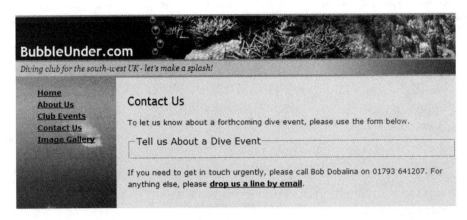

Figure 7.17. An empty form

IE and Empty `fieldsets`

If you're using a version of IE *earlier* than IE8, it's unlikely you'll see the `fieldset` border. In IE7 and previous versions, the `fieldset`'s border won't display if there's nothing (apart from the `legend` element) inside the `fieldset`; other browsers will show the border even when `fieldset` is without content.

If you're using IE7 (or earlier), add some temporary content so that you can see the border. Then, we can start to play around with it:

chapter7/website_files/03_temporary_form_content/contact.html *(excerpt)*

```
<form action="" method="post" class="contact">
  <fieldset>
    <legend>Tell Us About a Dive Event</legend>
    <!-- some temporary content -->
    <p>Form elements go here</p>
  </fieldset>
</form>
```

Figure 7.18 now shows the unstyled `fieldset` border as it appears in IE on Windows Vista.

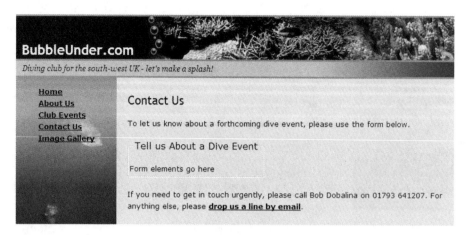

Figure 7.18. An unstyled `fieldset` displayed in IE

Styling `fieldset` and `legend` with CSS

If you wish, you can leave the styling of form controls until later (that is, after you've built the actual form and have all the controls in place). However, I prefer to jump right in there and apply CSS to forms as I go, mainly because I use CSS to set the widths of text boxes and so on, and I like to make sure each part looks right before I move to the next.

While the default appearance of the `fieldset` looks well enough in Figure 7.18, other browsers don't display the curved border that IE provides, which, as a result, can look a little dull. With CSS, though, it's possible to apply some styles that improve the look of our form, as well as standardizing the page's appearance across different browsers. Let's sort out the `fieldset` and `legend` elements in one hit. Open **style1.css** in your text editor and add the following style rules:

```
chapter7/website_files/04_styled_fieldset/style1.css (excerpt)
```

```
form.contact fieldset {
  border: 2px solid navy;
  padding: 10px;
}

form.contact legend {
  font-weight: bold;
  font-size: small;
```

```
    color: navy;
    padding: 5px;
}
```

Save **style1.css**, and take a look at the Contact Us page in your browser. The result should look like Figure 7.19.

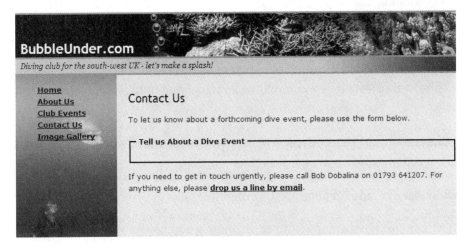

Figure 7.19. The `fieldset` styled in CSS

 class-ified Forms

We're using the `contact` class to style the elements in this form in the same way that we used the `events` class to style our table in Chapter 6. This is in case we decide to add other kinds of forms to the site later on. For example, we may add a search form in the future, and we may wish that form to have a vastly different appearance from this one.

The only problem I can see with this page is that there seems to be a little too much space between the first paragraph and the form. This can be fixed with a negative margin, which we apply to the `form` element like so:

chapter7/website_files/05_contact_name/style1.css *(excerpt)*

```
form.contact {
  padding: 0;
  margin: 0;
```

```
    margin-top: -15px;
    line-height: 150%;
}
```

In the above rule, I've also taken the opportunity to remove any default `padding` or `margin` values that the browser might want to set on the `form` element. Additionally, I've increased the default line height.

Adding Text Input Controls

Now we're going to add a couple of items to the form that will allow us to obtain some information—such as a contact name, telephone number, and so on—from the user.

1. In **contact.html**, add a `div` element just after the `legend`. If you added some temporary content for IE, you should remove it now.

2. Inside that `div`, add an `input` with `type="text"`.

3. Give the `input` element `name` and `id` attributes, both with a value of `contactname`.

4. Place a `label` that reads "Contact Name" before the `input`. Remember to add the `for` attribute, giving it a value that matches up with the `id` attribute of the `input` element.

5. Save the web page, and take a look at it in your browser.

How does it look? Does it resemble a text input? If not, check your HTML to see if it's right:

chapter7/website_files/05_contact_name/contact.html (excerpt)

```
<form action="" method="post" class="contact">
  <fieldset>
    <legend>Tell Us About a Dive Event</legend>
    <div>
      <label for="contactname">Contact Name</label>
      <input type="text" name="contactname" id="contactname"/>
    </div>
  </fieldset>
</form>
```

The div element will keep those items together and cause line breaks to appear before and after them; we'll use this approach on all the form elements on this page.

\<div\> or \<p\> elements to lay out your form?

I'm sure some people are passionate on this matter, but in the quest for semantic purity, there are arguments for either case. Some developers even like using lists to mark up their forms (considering each part of the form to be an item in a list of things to do). Use whatever works for you. Sometimes it makes sense to inherit the styles from a p like font color, or margin; at other times, it will be preferable to start with the blank canvas that a div offers.

We'll be using \<div\>s on the Bubble Under website.

Next, I'm going to address the styling of the text that sits inside the label element. With these minor tweaks, Figure 7.20 shows our progress so far:

chapter7/website_files/05_contact_name/style1.css *(excerpt)*

```css
form.contact label {
  font-weight: bold;
  font-size: small;
  color: blue;
}
```

Figure 7.20. Adding a contact name text input control to the form

Okay, let's add a bunch of other text input controls in one fell swoop. Here's the HTML you need, with new parts shown in bold:

chapter7/website_files/06_other_controls/contact.html *(excerpt)*

```html
<form action="" method="post" class="contact">
  <fieldset>
    <legend>Tell us About a Dive Event</legend>
    <div>
      <label for="contactname">Contact Name</label>
      <input type="text" name="contactname" id="contactname"/>
    </div>
    <div>
      <label for="telephone">Telephone Number</label>
      <input type="text" name="telephone" id="telephone"/>
    </div>
    <div>
      <label for="email">Email Address</label>
      <input type="text" name="email" id="email"/>
    </div>
    <div>
      <label for="eventname">What's the event called?</label>
      <input type="text" name="eventname" id="eventname"/>
    </div>
    <div>
      <label for="eventdate">When's the event happening?</label>
      <input type="text" name="eventdate" id="eventdate"/>
    </div>
  </fieldset>
</form>
```

Figure 7.21 shows how it looks.

Figure 7.21. Building up the form with several text inputs

Tidying Up `label` Elements with CSS

That form might work well, but the misalignment of the text input controls is a little ugly. Thankfully, you can correct this issue using CSS. Rather than apply the style to *all* label elements inside the form, we'll add a `class` attribute to all the `label` elements, so that we can style only the current `label`s. (We'll need to add some different style rules to other `label`s later on.) Add the following code to **style1.css**, just after the previous `label` selector:

chapter7/website_files/07_aligned_inputs/style1.css (excerpt)

```
form.contact label.fixedwidth {
  display: block;
  width: 240px;
  float: left;
}
```

Next, add the `class` attribute to the `label`s that you have in **contact.html**. Your HTML should now look like this:

chapter7/website_files/07_aligned_inputs/contact.html *(excerpt)*

```html
<form action="" method="post" class="contact">
  <fieldset>
    <legend>Tell us About a Dive Event</legend>
    <div>
      <label for="contactname" class="fixedwidth">Contact
        Name</label>
      <input type="text" name="contactname" id="contactname"/>
    </div>
    <div>
      <label for="telephone" class="fixedwidth">Telephone
        Number</label>
      <input type="text" name="telephone" id="telephone"/>
    </div>
    <div>
      <label for="email" class="fixedwidth">Email Address</label>
      <input type="text" name="email" id="email"/>
    </div>
    <div>
      <label for="eventname" class="fixedwidth">What's the event
        called?</label>
      <input type="text" name="eventname" id="eventname"/>
    </div>
    <div>
      <label for="eventdate" class="fixedwidth">When's the event
        happening?</label>
      <input type="text" name="eventdate" id="eventdate"/>
    </div>
  </fieldset>
</form>
```

Refresh the page of your browser, and it should look like Figure 7.22.

Figure 7.22. A more orderly look for our labels

What just happened there?

Sorry, I glossed over that CSS a bit! What we just did was a little clever (even if I do say so myself, ahem)—veering into *advanced* CSS territory. Essentially, the declarations we used told the browser to display the following:

display: block

This declaration converts an inline element (such as a `label` element) into a block-level element. Once it's treated as a block-level element, we can start doing a little more to it; for instance, setting a `width`.

width: 240px

Ah, there we go! By setting the `width`, we've reserved a certain amount of space for the `label` text. Nothing's going to encroach upon that; however, normally a break appears before and after a block-level element.

float: left

Remember this? We used it on the home page to move the feature image over to the right. In this case, we'll use it to place the `label` on the left; the content that immediately follows (the form input field) aligns to the right of it, in much the same way text in a newspaper wraps around photos in the page layout. Without this declaration, the text input control would appear beneath the `label` text.

Adding a `select` Element

Now, let's add a `select` element. Where could we use this on our page? We could make a control to specify the region of the country in which the diving event or trip will take place:

1. Add another `div` at the end of your `form` in `contact.html`.

2. Insert a `select` element into the `div` element you just added.

3. Give the `select` element `id` and `name` attributes with the value `region`.

4. Add a `label` that has some appropriate text.

5. Add an `option` element inside the `select` element for each region following:

   - South-west

   - South-east

   - Midlands

   - Central

   - London

   - East

   - North

   - Scotland

   - Northern Ireland

   - Wales

   - International (see details below)

Your HTML should now look like this:

chapter7/website_files/08_region_dropdown/contact.html *(excerpt)*

```
<div>
  <label for="region" class="fixedwidth">What region is the event
    in?</label>
  <select name="region" id="region">
    <option>South-west</option>
    <option>South-east</option>
    <option>Midlands</option>
    <option>Central</option>
    <option>London</option>
    <option>East</option>
    <option>North</option>
    <option>Scotland</option>
    <option>Northern Ireland</option>
    <option>Wales</option>
    <option>International (see details below)</option>
  </select>
</div>
```

And, of course, Figure 7.23 shows the obligatory screenshot.

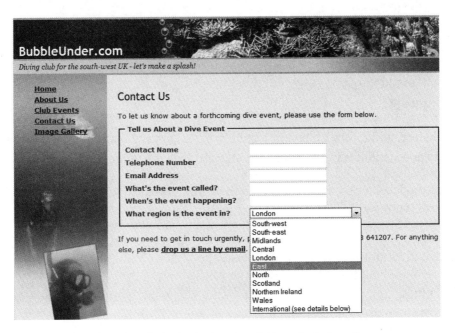

Figure 7.23. Activating the drop-down list (or `select` element)

Adding a `textarea` Element

We have the basics. Now it's time to let the users go a bit wild! Let's move beyond the noticeably restrictive inputs we've created so far. The `textarea` will let users enter as much text as they like, so we'll need to create extra space for this element.

Because a `textarea` is an "anything goes" kind of input, you might like to insert some guideline text before it. This is just to let people know what they should enter, such as:

> "Please provide any other details you think will be useful to us in the text area below (it may save us calling or emailing you, and help to avoid delays)."

Now, let's add a `textarea` to the form:

1. In **contact.html**, add an opening `<textarea>` tag and a closing `</textarea>` tag. Be sure to leave *no space between them*, as any spaces or carriage returns in the source code will appear inside the `textarea`, which can be annoying.

2. Add the following attributes with the values indicated:
   - `id="details"`
   - `name="details"`
   - `cols="30"`
   - `rows="7"`

3. As before, add a `label` element just before the `textarea`. Tie that in with the `id` and `name` attributes in the `textarea` element (use the value `details`).

4. Give the label a `class` attribute with the value `fixedwidth`.

5. Save your work, and take a look at the web page in your browser.

The HTML for this text area is as follows:

chapter7/website_files/09_text_area/contact.html *(excerpt)*

```
<div>
  <p>Please provide any other details you think will be useful to
     us in the text area below (it may save us calling or
     emailing you, and help avoid delays).</p>
```

```
<label for="details" class="fixedwidth">More details (as much as
    you think we'll need!)</label>
<textarea id="details" name="details" cols="30"
    rows="7"></textarea>
</div>
```

Figure 7.24 shows the intended result.

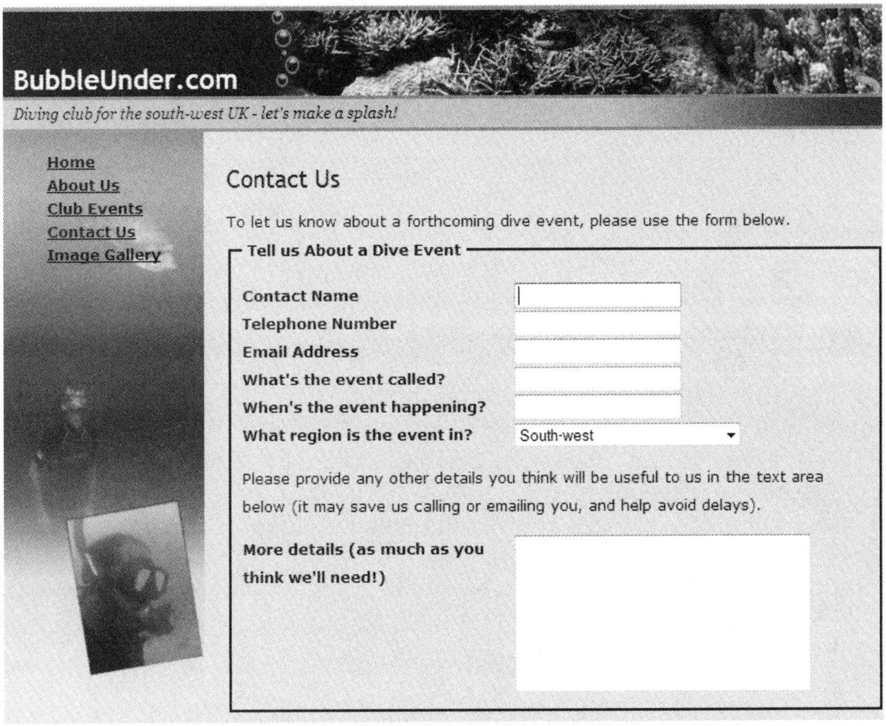

Figure 7.24. The `textarea` with room to type

Our form's nearly complete. Truth be known, it's probably detailed enough in its current state, but it's better to see a working example of *all* the input controls that you're likely to want to use. So let's fast-track through the last task: adding checkboxes and radio buttons.

Adding Radio Buttons and Checkboxes

As you know, we use radio buttons to allow users to choose one option from a group of options. With checkboxes, each option is independent of the others, so, if you have ten checkboxes, your users may check:

- all of them
- none of them
- any number of them

We'll utilize radio buttons so that users can choose a convenient time for a callback (just in case the information they supplied in the form is unclear). A checkbox will be employed for the user to confirm whether the information entered in the form can be shared—a very common use of checkboxes.

As I mentioned, we're going to speed through this section. Here's the HTML you need to add for the radio buttons:

chapter7/website_files/10_radios_and_checkboxes/contact.html *(excerpt)*

```
<div>
  <p>If we need to call you back for any more info, what would be
     the best time to call you on the number supplied?</p>
  <input type="radio" name="timetocall" id="morning"
     value="Morning" />
  <label for="morning">In the morning</label>
  <br/>
  <input type="radio" name="timetocall" id="afternoon"
     value="Afternoon" />
  <label for="afternoon">In the afternoon</label>
  <br/>
  <input type="radio" name="timetocall" id="evening"
     value="Evening" />
  <label for="evening">In the evening</label>
  <br/>
  <input type="radio" name="timetocall" id="never" value="Never"
     checked="checked" />
  <label for="never">No calls please</label>
</div>
```

Here's the final part of the code, which deals with the checkbox:

chapter7/website_files/10_radios_and_checkboxes/contact.html *(excerpt)*

```
<div>
  <p>Bubble Under may share information you give us here with
     other like-minded people or websites to promote the event.
     Please confirm if you are happy for us to do this.</p>
  <input type="checkbox" name="publicize" id="publicize"
```

```
        checked="checked"/>
    <label for="publicize">I am happy for this event to be
        publicized outside of and beyond BubbleUnder.com, where
        possible</label>
</div>
```

Figure 7.25 reveals how the form displays in Firefox.

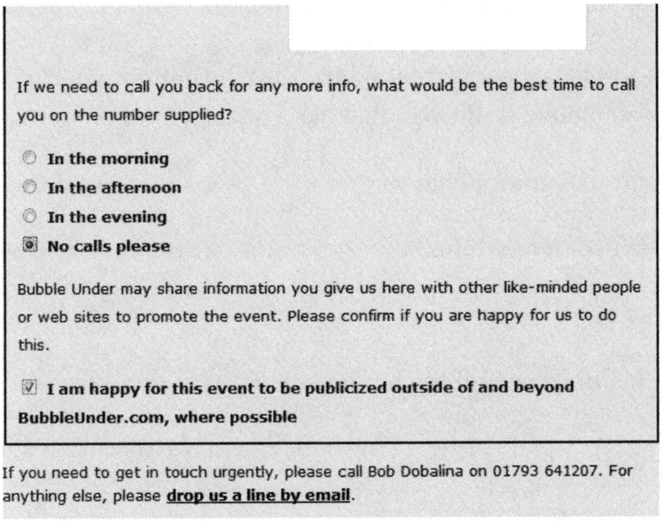

Figure 7.25. Radio buttons and checkboxes in the form

Now, go type all that in! Seriously, though, there's only one aspect here that you've yet to see: when you use a checkbox or a radio button, the control comes *before* the text that's associated with it. This is common practice with forms for the purpose of accessibility, so please don't break the convention by putting your text first, before the form control—no matter how much you might be tempted. You'll see that we have deliberately omitted the `fixedwidth class` on the labels we want to appear after the `input` elements, as we want to avoid them floating or displaying as a block.[17]

Completing the Form: a Submit Button

This really is the last step, and it will take but a moment. Add the following markup before the closing `</fieldset>` tag:

---

[17] Read more at http://webstandards.org/learn/tutorials/accessible-forms/01-accessible-forms.html on how the order of a control's text affects form accessibility.

```
<div class="buttonarea">
  <input type="submit" value="Send Us the Info"/>
</div>
```

I've added a `class` attribute to the `div` element that contains the submit button, and I've given it the appropriate value: `buttonarea`. I've done this because I want to be able to style the button area (the button and its containing `div`) in CSS, to make it stand out from the page a bit.

1. In **style1.css**, add a new contextual selector for the button. We want it to affect an `input` that's contained in the `div` that has a `class` of `buttonarea`.

2. Set the background color to navy.

3. Adjust the text color to white.

4. Make the font bold.

5. Add a little padding around the button—five pixels should do it.

6. Finally, add a one-pixel border on the button to make the border solid and white.

The CSS for these steps is shown here:

chapter7/website_files/11_submit_button/style1.css (excerpt)

```
form.contact .buttonarea input {
  background: navy;
  color: white;
  font-weight: bold;
  padding: 5px;
  border: 1px solid white;
}
```

Check the effect of this markup by saving **style1.css**, and refreshing the view in your browser. Are you looking at a blue button instead of a gray one? If it's gray, are you using an older version of Safari? Remember, some browsers don't support styling of all form controls. IE, Firefox, Chrome, and Opera should render the colors as specified, though.

Our button looks a little lost, I think. I like to create a special area for buttons like this. After all, they're special. They're the final part of the form. Besides, a special area helps to draw attention to them—that they're there to be clicked. Let's add a class selector for the button area:

```
form.contact .buttonarea {
  text-align: center;
  padding: 4px;
  background-color: #0066ff;
}
```

The button now sits in the middle of an eye-catching blue strip, rather than displaying at the bottom of the form all alone. Figure 7.26 shows the final product; our form from start to finish.

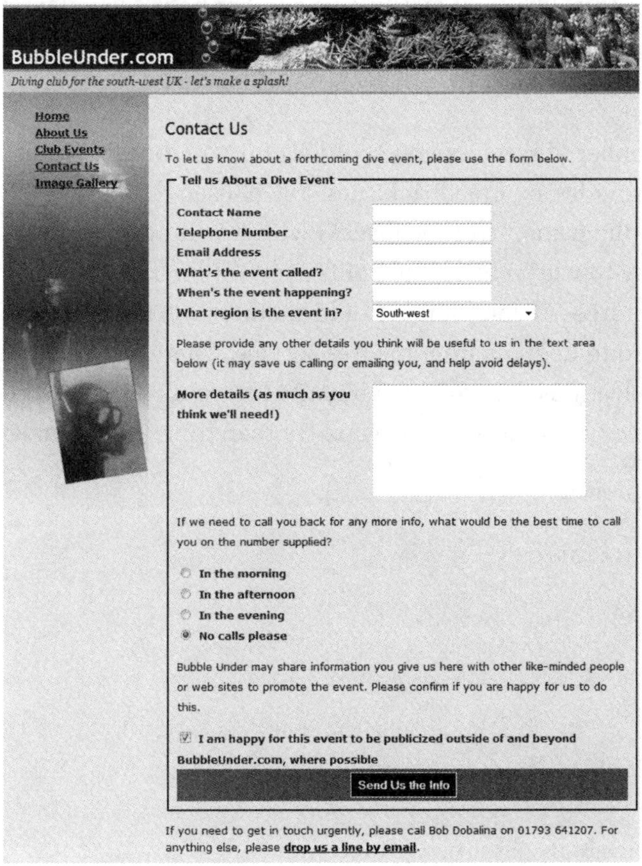

Figure 7.26. Highlighting the submit button with CSS styling

So far, you've learned what different form elements are used for, and which types of controls are suitable for particular purposes. Together, we've stepped through the process of building a form, and we've styled it with CSS along the way. But, what now? Where's this data going?

For the last part of the chapter, I'll walk you through the steps involved in signing up for a free form-processing service that will handle your data for you.

Processing the Form

As I said earlier, handling form data is a skill that requires programming. I'm unable to teach you how to program in PHP, Perl, or some other server-side language that can manipulate this data, as it would take another book to explain it. Fortunately, others have acknowledged the need for a simple form-processing service that costs little, or is free.

There are a number of services you could sign up for, but I'm going to walk you through one provided by Freedback.com. I've chosen this one as it offers a free service (hence the name, "free feedback") with few limitations and, at the time of writing, an easy-to-use website that guides you through the process. You may only use one form for free—if you wanted to add another form later for a different purpose, you would need to upgrade from the free service. There are numerous services out there, so if the features they offer are unsuited to your needs, your best bet is to head to your search engine of choice and try searching "free form email service," or similar.

Signing Up for Form Processing

The steps below explain the process of setting up a form for our project site. Naturally, you'll provide your own sign-on details for your site.

Head on over to the Freedback website[18] and register an account—it takes just a few moments. Now click the *Create a Free Form Now* button, seen in Figure 7.27. You'll need to provide a valid email address to verify the new account.

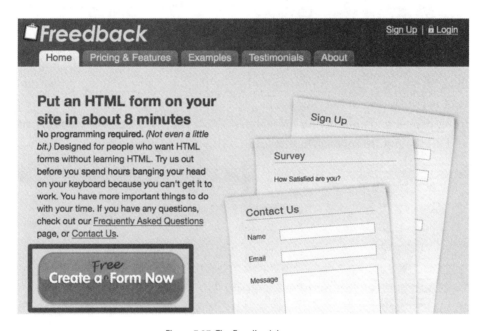

Figure 7.27. The Freedback home page

Once you've dealt with that, you'll be logged in to the service, where you can start to build your form. The system should take you straight there; otherwise, click on the **New Form** link. (If you start building a form, leave it unfinished, and then return to the site, you should have a form showing at the bottom of the screen, as marked in Figure 7.28. In that case, select the **Questions** button—to edit the existing form questions—and continue.)

---

[18] http://www.freedback.com/

Figure 7.28. The Freedback interface for creating a form

The service automatically sets up a name and email address field, marking them both as "required." Then simply add other fields (for example, telephone number, date of event, and so on), as shown in Figure 7.29. If you make a mistake, you can reorder, delete, and amend any fields later. Work your way through, making sure to add all the fields required in our form.

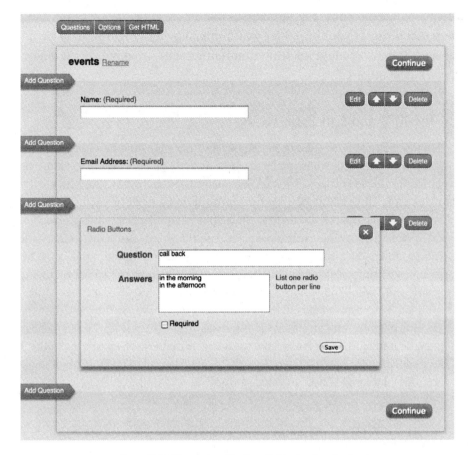

Figure 7.29. It's easy to add a form field using Freedback

After adding the form fields, there will be further options to complete. Choose the option to show Freedback's *Thank you* page. Alternatively, you can send the user to your own customized "Thank you" page, which can be done at a later stage if you prefer. You will also need to select the option to **Email a copy of each form submission to you**, as shown in Figure 7.30—otherwise there's little point to this service!

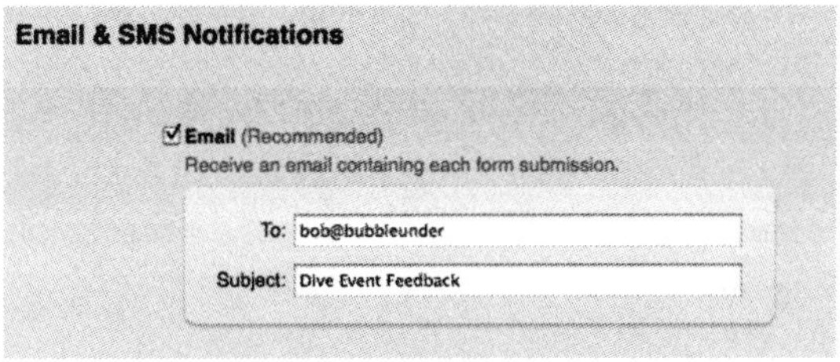

Figure 7.30. Directing the form your way

Once you've worked your way through all the fields, Freedback will present the markup that it *thinks* you'll need for your form, shown in Figure 7.31. I say *thinks*, because we'll have to adapt it a little to suit our needs—making sure it meets our high markup standards!

The X, Y, and Z of Form Fields

Another point to note—and I can't emphasize this enough, otherwise you'll be scratching your head when it fails to work—is that in all my examples below, the values for the `acctid` and `formid` fields have been set to XXXXXXXXXXX, YYYYYYY, ZZZZZZZZZZZ, and so on. What do these mean? Actually, they mean nothing! They're just there to draw attention to the fact that, once you've set up your own account with Freedback, you'll need to ensure that you use the values provided for you by Freedback—these are just examples in this book. In previous editions of this book, the values I used were from my own form that I set up, and I would often have feedback forms sent directly to me. Meanwhile, the budding web developer out there is checking the markup in the book, thinking, "I know this is right! I've entered it exactly as stated. Why is my form data not being sent to me?!" And the reason, of course, is that Freedback was tying the account and form identification up to my personal account and mailing it to me. So please, be sure to check the values over.

Figure 7.31. The form HTML that Freedback provides

In the figure, you'll notice that below the HTML that you should copy is a warning not to edit it. Guess what? We're going to ignore that warning! There are a few reasons why: it has produced the markup in a `table` layout (bad), it's missing `label` elements (also bad), and it commits the most heinous crime of using `<font>` tags! Rather than attempting to kick the Freedback markup into shape, we'll simply take what we need from it and apply it to the form that we built earlier in this chapter.

Inserting the Form Code

Freedback provides the following complete markup (note that I've removed some spacing and indents to save space here). We'll have to pluck out the parts that we'll copy and then paste into our own form. The parts you need are marked in bold:

Freedback-generated markup (excerpt)

```
<!-- Begin Freedback Form -->
<!-- DO NOT EDIT YOUR FORM HERE, PLEASE LOG IN AND
  EDIT AT FREEDBACK.COM -->
<form enctype="multipart/form-data" method="post"
  action="http://www.freedback.com/mail.php" accept-charset="UTF-8">
<div>
<input type="hidden" name="acctid" id="acctid"
  value="XXXXXXXXXXXX" />
<input type="hidden" name="formid" id="formid" value="YYYYYYY" />
<input type="hidden" name="required_vars" id="required_vars"
  value="name,email,field-ZZZZZZZZZZZZ" />
</div>
<table cellspacing="5" cellpadding="5" border="0">
<tr>
<td valign="top">
<strong>Contact Name</strong>
</td>
<td valign="top">
<input type="text" name="name" id="name" size="40" value="" />
</td>
</tr>
<tr>
<td valign="top">
<strong>Telephone Number</strong>
</td>
<td valign="top">
<input type="text" name="field-ZZZZZZZZZZZZ"
  id="field-ZZZZZZZZZZZZ" size="40" value="" />
```

```
</td>
</tr>
<tr>
<td valign="top">
<strong>Email Address</strong>
</td>
<td valign="top">
<input type="text" name="email" id="email" size="40" value=""/>
</td>
</tr>
<tr>
<td valign="top">
<strong>What&#39;s the event called?</strong>
</td>
<td valign="top">
<input type="text" name="field-ZZZZZZZZZZZZZ"
  id="field-ZZZZZZZZZZZZZ" size="40" value=""/>
</td>
</tr>
<tr>
<td valign="top">
<strong>When&#39;s the event happening?</strong>
</td>
<td valign="top">
<input type="text" name="field-ZZZZZZZZZZZZZ"
  id="field-ZZZZZZZZZZZZZ" size="40" value=""/>
</td>
</tr>
<tr>
<td valign="top">
<strong>What region is the event in?</strong>
</td>
<td valign="top">
<select name="field-ZZZZZZZZZZZZZ"
  id="field-ZZZZZZZZZZZZZ">
  <option value="South-west">South-west</option>
  <option value="South-east">South-east</option>
  <option value="Midlands">Midlands</option>
  <option value="Central">Central</option>
  <option value="London">London</option>
  <option value="East">East</option>
  <option value="North">North</option>
  <option value="Scotland">Scotland</option>
  <option value="Northern Ireland">Northern Ireland</option>
  <option value="International (see details below)">International
```

```
    (see details below)</option>
</select>
</td>
</tr>
<tr>
<td valign="top">
<strong>More details (as much as you think
  we&#39;ll need)</strong>
</td>
<td valign="top">
<textarea name="field-ZZZZZZZZZZZZZ"
  id="field-ZZZZZZZZZZZZZ" rows="6" cols="40"></textarea>
</td>
</tr>
<tr>
<td valign="top">
<strong>If we need to call you back for any more info,
  what would be the best time to call you on the number supplied?
</strong>
</td>
<td valign="top">
<input type="radio" name="field-ZZZZZZZZZZZZZ"
  id="field-ZZZZZZZZZZZZZ" value="In the morning"/>
  In the morning<br/>
<input type="radio" name="field-ZZZZZZZZZZZZZ"
  id="field-ZZZZZZZZZZZZZ" value="In the afternoon"/>
  In the afternoon<br/>
<input type="radio" name="field-ZZZZZZZZZZZZZ"
  id="field-ZZZZZZZZZZZZZ" value="In the evening"/>
  In the evening<br/>
<input type="radio" name="field-ZZZZZZZZZZZZZ"
  id="field-ZZZZZZZZZZZZZ" value="No calls please"/>
  No calls please<br/>
</td>
</tr>
<tr>
<td valign="top">
<strong>Bubble Under may share information you give us here
  with other like-minded people or websites to promote the event.
  Please confirm if you are happy for us to do this.</strong>
</td>
<td valign="top">
<input type="checkbox" name="field-ZZZZZZZZZZZZZ"
  id="field-ZZZZZZZZZZZZZ" value="I am happy for this event to
  be publicised outside of and beyond BubbleUnder.com where
```

```
  possible"/> I am happy for this event to be publicised outside
  of and beyond BubbleUnder.com where possible<br/>
</td>
</tr>
<tr>
<td colspan="2" align="center">
<input type="submit" value=" Submit Form "/>
</td>
</tr>
</table>
</form>
<br><center><font face="Arial, Helvetica" size="1"><b>
<a href="http://www.freedback.com">create web form</a>
</b></font></center>
<!-- End Freedback Form -->
```

Well, let's get cracking! Open **contact.html** in your text editor.

First take Freedback's opening form tag and paste it over the opening <form> tag in **contact.html**. Take all the hidden inputs just after Freedback's opening <form> tag and paste them inside a div element, just after the opening form tag in **contact.html**. It should look similar to the following markup (although the acctid, formid, and required_vars values will be the unique values that Freedback has assigned for your form. So avoid copying the values below):

contact.html *(excerpt)*

```
<form enctype="multipart/form-data" method="post"
action="http://www.freedback.com/mail.php" accept-charset="UTF-8">
  <div>
    <input type="hidden" name="acctid"
    id="acctid" value="XXXXXXXXXXXX"/>
    <input type="hidden" name="formid" id="formid" value="YYYYYYY"/>
    <input type="hidden" name="required_vars" id="required_vars"
    value="name,email,field-ZZZZZZZZZZZZZ"/>
  </div>
  <fieldset>
  ⋮
```

Now go through each of the form fields—telephone number, best time to call, and so on—taking the parts of the markup to which I previously drew your attention. Copy each of these pieces of information and paste them over the equivalent section on the contact form. There's no need to concern yourself with the text that appears next to each form control; just copy and paste the respective `input`, `select`, and `textarea` elements. Once you've completed all the steps, your contact form should look something like this (again, I say *something* because the `id` attributes' values will be the unique values for your account and form):

contact.html *(excerpt)*

```
<form enctype="multipart/form-data" method="post"
  action="http://www.freedback.com/mail.php" accept-charset="UTF-8">
<div>
<input type="hidden" name="acctid"id="acctid"
  value="XXXXXXXXXXXX"/>
<input type="hidden" name="formid" id="formid" value="YYYYYYY"/>
<input type="hidden" name="required_vars"
  id="required_vars" value="name,email,field-ZZZZZZZZZZZZ"/>
</div>
<fieldset>
<legend>Tell us About a Dive Event</legend>
<div>
<label for="contactname" class="fixedwidth">Contact Name</label>
<input type="text" name="name" id="name" size="40" value=""/>
</div>
<div>
<label for="telephone" class="fixedwidth">Telephone Number</label>
<input type="text" name="field-ZZZZZZZZZZZZ"
  id="field-ZZZZZZZZZZZZ" size="40" value=""/>
</div>
<div>
<label for="email" class="fixedwidth">Email Address</label>
<input type="text" name="email" id="email" size="40" value=""/>
</div>
<div>
<label for="eventname" class="fixedwidth">What's the
  event called?</label>
<input type="text" name="field-ZZZZZZZZZZZZ"
  id="field-ZZZZZZZZZZZZ" size="40" value=""/>
</div>
<div>
<label for="eventdate" class="fixedwidth">When's the event
  happening?</label>
<input type="text" name="field-ZZZZZZZZZZZZ"
  id="field-ZZZZZZZZZZZZ" size="40" value=""/>
</div>
```

```
<div>
<label for="region" class="fixedwidth">What region is
  the event in?</label>
<select name="field-ZZZZZZZZZZZZZ" id="field-ZZZZZZZZZZZZZ">
  <option value="South-west">South-west</option>
  <option value="South-east">South-east</option>
  <option value="Midlands">Midlands</option>
  <option value="Central">Central</option>
  <option value="London">London</option>
  <option value="East">East</option>
  <option value="North">North</option>
  <option value="Scotland">Scotland</option>
  <option value="Northern Ireland">Northern Ireland</option>
  <option value="International (see details below)">International
    (see details below)</option>
</select>
</div>
<div>
<p>Please provide any other details you think will be useful to us
  in the text area below (it may save us calling or emailing you,
  and help avoid delays).</p>
<label for="details" class="fixedwidth">
  More details (as much as you think we'll need!)</label>
<textarea name="field-ZZZZZZZZZZZZZ"
  id="field-ZZZZZZZZZZZZZ" rows="6" cols="40"></textarea>
</div>
<div>
<p>If we need to call you back for any more info, what would be
  the best time to call you on the number supplied?</p>
<input type="radio" name="field-ZZZZZZZZZZZZZ"
  id="field-ZZZZZZZZZZZZZ" value="In the morning"/>
<label for="morning">In the morning</label>
<br/>
<input type="radio" name="field-ZZZZZZZZZZZZZ"
  id="field-ZZZZZZZZZZZZZ" value="In the afternoon"/>
<label for="afternoon">In the afternoon</label>
<br/>
<input type="radio" name="field-ZZZZZZZZZZZZZ"
  id="field-ZZZZZZZZZZZZZ" value="In the evening"/>
<label for="evening">In the evening</label>
<br/>
<input type="radio" name="field-ZZZZZZZZZZZZZ"
  id="field-ZZZZZZZZZZZZZ" value="No calls please"/>
<label for="never">No calls please</label>
</div>
```

```
<div>
<p>Bubble Under may share information you give us here with
  other like-minded people or websites to promote the event.
  Please confirm if you are happy for us to do this.</p>
<input type="checkbox" name="field-ZZZZZZZZZZZZZ"
  id="field-ZZZZZZZZZZZZZ" value="I am happy for this
  event to be publicised outside of and beyond
  BubbleUnder.com where possible"/>
<label for="publicize">I am happy for this event to be
  publicized outside of and
beyond BubbleUnder.com, where possible</label>
</div>
<div class="buttonarea">
<input type="submit" value="Send Us the Info"/>
</div>
</fieldset>
</form>
```

We're almost done, but if you're looking at the markup above and thinking, "There's something wrong with that," then give yourself a well-deserved pat on the back! What's the problem with the previous block of markup? Earlier in the chapter, I pointed out that each form control needs to have an associated `label` element. The `label` element is linked to the related form control with a `for` attribute that matches the form control's `id` attribute. By originating the form on Freedback.com, some unique `id` attributes have been created to manage the form handling, and these are completely different from those we set earlier. There's no working around this, so we'll have to accommodate these values by amending the `for` attribute for each control. In the markup below, I've highlighted the parts that have changed (again, the values will be unique to you, not *exactly* as shown below):

contact.html (excerpt)

```
<form enctype="multipart/form-data" method="post"
  action="http://www.freedback.com/mail.php" accept-charset="UTF-8">
<div>
<input type="hidden" name="acctid"
  id="acctid" value="XXXXXXXXXXXX"/>
<input type="hidden" name="formid"
  id="formid" value="YYYYYYY"/>
<input type="hidden" name="required_vars"
  id="required_vars" value="name,email,field-ZZZZZZZZZZZZZ"/>
</div>
```

```
<fieldset>
<legend>Tell us About a Dive Event</legend>
<div>
<label for="name" class="fixedwidth">Contact Name</label>
<input type="text" name="name" id="name" size="40" value=""/>
</div>
<div>
<label for="field-ZZZZZZZZZZZZ"
  class="fixedwidth">Telephone Number</label>
<input type="text" name="field-ZZZZZZZZZZZZ"
  id="field-ZZZZZZZZZZZZ" size="40" value=""/>
</div>
<div>
<label for="email" class="fixedwidth">Email Address</label>
<input type="text" name="email" id="email" size="40" value=""/>
</div>
<div>
<label for="field-ZZZZZZZZZZZZ"
  class="fixedwidth">What's the event called?</label>
<input type="text" name="field-ZZZZZZZZZZZZ"
  id="field-ZZZZZZZZZZZZ" size="40" value=""/>
</div>
<div>
<label for="field-ZZZZZZZZZZZZ"
  class="fixedwidth">When's the event happening?</label>
<input type="text" name="field-ZZZZZZZZZZZZ"
  id="field-ZZZZZZZZZZZZ" size="40" value=""/>
</div>
<div>
<label for="field-ZZZZZZZZZZZZ"
  class="fixedwidth">What region is the event in?</label>
<select name="field-ZZZZZZZZZZZZ" id="field-ZZZZZZZZZZZZ">
  <option value="South-west">South-west</option>
  <option value="South-east">South-east</option>
  <option value="Midlands">Midlands</option>
  <option value="Central">Central</option>
  <option value="London">London</option>
  <option value="East">East</option>
  <option value="North">North</option>
  <option value="Scotland">Scotland</option>
  <option value="Northern Ireland">Northern Ireland</option>
  <option value="International (see details below)">International
    (see details below)</option>
</select>
</div>
```

```
<div>
<p>Please provide any other details you think will be useful to us
in the text area below (it may save us calling or emailing you,
and help avoid delays).</p>
<label for="field-ZZZZZZZZZZZZ" class="fixedwidth">
  More details (as much as you think we'll need!)</label>
<textarea name="field-ZZZZZZZZZZZZ" id="field-ZZZZZZZZZZZZ"
  rows="6" cols="40"></textarea>
</div>
<div>
<p>If we need to call you back for any more info, what would be the
  best time to call you on the number supplied?</p>
<input type="radio" name="field-ZZZZZZZZZZZZ"
  id="field-ZZZZZZZZZZZZ" value="In the morning"/>
<label for="field-ZZZZZZZZZZZZ">
  In the morning</label><br/>
<input type="radio" name="field-ZZZZZZZZZZZZ"
  id="field-ZZZZZZZZZZZZ" value="In the afternoon"/>
<label for="field-ZZZZZZZZZZZZ">
  In the afternoon</label><br/>
<input type="radio" name="field-ZZZZZZZZZZZZ"
  id="field-ZZZZZZZZZZZZ" value="In the evening"/>
<label for="field-ZZZZZZZZZZZZ">
  In the evening</label><br/>
<input type="radio" name="field-ZZZZZZZZZZZZ"
  id="field-ZZZZZZZZZZZZ" value="No calls please"/>
<label for="field-ZZZZZZZZZZZZ">
  No calls please</label>
</div>
<div>
<p>Bubble Under may share information you give us here with other
  like-minded people or websites to promote the event. Please
  confirm if you are happy for us to do this.</p>
<input type="checkbox" name="field-ZZZZZZZZZZZZ"
  id="field-ZZZZZZZZZZZZ" value="I am happy for this event to
  be publicised outside of and beyond BubbleUnder.com where
  possible"/>
<label for="field-ZZZZZZZZZZZZ">I am happy for this
  event to be publicized outside of and beyond BubbleUnder.com,
  where possible</label>
</div>
<div class="buttonarea">
<input type="submit" value="Send Us the Info"/>
```

```
</div>
</fieldset>
</form>
```

You may have also noticed that Freedback has applied a `size` attribute to the text inputs of `size="40"`. It's not *critical* that you remove this, but I'd recommend that it's better to set widths of text inputs using CSS, rather than the `size` attribute.

Save the page, and try it out in your browser—and this time *really* try it out! Enter data and then submit the form (assuming that you're online, of course). If you've done it correctly, you should be sent to a confirmation page, as shown in Figure 7.32. And here you can see the only real downside of using this kind of service—the confirmation page includes an advert underneath the oh-so-small-you-almost-miss-it progress bar/confirmation and continue link.

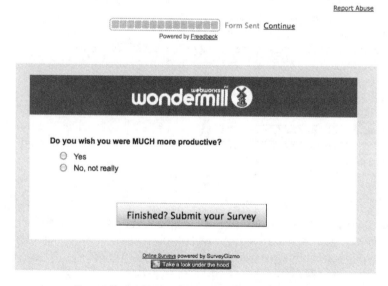

Figure 7.32. Freedback reports that the form has been sent

Feedback By Email

You've built your form and submitted some data. Now all you have to do is open up your mail client and wait for the post to arrive. Based on the form that we've built in this chapter, and using the form processing service, this is what you can expect to receive:

```
Contact Name: Jill Smith

Telephone Number: 01793 654834

Email Address: jsmith@someisp.net

What's the event called? Murder Mystery Weekend

When's the event happening? 12th August

What region is the event in? South-west

More details (as much as you think we'll need): Murder mystery
weekend, Cotswolds (no diving!) £65 per person, accom. included

Best time to call: In the afternoon

Bubble Under may share information you give us here with other
like-minded people or websites to promote the event. Please
confirm if you are happy for us to do this. I am happy for this
event to be publicized outside of and beyond BubbleUnder.com
where possible.


--
Date/Time: 2008-08-09 11:40:09 PDT
Sender IP: 81.109.255.237 [United Kingdom] | 4784f33t1rcqsOic
Referrer:
```

So that's basically all that's required to direct your form data into your inbox. You might still want to change some settings, though. For example, that last part where the user has accepted the terms and conditions? One little checkbox on the web page seems to create an awful lot of blurb in the email that's sent through! Just look at all this:

```
Bubble Under may share information you give us here with other
like-minded people or websites to promote the event. Please
confirm if you are happy for us to do this. I am happy for this
event to be publicized outside of and beyond BubbleUnder.com
where possible.
```

Surely it would be preferable to have this:

```
T&Cs accepted: yes
```

You can adapt the form markup so that it doesn't output this long wordy response by changing the `value` attribute. Compare the checkbox markup below with the previous version:

```
                                                        contact.html (excerpt)
<input type="checkbox" name="field-ZZZZZZZZZZZZZ"
id="field-ZZZZZZZZZZZZZ" value="yes"/> <label
for="field-ZZZZZZZZZZZZZ">I am happy for this event to be
publicized outside of and beyond BubbleUnder.com, where possible.
</label>
```

Similarly, you can edit the questions in Freedback.com afterwards to generate less wordy text in the final email sent through; what's displayed to the person filling in the feedback form isn't affected. So, if we wanted the checkbox answer to come through as "T&Cs accepted: yes," we'd have to amend the question, as shown in Figure 7.33.

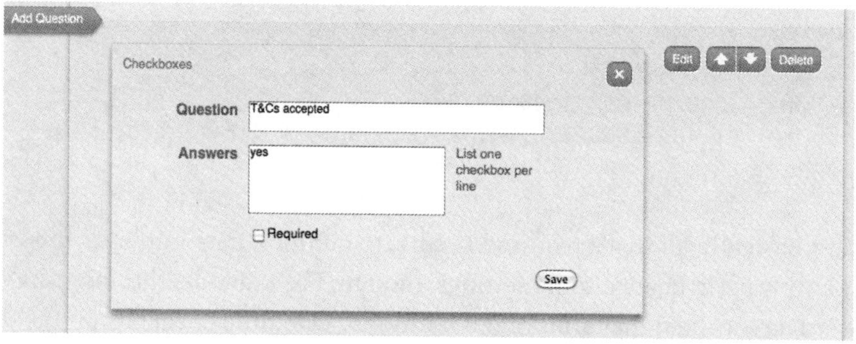

Figure 7.33. Amending existing questions for brevity

Once the form handler is set up and you have taken the essential values that we previously identified and put them into your form markup, you can continue fine-tuning the questions in Freedback until it produces just the right email. Don't be shy—feel free to experiment.

Finally, one more handy feature that's worth mentioning with Freedback: if you have email issues and lose some of your messages (it happens to the best of us!), you can log in to Freedback and retrieve previous form submissions. They are stored for six months.

Summary

In this chapter, we've explored the different types of form input controls, discussed what we'd use them for, and covered their limitations. We've stepped through the process of building a practical form, before styling it with CSS to make it more attractive. Finally, we've discovered that you don't need to be a programming whiz to deal with form data. But if you *do* want to have more control over how form data is handled—for example, you might want it stored in a database somewhere—you could consider learning a language like PHP. SitePoint published a book on that very topic, *Build Your Own Database Driven Website Using PHP & MySQL,*[19] written by Kevin Yank—you might want to check it out.

For now, though, the bulk of the work on our project site is done. We have content, some pretty pictures, tabular information, and a working form—and it's all styled in CSS, offering great flexibility for future redesigns. Now we can make these files live, so that the world at large can see our website. Let's set those wheels in motion right away!

---

[19] http://www.sitepoint.com/books/phpmysql1/

Interacting with Social Media

In previous editions of this book, we'd be looking at how to implement a blog on the site that we're working through by this stage. But since the second edition, our chosen method of updating the site with a blog changed drastically.[1] So drastically, in fact, that it was only possible to add a blog by doing either of the following:

▨ hosting the blog separately from the main pages on your site (which would make it look different, or take great effort to have it look the same, resulting in lots of duplicated work)[2]

▨ installing and customizing your own blogging software (such as Wordpress[3]), which is no easy feat for a beginner

---

[1] Previously, we suggested Blogger.com, specifically for its FTP service, where it could publish updates directly to your website. That handy option was, unfortunately, under-utilized by the masses, so Blogger withdrew the service in March 2010.

[2] Hosted blog solutions include Typepad (http://www.typepad.com/, but it's not free), Wordpress.com (http://wordpress.com/), and Blogger (http://www.blogger.com/). While Blogger withdrew our preferred FTP solution, they still offer the hosted option.

[3] http://wordpress.org/

In most cases, it requires having a solid understanding of technologies such as PHP and MySQL—definitely out of reach for beginners. What's also become abundantly clear since the last edition of the book went to press is that people LOVE **Facebook**! How do I know this? Because I asked!

In this chapter, we're going to investigate how to make use of opportunities that services like Facebook[4] and Twitter[5] offer you and your website with a minimum of fuss and bother. We'll discover ways you can easily use these services to put updates on your website quickly, whether you're beavering away on your computer in the study, or waiting for a bus with nothing more than a phone in your hand.

But Facebook is the Internet, right?

The fact that you've reached Chapter 8 of this book suggests you know this not to be true, but for many people, this is what they believe. Technically speaking, Facebook is most definitely not "The Internet." The Internet as a whole comprises many different networks—millions of networks, in fact—and the World Wide Web (WWW) is just part of that whole. And inside that WWW are all the websites that you know and love, including Facebook.

Just as Jupiter sits there in our solar system, sucking in most of the errant space dust and asteroids that swing past it like some *astronomical* vacuum cleaner, Facebook is this monstrous (in size, not nature … or not always!) presence, drawing in ever more people. And for many people, once they arrive, they're content to never leave. To use another astronomy reference, it's a bit like sitting on your front porch with a high-powered telescope, looking at everything going on around you, but never venturing beyond that front porch.

Facebook has become, for many people, the proverbial front porch. All the news they find, all the pictures they view, all the interactions they make—or at least a large proportion—are done through their Facebook profile, wall, or message pages. With that in mind, what are you going to do? Wait for them to be brave and venture beyond the "porch"? Whoah, crazy thinking there, cowboy! One way or another, it's inevitable; you need to put yourself in front of the Facebook masses.

---

[4] http://www.facebook.com/
[5] http://twitter.com/

Go Where the Audience Is

Now, I have no idea what kind of site you hope to build—or are already building—while reading this book. I'm unaware of what your business might be, or voluntary organization, or anything. But even as a non-betting man, I'd wager that your audience is on Facebook. And I'm not alone.

An increasing number of businesses are moving large portions of their websites onto Facebook—lock, stock, and barrel. In my opinion, this is taking it too far with the whole "let's get it on Facebook" ideology, because when you put all your time and effort into one outlet, you face problems. Let's run through a few what-ifs:

- visitor is unable to access the site because of a security policy blocking social networks (very common in workplaces)

- visitor is anti-Facebook for whatever reason (many people opt out because of privacy reasons)

- Facebook collapses because of a lack of funds.

You might be laughing at me about this last point or, at the very least, gagging on the warm coffee that you have just supped to keep the old brain ticking over. It may seem unlikely—unthinkable even—but sometimes businesses can become victims of their own success. I am not one for scare tactics, honestly, but as Facebook costs nothing to use and be part of, yet has millions of people around the globe constantly downloading photos from it, hitting the refresh buttons on their browsers, and generally giving its servers a solid workout, the money has to come from somewhere. I personally have no concerns that Facebook is about to go under in the short term, but to put my Disaster Recovery Expert hat on for a moment[6], I'd be wary about putting all my web presence into Facebook alone, for all the reasons above.

So, we're going to opt for a light touch where Facebook is concerned. But hang on a minute, Facebook isn't the only forum, is it? What about that other cute little birdy, Twitter?

---

[6] I'm not really a disaster recovery expert. I do, however, own a hat but only wear it at weekends so I can be lazy about combing my wispy hair.

A Two-pronged Attack: Facebook and Twitter

I'll give you an example of why I think a two-pronged attack on the social media front is a good idea, using a typical exchange at my house of an evening. The scene: my wife and I sit on the sofa, each with a laptop, the dog in between us being dutifully ignored (like all house pets are in this age of social media). I'm flicking through friends' Twitter updates; she is looking at friends' Facebook posts.

Me: "I don't know how you find your way around Facebook. It's really confusing."

Wife: "At least there's something to see—Twitter is just like Facebook's status update, but with everything else removed."

Me: "Exactly! And that's why I like it."

Wife: "And that's why I don't like it."

Dog: "Will you please shut up and just take me out for walkies?"

Everyone's different, after all. And that's why there are large camps of Facebook people and large camps of Twitter people and, of course, a certain amount of overlap where people are on both networks. If you want to reach the largest amount of people, you really have to dabble in both.

Let's not take sides, eh?[7] We'll begin by running through some of the features that Facebook offers; then we'll move on to Twitter. Finally, we'll pull it all together and see how it looks on our project site. We might decide that it's all a bit too much on the page. If there's one downside to all this easy-to-embed social stuff, it's that web pages can end up looking like they're plastered with adverts for other people's sites. We'll deal with that one later. For now, though, let's get busy with Facebook!

 Hey—Facebook Moved Everything Around!

> If there's one thing that Facebook does that causes a massive outcry, it's that it "moves stuff around." Like any website, as features are added, sometimes you have to rethink how it all hangs together. Facebook regularly gets new features, and it has a lot of users, so when changes are made, they seem to multiply greatly. It's inevitable. It's going to happen, and there's nothing you or I can do about it.

---

[7] <biased>Twitter for the win! Twitter for the win! Twitter for the win!</biased>

Unfortunately, I'm unable to predict what these changes might entail, so the instructions and screenshots that follow might change at some point after going to press (possibly about 10 minutes after the print run has ended, knowing my luck!). If this is the case, please accept my apologies. Facebook can be a bit of a moving target like that.

Setting Up a Facebook Page

I'm going to make an assumption before we move on, and that is you're already on Facebook. If I'm wrong, your first task is to sign up for Facebook. As I'm quite confident in that first assumption, though, I won't be running through all the steps you need to take to sign up—except to say, "Go to Facebook[8], click the **Sign Up** button, and take it from there."

[Pauses for a moment] All signed up then? Good! Let's continue.

We're setting up a Facebook Page. That sounds awfully generic, doesn't it? After all, every web page is a page, really. But no! This one has a capital P. It's a special kind of page.

Joking aside, Facebook's concept of a **Page** is really to differentiate it from a personal profile or a wall. A Page is used for the purposes of promoting a business, product, band, cause, and more. It's not particularly easy to find where to do this, though, so here's the secret[9] address: http://www.facebook.com/pages/.

Figure 8.1. The button to create a Facebook Page ...

---

[8] http://www.facebook.com
[9] It's not really a secret. But let's just pretend. It's more fun that way.

✴ Create a Page
Connect with your fans on Facebook.

Figure 8.2. … and the menu you'll see when you click the Page button

Pick the most appropriate category for you. For the dive site, I've chosen **Company, organization or institution** > **Travel/Leisure**.

Figure 8.3. The menu for creating a "Company, organization or institution" Page

You'll then be presented with a number of steps to work through. There's actually a lot of information to enter if you really want to make the most of this. We won't go through it all here—you can fill in the rest of the blanks quite easily. Let's focus on some key sections, though: **Add an image** is fairly straightforward. You just need a signifier to make it obvious what the Page represents. I've grabbed a screenshot of the site branding, cropped it, and uploaded.

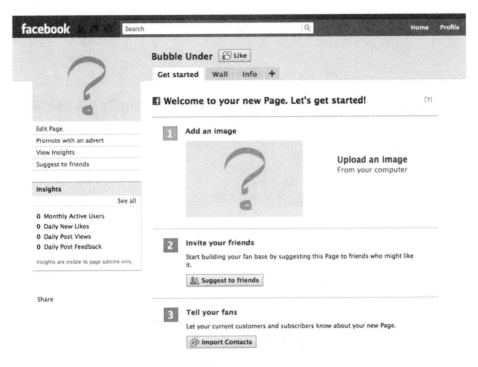

Figure 8.4. First stop: let's add an image

Figure 8.5. Our Bubbleunder.com branding is the ideal image

Invite your friends/Tell your fans: if you've been on Facebook for a while, there's probably people who you want to tell about your group/product/service. That's what these tools are for.

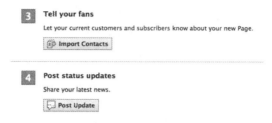

Figure 8.6. Tell your friends about your new Page

Promote this Page on your website: Now we're onto the good stuff! Click **Add Like Box**, and you will be presented with some options on how to customize it. This menu includes a preview that updates as you make changes.

Figure 8.7. By sticking a "Like" box on your Page, you encourage people to like you

We're up to the trickiest step to perform. It's ironic, as it's the single most important piece of information required for this to work—gaining the URL required.

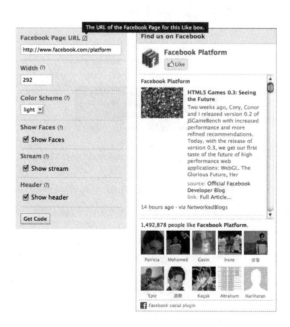

Figure 8.8. The URL is the crucial part of creating a Page

It tells you that you need a "URL for the Facebook Page," but doesn't explain where to find it! Here's what I suggest:

1. Return to your Profile Page.

2. Go to the search field at the top, and start typing the name of what you called your Facebook Page. When it appears in the results, click to select it.

Figure 8.9. Search for the name of your Facebook Page for the URL

3. Click the **Wall** link on the left-hand side.

Figure 8.10. Click on the **Wall** link

4. When the Page has loaded, go to the address bar and copy the whole address.

5. Click the **Get Started** link.

6. Now click on **Add Like Box**.

Figure 8.11. Now you can add your "Like" Box

7. You are now back to where you (almost) started, only this time you have the address (or URL) of the Page at the ready. Paste that over the one already in the field.

• Like the Page with one click, with

Figure 8.12. Paste your URL over the existing one

8. Press the **Get Code** button.

9. Copy everything in the **iframe** section.

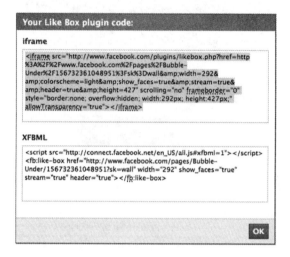

Figure 8.13. Copy the text in the **iframe** section

10. Now paste this in an empty text file. We'll be coming back to this in a bit.

11. Save the file as **FacebookLikeBox.html** (**Chapter8/examples/FacebookLikeBox.html**) somewhere handy. It doesn't matter where, as it's only a temporary location for now.

Phew! That was a bit of a runaround, as is Facebook's way. Let's return to setting up more key sections.

Set up your mobile phone: By following these straightforward steps, you'll be able to update your Facebook page with a simple text message (SMS, which stands for Short Message Service) or email sent to a specific email address. Figure 8.14 shows what you'll see.

6 **Set up your mobile phone**

Send Mobile Email
To upload photos or post status updates

Send text messages
To post status updates

Figure 8.14. You can update your Page via SMS

The steps required will depend on which country and which carrier you are with, so I won't cover that here. Figure 8.15, Figure 8.16, and Figure 8.17 should give you some idea, though, of what's involved. This is set up via Vodafone in the UK, with a screenshot taken off my iPhone showing the SMS confirmation.

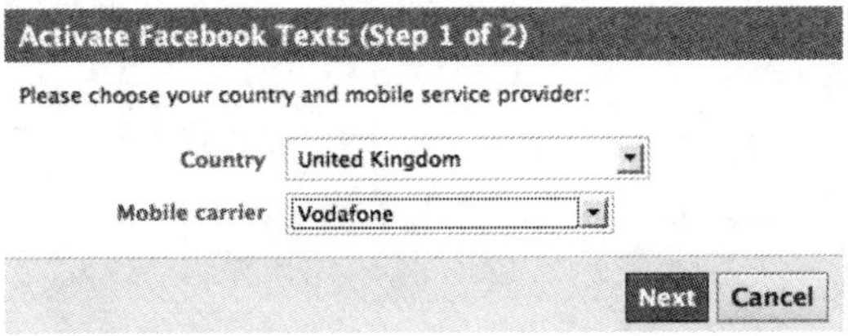

Activate Facebook Texts (Step 1 of 2)

Please choose your country and mobile service provider:

Country   United Kingdom

Mobile carrier   Vodafone

Next Cancel

Figure 8.15. Choose your location and service provider

Activate Facebook Texts (Step 2 of 2)

Text the letter F to 32665

When you receive a confirmation code, enter it here:

t8z4ws

Facebook does not charge for this service. Standard messaging rates apply.

vodafone   This service brought to you by Vodafone. By signing up to mobile texts, you also agree to Vodafone's Terms, available at www.vodafone.co.uk/facebook

Next Cancel

Figure 8.16. Enter your confirmation code

Figure 8.17. The SMS confirmation as shown on an iPhone

It might seem like we're veering off course a little here. I mean, we've gone from building up our own website to doing all this stuff on Facebook. "What's that all about then?" I hear you say. Fear not, it will all make sense soon. We're just in the setting up stage for now.

To summarize, what we've done is:

- established a Facebook Page
- created a **Like** box to use on your own site that will refer to this Facebook Page
- enabled simple updates to your Facebook page via mobile phone

Now we'll start to stitch all this together.

Adding a Like Box to Your Site

Not so long ago, you grabbed the necessary HTML to create a Facebook **Like** box. We're going to add that to the project site now. These can appear site-wide, but we'll limit it to just the home page.

1. Open the previously saved **FacebookLikeBox.html** file.

2. Select everything in that file and copy it.

3. Open **index.html** (the project site's home page).

4. Paste the **iframe** markup that you just copied after the image of the divers (**divers-circle.jpg**).

At the end of the page, we'll add some extra wording to explain the Facebook box. Add this in a new paragraph:

> All details of the group's diving activities, trips, and so on will be available from the various pages on this site but, in addition, we've got a Facebook page! If you're on Facebook, please do check it out. All the updates we post on Facebook will also appear here in this little box on the right (so even if you're not a Facebook fan, you can see our latest updates).

The markup should look like this:

chapter8/website_files/01_FacebookLikeBox/index.html

```
<h2>Welcome to our super-dooper Scuba site</h2>
<p><img class="feature" src="divers-circle.jpg" width="200"
   height="162" alt="A circle of divers practice their skills" />
</p>
<iframe src="http://www.facebook.com/plugins/likebox.php?➥
   href=http%3A%2F%2Fwww.facebook.com%2Fpages%2FBubble-Under%➥
   2F156732361048951%3Fsk%3Dwall&amp;width=292&amp;➥
   colorscheme=light&amp;show_faces=true&amp;stream=true&amp;➥
   header=true&amp;height=427" scrolling="no" frameborder="0"
   style="border:none; overflow:hidden; width:292px;
   height:427px;" allowTransparency="true"></iframe>
<p>Glad you could drop in and share some air with us! You've passed
your underwater navigation skills and successfully found your way to
```

```
the start point — or in this case, our home page.</p>
<p>All details of the group's diving activities, trips, and so on
will be available from the various pages on this site but, in
addition, we've got a Facebook page! If you're on Facebook, please
do check it out. All the updates we post on Facebook will also
appear here in this little box here on the right (so even if you're
not a Facebook fan, you can see our latest updates).</p>
```

Save the page, and check it in your browser. It should look … well, a little bit broken at the moment, as Figure 8.18 reveals.

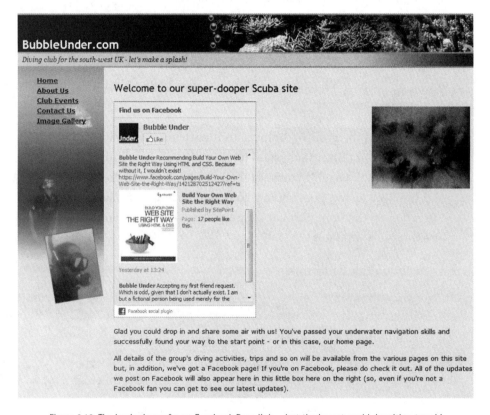

Figure 8.18. The beginnings of your Facebook Page link … but the layout could do with a tweak!

There's an awful lot of dead space. And that box really is a poor fit. I purposely threw this in so that you can see what's required to clean it up!

What we'll do is this:

▨ Make the **Like** box fit nicely with the image of the divers.

▪ Float both items—the image and the Facebook box—over to the right-hand side so that the rest of the content flows around it, just as it did previously.

Our first task is to make the box the same dimensions as the image. A quick look at the <img> tag shows that it is 200 pixels wide. To make the **Like** box the same size, we change two settings. These are highlighted (and changed to a value of 200) below:

```
<iframe src="http://www.facebook.com/plugins/likebox.php?➥
   href=http%3A%2F%2Fwww.facebook.com%2Fpages%2FBubble-Under%➥
   2F156732361048951%3Fsk%3Dwall&amp;width=200&amp;➥
   colorscheme=light&amp;show_faces=true&amp;stream=true&amp;➥
   header=true&amp;height=427" scrolling="no" frameborder="0"
   style="border:none; overflow:hidden; width:200px;
   height:427px;" allowTransparency="true"></iframe>
```

Our second task is make the **Like** box and the image appear on top of each other. To do that, we wrap both inside a div. Previously, we had a class of `feature` applied to the image. We'll remove that and, instead, apply a class of `aside`. The changed HTML should look like this:

```
<div class="aside">
   <img src="divers-circle.jpg" width="200" height="162"
   alt="A circle of divers practice their skills" />
   <iframe src="http://www.facebook.com/plugins/likebox.php?➥
   href=http%3A%2F%2Fwww.facebook.com%2Fpages%2FBubble-Under%➥
   2F156732361048951%3Fsk%3Dwall&amp;width=200&amp;colorscheme=➥
   light&amp;show_faces=true&amp;stream=true&amp;header=true&amp;➥
   height=427" scrolling="no" frameborder="0" style="border:none;
   overflow:hidden; width:200px; height:427px;" allowTransparency➥
   ="true">
   </iframe>
</div>
<p>Glad you could drop in  ... </p>
```

Finally, we'll need to change the CSS that previously applied to the image (in **style1.css**). Currently, it is:

```
img.feature {
  float: right;
  margin: 10px;
}
```

Insert the following CSS:

```
.aside {
  float: right;
  margin: 10px;
  width:200px;
}
```

Having saved the files, and with a quick wave of a magic wand and a refresh of the browser (okay, magic wand not really required), it should look like this Figure 8.19.

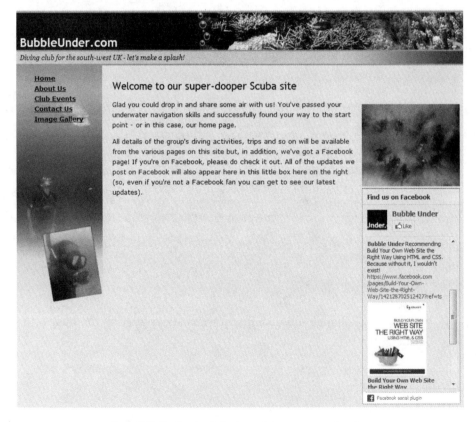

Figure 8.19. Floating has helped our diving page come together

That looks much better! However, with so little content on the home page, that tall **Like** box is a bit out of sorts. You could add more content, for sure. But a quick—and perfectly acceptable—fix would be to adjust the height of the **Like** box. This time, I'll leave it to you to find where in the HTML you can change that. If you've got it right, it should look like Figure 8.20.

Figure 8.20. Having adjusted the **Like** box, our page is now a neat fit

Remember, if you need some guidance, your old friend the Code Archive is there to help you (**Chapter8/website_files/03_FacebookLikeBox_ResizedHeight/index.html**)!

 Adjusting Width and Height the Easy Way

In the previous examples, I showed how you can hack at the generated markup for the **Like** box to make it fit the site better. You can actually set these heights and widths right up front, at the point where you initially asked Facebook to generate the markup. If you know these dimensions to begin with, that's the place to do it. (I just wanted you to get your hands dirty a bit—so much of what web developers do is about hacking and bending the markup to your will).

Yes! People Like Me! They Really Like Me!

Well, they can now—provided they press the **Like** button on the embedded Facebook content on your website, and they have a Facebook account. When they press the **Like** button, it will display a notification in their News Feed to say "Fred Likes Bubble Under," which will link directly to your Facebook Page. The trick now is to use your Facebook Page to inform friends about your *real* website, using posts to link to updates that you've made, or anything else you want to draw people's attention to.

 Liked, but Not Live

We're yet to discuss how you go about getting your site online. Facebook is already up and running but, at this stage, your website is still just a collection of files sitting on your computer's hard drive, invisible to the outside world. Setting up Facebook is just that—setting it up. In Chapter 9, we'll learn how to put your site online, and only then can you really tie up all the loose ends, and point your Facebook friends in the direction of your website.

Let's Sprinkle on Some Twitter Glitter

We've focused on what Facebook can offer—and indeed there's a lot more that you can do with it, particularly if you want to go beyond the basics—but now it's time for that other lovely social networking service, Twitter.

As I hinted at earlier when discussing the merits of Twitter versus Facebook, Twitter is a much simpler service to get your head around. It consists of status updates, better known on Twitter as **tweets**. And that's it![10] As with Facebook, it's easy to place tweets on your website. We'll also see how you can add a **Follow** button to your site, and, finally, look at the mobile aspect of Twitter, which is where it really comes into its own.

---

[10] Okay, okay, so there's also lists, trending topics and direct messages. But we're not interested in them here!

Adding Your Twitter Updates to the Site

Just like before, I'm going to assume that you already have a Twitter account. If you haven't registered for Twitter, head over to twitter.com[11] now and sign up, as in Figure 8.21. I'll make myself a cuppa and put my feet up for a bit while you do that.

Figure 8.21. Twitter's sign-up screen

Okay, so you're all Twittered up—you've set up a username, written some "About you" details, picked a photo for your profile—and we can now move on to the good stuff.

Head over to Twitter's Resources page,[12] seen in Figure 8.22.

---

[11] http://www.twitter.com

[12] http://twitter.com/about/resources

Figure 8.22. Twitter's Resources page

There is a selection of easy-to-use features here. For now, try the widgets, specifically **Widgets for** > **My Website**, as Figure 8.23 shows.

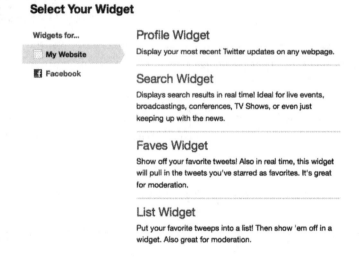

Figure 8.23. There are several choices when selecting a widget for your site

Select the **Profile Widget**, as Figure 8.24 illustrates.

Figure 8.24. The Profile Widget screen

You can now personalize the Profile Widget. Given that this will be embedded in our project site, we'll make some changes to the colors using the **Appearance** button. Figure 8.25 shows what the screen looks like.

Customize Your Profile Widget

Settings	Widget Colors	
Preferences	#061e52 ■ shell background	#ffffff □ shell text
Appearance	#000084 ■ tweet background	#ffffff □ tweet text
Dimensions	#b8e6e1 ▣ links	

Figure 8.25. Customize your Profile Widget's color scheme

Finally, adjust the size (to 200 pixels wide) in the **Dimensions** page; then you can **Finish & Grab Code**. Copy the code that appears in the text box, open **index.html** in the project site, and paste under the Facebook **Like** box (the `iframe`), before the closing `</div>`.

Your markup and script should now look like this:

```
<script src="http://widgets.twimg.com/j/2/widget.js"></script>
<script>
new TWTR.Widget({
  version: 2,
  type: 'profile',
  rpp: 4,
  interval: 6000,
  width: 200,
  height: 300,
```

```
    theme: {
      shell: {
        background: '#061e52',
        color: '#ffffff'
      },
      tweets: {
        background: '#000084',
        color: '#ffffff',
        links: '#b8e6e1'
      }
    },
    features: {
      scrollbar: false,
      loop: false,
      live: false,
      hashtags: true,
      timestamp: true,
      avatars: false,
      behavior: 'all'
    }
}).render().setUser('bubbleunderclub').start();
</script>
```

That's Not in the Script!

We are yet to use any scripts, so I will forgive you for being a little daunted by the script here. What's key here is that you don't need to know how it works or understand what it's doing—you only need to know that it works! Actually, all that's required for now is knowing how to copy and paste it. Learning **JavaScript**—which is what we have here—is a skill set in itself. I'll be touching on it briefly again in Chapter 14, where I'll provide some basic examples of cool stuff you can do with JavaScript with very little effort.

With a flourish of the old magic wand again—or a save and a refresh in the browser—your home page should now include both a Facebook **Like** box showing recent updates, and your latest Twitter updates, as in Figure 8.26.

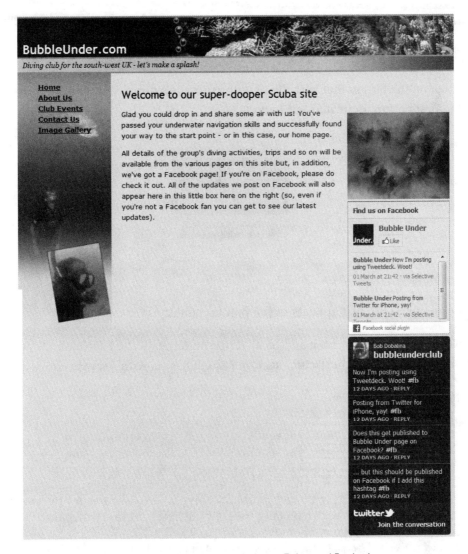

Figure 8.26. Our website now hooked up to Twitter and Facebook

Hmm. The layout is appearing a little shabby. It's lined up all right, but the right-hand side looks cluttered. Trust me, we'll return to that soon! For now, we'll just keep stacking more on. Crazy times!

Getting a Follow Button

The Twitter Profile Widget has a link to your Twitter page, but it's less obvious than saying, loud and proud, that you want people to follow you. This is what we do:

1. Head back to the Resources page.[13]

2. Select **Follow Buttons**.

3. Click on the button that best fits in with your site's design. For the dive site, it's the first button, indicated in Figure 8.27.

Figure 8.27. Choose the button that best suits your own website

4. Copy the HTML that appears in the pop-up panel.

5. Now go back to **index.html** and paste it just underneath the Facebook `iframe` markup, but above the Twitter section (which begins with `<script>`).

It should nestle like this:

```
<iframe src="http://www.facebook.com/plugins/likebox.php?➥
    href=http%3A%2F%2Fwww.facebook.com%2Fpages%2FBubble-Under%➥
    2F156732361048951%3Fsk%3Dwall&amp;width=200&amp;colorscheme=➥
    light&amp;show_faces=true&amp;stream=true&amp;header=true&amp;➥
    height=250" scrolling="no" frameborder="0" style="border:none;
    overflow:hidden; width:200px; height:250px;" allowTransparency=➥
    "true"></iframe>
<a href="http://www.twitter.com/bubbleunderclub"><img src="http://➥
    twitter-badges.s3.amazonaws.com/follow_me-a.png" alt="Follow
    bubbleunderclub on Twitter"/></a>
<script src="http://widgets.twimg.com/j/2/widget.js"></script>
```

If you save and check the file now, it almost looks the part. Almost. There are some styles elsewhere on the page for links that are interfering with the display of this Twitter button, which, as Figure 8.28 shows, has a border around it. In addition, when you hover over the link, a blue background appears.

---

[13] http://twitter.com/about/resources

Figure 8.28. The Twitter **Follow** button with a border

We're not going to change the link styles for the rest of the site, so we can simply override these styles by adding an `id` to the link, and then making use of that `id` in the CSS. So in **index.html**, we change the link as follows:

```
<a id="twitImageLink" href="http://www.twitter.com/bubbleunderclub">
  <img src="http://twitter-badges.s3.amazonaws.com/follow_me-a.png"
  alt="Follow bubbleunderclub on Twitter"/>
</a>
```

In **style1.css**, we're going to refer to that image using its `id` attribute. Then we'll make a few tweaks, all of which I'll explain in just a moment:

```
#twitImageLink img {
  border:none;
  display:block;
  margin:15px 0;
}
```

Looking at the CSS selector, we're picking an `img` that's inside the element with the `id` of `twitImageLink`. To remove the border (which appears because it's the default behavior for an image inside a link), we set it to none.

The next two lines deserve more explanation. An image is an inline object, and link styles (including `:hover` styles) often cause adverse effects. Depending on the placement of the image, you may be able to fix these issues by setting the image to `display:block`. In addition, once you've set it to be a block-level element, you can then set margins to it. I've suggested a 15-pixel margin on the top and bottom here, just to space it out a little, as the **Follow** link is sitting very close to the Facebook and Twitter boxes above and below it.

We can use a shorthand of `margin:15px 0`, which is the same as stating `margin:15px 0 15px 0`. (The four values represent the margins for top, right, bottom, and left—just refer to it in a clockwise direction. Easy!) With that in place, Figure 8.29 reveals the improved image.

Figure 8.29. With margins added, our **Follow** button is looking much tidier

Updating from a Twitter Client on Your Smartphone

Just as Facebook allows you to set up a way of updating your Page using your cell phone, Twitter does too. I'll skip the fine details on this one; the settings are self-explanatory, as a quick glance at Figure 8.30 shows (and no, that's not my real number!).

Figure 8.30. Twitter's settings for updating your Page via SMS

Once the phone is verified, you'll be able to send a text message to Twitter, where it automatically updates your Twitter status. So easy!

But the Page Looks Really Messy Now!

Ah, yeah. Sorry about that. On pages where there's a lot of content, it can be quite common for people to throw everything at the page—the proverbial "everything but the kitchen sink." On our project site, though, it's all a bit too much for that small space. So here's what I'm going to suggest:

- The small image of the divers will be moved into the body of the page.
- The sidebar will be used just for displaying the Facebook **Like** box and a **Follow on Twitter** link.
- We'll delete the Twitter Profile widget entirely but, before you lament its departure, we'll use Twitter to power the Facebook updates. Cunning.

So, let's do to it!

1. Move the image so that it appears just above the first paragraph.
2. Give the image an id of `homeImage` (we'll use that in just a moment).
3. Delete the script related to the Twitter Profile Widget, but leave the **Follow** link and image.
4. Finally, in **style1.css**, add in some new CSS as follows:

```css
#homeImage {
  float:left;
  margin:0 10px 10px 0;
}
```

As for the HTML, it should look like this:

```html
<h2>Welcome to our super-dooper Scuba site</h2>
 <div class="aside">
  <iframe src="http://www.facebook.com/plugins/likebox.php?➥
     href=http%3A%2F%2Fwww.facebook.com%2Fpages%2FBubble-Under%➥
     2F156732361048951%3Fsk%3Dwall&amp;width=200&amp;colorscheme=➥
     light&amp;show_faces=true&amp;stream=true&amp;header=true&amp;➥
     height=250" scrolling="no" frameborder="0" style="border:none;
     overflow:hidden; width:200px; height:250px;" allowTransparency=➥
     "true"></iframe>
  <a id="twitImageLink" href="http://www.twitter.com/bubbleunder➥
     club">
   <img src="http://twitter-badges.s3.amazonaws.com/follow_➥
     me-a.png"
```

```
     alt="Follow bubbleunderclub on Twitter"/></a>
</div>
<img src="divers-circle.jpg" width="200" height="162"
alt="A circle of divers practice their skills" id="homeImage" />
<p>Glad you could drop in and share some air with us! You've
     passed your underwater navigation skills and successfully found
     your way to the start point - or in this case, our home page.
</p>
```

We should now have a much tidier home page, with just one Facebook and Twitter feature each. Try resizing the window—you should see the text reflow around the image of the divers in a circle nicely, as in Figure 8.31.

Figure 8.31. A neat web page with Facebook and Twitter links, and text that reflows

Get Twitter to Update Facebook to Update Your Site

Yes, you read right! We dropped the Twitter profile because we're going to kill two birds with one stone (or kill off one bird—the tweeting kind—to avoid duplicating effort). We can set it up so that an update to Twitter automatically updates Facebook. And because your site includes the Twitter **Like** box and most recent updates, your site receives that update too. How easy is that?

There are a number of ways to update Facebook from Twitter. My personal preference is to use a Facebook app called Selective Tweets. As the name suggests, it allows you to decide when a Tweet should be pushed to Facebook, and when it should just go to Twitter. Here's what you need to do:

1. Head up to the search box and look for Selective Tweets. It should be quick to find (no need to type it all in, as Figure 8.32 demonstrates). Choose it from the options.

Figure 8.32. Search for the Selective Tweets input

2. Click on the **Go to App** button on the Selective Tweets page that appears.

3. Enter your Twitter username and **Save**.

That's it! You're linked. Now, to send an update that's published on Twitter, then Facebook, you just need to enter a **hashtag** at the end of your Twitter update: **#fb**. Hashtags are conventions for adding extra context and metadata to your tweets. Take a look at Figure 8.33 and Figure 8.34, and you can see that of the two most recent Twitter updates, only the top one with the **#fb** hashtag was published on Facebook.

Figure 8.33. Only the top tweet, with the hashtag, should publish to Facebook

Figure 8.34. Success! Our update has appeared

Now go and check your project site, and you should see that the Facebook **Like** box has ... ah, nuts. It hasn't updated. What's happened here? We did everything right, right?

Well, almost. When you set up Selective Tweets, by default it's set up to publish to your personal profile. It needs another slight adjustment to publish to your Page, and here's how:

1. Bring up the Selective Tweets App page using the search field, as in Figure 8.35.

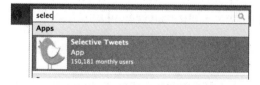

Figure 8.35. Letting the autofill function do its stuff

2. Select the **Your Fan Pages** tab.

3. You should see your Page here, so enter your Twitter name in the text input (as in Figure 8.36), and then click **Grant Permission**.

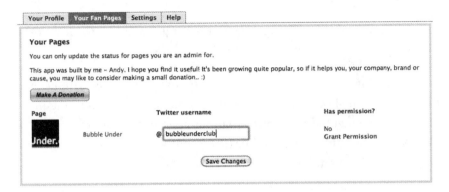

Figure 8.36. Enter your Twitter name under the **Your Fan Pages** tab

4. When asked, as per Figure 8.37, allow Facebook access to your tweets. Then click **Save changes**.

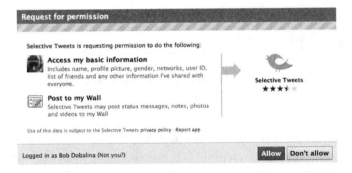

Figure 8.37. Allowing Facebook to access your Twitter feed

Now try another test message: posting on Twitter with the **#fb** hashtag. Did it appear on your Fan Page as well as your Profile page? Good! Now check the home page of the project site. Did the update appear here too? Excellent work!

Now the Training Wheels Are Off ...

There's been a lot going on here—and I could go on for many more pages if I wanted to. For example, I could show you how to:

■ have Facebook status updates automatically update Twitter (the reverse of what we're currently doing)

■ place a simple Facebook **Like** button on the page without the status updates showing

■ put a **Tweet this** prompt on any page in the project site to encourage others to promote it

And so much more. The truth is, there's plenty that you can do with Facebook and Twitter if you learn about using their **APIs** (Application Programming Interface), an interface implemented by a software program to enable interaction with other software; however, this is advanced territory, and would require a good working knowledge of a server-side programming language such as PHP.

Even without venturing into the world of APIs, there are still loads of other things you can try with Twitter. For example, you might have spotted earlier on the Twitter Resources page that there is also a collection of Facebook tools you can try out—and by all means do just that! I've picked a few to get you going, but you may find some of the other tools are a better fit for you personally. And there's only one way to find out.

Get Smart!

Before we leave Facebook and Twitter once and for all (or at least for this chapter), a final suggestion. If you have a smartphone—be that an iPhone, Android-supported phone, or Blackberry—be sure to check out the applications available for Facebook and Twitter. While each site comes in a mobile version, the native applications you can install on your phone have unique features and capabilities. I'll avoid picking one out in particular, as I change my mind about which one is best all the time, especially as they update with new features. So try some out and see how you go.

Figure 8.38, Figure 8.39, and Figure 8.40 show how easy it is to do two updates on different phone apps, using Selective Tweets. Both are published to Twitter, and to Facebook and then onto the site itself in the **Like** box. And all while I was waiting for a bus.[14]

---

[14] Well, I'm in the study, really ... but I could have been!

Figure 8.38. Using Selective Tweets to post from Twitter for iPhone and Tweetdeck (also on iPhone), respectively

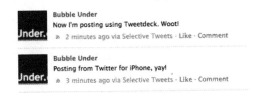

Figure 8.39. How the Tweets appear on Facebook (thanks to Selective Tweets and use of the **#fb** hashtag)

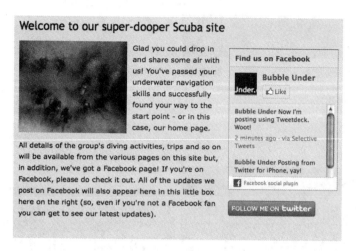

Figure 8.40. Finally, the Tweets showing on your site, via Facebook. Now that's efficiency!

Summary

We've covered how the big two social networks, Facebook and Twitter, can provide the tools for you to quickly embed content from these services into your own site. We've also seen how it's possible to tie these services together, so that you can update once and see the results appear in several places with minimal additional effort. And if that weren't enough, we've learned that it's possible to make these updates using little more than a phone, from the humble SMS to dedicated Facebook and Twitter apps on your fancy smartphones.

Now, if only your site was actually online and you were able point people to it. Perhaps it's time to move on to the next chapter, where we'll learn what's involved to make this happen.

Launching Your Website

Creating web pages can be great fun. It's relatively easy to learn (compared to brain surgery and rocket science, at least)—and you can experiment until your heart's content with little more than a standard computer and some fiendishly good typing fingers. Spend as little or as much time as you like building and viewing web pages, but remember: in the end you'll have to make these babies "live" on the Internet. How you achieve this—including the tools you'll need to make it happen—is the subject of this chapter. Let's begin by reminding ourselves of some of the basics of the Internet and how it's possible to see all these lovely web pages.

The Client–Server Model

The relationship between the browser you use and the websites you visit is known in technical circles as the "Client–Server Model." This is depicted in Figure 9.1.

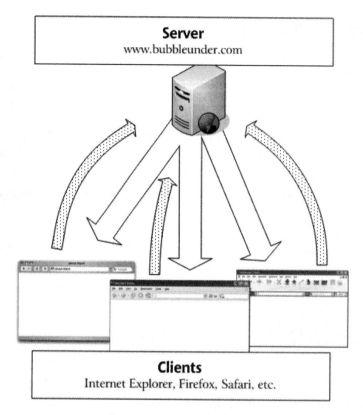

Figure 9.1. The Client-Server Model

The Client   That's you. You're the client (or rather, your browser is) and you want web pages. You send these requests for web pages via your ISP (Internet Service Provider), which provides the connection between you and the server.

The Server   That's the other party. Okay, it's another computer (and probably a hugely complicated, big fat beastie of a computer, at that) and its job is to meet all your requests for web pages.

That's the basics of the relationship. You and many others can ask that server for lots of different web pages and files at the same time—it's a very busy machine! The busier the website, the greater the demands placed on the server—and the more expensive it can be; but your website would need to receive *a lot* of visitors for this to become a problem. That's not for you to worry about now—after all, we're trying to do this on the cheap!

Web Hosting Jargon

To start with, here are a few words of jargon that will help you up front. (I'll expand on each of them further on in the chapter):

Bandwidth This is the size of the metaphorical pipe that runs between the client and the server, along which all the data travels. The wider the pipe, the more data can fit through it. The size of the pipe is usually measured in megabytes or gigabytes per month. You can now see where the term *broadband* evolved from—it's a big fat data pipe!

FTP This is the method used for transferring files from the client to the server and vice versa—and it's useful for putting your website on the server in the first place! FTP stands for **File Transfer Protocol**.

Domain Name Within the http://www.bubbleunder.com web address, this is the "bubbleunder.com" part. You can buy the rights to use a domain name for a fixed period—usually one or two years at a time, as it's not yours to own forever. This is referred to as **registering** the domain.

Hosting Hosting refers to the storage of your website files on an internet-connected server. Hosting is entirely separate from the registering of your domain name, although many hosting companies offer both services. Site owners use web hosts to eliminate exposing their own hard drives to potentially malicious web surfers. Oh, and it beats having to maintain their own computers so that their site can be accessed!

Hosting Your Website—Finding Server Space

The expression that there's no such thing as a free lunch is mostly true. Mostly. However, you can acquire many services for free on the Web, including hosting. Well, you can pick up hosting *almost* for free. We have to be realistic about this.

The cost for web hosting can vary from around US$10, to hundreds or thousands of dollars, each month. You get what you pay for, it has to be said.

- A cheap hosting plan is likely to have a limited monthly bandwidth allowance and may exclude advanced features. For example, website statistics that allow you to see how many visitors your website has attracted, and so on.

- A more expensive hosting plan will offer all the basics, plus more advanced features such as those statistics. Usually, it will allow you to do more with your website as it grows, or as your web programming skills improve.

However, it's folly to spend lots of money on features or bandwidth that you'll never use—especially a small website that you don't expect will attract masses of visitors. It's a bit like buying a double-decker coach to drive your auntie to work each day. I'll point out the web hosting features you'll need to consider shortly.

Free Hosting—with a Catch!

A sensible approach for beginners is to sign up for a free hosting service. Conditions will still apply to the service; perhaps you'll have pop-up ads forced upon your users, or be asked to include a link to the hosting company on your website. These shouldn't be big obstacles, though, but be sure to check out the conditions thoroughly before you sign up; a service that causes a pop-up ad to appear on every page of your site might well deter visitors from returning. Regardless, free hosting can at least help at the start, letting you share your website with others.

Of course, it pays to shop around. The best advice would be to conduct a search for the phrase **free hosting "no ads"** (be sure to wrap the "no ads" part in quotation marks), and check out the options available. Bear in mind that these change quite frequently; many companies that offer free hosting close their virtual doors after they have enough sign-ups. The best deals might last but a short time!

Beware of Ugly Addresses

If you do opt for free hosting, you may find that the website address for your files is a little on the ugly side; http://www.freespaceforall.net/users/~bubbleunder/, for example. However, there are ways to mask this ugliness, as I'll explain later in the section called "What is Web Forwarding?"—so don't let this rule you out of using free hosting.

Free Hosting with Your ISP

If you have a web connection, the chances are that your Internet Service Provider already offers you some free web space. Again, one could argue that this isn't truly "free," but if you're already paying for the connection, having the hosting thrown in will at least mean you can host your website at no extra cost. Well, almost—you'll still have the issue of an ugly domain name to deal with, but that can be resolved using a web forwarding service.

 Try the Forums

Make use of the expertise already out there. Be sure to pay a visit to SitePoint's online forums where you'll find a forum dedicated to web hosting.[1]

Free Hosting—with a Domain Name at Cost

Another option is to use a service that provides free hosting on the condition that you first register a domain name with them. This may be an economical option, as you'll have to pay for a proper domain name at some point; it's unavoidable, unless you're happy using a longer, less professional domain name offered through the free-with-a-catch services mentioned just previously.

Be a little wary, though. A service may claim to offer free hosting if you register the domain name with them, but the cost of registering may be higher than usual to offset the lack of hosting charges. In short, *free* may not be anything of the sort!

What is Web Forwarding?

If you opt for free or low-cost hosting, you'll probably gain a user-*un*friendly web address (like the fictional **http://www.freespaceforall.net/users/~bubbleunder/** address I mentioned earlier). That hardly rolls off the tongue, does it?

What web forwarding allows you to do is register a sensible domain name—there's no hosting to be paid for—that points to the address where your web pages are *really* hosted. You can then reassure people that your site's address is easy to remember (such as www.bubbleunder.com), and your pages will be delivered successfully.

---

[1] http://www.sitepoint.com/launch/webhostingforum/

Many small businesses (particularly family businesses) use web forwarding when setting up their first company site. Cheap (or free) hosting combined with a paid-for domain name keeps the costs down and provides an outwardly professional appearance. However, while this seems like a good solution for a new venture, there are some issues of which you should be aware.

The Downsides of Web Forwarding

Often, web forwarding will make use of an older feature of HTML called **frames.**[2] These are normally used to split the browser display into more than one area, a bit like cutting up a cake. It's a technique that's used less and less frequently, though, and is not even covered in this book (most sensible people agree that frames are generally a bad idea, for a number of different reasons).[3] If you use web forwarding services, your website—regardless of how many pages it has—will be displayed in a single frame. On the surface, this is fine to the casual observer, as illustrated in Figure 9.2. But really, your site's hiding a few little secrets.

There are a couple of anomalies in Figure 9.2 that, if you've a keen eye, you might have noticed. The first is the URL: normally, the filename of each page of a website appears at the end of the domain name. For example, the address of the Club Events page (**events.html**) would be http://www.bubbleunder.com/events.html. However, web forwarding with frames means that all our pages will appear to have the same address: **http://www.bubbleunder.com/**. This causes a number of problems:

- When a user attempts to bookmark a certain page from the website, only the home page is bookmarked.

- It makes it tricky for other sites to link directly to a specific page in your site.

- When a user clicks the **Refresh** button, the home page reloads—regardless of which page the user was viewing.

---

[2] http://reference.sitepoint.com/html/frame

[3] "Who framed the web: Frames and usability" by Roger Johansson [http://www.456bereastreet.com/archive/200411/who_framed_the_web_frames_and_usability/] features a good discussion on why frames are bad.

Figure 9.2. A website that uses a web forwarding service—notice the subtle problems?

The second anomaly is the `title` that we so carefully crafted for every page of our site. Using this web forwarding service, no matter which page of our site the users visit, they'll see the same title—and we're unable to change it. Some forwarding services may even take the liberty of using your title to advertise themselves as our example does ("Cheap domains from only $9.95").

Finally, as if there weren't enough reasons to think again about using web forwarding, this one could be the deal-breaker. Some search engines may not index content on your website if it's referenced using frames this way—or not give the pages as much credit as those not embedded into a `frameset` (which contains `frame` elements). So if you want your site to be found easily, it's a consideration you need to bear in mind.

It's just as well, then, that paid-for web hosting can be relatively inexpensive.

Paying for Web Hosting

If you're willing to put your hand in your pocket and pay for hosting, your options increase immensely. You'll avoid being hobbled by restrictions, such as forced links to the hosting provider's site, weird address behavior, or compulsory domain registration. And don't be fooled into thinking that hosting fees are financially crippling or only big businesses can afford them. These days, there are many excellent hosting plans to be had, and for a relatively small amount (less than US$10 per month), you can obtain a good package. Naturally, the more you pay, the more features there'll be—most of which probably seem like gobbledygook if you're new to this arena. However, as we mentioned before, there's no need to pay for masses of features that you'll never use (think people carrier, not double-decker coach!).

Based on what you have learned so far in this book, and what our project site will require, I'll outline briefly the features you'll need to look for when researching hosting providers.

Hosting Essentials

If you want to launch your site online quickly and easily, you'll need the following:

FTP Access to Your Server

As mentioned, FTP stands for File Transfer Protocol, but nobody ever says it in full. It's a bit like saying Automated Teller Machine instead of ATM. Stick to FTP, and you won't stand out like a sore thumb! But what is FTP?

FTP is a method of transferring data over a network, and it's the primary method of transferring files between a server (where a website is hosted) and a personal computer. Using an **FTP Client**—a program that helps manage these transfers—you can drag and drop files to your server as easily as if you were moving files within your hard drive (albeit a little more slowly). In this chapter, I'll show how you can use a selection of FTP clients to upload your files to the Web. You may also come across the term **SFTP**—a more secure version of FTP, hence Secure FTP.

Given a choice between the two, the latter is the better one to use, but you may not have that choice; some web hosts won't let you use SFTP, and similarly, some FTP clients have no support for SFTP. But if you're lucky on both counts, SFTP is the way to go.

Adequate Storage Space

Once you've finished building your site, it's a good idea to work out the total size of all your site files. You can find this out quite easily:

Windows

Right-click on the folder you created back in Chapter 1 on your hard drive that contains all of your website's files (that's the **Web** folder inside **Documents Library** or **My Documents** for XP/Vista). Now choose **Properties**, and you'll be presented with a dialog like the one depicted in Figure 9.3.

Figure 9.3. Windows' file properties dialog

Look for the number next to **Size** (not **Size on disk**—that will give you a skewed figure indicating how efficiently the file has been saved on your hard drive!).

Mac OS X

Figure 9.4. File properties in Mac OS X

In Finder, select the folder containing your website files and select **File** > **Get Info**. Figure 9.4 displays the **Get Info** dialog on the Mac, showing files that add up to almost 700kB.

Armed with this knowledge, you can consider how many files you have in your completed website, and try to work out how much your site is likely to grow. I know that it's not an exact science. Let's try a basic exercise to see how this might work in practice.

Multiply the total size of your existing website files by ten, and then add a little extra for luck. Make sure that your host will allow you that amount of storage space. These days, most hosts will give you more than you need for your first website. A free host may provide as little as 30MB, while a low-cost, paid-for service may offer gigabytes of storage.

Calculating File Sizes

In the examples above, the combined size of the files used in the website was a measly 690 kilobytes (kB). No hosting company will tell you how many kilobytes they'll offer; it will be referred to in megabytes (MB) or, most likely, gigabytes (GB). As you perform your calculations, bear these figures in mind:

- 1 kilobyte = 1,024 bytes
- 1 megabyte = 1,024 kilobytes
- 1 gigabyte = 1,024 megabytes

A Reasonable Bandwidth Allowance

This is trickier to assess—it's the proverbial "how long's a piece of string" scenario. If you have 20MB of files on your website and you access each of them once a month, you'd need a 20MB monthly bandwidth allowance. Well, that's about as unlikely a figure as you'll ever find, after all, you'll want others to be able to view the website as well. But how many? Ten? 100? 1,000? What happens if another website links to your site and you suddenly have thousands of people visiting in a single day? Your bandwidth usage shoots up, that's what!

You should aim for a monthly bandwidth allowance of at least 5GB; this should be a comfortable allowance for your first website, unless people are downloading large photos or video files from your pages.

Be careful about exceeding your monthly bandwidth allowance (although, arguably, it's beyond your control—others visiting your website pushes your bandwidth usage up). Some hosting companies offer no warnings when you've exceeded your bandwidth allowance; they'll simply block any further traffic to your site until the next calendar month or billing period starts. Others will allow the excess traffic, but they'll charge you a premium for their *flexibility*. It pays to check the fine print in your hosting agreement. Most hosts will notify you if you come close to exceeding your bandwidth allowance, though—allowing some leeway to buy extra bandwidth to cope with your new-found popularity!

Hosting Nice-to-haves

Email Accounts

A free hosting service is likely to offer some free email facilities but, like the domain name that such hosts provide, the email addresses often look unprofessional. For example, which of these looks better?

- bob.bubbleunder@freespaceforall.net
- bob@bubbleunder.com

It's amazing, but even the email address you provide to others can suggest a lot about the operation you run (I'll admit to being an email snob and judging people by their email addresses. "Hotmail.com? Pfff!"). This may be reason enough to shell out for hosting.

When you're assessing the host provider's email services, make sure they offer the following features:

POP3/IMAP   If the hosts offer either of these services (and they should), you'll be able to download email to your computer using an **email client**, such as Outlook Express, Thunderbird, or Apple Mail, as well as on your smartphone's mail application, which is very handy to have.

Webmail   If you need to keep in touch with others about the site while you're away from your personal computer, check to see whether the host offers a **webmail** facility. This allows you to log in to a website and check your email from any computer, just as you might with a Yahoo or Hotmail account.

Email forwarding   If you already have an email address, you may want to have any mail for your new website sent directly to your existing email address. This is called **email forwarding**. It's a bit like an electronic version of the mail redirection service you can use when you move house, but it has no expiry date. The advantage of this service is obvious—no need to check multiple email addresses. The downside is that when a person emails you at your website email address (bob@bubbleunder.com, for example), and you reply, the email address they'll see is your real (and possibly uglier) email address. This might look a little unprofessional, or confuse the recipient.

Server Side Includes (SSIs)

You'll already be aware that building a project site involves a lot of copying and pasting—as a change to the navigation in one file necessitates a change in all of them. That may be manageable for sites with a handful of pages, but if you have more than that—or can foresee your website growing—it will become increasingly difficult to maintain these site-wide changes.

One solution is to use **Server Side Includes** (SSI), which let you create a file that's included automatically in all of your web pages; hence, a change to that one file will be reflected on every page of your site. This is a very useful feature that will save you time in the long term, but it requires you to learn how to set up your own computer to act as a personal web server. This is not the most straightforward of tasks, so it's one topic you'll have to investigate in your own time. A good place for Windows users to start would be to download the Apache web server software.[4] Apache is an open source product used for running web servers that serve websites of all sizes. Mac OS X users will already have Apache installed; if that's you, you'll need to start **Personal Web Sharing**, which is accessible from the **Sharing** screen of **System Preferences**.

For now, though, just make a mental note that SSIs exist, and that they'll make maintenance of your site much easier in the long term. A good introduction to SSIs and how they work in Apache is available at yourhtmlsource.com.[5]

Support for Scripting Languages and Databases

If you want to make your website more dynamic, you may want to make use of a **server-side scripting** language such as PHP (not covered in this book). Server-side scripting enables you to apply some logic within your pages, so that content can display differently depending on particular circumstances. For example (and this is not real code, I should point out, just *pseudo* code):

---

[4] http://httpd.apache.org/
[5] http://www.yourhtmlsource.com

```
If time is between 8pm and 6am then
  Show the night-time image
Else
  Show the day-time image
End
```

You'd be hard-pushed to find a host that doesn't support at least one scripting language, and many will allow you to use a number of languages, should you want to. Even if you're not currently using a server-side scripting language, choosing a host that supports a handful of server languages will make life easier later on, should you decide to dabble in server-side scripting and add dynamic content.

Often, database support goes hand in hand with support for a scripting language. If you start experimenting with a scripting language, you'll probably find that you need somewhere to store and read data—most likely a **database**. A database is a collection of data that you can access and present in many ways. For example, a database of customers could be listed alphabetically on one web page, by location on another, and by debtor on another—particularly useful information to have! By updating your database, you then make it available to any of these web pages, and any new pages that you create can also tap into the stored information.

If you want to learn more about creating dynamic websites, SitePoint has it all covered for you. You can learn online from the various dedicated forum communities (PHP[6] and MySQL[7]—a database technology), or pick it all up in one book—Kevin Yank's *Build Your Own Database Driven Website Using PHP & MySQL*[8] is a great place to start.

It's fair to say that the very cheapest hosting services (and most free ones) won't provide database access or allow you to use a scripting language.

 What if my hosting requirements change?

The features that I've suggested here will almost certainly suit the requirements of your first website. However, if later you find that you outgrow your hosting plan, don't worry—you won't be locked in with that company forever. You can

---

[6] http://www.sitepoint.com/launch/phpforum
[7] http://www.sitepoint.com/launch/mysqlforum/
[8] http://www.sitepoint.com/books/phpmysql1/

transfer your domain name between different hosts as your needs change. Bear in mind, though, that you may incur a small transfer or exit fee, depending on the terms of service.

Likewise, don't be fooled into thinking you should pay for services early on *in case* you need them later. For example, don't go paying for PHP and MySQL on the off-chance that you might need these technologies in eight months' time. Just make sure you're able to upgrade your current hosting plan when you actually need those facilities—it's preferable to moving to another hosting company.

Pre-flight Check: How Do Your Pages Look in Different Browsers?

If you build your web pages according to web standards (and if you've been following the advice in this book so far, you most definitely have), you should find that your website works well on all or most browsers—no tweaks required! Still, you should check your page design as early as possible, just in case you spot anything. It's better to fix your prototype or template in as many browsers as possible, before you create lots of web pages based on that first page. You should then check your entire site in a range of browsers before you put those files on a live web server for everyone else to see. Here are the browsers that I'd recommend you test against; the most important ones appear at the top of the list for each operating system. The version numbers stated were the most up to date at the time of writing, but if you spot a newer version for download, use that instead.

Windows
- Internet Explorer 9 (http://www.microsoft.com/windows/ie/). Bear in mind that there may be *a lot* of people still using older versions of IE, particularly as IE9 won't run on Windows XP, which is still very much prevalent. So you'll still need to check your pages in IE6, 7, and 8.
- Firefox 5 (http://www.mozilla.com/firefox/)
- Chrome 12 (http://www.google.com/chrome)
- Opera 11 (http://www.opera.com/)

Mac OS X
- Safari 5 (http://www.apple.com/safari/)
- Firefox 5 (http://www.mozilla.com/firefox/)
- Chrome 12 (http://www.google.com/chrome)
- Opera 11 (http://www.opera.com/)

That's Just How Chrome Rolls

While most major browser updates—for example, upgrading from a version 4 to version 5—are up to the user to do (that's you!), Google's Chrome browser is the odd one out. It automatically upgrades in the background.

Uploading Files to Your Server

So, you've done your homework and settled on an affordable hosting plan that does everything you need. You've filled out countless forms and received just as many confirmation emails—containing all kinds of gobbledygook—from your hosting service. Let's filter through that to focus specifically on your FTP details.

FTP Settings

Your host will give you FTP details that look similar to those below. This example shows some *fictional* settings for the Bubble Under site (try as you might, entering these details won't lead to the live files—they're for demonstration purposes only):

```
Hello Bob Dobalina,

Your FTP account 'bubbleunder' has just been activated, and you
can begin uploading your website's files to it.

When you have your software and are ready to connect, you will
need to provide it with a few settings: your username, password,
and where you want it to connect to.

        Hostname: ftp.bubbleunder.com
        Username: bobdobalina
        Password: fl1bbertyg1bbet
            Path: /home/bobdobalina
```

The hostname, username, and password will always be required, but the path may be unnecessary; in fact, it may not even be supplied. Carefully check the instructions provided by your host.

Now that we have these details handy, let's upload some files.

Uploading with FileZilla for Windows

You can download numerous free FTP clients for Windows, but one of the most popular is the open source FileZilla Client (there is also a FileZilla Server, but we won't be using this). To download FileZilla, visit the FileZilla home page[9] and click on the **Download FileZilla Client** button to go to the Client Download page, as shown in Figure 9.5. We're only interested in the setup program. Click the link for the **FileZilla_x_y_z_setup.exe** file (where x, y, and z make up the version number).

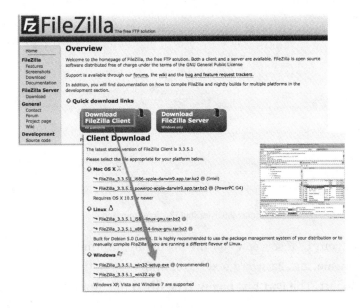

Figure 9.5. The FileZilla download pages

Once you've downloaded this file, run it to install FileZilla. In most cases, the default settings should serve you fine. Once it's finished installing, start it by selecting **Start** > **All Programs** > **FileZilla** > **FileZilla**. The FileZilla window shown in Figure 9.6 should appear.

---

[9] http://filezilla.sourceforge.net/

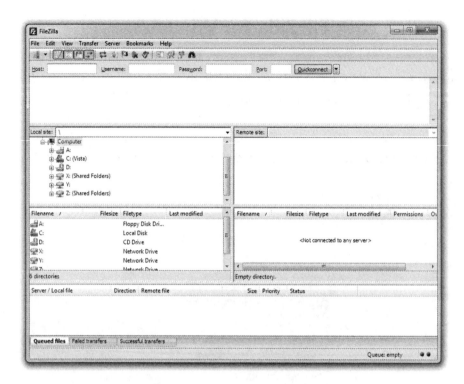

Figure 9.6. FileZilla FTP Client interface

To connect to your FTP server, enter the hostname, username, and password into the **Host**, **Username**, and **Password** text boxes at the top of the FileZilla window, and click **Quickconnect**. The **Port** text box will be filled in automatically.

You should now be connected to your FTP server. The files that reside on your computer will appear on the left-hand side under **Local Site**; the files on the FTP server will be shown on the right, under **Remote Site**, as you can see in Figure 9.7.

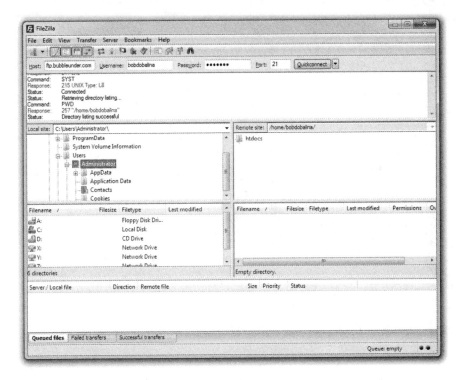

Figure 9.7. FileZilla, showing local files on the left, and server files on the right

To upload files, you need to follow three steps:

1. Locate the files that you want to upload using the left-hand panel (in the **Web** folder in the **Documents** library).

2. In the right-hand panel, navigate to the folder on the server to which want to upload the files. You'll need to refer to the hosting company's instructions to find out where your files need to go, but if you see a folder named **web**, **htdocs**, or **public_html**, it's a safe bet that your website files should go there.

3. To upload a file to the server, click and drag it from the left panel into the right panel, similar to how you would copy files in Windows Explorer. The progress of your upload will be displayed in the bottom of the FileZilla window, as shown in Figure 9.8. You can also drag an entire folder across; everything inside the folder will be copied over to the server.

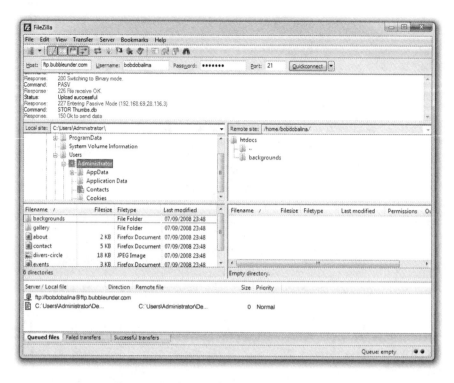

Figure 9.8. FileZilla uploading the **backgrounds** folder

 QuickConnect Recent Servers List

A handy feature of FileZilla is the **QuickConnect recent servers list**. It recalls the usernames and passwords for the last ten FTP servers you've connected to, so there's no need to re-enter those details every time you want to update your website. To activate this list, simply click the down arrow next to the **QuickConnect** button, and select the appropriate option—in our case, it would be **bob-dobalina@ftp.bubbleunder.com**.

Uploading with Cyberduck—Mac OS X

The Mac platform has fewer freely available FTP clients, but there's one nice tool (with an oh-so-cute icon) called Cyberduck.[10] Just like FileZilla (assuming you read the previous section, dear Mac user), Cyberduck will remember your login details, but you'll need to create an **FTP bookmark**. Here's how you do it:

---

[10] http://cyberduck.ch/

1. When you open Cyberduck, it should already show saved bookmarks. If this is the first time you've used it, you won't have any bookmarks saved yet, as Figure 9.9 illustrates.

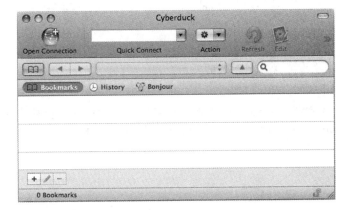

Figure 9.9. An empty **Bookmarks** screen in Cyberduck

2. Next, add a bookmark. Click on the little + button at the bottom of that application, and you'll be presented with the dialog shown in Figure 9.10.

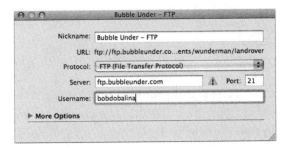

Figure 9.10. FTP server settings as seen in Cyberduck

3. Enter the FTP details (they're in the email from your hosting provider) into the **Server**, **Path** (under **More Options**), and **Username** text boxes. If you don't have a path, leave that field blank. Change the **Nickname** to anything you like—it's the name that will be displayed in the **Bookmarks** list. When you've done that, close the dialog, and the bookmark will be saved for future use.

4. To connect to the server, double-click on the bookmark. You may receive a warning about the host being unknown. Don't worry if it does appear—just hit the **Allow** or **Always** button.

Figure 9.11. Cyberduck warning about unknown host key

5. The next message you'll receive is one saying "Login failed"—this is because you've yet to set a password. Here's your chance to do it, and if you want it to be remembered for future reference, tick the **Add to Keychain** checkbox, seen in Figure 9.12.

Figure 9.12. Cyberduck's password prompt

6. If all the details are correct, you should connect straight through to your server; the main window of Cyberduck should have changed to display the files and folders stored on the server as well, as Figure 9.13 shows.

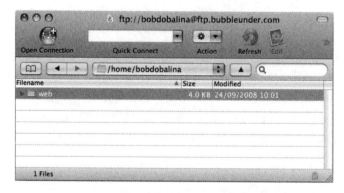

Figure 9.13. The **Web** folder on the live server, as displayed in Cyberduck

Uploading files to the server is now a simple case of dragging files or folders straight onto the Cyberduck window. If you treat this window like a Finder window, you won't go wrong.

Other Uploading Tools

As I mentioned previously, there are loads of stand-alone FTP clients that you could use (by stand-alone, I mean that's all they do—FTP and FTP only). More full-featured web development software packages like Dreamweaver include FTP facilities among their site management tools.[11] The procedure for uploading files using these services is exactly the same as the process I've outlined here; just make sure you enter the right details, as supplied by your web hosting company, into the correct boxes in the program's FTP dialogs.

Where's Your Site At?

Where's it at? It's on the Internet, that's where! If you've installed and run an FTP client, then uploaded your files, they should now be online for all to see. But the job's unfinished: you must make sure there are no broken links, and that your HTML and CSS are up to scratch.

Checking Links

In our project site, there are very few web pages, and images, to deal with. However, it only takes one careless typing error to break a link between your web pages or a reference to an image. Many web design and authoring programs include built-in link checkers, but there's no need to buy expensive software for this facility. Once again, there are oodles of free link checkers that you can download, or you can use an online service free of charge.

The first choice for checking your web pages is the W3C's Link Checker.[12] Enter the address for the website in the box and press the **Check** button. I've used another website in this example—my own supporting site for SitePoint's Ultimate HTML Reference[13] (one that really should have zero errors, or I'll be eating humble pie in large helpings)—as shown in Figure 9.14.

---

[11] http://www.adobe.com/products/dreamweaver/
[12] http://validator.w3.org/checklink/
[13] http://htmlreferencebook.com/

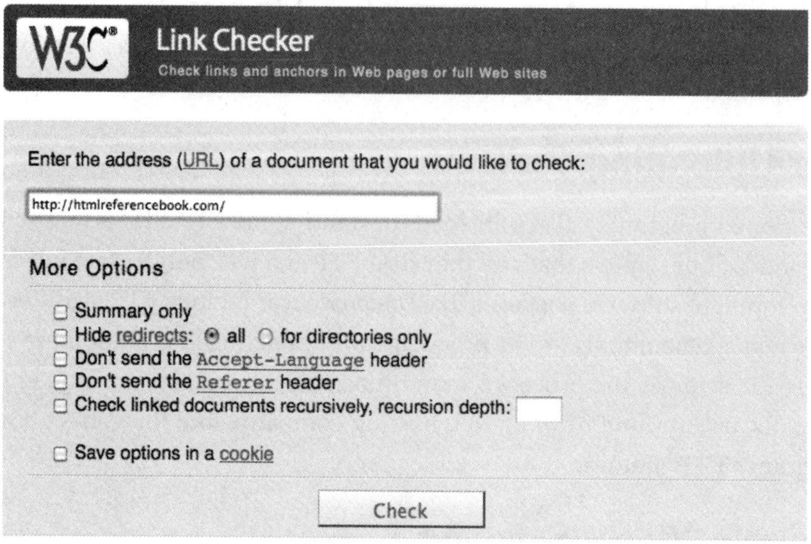

Figure 9.14. The W3C Link Checker service

The service will investigate all your links, and provide you with a report of all the links it found. More importantly, it will report any links that were broken.

Opt for a Summary Version

The report may be quite long if you have a lot of web pages, images, stylesheets, or other dependencies linked to the page you submit. In such cases, you might like to check the **Summary Only** option—then you'll only be told what's broken.

Validating Your Web Pages

Another important step before telling the masses to visit your new website is to **validate** your web pages. This is the process of checking your markup to see if it conforms to the rules of the language you specified in the Document Type Declaration (otherwise known as the doctype).

As you'll recall back in Chapter 2, the Document Type Declaration is the first line of your file's HTML:

chapter9/website_files/index.html (excerpt)

```
<!DOCTYPE html>
```

For the project site, we're using the HTML5 doctype, which is much simpler than previous doctypes (a list of which is available on SitePoint[14]). By validating your site, you're confirming that your pages follow the rules of HTML, and that there are no errors that might cause your page to fail in any given browser. This is important to check, because although a web page may *appear* to be fine to you, if there's an error in the HTML document, it may appear incorrectly for a user of a different browser. Validation gives you a heads-up about anything that may be problematic in another browser on which you haven't checked your website.

Another reason why it's important to validate your HTML is that the associated CSS is intrinsically linked to it. An error in the HTML can cause problems with the CSS; this can range from the minor—like the wrong link color displaying—to the much more drastic, such as a broken page layout.

How to Validate Your Live Web Pages

Again, specialist web development software like Dreamweaver has this functionality built-in, but there's always the W3C Markup Validation Service[15] if you don't have access to other tools. As with the link checker, simply type into the **Address** text box the address of the live web page that you want to check, and click the **Check** button. If you've followed the instructions in this book, you should see a nice message like the one depicted in Figure 9.15.

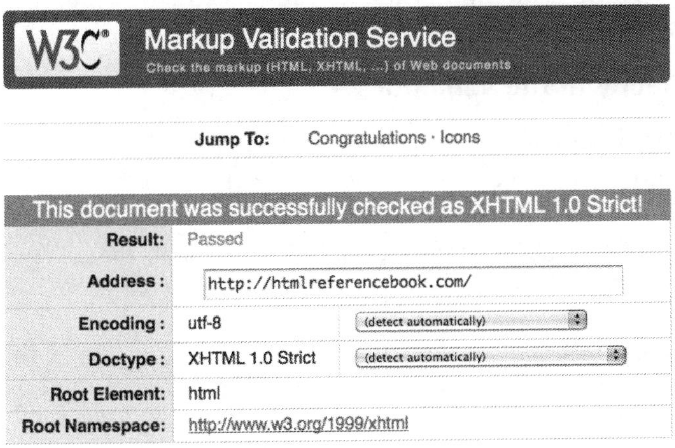

Figure 9.15. A pass mark for your markup!

---

[14] http://reference.sitepoint.com/html/doctypes

[15] http://validator.w3.org/

If you aren't seeing this (try scrolling down a little, just in case it's offscreen), your web page probably has errors that need to be fixed. The good news is that the validator will point out the problem, providing some explanation about why it's wrong. A typical validation failure looks like the page shown in Figure 9.16.

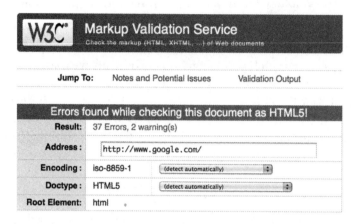

Figure 9.16. Highlighting and explaining validation failures

You'll need to check more than just one page on your website, and this is a one-page-at-a-time affair; unfortunately, it's not possible to check an entire site at once using this validator. To ensure that your site is valid, you'll need to validate every page individually. The W3C validator, however, is not the only online tool; the Web Design Group's HTML Validator is able to validate an entire site in one pass.

Go Directly to the Validator

With the W3C validator, you can check your markup before it's uploaded and publicly available. You can also choose the **Direct Input** option, which basically means you can copy and paste the HTML from any page and then validate it. If you try validating one of our project pages—for example, the gallery page—you should find that:

- the page validates (this is good)

- you receive a warning about the use of the HTML5 doctype, stating "Using experimental feature: HTML5 Conformance Checker". This is no cause for alarm; in fact, it may have ceased by the time you read this. Because HTML5 is still in a state of development, the validator that checks for conformance against HTML5 is too. The warning is just that—a note to let you know that it's trying its best, but isn't 100% sure!

 Using Third-party Markup

If you use a piece of third-party markup or code—for example, the Facebook **Like** box markup that we added to the home page in the previous chapter—it's very likely that there will be one or two nasties in there where validation is concerned. Sometimes it's possible to tidy up the third-party markup, but more often than not, it's safer to leave it as is.

The Facebook **Like** box example causes three errors by using nonstandard attributes in the `iframe` tag. If you're unsure what the effect of removing or changing these will be, leave it as is (additionally, you could curse the developers, and be content in the fact that, "It wasn't my work that failed to validate!"). The chances are that you will do more damage to the page by striving for 100% validation, while the invalid markup supplied will work perfectly well in all modern browsers. As much as I dislike invalid markup, there are times when you have to be flexible and try not to let it concern you too much.

Validate Everything

Validation is not just about your HTML—you can (and should) validate your site's CSS using the W3C's CSS Validator.[16] You can even run an automated test to see if your page is accessible to people with disabilities.[17] I must point out, however, that automated tests can only really point out *possible* problems—rather than confirm that your web page is *truly* accessible. Once again, if you find that the results are too detailed to make sense of (it's a common complaint), try seeking clarification in an online forum. SitePoint's CSS forum[18] members will be able to explain most CSS validation failures; for answers to web accessibility problems, register an account at the Accessify Forum[19] and post your question there.

---

[16] http://jigsaw.w3.org/css-validator/

[17] The most popular accessibility validator is Cynthia Says [http://www.contentquality.com/].

[18] http://www.sitepoint.com/launch/cssforum/

[19] http://www.accessifyforum.com/

What are all these errors?

An automated validation service has no feelings. If you were to ask it, "How's my hair looking?", it might bluntly reply, "Well, it's bad—it's uneven at the back, there are tangles here, here, and *here*, and the color's all wrong." My point is that an automated service of this type won't go easy on you—all errors will be reported in a matter-of-fact way.

Don't let this get you down—it happens to all web designers and programmers. And don't be annoyed with yourself if you fail to understand everything you're being told. It really can be a case of information overload.

The trick is to fix the obvious faults—those that you can easily identify—first. Then, when you've uploaded the amended pages, try validating again. You may find that fixing some standard problems also resolves others that you were struggling with. One simple dilemma is often the cause of many other problems.

If you're still unable to pass validation, make your way over to the SitePoint forums, specifically the HTML forum,[20] and post your question there. Tell the people you're a newbie after some advice, and you should receive that more caring, tactful approach that the validator so sorely lacks!

Promoting Your Website

If you've confirmed that your web pages are using valid HTML and CSS, and you're confident that they're widely accessible and look good on different browsers, you should now think about how you'll promote your website.

Promoting your site can be a project in its own right. SitePoint offers kits for those with a marketing budget, including *The Search Engine Marketing Kit*[21] and *The Web Design Business Kit.*[22] As a newcomer to the world of web design, though, these are probably too ambitious for the time being; I mention them to indicate how big this topic is in its own right (not to give you the big sales pitch!). So, what promotions can you undertake that won't cost you an arm and a leg?

---

[20] http://www.sitepoint.com/launch/htmlforum/
[21] http://www.sitepoint.com/books/sem1/
[22] http://www.sitepoint.com/books/freelance1/

Submit Your Website to Search Engines

An extremely high percentage of visitors to my personal websites arrive through searches on Google, Bing, and Yahoo (in that order), and the same will probably be true for your website. However, a search engine will not know that your website is there, unless either:

- there is a link to your website from another website that the search engine knows about (this is how search engines crawl the Web—by finding links in pages that it knows about, and adding these pages to its database of pages)

- you fill in a form on the search engine to instruct it to visit and index the content of your website (Google,[23] Bing,[24] and Yahoo[25] offer such pages)

Another good place to start is the Open Directory Project,[26] which aims to become a comprehensive directory of the Internet. It's structured hierarchically, so you'll need to work out where your site fits within the hierarchy before you submit it.

These are just a few tips to help you start. For further advice about search engine submissions, pay a visit to SitePoint's Internet Marketing forum.[27]

 Cleaner Markup, Better Search Results

It's worth noting that web pages that conform to standards, and are lightweight and accessible, attract better search engine results. Without going into too much detail, search engines find it easier to retrieve search terms from a well-structured web page than one that fails to adhere to web standards. You can learn more about how and why this is the case from the forum mentioned above.

Tell Your Friends and Colleagues

Well, it seems like an obvious idea, but it's worth mentioning. Your friends and colleagues could be your biggest fans—even if they've never seen your website. And

---

[23] http://www.google.com/addurl/
[24] http://www.bing.com/
[25] http://search.yahoo.com/info/submit.html
[26] http://dmoz.org/add.html
[27] http://www.sitepoint.com/forums/internet-marketing-2/

if you give them your website address on a handy-to-keep card or similar, you never know how many times they might visit, or who they might mention it to.

Craft an Email Signature with Your Website Details

Consider creating a default signature that's applied to every email message you compose. It's a marketing technique that's basically a no-brainer. A simple line or two at the end of each email you send can generate a surprising number of visits to your website:

```
Hi Dad,

What time should we should expect you for dinner on Tuesday? Also,
have you had a chance to check out the new website? Pretty
spiffy, eh?


--
Bob Dobalina
President of Bubble Under -- the diving club for the south-west UK
Visit our website at http://www.bubbleunder.com/
```

Once you've added it to your signature, there's no real ongoing maintenance required, and every message you send could attract a new visitor to your website!

Post on a Related Forum

Similarly, you can usually add a signature to posts you make in discussion forums that are related to your website's topic. It could even include a clickable link to your website. The advantage is that the others who post and read these forum messages have the same interest. So, rather than the signature being a hit-and-miss affair, it's being presented to those most inclined to take a look.

Of course, this means that you'll need to be more prolific with posting on such sites, but that's no hardship if it's a topic of interest to you.

Link Exchange

Finally, I'd recommend that you look into swapping links with similar websites. Be mindful of taking the right approach; emailing a site with "Hey, can you link to my website—it's really good!" isn't considered the best etiquette. However, if you've already included a link to a site, and you approach them nicely with this fact, asking whether they'd they be willing to link back, you may have more luck.

Link exchange programs that automate the process are available, but I'd recommend against using them. You can't be sure of the quality of links that will appear automatically on your website, nor the quality of sites that link to you through these services. Additionally, link exchange programs often require you to display ugly banner ads or badges, making your website look unprofessional. It's better to remain a little choosy and stay in control of your site.

Summary

In this chapter, we've focused on the process of placing your website files online, from the initial choices about where to host your website, to the nuts and bolts of putting your files up onto the live server. I've explained how you can use free online services to check whether your web pages are in good shape, and suggested some ways that you can begin to promote your new online venture.

It may have been fun building your site. Perhaps at times you've found it difficult, yet you've battled on and seen your way through to the end result. But is this the end of your website's development? Probably not—shortly after making your files live, you'll no doubt think of new additions. Fortunately for you, our next chapter is all about adding extra little tidbits of functionality to your site. So, what are we waiting for?

10

Enhancing the Site with HTML5 and CSS3

Although you might be unaware of this—or may have forgotten—but throughout this book we've actually been creating HTML5 documents. But that's only because we've used the HTML5 doctype. In all other respects, we've been using HTML4 (or earlier) elements, and have been writing the markup in an XHTML syntax. This includes lowercase tags and attributes, quoted attributes, and symmetrical opening and closing HTML tags.

We've been steering clear of using some real, honest-to-goodness, brand-spanking new HTML5 elements, but that's going to change in this chapter. I've also avoided covering some of the newer CSS features that people are making more use of in the world of web design, namely CSS3. Like HTML, all the CSS that you've learned up to this point has been safe and predictable. This is deliberate—after all, you're new to this. The last thing we want is for you to trip up too much in the early stages and then, in a fit of rage, throw the book out the window.

So in this chapter, we're going to learn about HTML5 and CSS3—just a moderate amount—and see how we can apply it to the project site. We will also learn how different browsers handle the various new elements and features. (And importantly, we'll learn to relax about the possibility of rendering differences between the browsers). Let's begin by finding out what is new in HTML5.

HTML5: A Brief History

There's a lot that I could write about the various groups that were involved in the making of HTML5, including the politics, infighting, and scandals, too. Okay, these "so-called scandals" would no-doubt fail to make the front page of your major newspaper, but my point is that you probably don't need to know *all* the background.[1] So here's my super-simple summary: In 1998 the W3C (who are responsible for the documentation and standards on the Web[2]) effectively parked HTML at version 4.01. An XHTML specification came after that, but it was simply an update on HTML with XML syntax and rules. Later, work began on a specification called XHTML2.0, but it lacked backwards compatibility. This striving to create a more rigid system meant that it would be unforgiving towards older web documents that were built with sloppier markup. So if a browser were set to only render a page created in valid XHTML2.0, it would shut out a huge proportion of the Web. Most of it, to be honest.

Realizing this was a bad course of action, a group of like-minded people from Opera, Mozilla, Apple, and Microsoft (collectively known as WHATWG[3]) worked on what would eventually become HTML5. In the meantime, the W3C saw sense, and XHTML2.0 was dropped like the dead donkey that it was. Now HTML5 is a collaborative (and occasionally combative) affair between the W3C and WHATWG. More importantly, it's the *agreed* way forward for HTML, rather than the breakaway effort from a disgruntled group of bearded and bespectacled nerds that will never gain traction. HTML5 is here to stay!

But what exactly is HTML5?

---

[1] For the backstory, some good in-depth articles can be found at http://diveintohtml5.org/past.html and http://en.wikipedia.org/wiki/HTML5.

[2] Actually, this is another thorny issue. The W3C don't really create standards, they make "recommendations," but the average person in the street would refer to them as standards. It's not technically correct, but at least everyone knows what everyone else is talking about. And that's a good thing!

[3] Web Hypertext Application Technology Working Group—catchy, huh?

Paving the Cow Paths

I love this expression. It explains to me what HTML5 is about in a neat little nutshell. Perhaps you haven't heard it before, though. The idea is that regardless of where you set out paths in a given area, people (or cows!) will find their own way. Often they are referred to as desire paths.[4] "Paving the cow path" is an admission that the path you set is being ignored, so you might as well "go with the flow". Pave that cow path and make it the official route! In HTML, paving the cow path can be demonstrated with a few simple comparisons, as Table 10.1 illustrates.

Table 10.1. The cow path from HTML4 to HTML5

HTML4	HTML5
`<div id="header"></div>`	`<header></header>`
`<div id="footer"></div>`	`<footer></footer>`
`<div id="nav"></div>`	`<nav></nav>`

That looks simple, right? If everyone is calling a particular element a header (using the id attribute), why not just create an element called header? Likewise footer and nav. Be assured that this wasn't conducted as some "finger in the air, best guess" approach. A couple of pieces of research formed the basis. First, in 2004, when a billion web pages were analyzed in the Google index to see which class names were most used on the Web.[5] Then, in 2009, Opera did a similar scan of approximately 2 million pages, chosen at random.[6] This research helped to form opinion about what HTML elements should be named (or reinforced already held beliefs). At the time of writing, the list of new HTML5 elements not rejected during the ratification process are: article, aside, audio, bdi, canvas, command, datalist, details, embed, figcaption, figure, footer, header, hgroup, keygen, mark, meter, nav, output, progress, rp, rt, ruby, section, source, summary, time, video, and wbr.

Now, we won't be covering all those elements here. Instead, I've picked a handful for now so that you can gain an idea of what you can do to update the site. But fear not! In the final chapter, I'll be recommending how and where you can learn more about a range of topics, including HTML5. I hope this chapter will give you enough

---

[4] http://en.wikipedia.org/wiki/Desire_path
[5] http://code.google.com/webstats/2005-12/classes.html
[6] http://devfiles.myopera.com/articles/572/idlist-url.htm

of a taste, and there's nothing to stop you from reading one of the many excellent online tutorials on HTML5 for free.[7]

Browser Support for HTML5

Before we go on, I should explain where the various browsers stand on support. The answer is: they have a very different stand on browser support! The problem is that, at the time of writing, HTML5 is still in a state of flux. And because the specification itself is a moving target, the various browser manufacturers have implemented and supported different features, depending on either their understanding (or agreement) of how certain elements should be rendered or treated, or based on their release schedule.

As such, it's not even worth stating a browser support chart here, as it will no doubt be out of date the moment this book goes to print. I would, however, recommend referring to http://caniuse.com/, which states various browsers' support for HTML5 and CSS3 features. So, browsers vary in their level of support for HTML5 features. But some are *more* different from others. I'm looking at you, Internet Explorer!

Fixing IE Support

Until IE9 came out, Internet Explorer had no support for any of the new HTML5 elements (and only the tiniest amount of support for more obscure HTML5 features). However, there are ways to make earlier versions of IE behave, at least from the point of view of allowing us to style these new HTML5 elements. The problem is that earlier versions don't know, for example, what a header element is:

- Is it a block-level element?
- Should it have any padding or margins?
- How should any text inside be presented?
- Can it be contained inside a list item?
- Is it allowed to be wrapped around a table?

---

[7] An excellent start would be Dive Into HTML5: http://diveintohtml5.org/introduction.html, and there are some excellent articles on HTML5 Doctor: http://html5doctor.com/. For those who can handle a bit of swearing and cheeky humor, Bruce Lawson's personal site (http://www.brucelawson.co.uk/category/accessibility-web-standards/html5/) has a number of excellent HTML5 articles, too.

IE8 and earlier simply doesn't know what to do with it! If you try to apply a simple style in the CSS, it won't apply that either, for example:

```
header {background:red; padding:10px; color:white;}
```

However, there is a way of forcing IE to recognize the header element and all the other HTML5 elements, letting you style it to your heart's content. We can thank Remy Sharp for this, the HTML5 enabling script:[8]

```
<!--[if lt IE 9]>
  <script src="http://html5shim.googlecode.com/svn/trunk/html5.js">
  </script>
<![endif]-->
```

Simply place this script between the opening <head> and closing </head> tags, and it's all taken care of for you. This is what it's actually doing:

1. First of all, it detects whether you actually need it. It's wrapped inside conditional comments, a way of serving out additional CSS or scripts to specific versions of Internet Explorer. In the example, it directs versions less than IE9—as shown by lt IE 9—to download this script.

2. The script is hosted at Google. You could always download it and self-host, but it's beneficial to refer to this Google version, because it's likely to be served more quickly than your own server. The other benefit is that many sites also refer to this same piece of code. So if your site visitor has already been to another site that uses this script, they'll already have it in their browser's cache, and will not need to download it again.

3. Inside the script that's downloaded, the older versions of IE are (to put it very simply) informed about the new HTML5 elements. This is done by having one of each of these items dynamically generated and inserted into the document.

4. These items that are dynamically generated won't appear at all, but it's enough for IE to understand that the elements exist, and you're then able to apply styles as you see fit.

---

[8] http://remysharp.com/2009/01/07/html5-enabling-script/

This is a super-simple addition to have on your site, so that's our next task with our project:

1. Open the home page of the site in your text editor: **index.html**.

2. Just after the `<meta>` tag and before the `<link>`, add the HTML5-enabling link in the `<script>` tags. It should look like this on your screen:

```
<!DOCTYPE html>
<html lang="en">
  <head>
    <title>Bubble Under - The diving club for the south-west UK
    </title>
    <meta charset="utf-8" />
    <!--[if lt IE 9]>
      <script src="http://html5shim.googlecode.com/svn/trunk/➥
        html5.js"></script>
    <![endif]-->
    <link href="style1.css" rel="stylesheet" type="text/css" />
  </head>
```

3. Repeat this for all pages in the site.

If you refresh the page in any browser, you'll see no discernible difference, but there's an easy answer to that—we're yet to try using any HTML5! For all the other non-IE browsers (and IE9), the script is entirely ignored, just as it should be.

Replacing Generic `divs` with Proper HTML5 Elements

The next step is to make some replacements in the site structure. I've mentioned the research into what people were commonly naming certain parts of the page. Well, this project site is no different. Remember these sections?

```
<body>
  <div id="header">
    <div id="sitebranding">
      <h1>BubbleUnder.com</h1>
    </div>
    <div id="tagline">
      <p>Diving club for the south-west UK - let's make a splash!
      </p>
    </div>
```

```
</div> <!-- end of header div -->
<div id="navigation">
  <ul>
    <li><a href="index.html">Home</a></li>
    <li><a href="about.html">About Us</a></li>
    <li><a href="events.html">Club Events</a></li>
    <li><a href="contact.html">Contact Us</a></li>
    <li><a href="gallery.html">Image Gallery</a></li>
  </ul>
</div> <!-- end of navigation div -->
  ...
</body>
```

One of them is a perfect match for an HTML5 replacement—namely the div with an id of header. The other is close; we have it as a div with an id of navigation, while in HTML5, the equivalent would be the shorter and simpler nav element.

Let's start by changing these in the markup:

▨ In **index.html**, take the div with an id of header and replace it with a <header> tag. Be sure to replace the closing tag for this element too.

▨ Take the div with an id of navigation and replace it with a nav element (and closing tag, too).

▨ You can also remove the comments that say end of header div and end of navigation div. By replacing the div with more meaningful tags, it becomes so much clearer in the markup what's being closed off, so the comments are now unnecessary.

I hope you're looking at markup like this:

```
<body>
  <header>
    <div id="sitebranding">
      <h1>BubbleUnder.com</h1>
    </div>
    <div id="tagline">
      <p>Diving club for the south-west UK - let's make a splash!
      </p>
    </div>
  </header>
```

```
<nav>
  <ul>
    <li><a href="index.html">Home</a></li>
    <li><a href="about.html">About Us</a></li>
    <li><a href="events.html">Club Events</a></li>
    <li><a href="contact.html">Contact Us</a></li>
    <li><a href="gallery.html">Image Gallery</a></li>
  </ul>
</nav>
...
</body>
```

That's a little easier on the eye. But how does it look on the web page? Save any changes and go take a look.

Um, okay ... how bad was it for you?

Figure 10.1. Our web page with nav and header tags

Depending on which browser you tried it in, the differences may range from minor issues (for example, a background image missing in the left navigation area), to a horribly broken layout (which will basically be down to IE!). The main reason for this is that you've broken the relationship that existed between the old structure of markup and CSS when you changed the tag names:

```
#header {
   border-top: 3px solid #7da5d8;
}
```

This markup no longer applies to anything, because there's no element with an id of header (as indicated by the # symbol). By removing the #, we're telling the CSS to style the header element as so:

```
header {
   border-top: 3px solid #7da5d8;
}
```

Similarly, the navigation is no longer styling properly, so we need to take this:

```
#navigation {
   width: 180px;
   height: 484px;
   background: #7da5d8 url(backgrounds/nav-bg.jpg) no-repeat;
}
```

And change it to:

```
nav {
   width: 180px;
   height: 484px;
   background: #7da5d8 url(backgrounds/nav-bg.jpg) no-repeat;
}
```

Go ahead, try this for yourself and see if it corrects the problems as you would expect. In most browsers, this is all we need to put it right again. In IE—or rather, versions older than IE9—we need to tell it a little bit more about how these elements should appear, because they have no idea at all. If IE doesn't know how an element should be displayed, by default it treats it like inline content (such as a span); we need to tell it that we want it to display as a block-level element (just as it was when it was previously a div element):

```
header {
   border-top: 3px solid #7da5d8;
   display:block; /* Only for IE8 or less */
}
```

```
...
nav {
  width: 180px;
  height: 484px;
  background: #7da5d8 url(backgrounds/nav-bg.jpg) no-repeat;
  display:block; /* Only for IE8 or less */
}
```

Make these simple changes, and then see how IE6, IE7, and IE8 behaves. Are we back on track? Good! We'll need to do this a few times, but thanks to Remy Sharp's HTML5 enabling script, IE will play ball no matter which version we're dealing with.[9] You may notice in some browsers that moving from the `div` to the `nav` version introduced a slight gap above the navigation, as seen in Figure 10.2.

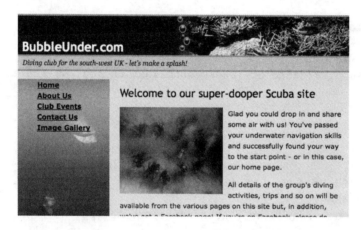

Figure 10.2. The nav element has caused a slight gap to appear above the navigation bar

This is the effect of the top margin of the unordered (`ul`) list inside the `nav`. We'll make a couple of slight changes to ensure all browsers play nice, so we'll remove the margin on that `ul` element, (but not others that may appear in the body copy), by adding in the following selector:

```
nav ul {margin:0;}
```

---

[9] That is, unless people browsing your site with IE have deliberately switched off JavaScript, in which case they'll receive the unstyled version. That said, if they've actively gone about disabling this, they're probably well used to websites breaking on a regular basis anyway!

This has removed the space above the navigation area so that the background imagery sits nicely, as Figure 10.3 shows.

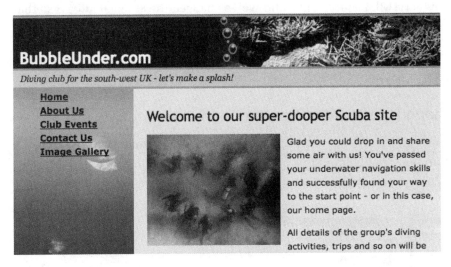

Figure 10.3. With the margin on our unordered list removed, it's looking a little better

Unfortunately, the space above the navigation links has been lost too. We can force those back down by adding some spacing inside the nav element. For that we use padding, giving us the following:

```
nav ul {margin:0; padding-top:15px;}
```

Okay, so now we're back on an even keel, as Figure 10.4 demonstrates!

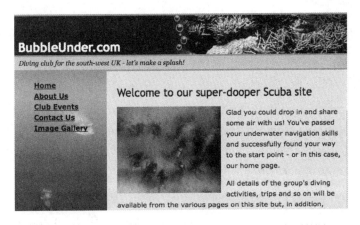

Figure 10.4. A bit of padding and our navigation bar is back to normal

So far, we've let older versions of IE know about the new elements that HTML5 contains so it can style them; we've changed a couple of elements on the page to their new HTML5 equivalents; and we've changed the associated CSS so that it matches up with this amended markup.

Let's take a look at some other sections on the web page, and see if more are ripe for an HTML5 update.

Marking Up the Main Content

As you scan through the markup on the project site's home page, you might well be thinking, "Well, there's this body content section on the page. If there's a `header` and a `nav` section, surely that's the next bit to be marked up?"

```
<body>
 <header>
   ...
 </header>
 <nav>
   ...
 </nav>
 <div id="bodycontent">
  <h2>About Us</h2>
  <p><span class="fun">Bubble Under</span> is
  a group of diving enthusiasts based in the ...</p>
 </div> <!-- end of bodycontent div -->
</body>
```

And if you're thinking this, I'd have to give you a congratulatory pat on the back and say, "Well done," before adding, somewhat regretfully, "But unfortunately, you're wrong." Sorry.

Strangely, there is no <content> element in HTML5, or <maincontent>, or <bodycontent>, or any other variation that you can think of. The HTML5 **parser** (that's the brain inside the browser that deciphers the structure of the web page) is clever enough to understand that after a `header` and a `nav`, the next piece of markup (which isn't an `aside` or `footer` element—more on these in a moment) must be the main content.

So, we can leave that for now. But what about these `aside` and `footer` elements?

The `aside` Element

If you've ever found yourself saying, "As an aside, I'd like to ...", you'll already have a good idea about the kind of content that goes into the `aside` element. It's information that's additional to what's being said, which could be easily removed without affecting the meaning of the main message.

In a web page, the `aside` element might be used for the following types of content:

- presenting a pullquote
- holding a sidebar for advertising
- a collection of links (for example, related websites), which would also be contained inside a `nav` element

We could tweak the About page to make use of the `aside` element, by removing the concluding quote from our man Bob and making it an `aside`. So we'd go from this:

```
<div id="bodycontent">
  <h2>About Us</h2>
  <p><span class="fun">Bubble Under</span> is ...
  <p>Or as our man Bob Dobalina would put it:</p>
  <blockquote class="fun"><p>"Happiness is a dip in the ocean
    followed by a pint or two of Old Speckled Hen. You can
    quote me on that!"</p></blockquote>
</div> <!-- end of bodycontent div -->
```

To this:

```
<div id="bodycontent">
  <h2>About Us</h2>
  <aside>
    <blockquote>
    Happiness is a dip in the ocean followed by a pint
    or two of Old Speckled Hen. You can quote me on that!
    </blockquote>
    Bob Dobalina, March 2011
  </aside>
```

```
<p><span class="fun">Bubble Under</span> is
a group of diving enthusiasts based in the ...
</div> <!-- end of bodycontent div -->
```

I've moved the aside further up the page so that, when floated with the CSS as shown, it appears in a sensible position, but in the source order—that is, the position it appears in the code. However, because it's marked up using the aside element, it effectively informs the browser that this is less important in the document flow.

To make the quote more visually appealing than it was before, I've applied a number of additional styles. I've made it so that the aside only takes up a certain percentage of the page width, so if you resize the browser window, the shape of the aside element changes accordingly. How you style a quote is entirely up to you, of course. The markup is below:

```css
aside {
    display:block;
    float:right;
    margin:10px;
    padding:10px;
    width:30%;
    background:white;
    font-style:italic;
    color:gray;
}

aside blockquote {
    font-size:1.2em;
    line-height:1.4;
    margin:0 0 0.5em 0;
    font-style:normal;
    color:#006;
}
```

The results can be seen in Figure 10.5 and Figure 10.6:

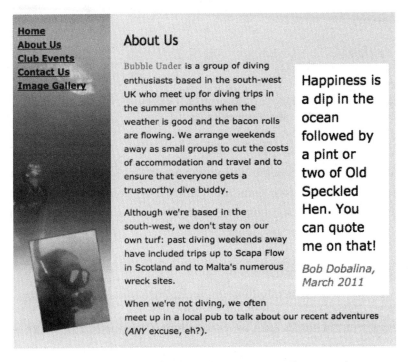

Figure 10.5. The About page with a narrow `aside` element ...

Figure 10.6. ... that stretches to a wide version when the browser window is resized

The `footer` Element

This should be quite obvious, but there is still more to the humble `footer` than you might first expect. Just as we were able to mark up the `header` of the web page, we can use a `footer` to group content that we might normally have at the end of the web page; for example, copyright messages, additional navigation items (to privacy policies, accessibility statements), site hosting information, and so on. Our project site lacks this sort of content that we could convert, but typically, it would be marked up like so:

```
<body>
  <header>…</header>
  <nav>…</nav>
  <h1>Main heading</h1>
  <p>Content </p>
  <footer>Copyright 2011. All rights reserved. Site maintained by
    bob@bubbleunder.com</footer>
</body>
```

It's a fairly easy one to remember, but you can actually have more than one footer on a page. You can have more than one header, too—as long as they are contained inside another new HTML5 sectioning element, such as the `article` element. So let's take a look at how that one works.

The `article` Element

Probably the best examples of when you would use the `article` element are:

- in a news website—with each news item being wrapped in an `article` element

- on a blog, where each blog post is wrapped in an `article`

Here's an example of how it might appear in a news site:

```
<article id="newsstory12534345">
  <h2>Police track down missing girl's kidnapper</h2>
  <p>Reporter: Fred Parker</p>
  <p>Police have reported ...</p>
  ...
  <p>Published on 24 March, 2011</p>
</article>
```

Web developers could take this a stage further by adding a `header` and `footer` element to each article they publish. It's usually quite clear which elements would appear inside a `header` and, in this example, the `footer` too. So, with a slight rejig, we have this:

```
<article id="newsstory12534345">
  <header>
    <h2>Police track down missing girl's kidnapper</h2>
    <p>Reporter: Fred Parker</p>
  </header>
```

```
  <p>Police have reported ...</p>
  ...
  <footer>
    <p>Published on 24 March, 2011</p>
  </footer>
</article>
```

Finally, it's possible to tweak the markup a little further with regards to the heading. In the news web page example, the heading is marked up as an h2. It's a fair assumption, therefore, that this article snippet is further down the document, underneath an h1 heading. This is logical, and good practice, but in HTML5 you can effectively treat each article as its own self-contained document. As such, the main heading here could change to an h1, and subsequent headings would be h2, h3, and so on:

```
<article id="newsstory12534345">
  <header>
    <h1>Police track down missing girl's kidnapper</h1>
    <p>Reporter: Fred Parker</p>
  </header>
  <p>Police have reported ...</p>
  ...
  <h2>Sub-heading goes here</h2>
  <p>In further developments ...</p>
  <footer>
    <p>Published on 24 March, 2011</p>
  </footer>
</article>
```

This means that your page as a whole could contain numerous h1 elements. This was previously frowned upon, but when they're contained inside the appropriate HTML5 element (article in this instance), it's perfectly okay to do this; the browser is able to ascertain the document structure, even with all these h1 elements.

The `figure` and `figcaption` Elements

Remember as far back as Chapter 5 when we learned all about images? I know, distant memories! Well, we'll revisit that again, dust it down and see what we can do with another couple of HTML5 elements: figure and figcaption. Let's remind ourselves how we marked up each image on the page:

```
<div class="galleryphoto">
  <img src="gallery/turtle-bite.jpg" width="400" height="258"
    alt="A turtle swims comfortably among the coral, despite its
    old injury - a large shark bite on one side" />
  <p>This turtle was spotted swimming around the Great Barrier Reef
    (Queensland, Australia) quite gracefully despite having had a
    large chunk taken out of its right side, presumably in
    a shark attack. <span class="photocredit">[Photographer: Ian
    Lloyd]</span></p>
</div>
```

So, we have a container (`div.galleryphoto`), which includes an image (`img`), and a paragraph (`p`), which is really acting as a caption. When we were putting this together earlier, I had a little moan about the `caption` element being used for an entirely different purpose—for tables. If only there was a suitable alternative that we could use for images, illustrations, and charts.

So you know where this is going. The new `figure` and `figcaption` elements are the perfect pairing for this kind of structure. Instead of a generic `div` (with a `class` of `galleryphoto` in our example), we can replace it with the `figure` element. And the paragraph can be replaced with the `figcaption` element, transforming the markup like so:

```
<figure>
  <img src="gallery/turtle-bite.jpg" width="400" height="258"
    alt="A turtle swims comfortably among the coral, despite its
    old injury - a large shark bite on one side" />
  <figcaption>This turtle was spotted swimming around the Great
    Barrier Reef (Queensland, Australia) quite gracefully,
    despite having had a large chunk taken out of its right
    side, presumably in a shark attack. <span class=➥
    "photocredit">[Photographer: Ian
    Lloyd]</span></figcaption>
</figure>
```

We'll also need to make some changes to the CSS, to ensure that our amended markup still displays on the page properly. The references in the stylesheet to our class of `galleryphoto` and the paragraph used as a caption will change from this:

```
.galleryphoto {
  padding-bottom: 10px;
  border-bottom: 1px solid navy;
  margin-bottom: 20px;
}

.galleryphoto p {
  font-size: 65%;
  font-weight: bold;
  margin-top: 0;
  width: 430px;
  line-height: 1.4em;
}

.galleryphoto p span {
  font-weight: normal;
  color: gray;
}

.galleryphoto img {
  border: 15px solid white;
}
```

To this:

```
figure {
  display:block;
  padding-bottom: 10px;
  border-bottom: 1px solid navy;
  margin-bottom: 20px;
}

figcaption {
  display:block;
  font-size: 65%;
  font-weight: bold;
  margin-top: 0;
  width: 430px;
  line-height: 1.4em;
}

figcaption span {
  font-weight: normal;
  color: gray;
```

```
}

figure img {
  border: 15px solid white;
}
```

Simple Selectors

Did you spot that we changed the selector `.galleryphoto p {}` to simply `figcaption {}`, instead of `figure figcaption {}`? We were able to just state `figcaption` because in HTML5, the `figcaption` can only appear inside a `figure` element; stating it in the CSS as `figure figcaption {}` is fussier than it needs to be, as the first part would be superfluous. I also added `display: block` to `figure` and `figcaption`, as Safari was having, shall we say, "issues" without this, causing the page to render poorly.

With these changes, the gallery looks almost as it did before, as Figure 10.7 shows.

Figure 10.7. A gallery image with the `figure` and `figcaption` elements

The one difference is that by changing from a `p` to a `figcaption`, the text color has changed from navy to black, because it no longer applies the following CSS rule:

```
p {
  font-size: small;
  color: navy;
}
```

Now, we could change the color back to navy by adding the color reference in the `figcaption` CSS, but hey, you know what? I think I prefer the caption with a different color to the usual body copy. After all, a web developer is allowed to change his mind now and again.

And There's Still More to HTML5

Oh yes, there's more—a LOT more! I've run through some of the HTML5 elements that you're most likely to find a use for (and which have the fewest problems when implemented in the browsers available). But there are still many more elements with which you could be experimenting.

HTML5 Forms Will Rock ... Soon

One section in particular revolves around forms. In Chapter 7, we built up a form using a range of controls, and in HTML5 there are even more types of controls available. These include sliders (`<input type="range">`), and special types of text inputs for capturing certain data such as email addresses (`<input type="email">`) and dates (`<input type="date">`). The benefit of using these specific input types is that it allows the browser to do a number of tasks, such as:

- validate that an email address is correct before submitting, and alert the user when it needs amending

- provide a simple date picker for any date field, rather than force the user to enter it as text in a specific format

- customize the pop-up keyboard that appears on touchscreen devices, so it's relevant to the type of data being entered; for example, when entering a web address, displaying a keypad with a **.com** button, as the iPhone does when encountering `<input type="url">`

Arguably, these are some of the most compelling features of HTML5, but I won't be going into any more depth here because of the (at present) rather patchy support for these features. There's not a lot of benefit in reworking our contact form example with all these new features for now. That said, it's definitely worth finding out more, and Mark Pilgrim's *Dive into HTML5* [10] has an excellent section on forms that you can read.

---

[10] http://diveintohtml5.org/forms.html

More Complex HTML5 (and Related) Technologies

In addition to new HTML5 elements and the enhancements to existing HTML elements (like the new types of input mentioned), there are a slew of further changes and more complex additions. Some have even been split into their own respective specifications so they could be developed independently of HTML5 (but still very much related to it). Some of these more complex additions include:

- Geolocation: the ability to pinpoint physical location in the browser[11]

- Offline storage: capability in the browser to download required files in advance, which it can make use of in the event of a lack of network connection (hence "offline")[12]

- The canvas element: a "resolution-dependent bitmap canvas which can be used for rendering graphs, game graphics, or other visual images on the fly" (http://www.w3.org/TR/html5/the-canvas-element.html)[13]

These are not covered at all in this book because they are all big topics in their own right and, as with the forms, support for them at present is still somewhat varied.

I trust that the changes we've covered in this chapter give you an idea about some of the new features HTML5 has introduced. If you follow the same steps—adding the HTML5 enabling script for older versions of IE, and using the new structural HTML5 elements (header, footer, nav, article)—you should have few problems in creating clean, easy-to-read markup that works in all modern browsers.

But perhaps, having re-engineered some of the underlying markup, you could add some further enhancements that the person looking at the web page will appreciate? An extra little sprinkle of magic, in the form of CSS3!

CSS3 ... CSS2 ... what's the difference?

As with the HTML5 section, I'm going to keep the history on this brief. Suffice to say that, up to this point, all the CSS you've read about is actually CSS2 (or 2.1, in

---

[11] Geolocation has its own specification [http://www.w3.org/TR/geolocation-API/]. This is not, I warn you, bedtime reading!

[12] Once again, Mark Pilgrim's online HTML5 book (above) is a good place to learn more about the topic.

[13] And once again, Mark Pilgrim will do the explaining regarding canvas in the section "Let's call it a Draw(ing surface)."

which certain aspects were removed from the CSS2 spec). CSS3 introduces a range of new options to improve text, colors, border styles, and various shadow and gradient effects. It also has entire "modules" (separate chunks of specifications that browsers will implement over time) dealing with such items as multicolumn layouts, fonts, and media queries, in which the browser is able to identify the type of medium (smartphone, desktop computer, tablet, and so on) the web page is being rendered on and adapt accordingly.

The CSS you've learned so far is fairly safe. Granted, there may be one or two slight quirks with browsers in certain circumstances but, by and large, everything works well across all modern browsers, and many of the older versions too (I'm looking at you, IE6!). With CSS3, the picture is a little different.

CSS3: Not Yet Universally Supported

The truth is that, at the time of writing, you do still need to keep your wits about you when using CSS3. No browser supports CSS3 in its entirety—not one—and the support they do offer for CSS3 differs in the features available, as well as how they make it possible to achieve the same effect.

We'll see this in action in a moment, but essentially what it means is that to apply a certain style on a given element on the web page (for example, if you want to have rounded corners on a block of content) you'll need to write the CSS a few times over to ensure it works for all. The main reason for this is **vendor prefixes**.

In Support of Vendor Prefixes

Some people have a real issue with vendor prefixes in CSS, because it means duplicating effort, making the stylesheet more bloated than it needs to be. But first, what is a vendor prefix?

The vendor prefix is a small piece of text that sits directly in front of the CSS property, identifying the browser vendor. So Firefox, the work of the Mozilla Foundation, has a vendor prefix of –moz-. If you want to set a border-radius (the property used to set rounded corners), you'd need to state it like this for older versions of Firefox:

```
-moz-border-radius: 5px;
```

This ensures that the style is only applied to Mozilla-based browsers. Other prefixes include `webkit`, `o`, and `ms`, which relate to Safari/Chrome (based on the WebKit rendering engine), Opera, and Microsoft respectively. So, if you want to set a five-pixel rounded corner for all browsers on a `blockquote` with a two-pixel border, you'd need to write the following:

```
blockquote {
  border:2px solid blue;
  padding:10px;
  -moz-border-radius:5px;
  -webkit-border-radius:5px;
  -o-border-radius:5px;
  -ms-border-radius:5px;
}
```

Now, you can see why vendor prefixes are unpopular. But we still need one more property/value here:

```
blockquote {
  border:2px solid blue;
  padding:10px;
  -moz-border-radius:5px;
  -webkit-border-radius:5px;
  -o-border-radius:5px;
  -ms-border-radius:5px;
  border-radius:5px;
}
```

Figure 10.8 shows what the effect would be in browsers that support it (the screenshot is taken from Firefox 4 on a Mac):

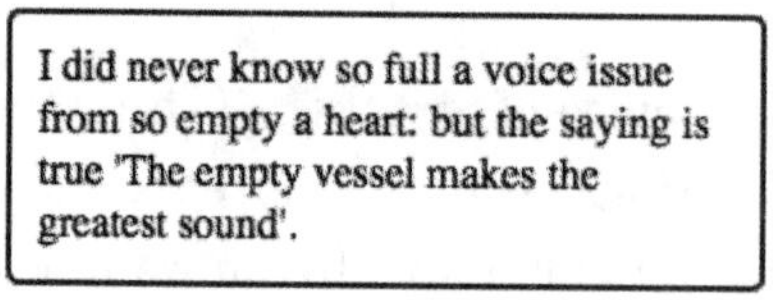

Figure 10.8. Rounded corners on a `blockquote`—all done in CSS!

The Reasoning Behind Vendor Jargon

Before you start yelling that people must be crazy to want to include all this code in their stylesheets, let me explain why it's like this. Browser vendors build their products based on specifications they receive from the World Wide Web Consortium (W3C). Each vendor has to read and fully understand the specifications; then bake that same knowledge into the browser itself. If the spec is slightly fuzzy or open to interpretation, or if there is some other reason for a misunderstanding along the way, the potential is great for four or five different browser vendors to treat the same CSS in their own unique way.

To avoid the possibility of a perfectly good CSS feature never being used because of the poor cross-browser support, browsers use these vendor prefixes. This in turn enables web developers to experiment with new CSS features. Through this experimentation and real-world usage, browser vendors are able to see what works. While several vendors might differ initially in how a feature should be implemented, over time they usually converge and agree on the best implementation. The idea is that, eventually, when the browsers all agree on the way forward, they can drop support for their respective prefixes on a given CSS property and just use the standard property name.

So, using `border-radius` as an example, we provide each browser with the same instruction using the vendor prefix first, and then the standard property name. Using Firefox as an example, in the CSS below, older versions that implemented the prefix will apply the first rule but ignore the second one. When a newer version comes out that drops the prefix, it will ignore the first rule and apply the second:

```
blockquote {
  -moz-border-radius:5px;
  border-radius:5px;
}
```

It's important to understand this, as we'll see some repetition in the CSS3 examples that follow. Try to take some solace that this is an intermediary stage in the evolution of browsers, and that at some point in the future, you'll be able to remove some of the repeated CSS.

The Good News on CSS3

Repetition aside, what's great about CSS3—or certainly the features that we'll learn about—is that there's already a lot that modern browsers support very well. The arrival of IE9 has boosted the support charts even further (traditionally it was always Internet Explorer that spoiled our fun by ignoring the cooler CSS3 styles!).

So, now that we know there are a range of browsers that permit CSS3 touches (albeit with us having to write some extra CSS), let's start to apply some to the project site.

Look at All Those Sharp, Pointy Corners!

The issue with laying the site out with CSS in boxes (well, `div` elements, mainly) is that it can end up looking a little boxy! If only there was a way to soften it up a little.

There are so many hard corners on the site, it's only a matter of time until someone says, "Watch out with those boxes—you could poke someone's eye out with them!" This looks like a job for `border-radius`! I showed the syntax for `border-radius` a short while ago to explain how vendor prefixes work, so this will be familiar. The style is now going to be applied to an `aside` element:

```
aside {
  border:2px solid gray;
  -moz-border-radius:5px;
  -webkit-border-radius:5px;
  -o-border-radius:5px;
  -ms-border-radius:5px;
  border-radius:5px;
}
```

We used the `aside` element to contain a quote on the About page (**about.html**):

```
<aside>
  <blockquote>
  Happiness is a dip in the ocean followed by a pint
  or two of Old Speckled Hen. You can quote me on that!
  </blockquote>
  Bob Dobalina, March 2011
</aside>
```

If we put that CSS in the **style1.css** file, save it, and then check it in the browser (take your pick, as long as it's after IE8!), we should see it transform as in Figure 10.9.

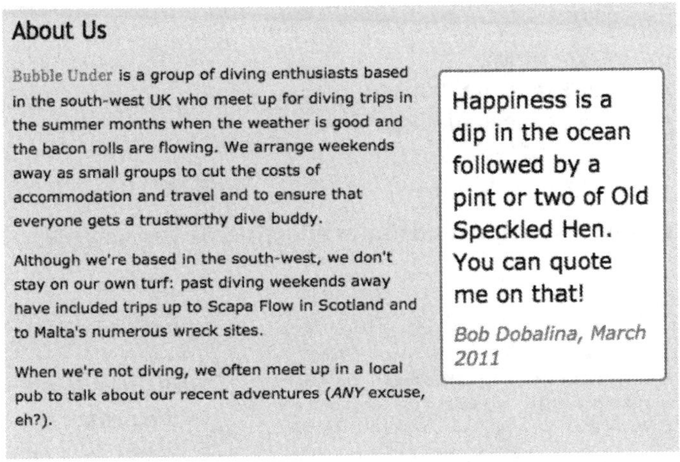

Figure 10.9. The quote with nice rounded borders

It's only the slightest of strokes, but it helps to add a touch of class. However, like anything, you can overdo it, so don't go applying rounded corners to everything.

To make the curve more pronounced, simply increase the border-radius value. We have used a 5px value, but what happens if we bump that up to 20px, as in Figure 10.10?

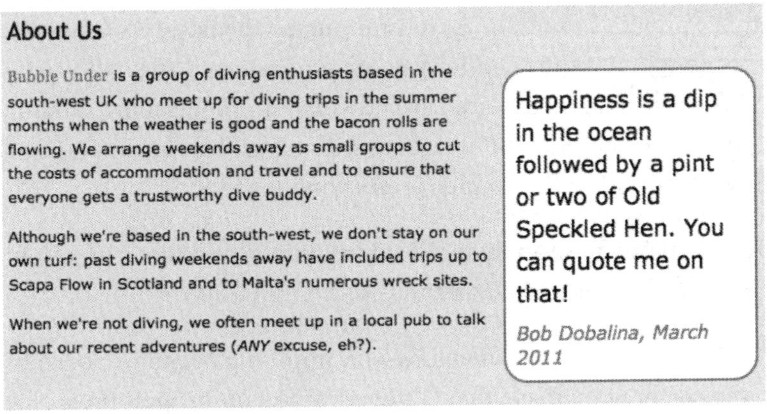

Figure 10.10. A more pronounced rounded-corner effect

It is even possible to set different curves to different corners of the one box. For example, if you wanted a rounded corner top-right and bottom-left, but the other corners to remain square, you'd have to do the following:

```
aside {
  border:2px solid gray;
  border-top-right-radius:20px;
  border-bottom-left-radius:20px;
}
```

The result is so easy to achieve and really effective, as you can see in Figure 10.11.

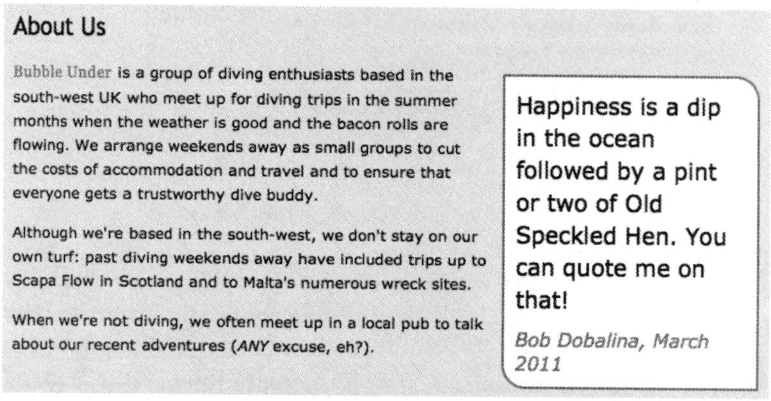

About Us

Bubble Under is a group of diving enthusiasts based in the south-west UK who meet up for diving trips in the summer months when the weather is good and the bacon rolls are flowing. We arrange weekends away as small groups to cut the costs of accommodation and travel and to ensure that everyone gets a trustworthy dive buddy.

Although we're based in the south-west, we don't stay on our own turf: past diving weekends away have included trips up to Scapa Flow in Scotland and to Malta's numerous wreck sites.

When we're not diving, we often meet up in a local pub to talk about our recent adventures (*ANY* excuse, eh?).

Happiness is a dip in the ocean followed by a pint or two of Old Speckled Hen. You can quote me on that!

Bob Dobalina, March 2011

Figure 10.11. Mixing up corner styles in the one box

Having talked about vendor prefixes, you might be asking why there are none showing in the previous example. As it turns out, all the latest browsers now support border-radius without the need for vendor prefixes, and they all use the same syntax. So the three lines above are perfectly okay by themselves, unless you know (or think) that some visitors to your site are still using older browsers, in which case you might want to add in the vendor prefix versions too.

Personally, I'm happy to drop them for this example, and that's precisely what the browsers would like you to do over time.

Feel free to play around with the values—try applying border-radius to different elements and see how it affects them. It even works on images. If we changed the CSS above to apply to the img element rather than the aside, the home page image would look like Figure 10.12.

Welcome to our super-dooper Scuba site

Glad you could drop in and share some air with us! You've passed your underwater navigation skills and successfully found your way to the start point - or in this case, our home page.

All details of the group's diving activities, trips and so on will be available from the various pages on this site but, in addition, we've got a Facebook page! If you're on Facebook, please do check it out. All of the updates we post on Facebook will also appear here in this little box here on the right (so, even if you're not a Facebook fan you can get to see our latest updates).

Figure 10.12. The `border-radius` property applied to an image

The Details in the Shadows

As a web developer, it's very common to receive web page mockups featuring lots of rounded corners from designers. Now we know that there are ways to achieve this with some simple CSS, but there's another feature of such mockups that's always been tricky to deal with—the drop shadow. In a graphics package such as Photoshop, applying a drop shadow is a supremely easy task, but making it work on a web page has always been difficult.

In the past, it's meant having to create images with the drop shadow as part of the image, but even this has its limits—such as what happens when the browser window is resized. Does the shadow part of the image move to a position on the page where the effect no longer works? Thankfully, there's a way to achieve a proper shadow effect with CSS, and the property is called `box-shadow`.

A good page to demonstrate it on is the photo gallery. We'll apply some extra rounded corner effects using `border-radius` while we're at it too. The new CSS3 styles are highlighted in bold:

```
figure img {
  border: 15px solid white;
  border-radius:10px;
  box-shadow:2px 2px 5px gray;
  margin-bottom:10px; /* added just to give the shadow some
  breathing space */
}
```

And in Figure 10.13, the effect is clear to see.

Figure 10.13. The box-shadow property takes care of drop shadows

How is this done? The box-shadow property takes four values to make it work, and they are (in order):

1. the offset along the *x* axis
2. the offset along the *y* axis
3. the amount of blur on the shadow
4. the color of the shadow

In our example, we have a shadow that's two pixels to the right and two pixels below the image, with a five-pixel blur and colored gray. Let's try a different set of values, and you'll see how easy it is to change:

```
box-shadow:10px 10px 20px black;
```

Which gives us Figure 10.14.

Jill was just snorkelling when she took this picture - the jellyfish was only a couple of feet under the surface, hence the light is excellent. Jill assures us that the jellyfish had no "nasty, stingy, dangly bits"!
[Photographer: Jill Smith]

Figure 10.14. A larger offset gives a deeper effect to the drop shadow

It's even possible to apply multiple box-shadows to one element—you simply place a comma between each set of four values. For example, you could apply a shadow bottom-right and top-left by using a mixture of positive and negative x and y values, like so:

```
box-shadow:2px 2px 15px black, -2px -2px 15px black;
```

The effect is that of an outer glow rather than a drop shadow, and it's particularly effective on elements such as buttons on forms. Figure 10.15 shows how it looks on our gallery images.

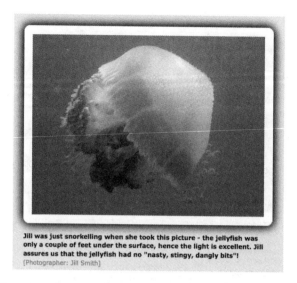

Jill was just snorkelling when she took this picture - the jellyfish was only a couple of feet under the surface, hence the light is excellent. Jill assures us that the jellyfish had no "nasty, stingy, dangly bits"!
[Photographer: Jill Smith]

Figure 10.15. A glow effect generated by clever use of the box-shadow

But what about the vendor prefixes?

In the previous examples, I didn't show the vendor prefix versions. At the time of writing, all but one of the modern browsers worked with the proper box-shadow property. Only my version of Safari (version 5) refused to apply the styles, so it was necessary to double up with the WebKit vendor prefix, for example:

```
-webkit-box-shadow:2px 2px 15px black, -2px -2px 15px black;
box-shadow:2px 2px 15px black, -2px -2px 15px black;
```

From box-shadow to text-shadow

Just as our friends from the world of web design like to provide mockups with drop shadows under panels, blocks, and so on, they often use similar techniques with text elements. Well, wouldn't you know it, CSS3 has its own way of doing that too. Say hello to the text-shadow property!

Now, for my first trick, I'm going to make an element look ugly, just to prove a point. How about the h2 heading on our project site? That should do it!

In **style1.css**, add the following (it's not important where you place it):

```
h2 {
   text-shadow:5px 5px 2px gray;
}
```

Then save it and have a look at the site. Does it look awful? Good! Well, kind of. It's good that it worked, but it's proof that the `text-shadow` property can easily be abused, creating ugly text that's often difficult to read, as Figure 10.16 shows.

Figure 10.16. When `text-shadows` diminish your web page's overall look

In my experience, `text-shadow` works best when you apply small values to the *x* and *y* offsets, a small amount of blur, and a complementary color (the syntax is actually the same as it is for `box-shadow`). Then, when it's applied to text on buttons and the like, it gives the effect of making the text appear chiseled or embossed.

We can use a subtle `text shadow` on the navigation text to bring it out against the dark blue background. In **style1.css**, find the section that deals with the navigation styles (look for the new HTML5 `nav` selector). Now add in the following:

```
nav a {
   text-shadow:1px 1px 2px white, -1px -1px 2px white;
   text-decoration:none;
}
```

Save the stylesheet, and then take a look at the page in the browser. (Note that I removed the underline using `text-decoration: none` on purpose, as the underline part also receives a shadow—a bit of an overkill). Does your page look similar to Figure 10.17?

Figure 10.17. Subtle use of `text-shadow` applies a glowing effect

We need to add in one more piece of CSS—to switch the shadow off when hovering over the link. Currently on the project site, the hover color for the text is white, the same as the `text-shadow` color. If `text-shadow` is left on, it makes the hovered-over text look fuzzy, as in Figure 10.18.

Figure 10.18. The "hover glow" effect: hardly user-friendly!

Here's the simple fix (and the result can be seen in Figure 10.19):

```
nav a {
  text-shadow:1px 1px 2px white, -1px -1px 2px white;
  text-decoration:none;
}

nav a:hover, nav a:focus {
  text-shadow: none;
}
```

Figure 10.19. The glow effect is removed from the hover, making the text readable

We Don't Serve Your Type Around Here!

A long-standing problem of the Web has been about displaying text in more interesting typefaces than the usual defaults: Times New Roman, Arial, Verdana, and Helvetica. There are only so many fonts installed on computers that you can absolutely rely on. And, sure, you can try to make the text more interesting by varying sizes, boldness, line spacing (the `line-height` CSS property), and the space between letters (the `letter-spacing` CSS property), but that only goes so far.

Many resort to the horrible solution of creating an image with your chosen font, and then putting that on the site instead of real text. That way, you guarantee that everyone will see the correct typeface. But it's poor in so many ways, including being inflexible, being a heavier download, and posing potential accessibility problems.

Fortunately, it's now possible to embed fonts in a web page, just as easily as you can place images on your pages, or link to external stylesheets. It's made possible by the `@font-face` construct in CSS, which allows you to link to a font, give it an easy name to remember, and then use the name in your stylesheet, applying that font to whatever you choose. For example, if I had a font called "monkeyfeatures" that I'd made myself, I could embed it on my site; I could even give it an abbreviated name ("mf"), making it easier and quicker to refer to anywhere in the CSS file:

```
@font-face {
  font-family: mf;
  src: url(/fonts/monkey-features.ttf);
}
...
h1 {
  font-family: mf, arial, sans-serif
}
```

It does come at a slight cost, however; namely the size of the download. Depending on the font file, it may mean a slightly larger initial download for people visiting your site.

There are many ways that you can embed fonts, including:

- utilizing a dedicated font service like Typekit[14] or Fontdeck,[15] which charge for the service but provide a rich set of resources
- creating your own font sets suitable for the Web using Font Squirrel[16]
- using one of the free ready-made font kits from Font Squirrel or Google Web Fonts[17]

These services have really taken off, thanks to widespread browser support, along with various legal issues having been resolved. (Fonts are subject to licensing conditions, always a problem area—the owners didn't want their fonts being downloaded freely.) The beauty of these services is that they hide a lot of the various workarounds that have built up over time, making it possible to provide the same font to numerous browsers.

We'll show just how easy it is to embed a font by using Google's offering.

Google Web Fonts

We'll perform a simple task: use Google's repository of fonts to change all h2 headings on the site. The steps are very easy to follow:

1. Head over to http://www.google.com/webfonts.

2. Scroll up and down until you find a suitable font. Decorative fonts might be tempting, but remember that people still need to read them! I've picked a fairly sensible font for now, Candal, seen in Figure 10.20.

3. As you hover over it, you're advised to "Click to embed." So do what the good people at Google suggest and click away!

---

[14] http://typekit.com/

[15] http://fontdeck.com/

[16] Font Squirrel's font generator can be found at http://www.fontsquirrel.com/fontface/generator, but you'll need to confirm that the font you want to use—which you supply by way of upload—is one that you have the rights to use.

[17] http://www.google.com/webfonts

Figure 10.20. Candal—a sensible font from Google's library

4. You'll then be presented with a preview window, as in Figure 10.21. If you like what you see, select the **Use this font** tab.

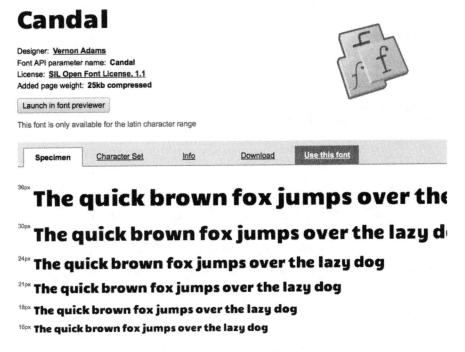

Figure 10.21. Previews of how the font will present on the page

5. You'll be presented with one line of HTML that you need to embed the font, and a second line of CSS that will apply the style to an h1 element, as in the markup below:

```
<link href='http://fonts.googleapis.com/css?family=Candal'
  rel='stylesheet' type='text/css'>

h1 {
  font-family: 'Candal', arial, serif;
}
```

Figure 10.22 displays the page you should see on screen:

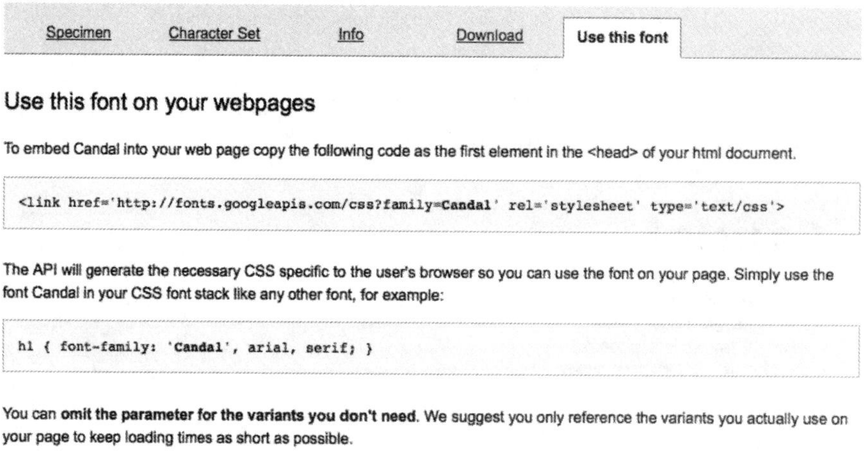

Figure 10.22. Simple instructions tell you how to embed the new font on your page

6. Copy that first line of HTML (the link element) and paste it into the head of your web pages (before the closing </head> is just fine); do that on all the pages.

7. In **style1.css**, we already have a style defined for h2 elements, so we'll just take the CSS property/value pair that Google suggests and paste it in like so (note that I've also boosted the font size):

```
h2 {
  color: navy;
  font-size: 130%;
  font-weight: normal;
```

```
    padding-top: 15px;
    font-family: 'Candal', arial, serif;
    font-size:2em;
}
```

Make sure everything is saved; then go check a few pages. You should have a nice-looking heading now—just like in Figure 10.23.

Figure 10.23. Google's Candal font appears in our h2 elements

I'd suggest you now check to see what happens when you resize the browser window. Does the heading look bad, as in Figure 10.24, when it wraps?

Figure 10.24. Nice font, bad text wrap

We can fix that by adding in a `line-height` property in the CSS. Adjust it up and down until it looks right (for this font, a setting of `line-height: 1` fixed it):

```
h2 {
    color: navy;
    font-size: 130%;
    font-weight: normal;
    padding-top: 15px;
    font-family: 'Candal', arial, serif;
    font-size:2em;
    line-height:1;
}
```

Figure 10.25 shows an improvement.

Figure 10.25. A bit of `line-height` and our heading looks super-dooper

Changing the font is easy, too—just follow the steps above, picking a different font. Figure 10.26 shows our page using a different font called Luckiest Guy.

Figure 10.26. Experiment with fonts to see which styles suit your site best

The only danger of this (aside from the aforementioned extra download required for each font file) is the possibility of overdoing it. Just because you can embed lots of fonts, doesn't mean you should. I mean, how far do you want to go? Figure 10.27 reveals what "too far" looks like.

Figure 10.27. You can, of course, get carried away with font embedding

My advice—stick to using embedded fonts for headings, primarily, or fonts that you know will display at a larger size (many of the embedded fonts look bad in small sizes). Body copy isn't ideal for this treatment, as there may be a delay when loading the page between the default font being displayed and the embedded one taking over. On headings this is less of an issue, but it can be jarring when an embedded font is used throughout.

As with all the other CSS3 properties we've seen in this chapter, there's a lot more you could learn if you want to; I trust that Google's Web Fonts service has provided enough of a taster of what's available to you right now, with a minimum of fuss and bother.

Other CSS3 Features to be Aware of

I would love to continue listing all the new features that you can try out with CSS3 but, honestly, there's a whole book there just by itself. So far, I've selected and demonstrated what I think are the safest and most useful aspects of CSS3 that you can start using now. You should, however, be aware of the following (and I've suggested further reading where it's genuinely useful):

- Multiple background images

- Opacity, demonstrated on the css3.info (http://www.css3.info/preview/opacity/) website.

- RGBA color (setting transparency levels on background colors); an introduction to opacity and RGBA can be found at http://www.css3.info/introduction-opacity-rgba/

- Additional attribute selectors—see SitePoint's CSS3 Attribute Selectors reference page: http://reference.sitepoint.com/css/css3attributeselectors

- Media queries (which let you apply different styles depending on the browser or device); SitePoint's CSS3 Media Queries reference page is at: http://reference.sitepoint.com/css/mediaqueries

IE as a Second-class Citizen

With all these changes we've made on the project site, I'd like to go back and revisit our old friend Internet Explorer. In particular, I'd like to see how the old and cranky IE6 fares with all the changes applied.

The simple answer is it doesn't really care. It doesn't break, though. The site will be just as usable in IE6 as it is in Firefox 5, Chrome 12, and so on; it just won't look quite so pretty.

In the code archive, you'll find that the final version of the website has had a few more CSS3 touches applied than we covered in this chapter, but they're all techniques that we've learned about.

Summary

Well done for staying the distance. There was a lot to cover in this chapter, and even more that I wasn't able to cover because of space (and I'm still fretting even now about the bits I missed as I write this). I hope that the new features of HTML5 and CSS3 have sufficiently whetted your appetite, and that you feel you can use them now.

In this chapter, we've seen how new HTML5 elements can be used and made to work visually, even in old browsers like IE6. We've learned a little bit of the history behind HTML5, and how we've ended up with a new set of elements that are very intuitive and easy to understand (such as nav, header, and footer).

With CSS3, we've realized that there's a lot you can do, design-wise, just within the browser: some tasteful touches of drop shadows and rounded corners, and a careful selection of fonts. We've also learned not to go too far with these new techniques, lest we overdo it! In Chapter 11, we'll learn how we can easily add a level of interactivity to the site using JavaScript and, specifically, a very popular library called **jQuery**.

Strap yourself in—this is going to be a fun ride!

Chapter 11

Adding Interactivity with jQuery

I hope that when you compare the progress made with each chapter that you're gaining a clear picture of how much the project site has moved on. Up until now, it's all been about having the right HTML for the job so that the document conveys the proper meaning, and making the best use of CSS to style the pages and elements on them.

In this chapter, however, we'll see how you can add a further layer to the site: the "behavior" layer. Just as you should be able to separate the presentation (CSS) from a document, so you should also be able to do the same with the behavior, and for this you need to use JavaScript. And use it *the right way*.

But what is behavior? It might be what happens as you hover your mouse over an item on a page, causing another item to pop up. It might be a prompt that appears when you choose a certain link, asking if you really wanted to do something; for example, "Did you really want to delete all these items?" It might be the way the navigation reacts as you move the mouse over it. In short, it could mean several things, and I'm sure you could come up with plenty of examples on your own.

JavaScript? jQuery? What's the difference?

I've mentioned JavaScript in passing—it's what's known as a client-side scripting language. **Client side** means that it runs in the browser on the client's computer, as opposed to logic that is processed on the server before the results are sent back to the client's computer. JavaScript is the only client-side language that runs on all browsers—there's no real competition or choice here—so we're quite safe using it.

You might have heard of jQuery; it's what's known as a **library**. Written in JavaScript, it allows developers to shortcut a lot of the processes to achieve certain effects. It works because the developers behind it have created a series of **functions**—code structures that are basically the central working units of JavaScript, and that in jQuery's case take care of any differences or oddities across browsers, keeping things as simple as possible. The jQuery home page can be seen in Figure 11.1.

Figure 11.1. The jQuery home page

To go back to a car analogy, you don't need to know how every car engine works—and they all differ in some way—but if you know that to make it go faster you just have to put your foot down on the accelerator, it's easier to move from car to car and just drive. jQuery takes the guesswork out of creating similar experiences in different browsers; it understands how each browser's engine works, but makes it easy so that you only have to give it a simple command—the coding equivalent of "put your foot down and it goes faster."

Standard JavaScript versus jQuery: A Simple Example

To give you an example of how jQuery can make life easier, I'm going to show you two ways of doing the same task. It may look like gobbledygook, but all you really need to see is the difference in the amount of effort necessary to achieve the same effect—in this case, hiding something from view. First, the standard JavaScript way of doing it:

chapter11/examples/01_hideHeadingStandardJS.html

```
document.getElementById("someThing").style.display="none";
```

Now, the jQuery way:

chapter11/examples/02_hideHeadingjQuery.html

```
$("#someThing").hide();
```

It's a basic example, but without knowing too much about how it works, I hope you can see that the second version is easier to understand.

Actually, it's a little too basic. For you to be able to do the second shorter bit of script, you first need to load the jQuery library. Inside that library are a lot of scripts that make this all possible for you. So the browser still has to do a certain amount of work but, as a developer, the process is massively simplified.

How do I get jQuery and use it?

It's actually very easy to use jQuery. The steps are:

1. Go to the jQuery website at http://jquery.com/ and download the latest version of the library (select the minified version), as you can see in Figure 11.2.[1]

---

[1] http://docs.jquery.com/Downloading_jQuery#Download_jQuery

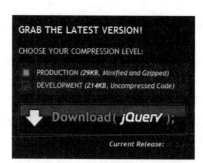

Figure 11.2. The download link for the jQuery library

2. You then save it in a suitable place with the rest of your site's files (for example, in the root folder, or in a folder called **js**, **javascript**, or **scripts**). Depending on the browser you're using, it'll either prompt you to save the JavaScript file, or simply show it in the browser window as a text file. If it does the latter, go to the **File** menu and choose **Save Page As** (or similar), as in Figure 11.3.

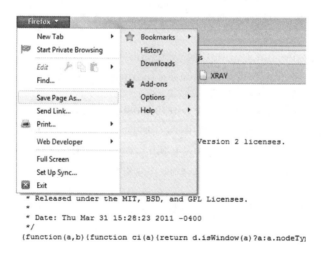

Figure 11.3. Save the download as a **.js** file

3. On your pages, refer to the script at the end of your page like so:

```
<script type="text/javascript" src="/pathto/jquery-X.X.X.min.js">
</script>
```

Note that `pathto` should be replaced with whichever folder you chose to save it in, and `X.X.X` will be the latest version of jQuery.

4. Finally, you need to actually make use of jQuery (all you've done so far is link to it). To do this, either put some script directly on your chosen page inside some `<script></script>` tags, or reference another external script that you'll share with all your pages.

Did any of that confuse you? I wouldn't blame you if it did—it's tricky to understand until you actually give it a go, so here are a couple of examples.

In the code archive, open the file **chapter11/examples/03_jQueryEmbeddedScript.html**, and you'll see the following:

chapter11/examples/03_jQueryEmbeddedScript.html

```
<!DOCTYPE html>
<html lang="en">
  <head>
    <meta charset="utf-8">
    <title>Embedded script example</title>
  </head>
  <body>
  <h1>Embedded script example</h1>
  <script type="text/javascript" charset="utf-8" src="js/➥
    jquery-1.5.2.min.js"></script>
  <script type="text/javascript" charset="utf-8">
    $("h1").after("<p>I've just inserted a paragraph</p>");
  </script>
  </body>
</html>
```

First, we link to the jQuery library; immediately the script adds a new paragraph to the document, with this line:

```
$("h1").after("<p>I've just inserted a paragraph</p>");
```

Try opening this file in the browser, and the additional paragraph should appear without any noticeable delay.

Another way of using jQuery is to have a common JavaScript file that you refer to on all pages—just like the single CSS file referred to on all pages—which would be as follows:

```
<!DOCTYPE html>
  <html lang="en">
  <head>
   <meta charset="utf-8">
   <title>Common script example</title>
  </head>
  <body>
  <h1>Common script example</h1>
  <script type="text/javascript" charset="utf-8" src="js/➥
    jquery-1.5.2.min.js"></script>
  <script type="text/javascript" charset="utf-8" src="js/➥
    common.js"></script>
  </body>
</html>
```

And in the **common.js** file:

```
$("h1").after("<p>I've just inserted a paragraph</p>");
```

Hang On a Moment!

In my usual way, I've glossed over a certain detail to avoid bombarding you with information. When using jQuery, it's important that you wait until the browser is good and ready to start running scripts. To do this, you need to ensure that all lines of script are contained inside a `document.ready` statement, which looks like this:

```
$(document).ready(function(){
  $("h1").after("<p>I've just inserted a paragraph</p>");
});
```

This is another one of those times when, as a beginner, I'd recommend you go easy on yourself with having to remember the exact syntax here. Instead, just copy and paste one that you know works, and you should be fine.

jQuery: Primed and Ready For Action

So, what can jQuery do? Perhaps the question is what can't it do. jQuery has made it possible for people who were uncomfortable writing long, detailed blocks of JavaScript to do some amazing stuff. In this short chapter—which offers but a mere taste of jQuery—I can only scratch the surface.

To put it concisely, jQuery works by saying to the browser:

- find this item/s on the page
- now perform this action/s

It does all this using the same syntax for selecting items that you use in CSS when choosing to style elements, as you can see in Table 11.1.

Table 11.1. Examples of jQuery's simple and effective functionality

`$("h3").hide();`	Hides all h3 elements on the page
`$("p").fadeTo('slow',0.5);`	Slowly fades all paragraphs (p elements) on a page to 50% opacity
`$("#navigation").show();`	Shows the element with the id of navigation (assuming it was previously hidden, either by script or with CSS `display: none`)
`$(".footnotes").hide();`	Hides anything that has a class of footnotes

Normally, these kinds of actions occur as a result of another action—for example, if the person looking at your page clicks on a link, hovers the mouse over an item, or presses a button. The syntax becomes a little more complicated, but it is still relatively easy to read and understand.

Let's look at a few more in Table 11.2.

Table 11.2. Statements that contain more advanced jQuery functionality

`$("input").focus(function(){` `$(this).select(); });`	When any `input` element receives focus, the browser should select that `input`'s contents (for example, when a text input is clicked on, all the text is selected, making it easier to overtype)
`$("#confirm").click(function(){` `$("#confirmationMessage").show(); });`	When the element with the `id` of `confirm` is clicked (most likely a button), the browser should show the element with the `id` of `confirmationMessage`

`$(".helpIcon").mouseover(function(){`
`$("#helpTips").fadeTo('medium',1);`
`});`
	When the mouse hovers over anything with a `class` of `helpIcon`, the browser will show the element on the page with the `id` of `helpTips` (fading it into view at medium speed, rather than showing it without delay)

There are many ways of triggering an action. The trigger points are known as **events** in JavaScript, and some common events that you'd use in jQuery are:

- `.mouseover()`
- `.mouseout()`
- `.click()`
- `.focus()`
- `.submit()`

The actions that you'd take are many and varied, but here are some of the more common ones you'll use (dealing with visual effects):

- `.hide()`
- `.show()`
- `.fadeIn()`
- `.fadeOut()`
- `.fadeTo()`
- `.slideUp()`
- `.slideDown()`

To do this proper justice would take a whole book's worth of attention. Thankfully, there is a perfect book for this: *jQuery: Novice to Ninja*.[2] If you like what you see throughout the remainder of this chapter as I add some jQuery to the project site, grab a copy of this jQuery book. It will guide you through the jQuery terrain and teach you heaps of good stuff. This chapter is merely here to whet your appetite!

Using jQuery on the Project Site

As the project site is a small one, there's a slight risk of adding bells and whistles to a site that doesn't really need it. So let's think of a couple of practical examples that are easy to understand. Here's what we'll do:

- On the contact form, we'll set up some default values as help tips that will automatically clear when they receive focus.

- For the gallery page, we'll use jQuery to suppress the caption that appears under each image by default, but show it when the mouse hovers over the image.

Setting Up References to jQuery

The first step is to adjust the site so that it references both the jQuery library (which you downloaded and saved earlier) and a common JavaScript file (with the extension of **.js**). We need to add the following two lines to the end of each of the pages in the site:

```
<script type="text/javascript" src="js/jquery-1.5.2.min.js">
</script>
<script type="text/javascript" src="js/common.js"></script>
</body>
</html>
```

I've chosen to store the JavaScript files in a folder called **js**, but you can choose what works best for you. Another point to note here: the two scripts are added at the end of the document, just before the closing `</body>` tag. Many websites reference all the scripts at the beginning of the document, between the opening `<head></head>` tags—and indeed many books teach you this, too. But it's a better technique to add them at the end, because loading the scripts upfront can delay the page from appear-

---

[2] http://www.sitepoint.com/books/jquery1/

ing. It's can be quite a complicated topic, with a fair amount of science and engineering to it!

If you want to learn more about why I suggest placing it here, I recommend that you read Steve Souders' article on the Yahoo Developer Network.[3] Otherwise, you can just take my word for it.

The Common JavaScript File

In case you're wondering how you create the **common.js** file, it's just another type of text file. Simply create a new empty document in your text editor, and save it with the extension **.js**.

Adding Default Form Value

We start by ensuring that the scripts that run in **common.js** do so only when the document is good and ready:

```
$(document).ready(function(){
  //scripts go here
});
```

Can I make a comment?

Just as you can add comments in HTML using `<!-- -->` and `/* */` in CSS, you can do the same in JavaScript. You can either comment out just one line by starting it with `//` (as shown in the markup), or do multiline comments using `/* */`.

We'll go through a few of the form inputs and give each of them a value. Let's begin with the name field:

```
$("#contactname").val("Please enter your full name");
```

Notice that the field is referenced by its id value (`#contactname`), and the value we want it to have is inside the parentheses, surrounded by double quotes. Enter that line *exactly* as is and place it inside the `$(document).ready(function(){ });`.

---

[3] http://developer.yahoo.com/blogs/ydn/posts/2007/07/high_performanc_5/

Now save it and refresh the browser on the contact page, and you should see that the first text input on the form now has help text, as in Figure 11.4.

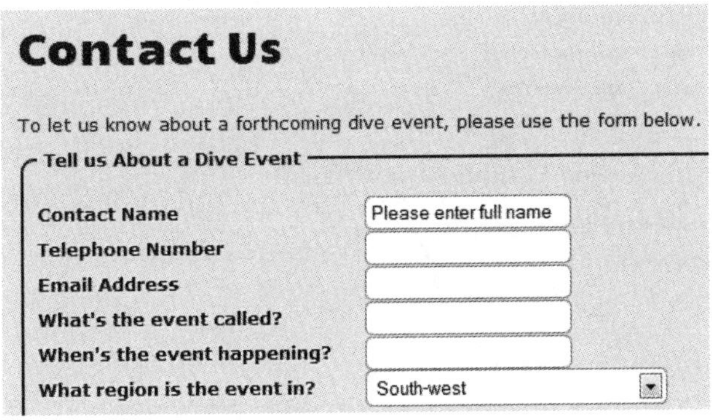

Figure 11.4. Our form comes loaded with prewritten text in the first field

Now let's stack a few of these up for the page:

```
$(document).ready(function(){
  $("#contactname").val("Please enter your full name");
  $("#telephone").val("Incl local dialling code");
  $("#eventdate").val("Format DDMMYYYY");
  $("#details").val("The more you can enter here, the less we have
  to check with you :)");
});
```

Save **common.js**, and refresh the contact page in the browser. Do the appropriate fields have this additional help text in place, as in Figure 11.5?

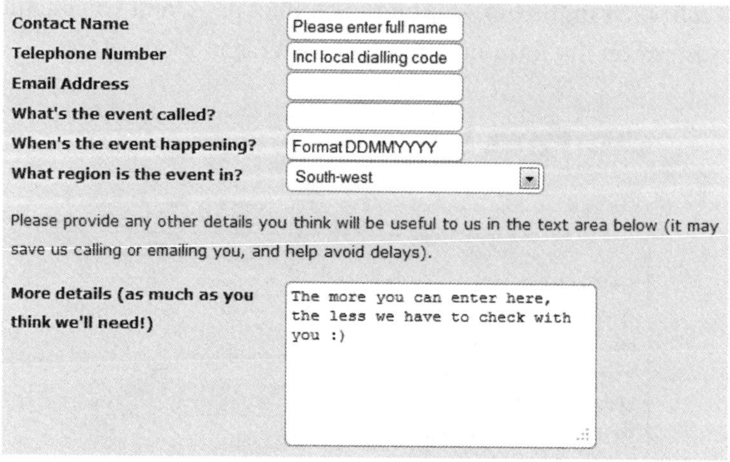

Figure 11.5. Adding more helpful information for users in subsequent fields

While this is quite helpful, it's also introduced a problem of its own: to enter data in these fields, it's now necessary for the user filling in the form to delete the text first, or type over it. We can help by adding the following line:

```
$(document).ready(function(){
  $("#contactname").val("Please enter your full name");
  $("#telephone").val("Incl local dialling code");
  $("#eventdate").val("Format DDMMYYYY");
  $("#details").val("The more you can enter here, the less we have
  to check with you :)");
  $("input, textarea").focus(function(){
    $(this).select();
  });
});
```

We've selected both input and textarea elements on the page with the use of $("input, textarea"). The comma acts exactly the same as it would in a CSS selector, and means "OR."

Now when a person filling in the form clicks on one of those fields, it's automatically selected, making it easier to type over or delete, as in Figure 11.6.

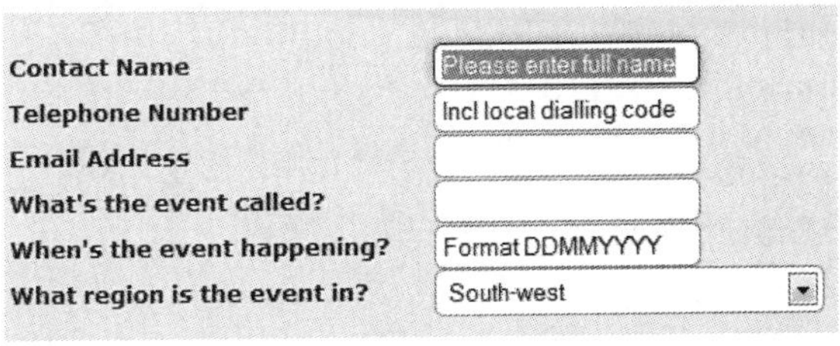

Figure 11.6. Typing over the placeholder text becomes easy with jQuery

If you tripped up anywhere on this one, there's no shame in it. It's much easier to make a mistake with JavaScript than HTML and CSS, as it's much less forgiving of errors. Remember that the code archive has all the answers (this one can be found at **chapter11/website_files/01_AddDefaultFormValues**).

Showing the Picture Gallery's Captions on Hover

For our second practical example, we'll make it so that each picture caption only shows when the mouse hovers over the image. Our first step is to hide the captions, like so:

```
$("figcaption").hide();
```

Nice and simple! But now it starts to become more complex. We now need to set it so that each `figure` element has its own behavior applied—so that when you hover over a `figure` element, only the caption that relates to that `figure` is shown. To do this, jQuery provides the `each()` function. For us, this means the following:

```
$("figure").each(function(){
    //add the behavior for each figure here
});
```

Let's flesh it out a bit more. For each of the `figure` elements, we want to:

- when hovered over, show the `figcaption` element for the image
- when hovered away from, hide the `figcaption` element for the image

Now we'll translate that into code that works for jQuery:

```
$("figure").each(function(){
  $(this).hover(function(){
    $(this).find("figcaption").show();
  },function(){
      $(this).find("figcaption").hide();
    });
});
```

Like before, don't be put off if this looks a little daunting. It's a taster—nothing more, and there's no test later. But take a look at the code and compare it to the two bullet points that I wrote in English. Can you see how the jQuery code closely matches the logic I expressed in normal everyday language? Sometimes the challenge of writing good jQuery code is not about knowing the syntax, but about thinking through the logic and the steps. If you can get that right, often the jQuery flows without too much difficulty.

While the previous block of code works okay, it's not quite as slick as I'd like it to be. Hovering over the image shows and hides the caption part, but it's a *sudden* show/hide effect. We can make it appear more smoothly by using one of jQuery's off-the-shelf effects. We'll use the slideUp and slideDown effect, and set a time for this to happen, so the code changes to this:

```
$("figure").each(function(){
  $(this).hover(function(){
    $(this).find("figcaption").slideDown('medium');
  },function(){
      $(this).find("figcaption").slideUp('medium');
    });
});
```

With this script in **common.js**, as well as the previous form help tips, the jQuery code in its entirety looks like this:

chapter11/website_files/02_GalleryCaptionHoverEffect

```
$(document).ready(function(){
  //Enhancing the form with helper text
  $("#contactname").val("Please enter your full name");
  $("#telephone").val("Incl local dialling code");
  $("#eventdate").val("Format DDMMYYYY");
```

```
$("#details").val("The more you can enter here, the less we have
    to check with you :)");
$("input, textarea").focus(function(){
    $(this).select();
});
//Making the gallery captions appear on hover
$("figcaption").hide();
$("figure").each(function(){
    $(this).hover(function(){
        $(this).find("figcaption").slideDown('medium');
    },function(){
        $(this).find("figcaption").slideUp('medium');
    });
});
});
```

If you've copied the code and it's exactly the same as the example I've just shown, save it, and then try out the gallery page and see how it reacts. Slick, huh? If it fails to work for you, remember you can grab the code from the code archive (and you'll be looking for **chapter11/website_files/02_GalleryCaptionHoverEffect**).

 Getting Specific with jQuery

As the effects in the examples just shown are specific to two pages, they're fairly uncommon pieces of JavaScript. As such, we could have just as easily placed these only on the pages affected. I've chosen to show you the method that uses a shared JavaScript file, as this is how you'd typically use this for site-wide effects. (In fact, we'll adapt the form help text script again in Chapter 13 to add one further enhancement, and this will be site-wide in its scope).

Summary

That's as much as I can realistically cover in this small chapter. It's been a lightning tour of jQuery, and in doing so, I know I've glossed over some details. My hope was only that it would give you an insight into how jQuery works, and what it might be used for. If it's started you thinking, "I like this—I want to learn more!" then I'll have done my job.

In Chapter 12, you'll learn how to identify the source of some CSS problems using a handful of free and useful tools. I mean, I can guide you through the steps for this project site, but at some point you're going to want to experiment. And when you do, you can expect a few slipups along the way (and I won't be around to help, sorry!). Just as well, then, that these tools I'm going to tell you about are simply awesome, and, without a lie, ones that I use every working day of my life.

Let's find out what they are ...

12

What to Do When Things Go Wrong

The old adage that you learn through making mistakes is pertinent when it comes to developing websites. Every developer—*every* one of them—will attest to making mistakes regularly in this line of work. And if it's not a mistake that you've made, perhaps it's a bug that's unique to a given browser that you're forced to find ways to deal with.

So it's quite normal to slip up along the way. The issue is how to address a problem when it occurs or, even better, work in such a way that prevents mistakes from happening in the first place. As they say in the medical world, prevention is better than a cure, but we'll be taking a look at how you can do both in this chapter.

Prevention

The best way of avoiding a major rework after you've spent a long time toiling is to check your work frequently as you develop. So my first tip is to develop using multiple browsers.

Keep Multiple Browsers Open While Developing

When working on a task that's more than just a simple content change, be sure to have a few browsers open at the same time, and have the page you're working on open in each of them. It could be a change to an existing CSS layout, a new page layout, or a new form or component that you're putting together. You don't need to have all browsers open at once, but I would recommend using these (with their rendering engines in parentheses):

- Internet Explorer (Trident)
- Firefox (Gecko)
- Google Chrome (WebKit)
- Opera (Presto)

Because they all have different rendering engines powering them, there may be differences between the way they present certain items on the page. As you make changes to the HTML and CSS (but it's mainly CSS changes that we're focusing on), save your work, and hit refresh in all these browsers. Then deal with any issues as they crop up, incrementally.

Internet Explorer is the real problem, though. Nine times out of ten, if I create a CSS layout or style and check it in Firefox, it's almost identical in Chrome, Opera, and Safari. Internet Explorer 9 is mostly fine, being a new browser, as it supports so much more of CSS2.1 and CSS3 than its predecessors did. Nonetheless, the older versions of IE cause a number of problems, none of which are easy to address. But we'll have a go.

Running Multiple Versions of Internet Explorer

It's possible to install different versions of most browsers, providing that you choose a different install location when you run the setup file. However, Internet Explorer is less cooperative. If you have IE9 installed, it's impossible to have a *proper* copy of IE8, or IE7, or IE6 installed.

Similarly, if you're running IE6 and are unable to install a newer version of the browser (and yes, this is still happening, mainly in the corporate world where it's not possible to upgrade for various reasons), you're going to have problems not knowing how your work looks in other versions of IE.

The bad news is that there can be substantial differences between versions of IE. The browser that you most need multiple copies of is the one that prohibits you from installing multiple copies. So what can you do?

- Buy three computers and install a different version of IE on each. (Like that's gonna happen!)

- Have one machine that's set up running three virtual machines. Of course, you'll still have to pay for three individual licenses for Windows XP/7, or whatever you choose to run. Additionally, it's more than likely that running a virtual machine inside your main operating system is going to slow everything down to a crawl. (Once again, I'm thinking this is unlikely to happen either!)

- Try to find a hacked version of the various IE versions. These are unofficial versions of the IE browsers that people have modified, so that they can be run independently of each other. Yet, because they're illegal, we'll refrain from further exploring this suggestion.

- Install an application that provides the CSS rendering and JavaScript engines of various browser versions. IE Tester[1] (in theory) allows you to try out your pages in IE6 through to 9. I say in theory, because in practice I've found numerous issues, which has meant I'm unable to truly trust what it shows me.

- Use an online service that lets you submit your site and try it in different browsers and operating systems; for example, BrowserCam[2] or Browsershots.[3] This does mean that the site must be online and available for the world to see. This is not exactly ideal for development—you really want to work out all your glitches before it's unleashed for everyone to see; post-live fixes are the devil's work.

It's less than ideal all round, isn't it? That said, you can—and should—use whatever statistics you have to hand about the users coming to your website; this will inform your decision on the level of effort required when making your site work in older browser versions. We'll be looking at adding Google analytics (which provides this kind of information for free) in Chapter 13. But if your website is showing that fewer than 1% of visitors are using IE6, is it really worth putting 80% of your bug-

---

[1] http://www.my-debugbar.com/wiki/IETester/HomePage
[2] http://www/browsercam.com/
[3] http://www/browsershots.org/

fixing time into rectifying this browser's problems? I think we both know the answer to that one.

Validate HTML and CSS as You Go

So you're making changes and using the approach of "save, refresh browser 1, refresh browser 2, refresh browser 3, and so on." Should you spot any problems along the way, you can first try to validate your markup or the CSS related to it. In Chapter 9, I showed you the W3C's validator, and explained that you can use it either by entering the URL of a live site, or by copying and pasting the HTML from your page. While you're developing your site, you will need to do the latter.

A missed closing tag, or one closing tag too many can play havoc with your page layout. A visit to the validator should highlight the issue. Check out this example:

```
<!DOCTYPE html>
<html lang="en">
  <head>
    <meta charset="utf-8" />
    <title>Broken Table example</title>
  </head>
  <body>
    <h1>Broken Table example</h1>
    <tabel>
      <tr>
        <th>Account Type</th>
        <th>Interest Rate</th>
      </tr>
      <tr>
        <td>Smart</td>
        <td>From 2%</td>
      </tr>
      <tr>
        <td>Young Saver</td>
        <td>From 1.6%</td>
      </tr>
    </table>
  </body>
</html>
```

Can you spot the problem? I deliberately put in a typo—a small one—but it means that your table will display incorrectly, as in Figure 12.1.

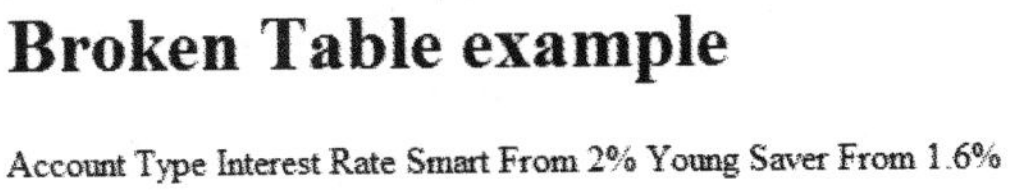

Broken Table example

Account Type Interest Rate Smart From 2% Young Saver From 1.6%

Figure 12.1. A broken table

When we copy and paste the HTML into the validator and run a test, it reveals 22 errors as Figure 12.2 shows.

Figure 12.2. The W3C validator identifies the errors in our markup

Scrolling down the page, we can see that it forbids you to have the `tabel` element inside the `body` element, as Figure 12.3 reveals. That makes sense—after all, there's no such thing as a "tabel." A `table` element, on the other hand, is quite all right!

⊗ *Line 9, Column 7*: **Element tabel not allowed as child of element body in this context. (Suppressing further errors from this subtree.)**

`<tabel >`

Content model for element body:
Flow content.

Figure 12.3. Fix that `tabel` element right away!

So the validator has alerted us to the problem. By changing it from `tabel` to `table` and running it through the validator again, we can see that the problem disappears. In fact, all of them—those 22 errors are really just one genuine error and 21 further errors because none of the elements inside are allowed inside our "tabel."

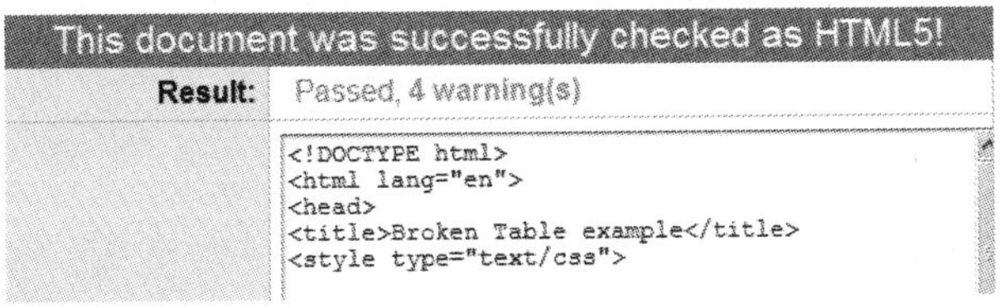

Figure 12.4. No more "tabel" means no more errors

That was a fairly basic example, but it shows how one error can have a knock-on effect, and when combined with CSS styles it can mean disastrous-looking results. Hence, the W3C validator is your friend.

Learn About Known Browser CSS Bugs

It would be unreasonable to expect you to know or learn all the various browser bugs that are out there, but it pays to be informed where Internet Explorer is concerned. It has the lion's share of problems but, thankfully, the problems are all very well documented.

A good source of knowledge of IE bugs and how to fix them is a site called Position Is Everything,[4] and for IE specifically, Explorer Exposed.[5]

Worth knowing about in advance—and bugs which I encounter all the time in my daily work on the Web—include the Double Float-Margin Bug,[6] the Guillotine Bug,[7] and the Peekaboo Bug.[8] There's no need to memorize the fix for these, but it's good to read up on them a bit; by experiencing the problem on these pages, you'll remember where to find the solution when you do see it on one of your pages.

Prepare Your Browser for Battle—with Extensions!

When I'm setting up a new computer at home or at work, the very first thing I do after installing the browsers is to install a few additional tools. My primary browser for developing is Firefox, because it was the first browser that truly allowed developers to create these add-ons (known as **extensions**). Very soon, these tools became indispensable in my day-to-day work. Now, there is support for extensions in a wider range of browsers (such as Chrome, Opera, and Safari), and the browsers also come with a good set of developer tools as part of the standard installation.

To be honest, we're spoiled these days! I'm going to show you a few extensions for Firefox, rather than use the default developer tools for a few reasons:

---

[4] http://www.positioniseverything.net/

[5] http://www.positioniseverything.net/explorer.html

[6] http://www.positioniseverything.net/explorer/doubled-margin.html

[7] http://www.positioniseverything.net/explorer/guillotine.html

[8] http://www.positioniseverything.net/explorer/peekaboo.html

- Familiarity—if you have questions about how these tools work, you're more likely to receive help because they're well-known and well-used.
- Functionality—generally they offer a lot more than the standard developer tools.
- Regularity—these extensions are updated regularly, sometimes to address bugs but also to add new features.

The tools I'm recommending you use are:

- Firebug (extension)
- Web Developer Toolbar (extension)
- XRAY (a **favelet**, which is a little piece of JavaScript that can be saved as a favorite in your browser)

Get Firebug

If you wanted to tell people to install Firebug on their browser, what web address would you send them to? How about http://getfirebug.com? That will do nicely!

1. Head on over to this site in Firefox, and click on the **Install Firebug** link on the home page.

2. Choose the most recent version suggested (unless it says "Alpha"). It should be clear which one to use, as evident in Figure 12.5.

Downloads: All Versions of Firebug

This page is for downloads from getfirebug.com. The links on this page lead to directories where you can select a version and click on it to install.

Addons.mozilla.org also distributes Firebug and you may prefer that site for downloads.

Firebug for Firefox

 Firebug 1.7 for Firefox 4: Recommended

Compatible with: Firefox 4
Release notes You may subscribe to this release on addons.mozilla.org

Firebug 1.6 for Firefox 3.6

Compatible with: Firefox 3.6
Release notes You may subscribe to this release on addons.mozilla.org

Figure 12.5. Pick Me! Pick Me! Selecting the latest version of Firebug

3. With luck, this should start the installation process; however, you may be taken to an index page and wonder what to do next. If this happens, look for the file that says **firebug-X.X.X.xpi** (where X.X.X is the version number), and click on that.

4. For security reasons, Firefox will block this installation initially (because **.xpi** files make changes to the browser, so it's being extra careful). You'll have to tell it that you trust the source of the installation file. This is a safe website, so press the **Allow** button and the installation should proceed, as in Figure 12.6.

Figure 12.6. Allowing Firefox to download Firebug

5. And yet, the browser checks one more time about allowing the install—seen in Figure 12.7. You know what to do.

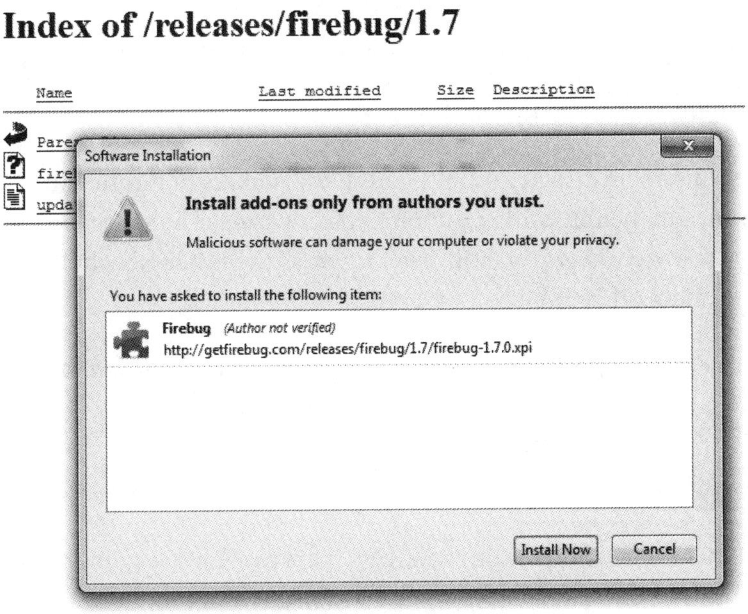

Index of /releases/firebug/1.7

Figure 12.7. Hit the **Install Now** button and you're almost there

6. Finally, restart the browser (but not your computer!).

That's Firebug installed. We'll start using it shortly, but there are a couple of more items to add first.

Install Web Developer Toolbar

The Web Developer Toolbar[9] (WDT) does many tasks that Firebug does—there's some overlap with all the tools available—but it also takes care of a bunch of stuff that Firebug doesn't handle. So we'll install this too.

I'm going to show you another source for extensions this time. With Firebug, we went to the developers' website. Mozilla has its own repository of extensions— approved and vetted versions—and you can get the WDT from here.[10]

---

[9] Actually, it's just called "Web Developer," but I've yet to meet anyone who doesn't refer to it as the "Web Developer Toolbar." Besides, a "Web Developer" is a person, not a browser addition, isn't it?

[10] You can also download the WDT from http://chrispederick.com/work/web-developer/, the developer's own page. Installing from there would cause Firefox to present the same warning about the site being blocked, which you can ignore, of course.

1. Head to the WDT page on the Mozilla add-ons site here: https://addons.mozilla.org/en-us/firefox/addon/web-developer/.

2. Click on the button that reads **Add to Firefox**.

3. Because it's come directly from Mozilla, the makers of Firefox, the first warning that showed when installing Firebug doesn't appear here because it's a trusted source. You will, however, still need to press the **Install Now** button on the warning dialog that appears.

4. As with Firebug, you'll need to restart the browser for the extension to work.

One more to go ...

Add XRAY

The final tool I'm recommending is XRAY. This time, we're going to be adding this tool as a browser favorite. Rather than installing to the browser, when you want to run it, you click on the favorite, and it grabs the necessary scripts to work on the fly. But I'm getting ahead of myself! Here are the steps you need to do:

1. Go to http://www.westciv.com/xray/.

2. Follow the instructions on that page as in Figure 12.8—dragging the link to your browser's bookmarks bar or equivalent.

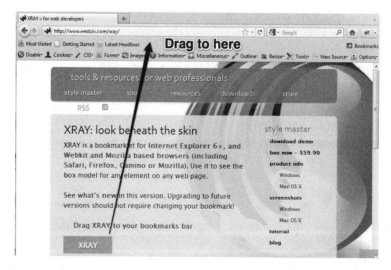

Figure 12.8. Follow the browser's instructions, and drag the XRAY link to the bookmarks bar

3. If you can't see your bookmarks bar, you may need to switch it on in **Options**, as shown in Figure 12.9.

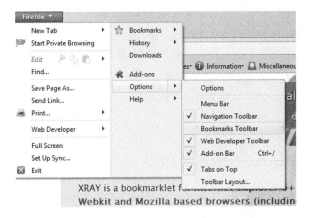

Figure 12.9. Switch on your Bookmarks Toolbar in **Options**

If you're adding XRAY to Internet Explorer, there'll be a warning to say that it may be unsafe (the wording differs depending on which version of IE you're using), as in Figure 12.10. Once again, click on the **Yes** button, as you know it's safe to use.

Figure 12.10. You can click **Yes**—XRAY is safe to use

So, with Firebug, Web Developer Toolbar, and XRAY installed and at the ready, we can now move on to the second part of this chapter. We've covered the prevention stage, now it's on to the cure. And these will be the perfect tools to diagnose all our web page ills.

Inspecting Problems with Firebug

Before I go any further, I will say this about Firebug: it is the veritable Swiss Army knife of web development tools! There's so much it can do, and we'll only be scratching the surface here. So don't be put off if you see a lot of options and think that you need to know what everything does—you don't. As time goes on, you'll learn about other features, but this is a light and gentle introduction.

So, the project site's gone a bit off course (in the code archive it's **website_files/01_FirebugExamples/about.html**). Nothing too catastrophic, but the header part of the page looks a bit wrong. The text in the tagline is too far to the left and no longer italicized, and the padding is all wrong.

Here's what we'll do:

1. Right-click on the tagline text (or **CTRL**-click for Mac users).

2. Choose **Inspect Element**—a new option that's appeared now that Firebug has been installed, as seen in Figure 12.11.

Figure 12.11. **Inspect Element** is a new addition to your right-click menu

3. The Firebug panel will appear at the bottom of the browser. On the left, you should see the markup (HTML) with the element that you inspected highlighted. On the right is any CSS that applies to it. Figure 12.12 shows what it looks like. Take a look around that left pane. Does anything seem odd to you?

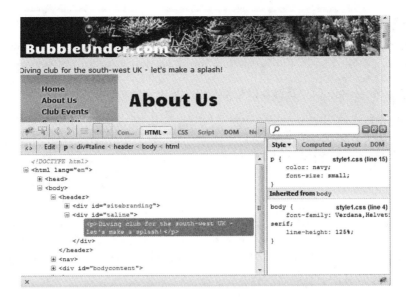

Figure 12.12. Firebug brings the pages' markup into view

4. Take a closer look, just above the highlighted paragraph. See the culprit? It's the class name of "taline." That should be `tagline`. Somehow, old clumsy-fingers here has accidentally deleted a character.

5. With the case of the typo solved, we simply change it in the offending page and save it. Then refresh the browser and the problem goes away. But here's where it becomes interesting. With the Firebug panel still open, you should see that as well as the HTML on the left having changed (to reflect the correct class name), the CSS on the right has also been altered, revealed in Figure 12.13. We can now see the styles that apply to that line, even the stylesheet (**style1.css**) and line number (16). This, in my opinion, is the absolute best feature of Firebug!

Figure 12.13. The HTML and CSS will change in the Firebug window once the problem is fixed

Let's try another example. In the gallery page, we're having some issues that need sorting out. The images have gone a bit awry, there's horizontal scrolling going on, and all sorts of issues … take a look at Figure 12.14. Firebug to the rescue!

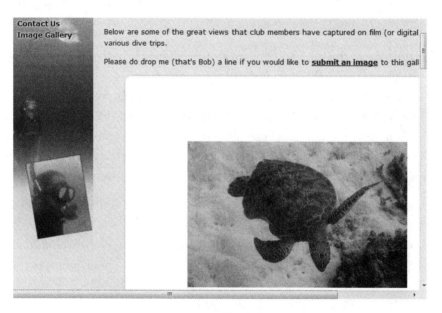

Figure 12.14. The Bubble Under gallery in a pickle

1. Right-click on the image and choose **Inspect Element**.

2. The styles that apply to the image will appear in the right pane of Firebug, as Figure 12.15 shows.

Figure 12.15. Firebug's right pane brings up the page's styles

3. Notice that there is a 115px-wide border being applied. Oops! Surely that should be 15px? Before we go to the stylesheet to make the changes, we can try a few techniques right here on the page to check our suspicions.

4. Click on the value for that piece of CSS and it should become editable. You can now type over the 115px part, changing it to whatever you want, as Figure 12.16 demonstrates. (Click anywhere outside of it once you're done to exit editable mode.)

Figure 12.16. Click on the CSS, and you can edit in the Firebug pane

5. You can also try disabling that style. Did you notice as you hovered over it that a little struck-through circle symbol appeared? Click on that symbol, and the style will be suppressed and grayed out, as in Figure 12.17. You should also see your massive image border disappear—more proof that this is the culprit!

Figure 12.17. Try disabling the style altogether

6. Finally, instead of typing over the whole value, you can adjust the px value by using your arrow keys on the keyboard. To do this, place the cursor so that it's somewhere in the middle of that 115px value, as shown in Figure 12.18. Now press the **up** or **down** arrows on your keypad. You should see the border width increase or decrease smoothly.

Figure 12.18. Changing the pixel value with the arrow key

None of the changes that you make in that CSS pane are permanent; it's just for you to see the effect of changing certain values or settings.

The last tip about using the arrow keys is one I use frequently. Sometimes, when crafting CSS, it can be guesswork what the best value is. So, I put in my best guess, load the page in Firefox and, if it looks wrong, I inspect the element and adjust the value this way. Once it looks good, I make a note of the figure showing in the CSS pane in Firebug; then I go back to my CSS file and use that value.

It really is a joy to gain instant feedback in this way, rather than the rigmarole of "guess a number, save the CSS, refresh the browser, and repeat ad infinitum." You can also edit portions of HTML on the page if you want to quickly see what the effect might be of a really long headline, or text in a navigation item.

For example, let's imagine that we wanted to change the link from "About Us" to "About Bubble Under," and then see how it might look. Here's how it's done:

1. Go to **Inspect Element** (you know how to do this now) on the "About Us" link.

2. Click inside the `<a>`element in the HTML pane so that the text becomes editable, as in Figure 12.19.

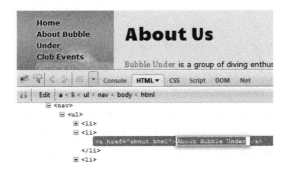

Figure 12.19. Making the `<a>` element editable

3. You can now type whatever you want and see the effect in the page. Once you're done, click anywhere else on the page to exit editable mode.

Instant feedback—it's great! It's a kind of digital playpen for developers where you can try stuff out to your heart's content without breaking anything.

Finally, as a way of becoming more familiar with Firebug, I'm going to let you explore by doing. To do is to learn, and all that, so have a go at this:[11]

1. Inspect any element on the page. Then, in the HTML panel, click on the parent element for the one that you've chosen. See how the right and left panels change.

2. Right-click on the CSS panel for any given CSS selector. Investigate the options that appear, and see how you can make changes.

3. Right-click on any element showing in the HTML panel. Try **Scroll into view**, **Delete element**, or **New attribute**.

Like I said, it's the veritable Swiss Army knife—a tool for everything here. So perhaps we should take a look at another tool we have at hand, the Web Developer Toolbar.

---

[11] What's great about this is that you can try it on any web page—not just this book's project site. You can do no harm at all!

Web Developer Toolbar

Or WDT, for the sake of brevity! As with Firebug, there are many tasks you can accomplish with this tool, but there's a handful that you'll find yourself using again and again. Here are my picks from this excellent tool that I couldn't be without.

Disable CSS

One of the first tests I do on any web page when trying to assess a developer's skill level is disable CSS. (For example, if I'm trying to establish whether a potential employee or contractor builds websites the right way and understands web standards.) If a page is correctly put together and uses CSS alone to control the layout, colors, sizing, and so on, disabling the CSS should reveal a basic version of the page. See Figure 12.20 for where you can disable it.

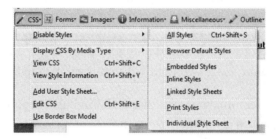

Figure 12.20. The WDT menu for disabling CSS on a web page

And the effect on the project site is as I would expect it to be, in Figure 12.21.

Figure 12.21. BubbleUnder.com sans CSS—looking rather bare

At this point, I'd normally include a screenshot of a high-profile website that still uses tables for layout, demonstrating just how little it changes when CSS is disabled. But it's growing harder and harder to find examples of this—which is good, because it means that people are finally getting with the program!

That said, if you try this **Disable CSS** feature on a few sites that you visit frequently, you're sure to see examples where disabling the styles has little to no effect on the page layout. (And that's bad, because it means CSS was bypassed, tables were used inappropriately, and all the styling is embedded right there on the page.)

This is a WDT feature that I use so often, I never actually use the mouse to select it; instead, I use the keyboard shortcut (**CTRL + Shift + S**, or **CMD + Shift + S** on a Mac), which allows me to quickly disable and re-enable the CSS.

Disable JavaScript

In Chapter 11, we had an introduction to JavaScript and, specifically, using the jQuery library. When you do start playing around with JavaScript in more depth, the **Disable JavaScript** feature will be a great time-saver—seeing how your pages behave with and without JavaScript. Figure 12.22 shows you how to disable JavaScript.

Figure 12.22. WDT lets you disable JavaScript on a web page

Note that with **Disable JavaScript**, you need to switch it on first; then refresh the page to see the effect. So, using the gallery example from Chapter 11, choose **Disable > All JavaScript**. You should see the default view of the gallery captions that we've seen all the way through the book—nobody misses out on any important information.

What often happens, though—and what this feature is great for identifying—is that people write their scripts in a way that means content is hidden by default. If such content is viewed in a browser with JavaScript switched off, whole blocks of useful content may be invisible. A quick check using this tool will reveal this poorly implemented JavaScript.

Outline Elements on the Page

In Firebug, I demonstrated that you can right-click anything on the page and select **Inspect Element**, which can reveal what element you're looking at, be it a `paragraph`, `table`, or `image`. Another way of viewing things is to have all elements of a certain type revealed to you. So, for example, if you wanted to see all the `paragraphs` on a page, you can do this in WDT by choosing **Outline > Outline Custom Elements**, and typing in **p**. Figure 12.23 indicates where you can find this menu feature.

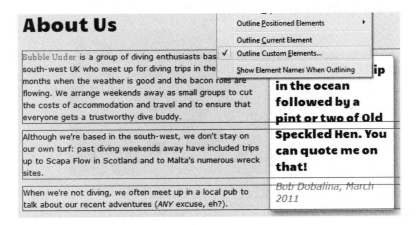

Figure 12.23. Select **Outline Custom Elements**, and type in the element you want

As you went down the options to **Outline Custom Elements**, you may have noticed some predefined choices, particularly for tables. This is because tables should never be used for layout, and this is a handy way of identifying a page that misuses tables this way. Figure 12.24 exposes a site using tables incorrectly, which WDT is able to outline quickly for us.

Figure 12.24. Tables being used for layout—that's a no-no!

Hide Images or Reveal `alt` Attributes

An `alt` attribute is supposed to be an alternative to the `image` element. In most browsers—but not IE—if the `image` is present, you can't see the `alt` attribute. This can lead to maintenance problems, as you might update the `image`, but forget to update the associated `alt` attribute because it's not obvious when you look at the page. By choosing **Images > Display Alt Attributes** in WDT, you can see the `alt` attributes alongside the `image` it relates to, which can really help identify mismatches, as shown in Figure 12.25.

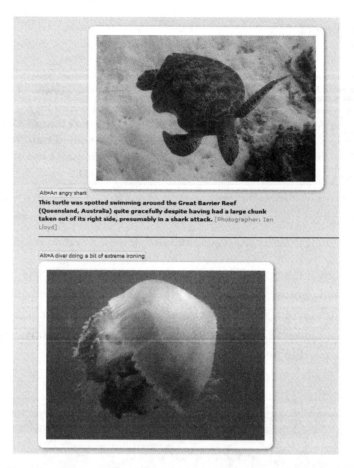

Figure 12.25. These are definitely not the `alt` attributes we want for these images

You can also hide images entirely, find broken images on the page, and—one that I use often—hide background images. This last one is particularly useful when you have text on a background image. If no background color has been set to complement the background image, you can get into trouble, as this tool quickly reveals.

For example, if you have white text over a dark blue background image, but no background color has been set, you're likely to have white text on a white background when images are disabled, making that section illegible. This tool can reveal this type of error very promptly.

Here's another example from the project site. The table headings and cells (`th` and `td`) have a purposely broken (missing) background color, and the table background color has been set to white. The top half of Figure 12.26 shows how it should look, while the bottom half reveals the effect of hiding background images.

Club events/dive trips for the next six months

Date	Event Description	Approximate Cost	Contact
12 July	Committee meeting, deciding on next year's trips	N/A	Bob Dobalina
19 July	7-day trip to Hurghada (package deal) - limited spaces	£260 pp (all inclusive), departing Luton	Bob Dobalina
5 August	Ocean & Sports Diver Theory Course	Call for details	Jeff Edgely
12 August	Murder Mystery Weekend, Cotswolds (no diving!)	£65 pp (accommodation included)	Jill Smith

Club events/dive trips for the next six months

12 July	Committee meeting, deciding on next year's trips	N/A	Bob Dobalina
19 July	7-day trip to Hurghada (package deal) - limited spaces	£260 pp (all inclusive), departing Luton	Bob Dobalina
5 August	Ocean & Sports Diver Theory Course	Call for details	Jeff Edgely
12 August	Murder Mystery Weekend, Cotswolds (no diving!)	£65 pp (accommodation included)	Jill Smith

Figure 12.26. With no background color set, the text in our table headers becomes unreadable

While the information in the table cells is readable, the table header text appears invisible, as it's white on white. WDT promptly revealed this problem in the purposely broken version of the events page (in code archive at **website_files/02_WebDevToolbarExamples/03_NoBackgroundColorSpecified/events.html**).

View Information about CSS and JavaScript

One final feature to mention on WDT is its ability to bring up a report on all the CSS or JavaScript that a page uses. You can do this using the following options:

- **CSS > View CSS**
- **Information > View JavaScript**

You'll then be presented with a new tab that lists all CSS or JavaScript on the page (depending which option you took); you can then expand or collapse the information to make it easier to read and find what you need. It may not be obvious now why you might need it but, trust me, this is a great tool to have on hand when you need to work out why a page is broken. It really saves you time trawling through the page's source code and picking out all the references to CSS and JavaScript.

And So Much More ...

As with Firebug, this tool has loads more to offer. And the best way to learn what it can do is to have a play. Forget the project site for now—go and visit a page that you know quite well and visit frequently, and start to have a poke around using this tool. Some suggestions for you:

- **Information > Display Block Size**
- **Information > View Document Outline** (a good way to check on a news/blog article)
- **Outline > Headings**
- **Resize > Resize the Window**

Oh, the power! Before you just looked at these web pages; now you can really have a good dig around and see exactly how they've been built—and (with a suitably smug look on your face) pick holes in all their little mistakes!

How to use XRAY

The final tool that I'm going to talk you through is the super-simple XRAY. Brought to you by the wonderful people at Westciv—long-standing supporters of web standards and doing things the right way—XRAY lets you quickly analyze any element on a page.

As I said earlier, this one isn't an extension that you install—it's a special kind of bookmark or favorite. Or, to use the parlance, a favelet. And just as you can call up a favorite page, you can summon up XRAY by clicking on this browser favorite. When you do, Figure 12.27 reveals what you'll see on the page.[12]

Figure 12.27. The XRAY start screen

Now just click anywhere on the page. Whichever element you click on will have its information displayed in this floating panel. It may not tell you everything that you need to know (that's where Firebug comes in), but for the purposes of quickly checking some HTML and CSS properties, it's a perfect, quick solution. For example, it will tell you:

---

[12] This is how it looks at the time of writing, but I know that a new version is in the pipeline that will add more features, but should, mostly, appear like this. So don't be too surprised if it looks a little different from the screenshots used here.

- border values
- margin values
- padding values
- height and width
- *x* and *y* coordinates
- whether the element is floated
- how the element is positioned (`static`, `relative`, or `absolute`)

The top of the panel reveals where in the document hierarchy it sits in a **breadcrumb-trail** style—a horizontal progression of elements. You can even use that "breadcrumb" to jump up a level (or several levels at a time) to see where the element is in context. Figure 12.28 shows an `hgroup` element selected, while in Figure 12.29 a parent element (`section`) two levels up is depicted.

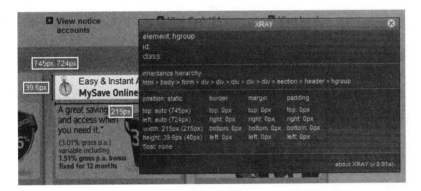

Figure 12.28. The hgroup element is selected

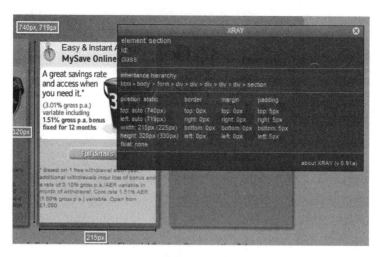

Figure 12.29. Two levels up, a parent element is selected

In addition, XRAY shows margin and padding amounts around the element selected using a color scheme. This may be deliberate (or not), but here's how I remember it:

- Padding = Pink
- Margin = Maroon[13]

Try it out for yourself. One particularly useful aspect of XRAY that I'd like to draw your attention to is where it shows the `top`, `left`, `width`, and `height` values.

Notice that there are two values (one in parentheses). Sometimes the values here differ. Why could that be? The first value is the amount that you've set it to; for example, take this CSS:

```
div.myBox {
  width:100px;
  padding:10px;
  border:2px solid red;
}
```

When clicking on a `div` with this `class` while XRAY is running, you will see the following, as shown in Figure 12.30.

---

[13] Okay, so it's really purple, but it helps me to remember!

Figure 12.30. Two values are shown in the XRAY window

The first value in XRAY says 100px (what was stated for the width property). The value in brackets is the actual width, and calculated as follows:

- 2px for border (left)
- + 10px padding (left)
- + 100px width
- + 10px padding (right)
- + 2px for border (right)
- *= 124px total*

This difference in the two figures can often pinpoint the cause of problems. If the layout is busted, perhaps something is too wide? XRAY might reveal the difference, and you then look to see if the clues are elsewhere in XRAY's floating panel (namely the padding, margin, or border values).

Let's look at a real example based on the project site. In the code archive for this chapter (**website_files/03_XRayExamples/01_BlockquoteWidthWrong**), look at the quote on the right-hand side. There's nothing obviously wrong with it, but if the total width needed to be 300px, it needs to be addressed. By bringing up XRAY and checking the aside element, it's showing the width value as 300px (322px), evident in Figure 12.31.

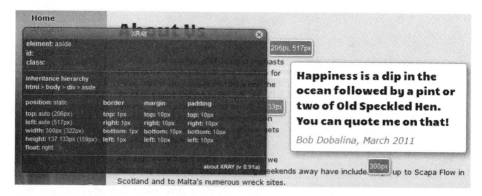

Figure 12.31. Bringing up XRAY will show you the true width of an element

What's happened is that the width has been set on the inner `blockquote` element to 300px. The `aside` element also includes 10px of `padding` either side and 1px of `border` either side, giving a total of 322px. So, because of the parent container's `border` and `padding` values, it's 22 pixels wider than desired. The easy solution is to subtract 22px, giving a value of 278px for the `blockquote`. With that in place, a quick check with XRAY on the parent `aside` element shows the two values of 278px and (300px), as in Figure 12.32.

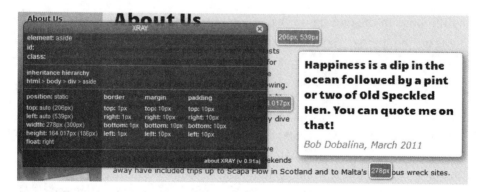

Figure 12.32. A bit of subtraction and the `blockquote` width is corrected

Sometimes XRAY may seem a bit limited, and you're forced to dig a little deeper using Firebug. But as a tool that you can quickly call up to check the most likely causes of problems, it's invaluable.

Summary

In this chapter, we've seen just how useful a handful of free but incredibly powerful tools can be in helping you resolve HTML and CSS issues. By using Firebug, we discovered that there is such a thing as a Swiss Army knife for web development debugging. The Web Developer Toolbar provides a quick way of gleaning all manner of information about a web page, as well as quickly disabling or removing features. Finally, XRAY shows that with just a small amount of information on hand, you can identify the source of problems.

Between the three, you have an excellent tool set to fix all your HTML and CSS woes. The great news is that this is just the tip of the iceberg. There are so many other tools out there that you could try for your browser. As you grow more confident with building your pages—or as you encounter more problems, new and more interesting than those you faced before—you'll find yourself wanting to add more tools to your browser, regardless of whether you're running Firefox, Chrome, Opera, or Safari. Even Internet Explorer users have a few choices to hand—and that's a rare opportunity!

But enough of all this pimping your browser. Let's get back to pimping up your site with all kinds of really useful free stuff.

Chapter 13

Pimp My Site: Cool Stuff You Can Add for Free

Your website looks great, and everything seems to be going tickety-boo. Your work's done, right? Well, no. There's always more to do!

When you first set up your website, you probably had a good idea of the audience you were building it for, and you may well have catered admirably to that audience. But within weeks of launching your site and promoting it to the world (using some of the suggestions I made in Chapter 8), you started receiving emails from strangers asking questions about the site that you hadn't expected:

> "Can you tell me who can service my air regulators in North Devon?"

> "I can't find details of your training courses—do you offer any?"

> "My name is Abdul Akinbobola and I am the son of the recently deposed president of Burkina Faso …"

Okay, so that last message has nothing to do with your website, but trust me, you'll certainly receive emails like this! The point is, no matter what sort of planning you've done, people beyond your expected audience will find your website, and it's likely you'll need to cater to them, too. This is where you should consider some add-ons to your site—extras that will:

- enable you to *discover how people are arriving at your website* (for example, through a Google search, or via another website's link where you've promoted your own site)

- reveal *which search terms people used* to reach your website, and provide some statistics about the most common ones

- let the visitor *search the contents of your website* (rather than click around the navigation in the hope of finding what they need)

- allow the visitor to *search a group of related websites* from the comfort of your website

- provide a way for you to *manage a list of your favorite websites* related to the topic of your own website, and provide them as a links resource for others

- let your visitors become part of your website community by *having a discussion forum*

All these goals can be achieved using free services, and in this chapter, I'm going to provide step-by-step instructions to help you add these services and truly pimp your site![1]

Getting the Low-down on Your Visitors

How can you be absolutely sure that what's on your website is the right content for your audience? Well, the truth is that you can't—everyone's different, after all, and each person's needs are unique. However, you can be given some indication about whether your website is serving the audience's needs through some simple statistics.

---

[1] For those who don't understand the reference, Pimp My Site is my little pun based on the MTV show *Pimp My Ride* [http://www.mtv.com/ontv/dyn/pimp_my_ride/series.jhtml], in which old, neglected cars are renovated (or "pimped") for their owners. That's not to say that your website is old or neglected, though!

Some hosting companies will provide statistics software as part of your package, so be sure to check. If your package includes a statistics service, you might wish to skip this next section, go to the section called "Registering a Google Account" and just use the tools your host has provided. Most free hosting services—and many of the cheaper hosting plans—won't provide statistics for you. And even if your hosts *do* provide such services, they're usually substandard. So it's up to us to ensure we receive the best information that we can.

Choosing a Statistics Service

As with a number of services I've mentioned elsewhere in this book, there are two ways that you could introduce a statistics service to your site:

- You could install and configure a statistics service on the web server that hosts your site. The web server keeps detailed records of every visit to your website: it records the time of the visit, which pages were viewed, which browsers were used, how visitors found the site, and much more. There are many programs you can install on your web server that will produce easy-to-read graphs based on this data. Installing this software is no easy feat, though, and I'd advise against it for beginners.

- Thankfully, the second option is much easier—you can sign up for a third-party solution that collects and stores the data on your behalf. All you're required to do is add a link to an image or script file (hosted by the service provider) into your web pages.

Many third-party statistics services are available, but to narrow it down, I advise you to look for one that offers the following features:

List of referring websites (recent referrers and totals)
This will tell you how your visitors found your website.

Number of visitors
You should be able to view a count of the number of visitors your site receives each day and each month, as well as the total number of visitors who have stopped by since the site launched.

Information about your visitors' computer setups

This will tell you whether your visitors are using PCs or Macs, which browsers they're using, and so on.

Any information beyond this is probably overkill for a small-scale website; too many statistics can muddy the waters, and there's a lot to be said for simplicity. There are a number of free hosted stats services you might want to consider using, including StatCounter,[2] Extreme Tracking,[3] and AddFreeStats.[4] However, for my money, the best solution you could opt for is Google Analytics.[5]

In the past, I used a number of the free services mentioned, but have since switched all of them across to Google Analytics. While the service is free, it doesn't *appear* to be cheap—in short, you're receiving a whole lot more than what you paid for! In addition, it's so easy to set up and then analyze the data that it captures. Let's start by signing up for an account.

Registering a Google Account

Make your way over to http://www.google.com/analytics/. It's a quick process to have Google Analytics up and running. If you already have a Google account—highly probable given the number of services they already offer, notably Gmail (Google Mail)—you can simply log in and sign up for Analytics. For now, though, I'll assume that you're without a Google account, so here's what you do:

1. Click on the **Sign Up Now** link, as shown in Figure 13.1.

---

[2] http://www.statcounter.com/

[3] http://www.extreme-dm.com/tracking/

[4] http://www.addfreestats.com/

[5] http://www.google.com/analytics/

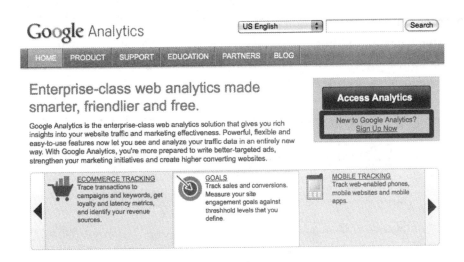

Figure 13.1. Google Analytics home page

2. This will take you to a login screen, as shown in Figure 13.2 (unless you're already logged in to your Google account). If you already have an account, you'd use the login panel on the right, but we're assuming you've never set up a Google Account. Click the **Create an Account Now** link (and yes, this does seem a bit like *déja vu*, doesn't it? Sign up now! Sign up now!).

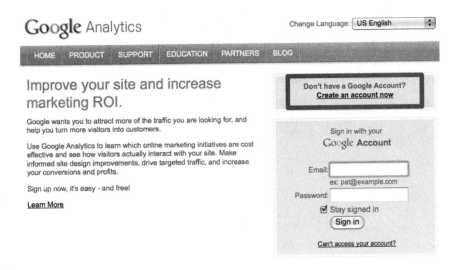

Figure 13.2. Google Analytics login/sign-up page

3. There are just a handful of details to input on this page—seen in Figure 13.3. Enter your email address, pick a sensible password, and attempt to read the almost indecipherable characters in the word verification box (good luck—it usually takes me a few tries!). Press the button that says **I accept. Create my account.**

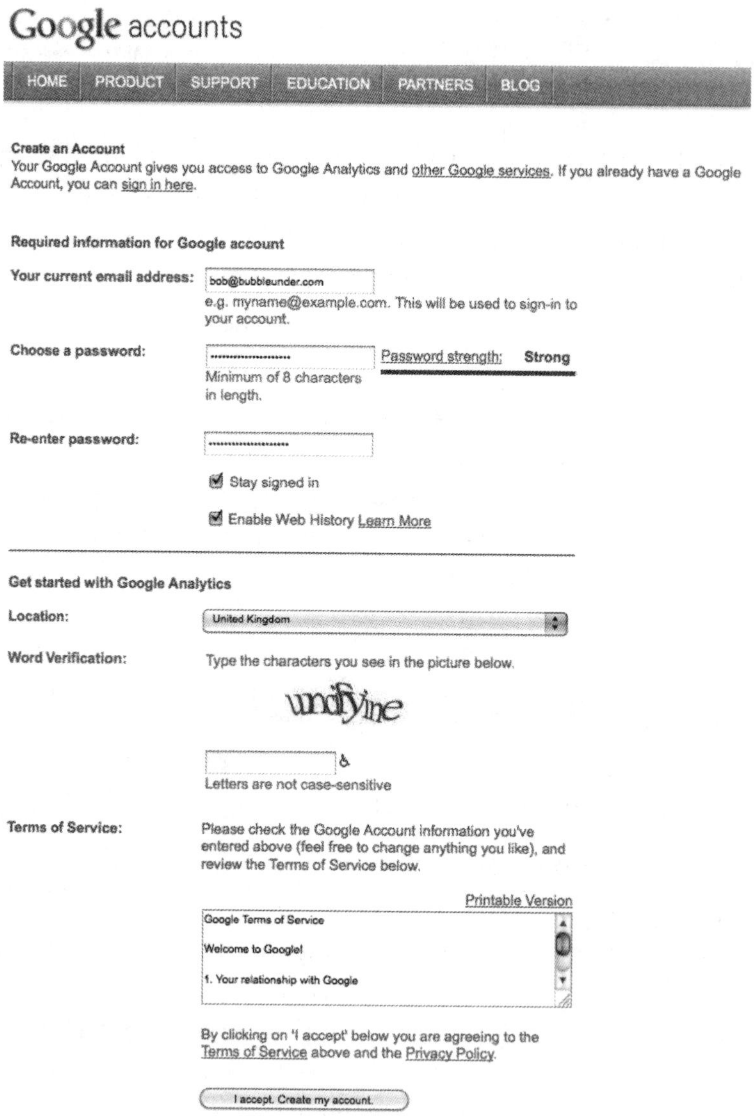

Figure 13.3. Creating the Google Account

4. Having sent the form, Google will ask where to send a verification code—either as a text message to a mobile phone, or a recorded message to a phone number of your choosing. Pick whichever is best for you, and enter the verification code that Google has created in the next page.

5. We're not quite done yet! Just to be absolutely sure, Google will then perform a second verification check by sending you an email. Click on the link in that email, and that's all the verification steps taken care of.

6. You now have a Google account, but you're yet to have a Google Analytics account set up. Log in to your Google account (using the http://www.google.com/analytics/ address from earlier). You'll see some more blurb about Analytics on the next page. Rather than read it all now (plenty of time for that later), head straight to the panel with the button that says **Sign Up**, as shown in Figure 13.4.

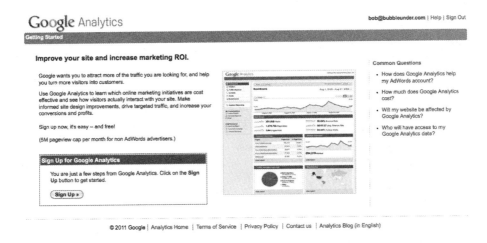

Figure 13.4. Logged in to Google, but still need to register for Analytics

7. There's nothing too taxing here at all, as Figure 13.5 shows. Google just needs to know a few details about your website, where you are in the world (for the time zone), and some personal information. You're also asked to tick a box confirming that you've read the lengthy list of terms and conditions; should you comply, this would probably make you the second person in history after Google's lawyer to *actually* have done this (read it, not tick the box, that is!).

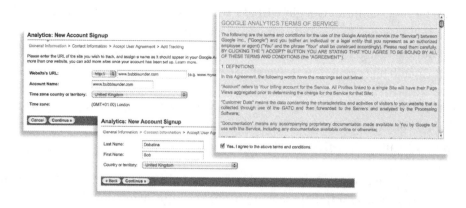

Figure 13.5. Some of the sign-up steps (and a beast of a Terms and Conditions page!)

8. In the final step of signing up, Google presents you with some code to copy and paste into your web pages. There are a few options that you can choose (relating to what you're wanting to track), but as a beginner, I'm going to assume that you're concentrating on your first and only site for now. For that reason, leave the default setting of **A single domain**; then highlight and copy the code provided in the text area on the right, as in Figure 13.6.

Figure 13.6. Copy the code that Google Analytics provides

That's it for the sign-up process. Now all you need to do is put the generated code—just a few lines of it—into your web pages.

Adding the Statistics Code to Your Web Pages

Your statistics code should look like this (though specific details relating to your account will differ, namely the unique ID that is highlighted in bold):

```
<script type="text/javascript">
  var _gaq = _gaq || [];
  _gaq.push(['_setAccount', 'UA-12345678-1']);
  _gaq.push(['_trackPageview']);
  (function() {
    var ga = document.createElement('script'); ga.type =➥
    'text/javascript'; ga.async = true;
    ga.src = ('https:' == document.location.protocol ?➥
    'https://ssl' : 'http://www') + '.google-analytics.➥
    com/ga.js';
    var s = document.getElementsByTagName('script')[0];➥
    s.parentNode.insertBefore(ga, s);
  })();
</script>
```

To start, paste this code in your web page *just before* the closing `</body>` tag. It's good practice to place it here, as it's the last item loaded on your web page; that way, if Google takes a while to send the data requested, it won't hold up your web page loading. Here's how it looks in the context of the About page (which I've truncated to a degree):

website_files/01_statcounter_code/about.html *(excerpt)*

```
    <p>When we're not diving, we often meet up in a local pub to
    talk about our recent adventures (<em>any</em> excuse, eh?).</p>
  </div>
<!-- end of bodycontent div -->
<script type="text/javascript">
  var _gaq = _gaq || [];
  _gaq.push(['_setAccount', 'UA-12345678-1']);
  _gaq.push(['_trackPageview']);
  (function() {
    var ga = document.createElement('script'); ga.type =➥
    'text/javascript'; ga.async = true;
    ga.src = ('https:' == document.location.protocol ?➥
    'https://ssl' : 'http://www') + '.google-analytics.➥
    com/ga.js';
    var s = document.getElementsByTagName('script')[0];➥
```

```
        s.parentNode.insertBefore(ga, s);
  })();
</script>
</body>
</html>
```

That's the About page taken care of, but you'll also need to add the code to the other pages in your website, and save them all.

Once you've added the tracking markup as described above, you'll need to upload the amended pages to your server by FTP (as described in Chapter 8). From now on, every user visit to your website will also place a request to Google's files that you inserted at the end of the page—what Google does is track these requests to build up a picture of your website usage. You can access these reports from the Google Analytics Settings page, shown in Figure 13.7. This is always the first page after logging in, so no hunting around is required!

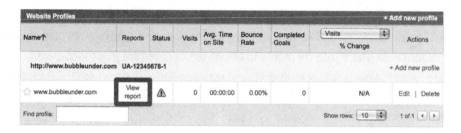

Figure 13.7. Google Analytics Settings page

Because we're using a dummy site in this book with no real users, it's a bit difficult to demonstrate real lifelike stats—so here's the Dashboard page from one of my own websites, Accessify.com, and a few examples. It's been around for quite a while, and has enough traffic to produce some statistics, as Figure 13.8 shows.

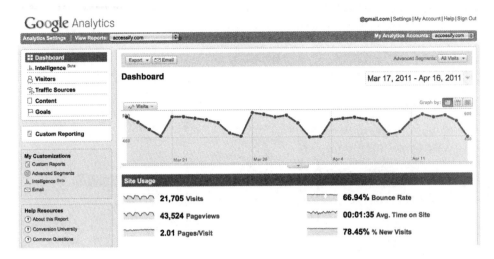

Figure 13.8. The Dashboard—showing an overview of visitor statistics

There are many other useful statistics here—too many to go into in more detail, in fact. My advice is to sign up, apply the statistics code, and upload your amended pages to your web server. Then, simply leave it for a few days—or weeks, even—before logging back in to check the statistics. By that time, you might have enough data to see some patterns forming (unless, of course, you've not told anyone about your site, and no one's linked to the site—in which case the usage statistics will point to just one user: you! New websites can take time).

An example of the range of information Google Analytics can provide is shown in Figure 13.9—a montage of the main site navigation with various features. Google Analytics is the jack-of-all-trades of free statistics, but like the famed knife, you'll barely use 20% of the tools on offer!

Figure 13.9. Examples of the Google Analytics navigation menu options

What to Look for—a Summary

The most illuminating statistics that you'll probably need will be on the front page —aka the Dashboard—and these are:

Visitors: How many people are using the site … and do they stay long?

It's great to know how many visitors your site receives, and see how that changes over time, too. But when they reach the site, do they stick around for long? Or do they just hit the back button on the browser and go elsewhere? The **Visitors** information tells you all of that and more.

Traffic Sources: Through which web pages do visitors arrive at your site?

If another site has linked to your website, and a user follows that link to your site, that information will be recorded in **Traffic Sources**. It's good to be aware of websites that have linked to you (if for no other reason than to give you an ego boost!), and why they've linked to you—it's easy enough to take a look at the *referring site* from these reports. In most cases, your key referrers will be search engines (and you can even find out what phrases people entered that led them to your website).[6]

Content Overview: **What are the most popular pages on the site?**

Are the pages that you want people to look at receiving the most hits? This simple list shows the top five visited pages, and tells you what percentage they account for; clicking through reveals a raft of additional information on each page.

A Search Tool for Your Site

This one's a cinch! We'll have you set up in minutes. And guess what? It's those people at Google that we again have to thank. It could barely be any easier.

Here's the basic markup you'll need to have (so that Google can provide search results based on the content of your website only):

```
<!-- SiteSearch Google -->
<form method="get" action="http://www.google.com/search">
<label for="q">Search:</label>
<input id="q" name="q" size="20" maxlength="255" value=""
    type="text"/>
<input name="domains" value="http://www.bubbleunder.com/"
    type="hidden"/>
<input name="sitesearch" value="http://www.bubbleunder.com/"
    checked="checked" id="mysite" type="radio"/>
<label for="mysite">Just this site</label>
<input name="sitesearch" value="" id="www" type="radio"/>
<label for="www">WWW</label>
<input name="btnG" value="Go" type="submit"/>
</form>
<!-- SiteSearch Google -->
```

All you need to do is change the text in bold to match your website's address.

Here's that same code implementing the Bubble Under website (at least, on a portion of the Events page):

---

[6] Sometimes, website managers talk about "checking their referrer logs." This is what that term means—looking through the lists of sites who have sent traffic to your website, including search engines, and reviewing the search phrases used to find your site.

```
<!DOCTYPE html>
<html lang="en">
<head>
  <title>Forthcoming club diving events and trips with Bubble Under
  </title>
  <meta charset="utf-8"/>
  <!--[if lt IE 9]>
  <script src="http://html5shim.googlecode.com/svn/trunk/html5.js">
  </script>
  <![endif]-->
  <link href="style1.css" rel="stylesheet" type="text/css" />
  <link href='http://fonts.googleapis.com/css?family=Candal'
  rel='stylesheet' type='text/css'>
</head>

<body>
  <header>
    <div id="sitebranding">
      <h1>BubbleUnder.com</h1>
    </div>
    <div id="tagline">
      <p>Diving club for the south-west UK - let's make a splash!
      </p>
    </div>
    <!-- SiteSearch Google -->
    <form method="get" action="http://www.google.com/search">
    <div id="search">
      <label for="q">Search:</label>
      <input id="q" name="q" size="20" maxlength="255" value=""
        type="text" />
      <input name="domains" value="http://www.bubbleunder.com/"
        type="hidden" />
      <input name="sitesearch" value=" http://www.bubbleunder.com/"
        checked="checked" id="mysite" type="radio" />
      <label for="mysite">Just this site</label>
      <input name="sitesearch" value="" id="www" type="radio" />
      <label for="www">WWW</label>
      <input name="btnG" value="Go" type="submit" />
    </div>
    </form>
    <!-- SiteSearch Google -->
  </header>
    ⋮
```

Note that we need to position the search form in an appropriate location, as well as format the text a bit. I've used CSS to achieve this, using absolute positioning to place the search box in the top right-hand corner of the page. To do so, I wrapped a `div` around the form elements and gave it an `id` attribute. That way, I can reference the form in the CSS, as shown below:

```
#search {
  position: absolute;
  top: 77px;
  right: 10px;
  font-size: x-small;
  font-weight: bold;
}
```

Figure 13.10 shows how the search box looks on the page itself.

Figure 13.10. The Bubble Under site with integrated search option (screenshot from Firefox/Mac)

Google Search Limitations

Using Google's service in this way is certainly a breeze, but you should be aware of its limitations:

- Google will only show search results if it *knows* about your website—and it will only know about it if you've submitted your website's address to Google in the past (and Google has indexed it),[7] or Google has found your website by following a link from another site.

- Search results may not be completely up to date. If you make changes to your site, and then upload those changes, Google may take days or even weeks to recognize that a change has been made—it really depends on when the search engine re-indexes your site.

- Search results are unable to be customized. The results page will look like a standard Google-search results page, but the linked search results will all be pages from your website (aside from sponsored links). However, people are familiar with Google, so this has its benefits.

Searching by Genre

If adding a Google search tool has no appeal, you might like to try another service called Rollyo, a *roll-your-own* search engine.[8] Rollyo allows you to create a custom search interface, one that lets you pick and choose which websites you want to search. This helps to ensure that the search results are more focused and closely related to your own website's content.

1. Click on the **Register** link in the top right-hand corner and complete the scant details requested of you by the registration page, shown in Figure 13.11.

---

[7] You can notify Google of your website's existence at http://www.google.com/addurl/.
[8] http://www.rollyo.com/

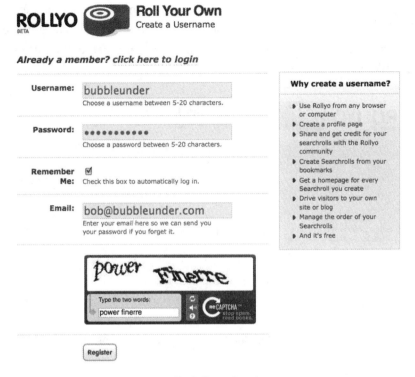

Figure 13.11. The Rollyo registration screen

2. Next, you'll be asked for profile information, and you'll see a big red arrow with the words, **Skip this for now.** You know what to do!

3. On the following page, select the **Create a custom searchroll** link, as illustrated in Figure 13.12.

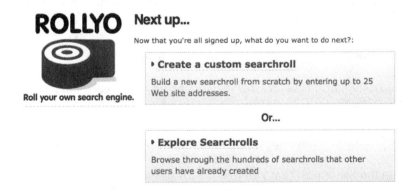

Figure 13.12. Choose **Create a custom searchroll**

4. In the page shown in Figure 13.13, you're asked to provide a name for your *Searchroll*, a list of websites that you want to include, and a category, and then identify any *tags* (keywords that describe your search facility's purpose) that you'd like to assign to your Searchroll.

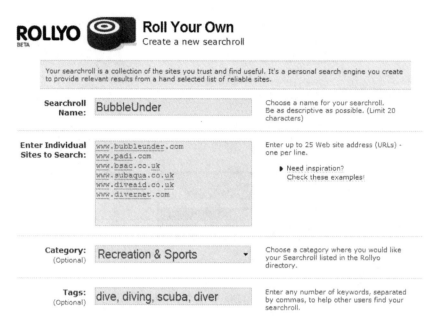

Figure 13.13. Adding sites that you want to search

Once you've saved these changes, Rollyo doesn't make it obvious what to do next. It displays a search box that now has a custom option (a radio button that matches the Searchroll name, in our case Bubble Under). To place a search box on your site that uses *only* the websites that you set up in Rollyo's "Individual Sites to Search," you need to do the following:

1. Click on the **Dashboard** link at the top of the page.

2. On the Dashboard page, look for the section entitled **Searchbox**, which should take you to http://rollyo.com/searchbox.html.

3. Add a title and include the address of the site, as indicated in Figure 13.14.

4. Include the Searchroll that you just set up so that it appears in the column. Do this by selecting its name in the left column, and pressing the >> button.

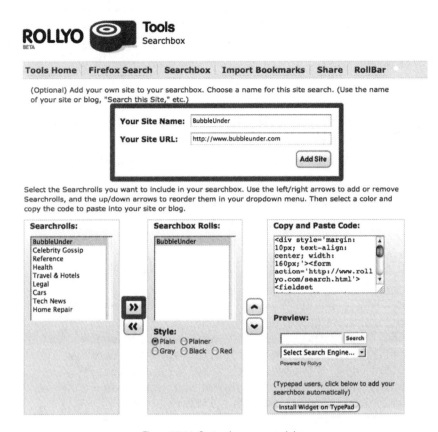

Figure 13.14. Customize your search box

Rollyo will create some HTML for you but ... it's HIDEOUS. It is full of nasty inline styles, so we'll take a slightly different approach. I've stripped this back to the bare minimum on the example site. Here's the markup for the Rollyo search I created for BubbleUnder:

```
<!-- SiteSearch Rollyo -->
  <form id="searchform" name="searchform" action="http://www.➥
    rollyo.com/search.html" method="get">
    <div id="search">
      <input type="text" name="q" value="" id="search-box" /> in
      <select id="searchmenu" name="sid">
        <option value="6170">Bubble Under</option>
        <option value="web">The web</option>
      </select>
      <input type="submit" value="Search" />
```

```
        </div>
      </form>
<!-- SiteSearch Rollyo -->
```

To make this work for you, you'd need to change the `<option>` element highlighted in bold so that it uses the correct value (here shown as 6170) and, of course, the text displayed to the user (here it's "Bubble Under"). Perhaps you're unsure what the value should be. Take a look at the nasty HTML that Rollyo tried to have you use. It's in there somewhere—just a case of sifting it out. Here's what Rollyo produced (and the lack of line breaks and spaces is exactly as it was when copied from the site) with the important value highlighted for you:

```
<div style='margin: 10px; text-align: center; width: 160px;'>
  <form action='http://www.rollyo.com/search.html'>
    <fieldset id='searchboxset' style='margin: 0 0 10px 0➥
      !important; padding: 4px 0 0 !important; height:➥
      62px; width: 160px; border: none;'>
      <input type='text' size='30' style='background:➥
      #fff; font-family: helvetica, arial, sans-serif;➥
      color: #000; font-weight: normal; float: left;➥
      width: 108px; height: 14px; margin: 3px 0 4px 0px➥
      !important; font-size: 13px !important;➥
      vertical-align: middle;' name='q' value="" />
      <input type='image' src='http://rollyo.com/remote/➥
      btn-togo-search-ph2.png' alt='Go' style='margin:➥
      2px 0 0 3px !important; float: left; border: none;➥
      ' /> <br />
      <select id='rolls' name='sid' style='float: left;➥
      width: 158px; margin: 0 0 2px 0 !important;➥
      font-size: 12px;'>
        <option value='698660' selected='selected'>Select
          Search Engine...</option>
        <option value='698660'>BubbleUnder</option>
        <option value='web'>Search
          The Web</option>
      </select>
      <input type='hidden' name='togo-v' value='1' />
      <div id='about' style='font-family: Arial, Helvetica,➥
        sans-serif; font-size: 9px;'>
        <div style='float: left;'>Powered by <a href='http:➥
          //www.rollyo.com/' style='color: #C00;'>Rollyo</a>
        </div>
      </div>
```

```
    </fieldset>
  </form>
</div>
```

Comparing the HTML that I recommended and what Rollyo produced, I hope you can see which is the neater option!

Figure 13.15 shows how the search interface displays on the web page. (I placed everything inside the form in the absolutely positioned `div`—in the same position as the Google search box in the earlier example.)

Figure 13.15. Adding a Rollyo search to the Bubble Under website (screenshot from Firefox/Mac)

Because the Rollyo search results are syndicated from Yahoo, the next step is to submit your site to Yahoo for indexing[9] if you're yet to do so. As with most search engines, it may take days or weeks before Yahoo visits your site and adds your pages to its database. Your Rollyo searchroll will still work during this time; it just won't include your site in the results it displays.

Finally, Figure 13.16 depicts the search results displayed on the Rollyo website.

---

[9] http://search.yahoo.com/info/submit.html

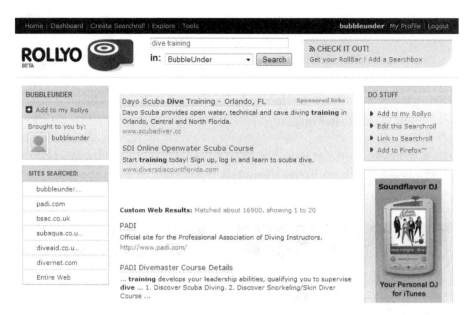

Figure 13.16. Displaying the search results on Rollyo

This is a novel way of adding search functionality to your site—but it's one that could potentially send people in another direction! However, if your website is more of a fun venture, than focused on making cold hard cash, this could be the ethical way to go. Believe me when I say it'll be good for your karma—you'll see!

Enhancing Search Further with jQuery

In Chapter 11, we showed how you could make enhancements to the site using some simple jQuery code. If you cast your mind back, I suggested placing the code in a common JavaScript file (in **js/common.js**), but admitted at the time that such code was uncommon. If you remember that, you might also recall that I promised it would be used site-wide in this chapter. It's only a slight amendment, but I'm going to add in one extra line to the form helper tip code that we set up for the Contact page, and it looks like this (shown in bold):

```
$("#contactname").val("Please enter full name");
 $("#telephone").val("Incl local dialling code");
 $("#eventdate").val("Format DDMMYYYY");
 $("#details").val("The more you can enter here, the less we have
   to check with you :)");
```

```
$("#q, #search-box").val("Enter search phrase");
 $("input, textarea").focus(function(){
  $(this).select();
});
```

With this additional line, we can set up the same effect for the search box. Note that it has two ids in the selector, one for an element with the id of q, and another with an id of search-box. I did this so that it covers whichever search solution you opted for—Google or Rollyo. The result can be seen in Figure 13.17.

Figure 13.17. Add a little guidance to your search field with jQuery

Because we set it up so that all pages refer to **common.js**, every page in the site will apply the effect—not just the Contact page. You can see the example in the code archive at **chapter13/website_files/04_rollyo_search_jquery/**.

Caution: Contents May Have Shifted in Transit

Rollyo was new at the time of writing the first edition of this book. Some five years later, when I was putting this third edition together, it still appeared to have had only the *tiniest* of changes. It was also still showing as a **beta** version, a software term used to denote a work-in-progress, although these days, it's used more as a liability waver! Like a volcano that's lay dormant for a while, my gut feeling is that it may be overdue for a change or two. Or perhaps everything's working so well, it will be kept as is for another couple of years. Who knows! So please bear in mind that it might change after this edition goes to print, and if that transpires, you may need to adapt some of the steps.

Discussion Forums

Arguably, one of the best ways to create a virtual community around your website —and to ensure that people come back time and time again—is to provide a chat forum. There is one small problem, though—forums aren't particularly straightforward to set up. Furthermore, once you start to have regular posts appearing, you'll face the issue of moderating the forum's content. Will you moderate it yourself? Will you just let the forum discussions take their own course?[10] Will you empower regular visitors to moderate the forums?

Most of the fully featured (and free) forum software products that you could use have some prerequisites that basically rule out my covering them in this book. For example, many packages require your hosting company to support PHP (a scripting language) and make a MySQL database available to you. At this stage, you probably find these quite foreign concepts.

In previous editions of this book, I've suggested using Yahoo Groups. For this edition, I was thinking of recommending Google Groups but, in the end, decided to skip both routes. In fact, I'm just going to say this: Facebook. Love it or hate it, most people you know will be on Facebook, and while the features that Facebook offers for discussion may be limited (compared to the more complex forum software), they are intuitive. People know how to use Facebook, so why make life difficult for yourself and others? It does mean that the solution isn't integrated into your site—you're using Facebook entirely for this—but you can still link to the Facebook Group from your own site (or even embed it using an `iframe`, but that may look a little ugly). All you need to do is **Create Group** in Facebook and then give it a name, as in Figure 13.18.

Figure 13.18. Using Facebook to create a community around your site

---

[10] The short answer to that is: no! If you give people the freedom to run wild, they may well do just that—which could even place you in hot water, legally speaking. For example, a forum member could slander another user on your forum, or link to copyrighted material for others to download, and you as the website owner could be responsible for those people's actions. Moderation is a *great* idea.

Be sure to set the **Privacy** option to **Open**, as in Figure 13.19, unless you actually want to create a closed group only available to certain members.

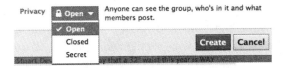

Figure 13.19. Select the **Open** option in the **Privacy** menu

You'll need to add some names to kick-start the process, and these people will receive invites to join, which they can accept or decline. Additional people can request to join the group at any time and you, as the administrator, have the power to approve or deny a request to join. You could also promote other people to the position of administrator, which can help to reduce the workload later.

Aside from managing who is in the group and what their respective administration rights are, the rest of it will be second nature for anyone who has ever posted a comment, link, photo, or video on Facebook.

Summary

In this chapter, I've shown that no matter how much work you put into building a website, there's always more you can do. I've focused on some add-ons that, I believe, really do improve a website and encourage you—as well as others visiting the site—to use it more. However, I would like to sound one note of warning at this point, and it is this:

Know when to stop!

There are many websites still kicking around today that were built in the mid-to-late nineties, when the motto seemed to be: the more flashing/spinning/bouncing widgets on the page, the better the website. Thankfully, as the art of web design has matured, people have come to realize that *less is more*. Please bear this in mind when adding features. Otherwise, before you know it, the bells and whistles will have taken over completely!

Avoid Being Too Reliant on Third-party Services

There's another reason not to go overboard adding third-party features to your website. If that third party's web server is slow for some reason, and your web page is trying to access that provider's server, your web page may appear to load slowly. In addition, you need to be careful about *putting all your eggs in one basket*. If the service you use is free, be prepared that one day the owners may decide to close the service down, or charge for it. Would your website be able to function properly if this happened?

At this point, your website should have all the features that it needs. If you've followed the advice I've given in this book, you'll have a well-formed, standards-based website that you can be proud of. If you've enjoyed designing and building your web pages, you might want to improve your skills even further. Instead of me leaving you to fend for yourself at this point, I'm going to make some suggestions about where you can acquire the skills you need; frankly, there are an awful lot of bad websites and books out there, and you could easily pick one up by mistake. I'd hate for you to undo any of the good work you've done so far! So, let's continue on to the final chapter, in which we'll explore the possibilities that now lie before you.

Chapter **14**

Where to Now? What You Could Learn Next

In the course of this book, I've given you a foundation for building websites that will set you in good stead for many years to come. The methods described here are not workarounds—they don't try to use HTML or CSS to cobble together effects never intended to be created using these technologies. The techniques we've used are based on well-established standards to which any new web browsers should conform. In short, by following the advice of this book, rather than another beginner's manual that could teach you numerous bad practices, you now have a good base from which to further develop your skills.[1]

But what exactly can you do from this point forward? What are your options for developing your skills even more, without erring from the path of high-quality,

---

[1] Actually, you can afford to smile at this point. Although some of the concepts in this book are, on the face of it, quite simple—for example, using CSS to control the page layout—a large number of people out there would consider them advanced. That's because those people have learned the old (wrong) methods, and rewiring their brains to another way of thinking can be demanding. You won't need to do that, though!

standards-based web design? These questions will direct what this short chapter is about—it's a road map to ensure that you learn from the best material out there.

Throughout writing this book, in every chapter, I had to know at what point I needed to rein things in.

- Had I said enough about a topic?

- Did I gloss over some fine details?

- Were those fine details important to know as a beginner, or would they perhaps confuse the reader?

This was always an issue, and I hope the parts I did choose to leave out were the right ones. These would invariably be more advanced techniques, or extra information about why tasks are done in a certain way that I felt were unnecessary to include. But, in the back of my mind, I knew that there was this final chapter in which I could fill in some of the blanks and provide further pointers.

I'm going to break the various options into five areas:

1. HTML—looking beyond the basics
2. CSS—discovering just how far your designs can go with some clever CSS
3. JavaScript—adding further interactivity to your website
4. High performance pages—moving beyond mere practitioner to the status of "front-end engineer"
5. Programming—opening up the possibilities with scripting languages and databases

Let's start with our web page building blocks: HTML.

Improving Your HTML

First, let's have another pat-yourself-on-the-back moment. You've already grabbed a head start by learning HTML (specifically, HTML5) with the more fussy XHTML syntax. As a result, you've been putting into practice such techniques as:

- declaring a doctype at the beginning of the document (an essential aspect of HTML)
- ensuring that all attributes are quoted properly (for example, `<div id="sitebranding">`)

- writing your markup entirely in lowercase
- closing all tags correctly (for example, `<p>This is a paragraph</p>`)—and that includes empty elements (for example, `<input type="input" name="q" value="" id="search-box"/>`)

You've learned some of these techniques by copying, though perhaps you haven't always understood *why* some aspects of HTML are achieved this way. To use the car analogy once again, when you first learn to drive, you know almost nothing about why you have to perform certain actions, but you follow the instructor's advice nonetheless. After you've been driving for a while, you stop thinking about *why* you do it a certain way; you just do it and know that's how it should be done. For some people, though, driving the car well isn't enough—they want to know how their car works, and understand how the engine, wheels, gearbox, and electrical system all fit together. If they can understand that, maybe they can make the car drive more smoothly (or faster), and look better—they can really make it their own. And this is the point we're at with HTML: now's the time to find out more about the nuts and bolts of what you've learned to date.

It's worth pointing out that you can be less strict when writing HTML5 markup than we've been in this book (for example, not worrying about what case the tags are written in, omitting quotes from attributes, and so on), and it's still valid. I chose XHTML syntax for this book because I believe it encourages better practices for the long term. Although I mentioned this at the start, it's prudent to remind you of the differences between HTML and XHTML again,[2] particularly as you now have a greater understanding than you did when you began!

The Official Documentation

Perhaps that heading should read *Recommendations*, which is what the World Wide Web Consortium (W3C) likes to call them. If our website was a car, the W3C recommendations would be the car's technical service manuals, complete with all the electrical wiring diagrams. In short, the recommendations don't make for light reading! However, in the search to truly understand how and why HTML works the way it does, you can't find a more complete or technically accurate documents than the W3C's.

---

[2] http://reference.sitepoint.com/html/html-vs-xhtml/

Because HTML5 is still a work in progress, you need to be aware that the document is subject to change. For this reason, I'm including links to the older (but stable) HTML 4.01 spec, as well as HTML5:

- HTML 4.01: http://www.w3.org/TR/html401/
- HTML5: http://www.w3.org/TR/html5/

If you do decide to attack the nuts and bolts of all things HTML by reading the W3C documentation, please note that with some elements in HTML 4.01 their purpose was redefined in HTML5 (for example, the b and i elements). So if it seems like you're receiving conflicting statements, the definition used in the later version is the one that you should go with, every time.

 Making W3C Specs a Little More Understandable

Because your first read of a W3C document will likely be a less-than-fun event (I'm being diplomatic here), it might be an idea to take a look at J. David Eisenberg's article "How to Read W3C Specs."[3] This author does a great job of explaining some of the terminology and structures that you'll encounter on the many and varied W3C documents. It won't make reading the documentation as enjoyable as, say, an adventure novel, but you will at least be able to glean the information you need with less head-scratching.

Other Useful HTML Resources

If the official documentation is simply too much for you to take on board right now, park it for the time being—you can always go back when you come across a problem, or want clarification on a specific issue. There are other sources of information that you'll probably find a lot easier to take in, some of which I've listed below.

The Ultimate HTML Reference

Perhaps it should come as no surprise that I mention this one first—the complete HTML reference that I wrote after writing the first edition of *this* book. It fills in many of the gaps present in this book.

The Ultimate HTML Reference is available as a hardback book from SitePoint (see http://www.sitepoint.com/books/htmlref1/). If you're unsure about buying the

---

[3] http://www.alistapart.com/articles/readspec/

complete reference just yet, you can still check your facts online. You may already have been, actually; many of the references to HTML elements in this book point to the online reference—known as the SitePoint HTML Reference and found at http://reference.sitepoint.com/html/ (and shown in Figure 14.1).

Figure 14.1. The SitePoint HTML Reference with the entry for "table"

HTML Dog

While slightly older than SitePoint's *The Ultimate HTML Reference*, Patrick Griffiths' site, HTML Dog (http://www.htmldog.com/guides/) offers a great way to further your skills. The site breaks HTML[4] and CSS into three levels: Beginner, Intermediate, and Advanced. The sections are short enough to learn in small bursts, and clearly marked examples illustrate each topic.

With the knowledge you've gained from reading this book, you can probably skip the Beginner and Intermediate sections; head straight to the Advanced information http://www.htmldog.com/guides/htmladvanced/, where you can learn a new set of HTML elements that we didn't cover in the earlier chapters.

HTML Dog doesn't include the newer HTML5 elements, but that's no major issue thanks to …

---

[4] Patrick refers to HTML, but all the examples shown are XHTML-compliant.

HTML5 Doctor

Moving on from HTML-teaching dogs, we're on to HTML5-specialist doctors. Okay, so they're not real doctors, but you can trust the team of people at HTML5 Doctor (http://html5doctor.com/) to deal with your HTML5-related ailments. The article archive is probably the best place to start, and each article is written in a more friendly and accessible way than any W3C document could ever manage.

A List Apart

A List Apart (ALA) is an old favorite among the web design community. Instead of teaching in modules (like the websites mentioned previously), it takes more of a magazine-like approach. Each feature is written as a complete piece that either tackles a known problem or explains a creative idea to inspire others.

The website sorts its various articles (of which there are many) into categories; look for *HTML and XHTML* at http://alistapart.com/topics/code/htmlxhtml/. You'll find links to a number of useful articles on this page. Some of the material will cross over into other technologies that you may not fully understand at this point (some of the articles focus on cutting-edge techniques), but you will almost certainly find inspiration from the articles on *A List Apart*.

HTML5 & CSS3 For The Real World

Of course, it would be remiss of me not to mention SitePoint's very own handy tome of all things HTML5 (not to mention CSS3), *HTML5 & CSS3 for the Real World* (http://www.sitepoint.com/books/htmlcss1/), released in May this year. It's a comprehensive look at where web technologies are right now, as well as where they're heading—semantic tags, form markup, a new approach to embedding audio and video on your site, as well as some nifty niche stuff like Microdata.

Advancing Your CSS Knowledge

At this point, I think I'm obliged by web design convention to blurt out the following web address for CSS Zen Garden: http://csszengarden.com/.

More than anything, this website demonstrates what CSS can do when it's placed in the right hands. I had intended to structure this section so that the official documentation was referred to first, followed by other examples. But like the many thousands who've tried to promote greater use of CSS on websites, I can't help but turn to this site first.

Canadian web designer Dave Shea created CSS Zen Garden back in 2003, because he felt at the time that the examples of CSS-based designs in existence were less than encouraging—they were boxy, boring, and generally unsexy. In short, the people who understood the CSS language were technical people first, and designers second (or even third or fourth). Dave approached CSS primarily as a designer; being a coder was secondary. He launched CSS Zen Garden with a handful of his own designs—all of them more inspiring than contemporary offerings—then encouraged others to contribute designs based on the same document. Many years later, the site's archives contain literally hundreds of designs that prove that when you separate the presentation of a document from its structural foundation, you have a very powerful tool at your disposal. Figure 14.2 shows just a few examples of designs from CSS Zen Garden. Dave Shea's first version—which kicked it all off—appears top left.

Figure 14.2. A selection of styles from CSS Zen Garden

What's key here is that all these designs use *the same underlying document*. All that changes between each design is the linked stylesheet, which refers to a different set of typographic styles, color palettes, and background images.

The CSS Zen Garden was intended to provide inspiration, and it does its job well! Despite being over eight years old—and the fact that it uses no HTML5 elements —it's still a very persuasive website for adopting CSS. If you see a design on the site that you like and want to look more closely under the hood to learn how it was done, just click on the link that reads **View This Design's CSS**.

The Official Documentation

We're back on track again with the official information. If you've looked at some of the work submitted to CSS Zen Garden, you might have spotted some fairly advanced CSS that you're eager to understand. As with HTML, no source of information is more complete than that maintained by the W3C in its Cascading Style Sheets (CSS) Specification, at http://www.w3.org/TR/CSS21/.[5]

As with the HTML document I mentioned earlier, the W3C CSS Specification is another highly detailed piece of documentation that's an involved read. It's very useful as a reference for those moments when you come unstuck with CSS, but where could you go for some information that's a little easier on the old brain-box? You know where this is going, don't you?

The Ultimate CSS Reference

Just as SitePoint offers a complete HTML reference for your reading pleasure, it also offers a complete—I'm sorry, I mean *Ultimate—CSS Reference*. This is also available as a hardback book from SitePoint—see http://www.sitepoint.com/books/cssref1/—so you can keep it open as you work to check anything that's bugging you.

It's also available as an online reference—known as the SitePoint CSS Reference and found at http://reference.sitepoint.com/css/—as shown in Figure 14.3. You can use the thoughtfully organized navigation menus, or type some text into the search field and see what it finds for you.

---

[5] This link refers to CSS level 2, revision 1. There are different versions of the CSS recommendations, as there are versions of other W3C documents. At the time of writing, the CSS2.1 documentation was labeled a *Candidate Recommendation*, which translates as "almost 100% approved." In other words, it's safe to use these as your benchmark.

Figure 14.3. The SitePoint CSS Reference

HTML Dog

HTML Dog also has a CSS section, found at http://www.htmldog.com/guides/. You'll know some of the CSS tricks in the intermediate tutorial, but it contains other useful tips that you should pick up before moving on to the advanced section.

CSS3.info

If you want to get up to speed on some of the newer (dare I say, sexier?) CSS3 effects that browsers are adding support for all the time, you should take a look at CSS3.info (http://www.css3.info/). It has examples of all the new CSS3 properties—such as `border-radius`, `text-shadow`, and `box-shadow`—as well as some more complex properties not covered in Chapter 10. These include RGBA background colors (which allow you to set opacity on colors), multiple background images, media queries, and multicolumn layouts. All very exciting stuff, and clearly demonstrated in a way that's easy to understand. Check out the CSS3 Preview section for a full list (http://www.css3.info/preview/).

CSS Discussion Lists

You can learn a great deal from website tutorials like those I've mentioned, but what happens if you have a question about a specific issue? In previous chapters, I've suggested that you raise issues on SitePoint's CSS forum.[6] If you explain that you're a newbie, you should find that forum members will make a real effort to assist you, providing clear instructions to help solve your problem. You'll probably find that this forum (along with the other SitePoint forums) has so many experts ready to respond to your questions, that it's likely that there's no need for you to venture much further afield for help.

There are other discussion lists that you could join if you want to further your CSS skills. The two that I'd recommend are:

- CSS-Discuss at http://www.css-discuss.org/
- Web Design-L at http://webdesign-l.com/

These lists tend to go more heavily into the nitty-gritty of CSS issues, and uninitiated observers can, at times, feel as if they've gate-crashed a rocket scientists' convention. These people really do know their stuff, but they don't always go easy on beginners. So my advice is:

1. Register first; then observe the discussions for a while, and see what goes on before contributing.

2. When you decide to ask a question, be sure to prefix it with "I'm a newbie."

3. When replying to comments, take care with your quoting style. The preferred style (which most email programs don't do for you automatically, unfortunately) is to use top-down quoting.[7]

 Discussion Lists versus Forums

Just what is the difference between a discussion list and a forum? A discussion list is a group that operates via email; subscribers receive either separate emails for each post made by a group member, or a digest of the communications on a daily, weekly, or monthly basis. A forum, on the other hand, is a web-based service. That is, you use a web browser to log in to the forum; then you pick and choose from the categories to read whichever posts take your fancy.

---

[6] http://www.sitepoint.com/launch/cssforum/
[7] Matt Haughey offers excellent advice in "How to Write Effective Mailing List Email" [http://www.digital-web.com/articles/how_to_write_effective_mailing_list_email], a piece written for *Digital Web Magazine*. Look for point two: Top Down Formatting.

Which is better? Well, that depends on the way you like to learn. Some people prefer discussion lists because they can store the emails they receive, searching through archived messages to find specific solutions as the need arises. Others prefer to dip into forums as they please, and avoid having their inboxes clogged up with messages.

My best advice is to try out a discussion list and see how it goes. If you find the amount of messages you receive too overwhelming, you could try sorting the mail into dedicated folders (check your mail client for rules that let you divert mail based on certain criteria). If that doesn't work out, you could try a digest, or even unsubscribe altogether. But you'll only find out whether discussion lists suit you if you give them a try, so be sure to do so!

The CSS Discuss List's Companion Site

The CSS Discuss list has a companion **wiki**—a page that can be edited or updated by anyone—that features an archive of best practices discovered in various email discussions. Members of the mailing list frequently update the content displayed here. The information is not as ordered as in the other sites mentioned in this chapter (namely SitePoint and HTML Dog), but it will make sense once you've had a little more exposure to intermediate and advanced CSS. On the wiki's front page, at http://css-discuss.incutio.com, you'll find links to explanations of a number of good practices, and tips for improving your CSS to expert level.

I recommend you take a closer look at these sections:

Sizing Text > Font Size	great advice on how to size fonts consistently across a range of browsers
CSS Layouts	methodologies and examples of various CSS layout techniques—such as two- and three-column layouts—and techniques to position footers that always align correctly
Switching > Style Switching	all the information and links you need in order to incorporate a *style switcher* into your website (so that you can have more than one stylesheet from which users can choose, according to their specific needs)

If you make websites like these your regular haunts, you'll be well on your way to becoming a CSS guru. Perhaps I'll be reading one of your books on the topic one day?

Learning JavaScript

The next logical step after you learn HTML and CSS is to take on a client-side scripting language, which really boils down to learning JavaScript.[8]

In Chapter 11, I demonstrated how you could use the jQuery library to achieve some impressive effects with a minimum of fuss. It's a quick way to do stuff, but if you reach straight for jQuery without understanding the underlying fundamentals of JavaScript, you'll never truly become an expert in JavaScript. If jQuery piqued your interest, I'd suggest a crash course in basic JavaScript.

Unusually, I'm going to recommend that you *don't* refer to any official documentation on this language because, frankly, I don't think it's the best way to learn JavaScript (it's the best way to be scared off, though!). I quite like the modular, step-by-step approach that W3Schools takes in teaching JavaScript, at its Learn JavaScript page[9]. I wish that I'd been able to learn in such a nice way when I began to tinker with this language!

With JavaScript, the possibilities are limited only by your imagination. If you find yourself thinking, "I'd like that part of the web page to be movable," or, "I want to be able to hide this part of the web page at the click of a button," JavaScript will let you do it.

Compared with HTML and CSS, though, JavaScript is quite complicated. This is partly because JavaScript is very unforgiving when it comes to typing errors—one missing semicolon, and your whole script may break—and partly because no one can anticipate what tasks you're going to ask JavaScript to perform on your site. Hence, teaching it can never be as focused or strictly defined as other topics.

To my mind, the budding JavaScripter would be best to do the following:

---

[8] It is possible to run a similar language called VBScript, but it's not widely supported as a client-side language, and I can't recommend it for use on a website as some browsers do not provide built-in support for it. I mention it here so that you are, at least, aware of its existence.

[9] http://www.w3schools.com/js/js_intro.asp

- Run through the W3Schools tutorial, and be sure to try out all the examples for a feel of what the language can do.

- Think about a practical use for JavaScript on your own website (having run through the tutorial, you should have a sense of how you might utilize this technology). Then, try putting it into action.

- Trawl through SitePoint's extensive back catalog of JavaScript-related articles.[10]

- Be sure to ask any questions you have about JavaScript at SitePoint's dedicated JavaScript forum.[11]

- Naturally, SitePoint has a great book for you: Kevin Yank and Cameron Adams have compiled everything you need for learning JavaScript from scratch in *Simply JavaScript*.[12]

Becoming a jQuery Guru

With the fundamentals of JavaScript under your belt, it's time to take another look at jQuery. You'll be amazed at how much easier writing good jQuery code will be with this understanding of JavaScript now firmly in place.

But where can you learn from? Thankfully, there are numerous jQuery resources that you can refer to. The official documentation can be found at jQuerys website at http://docs.jquery.com/, but it will present the same kind of challenges that the W3C's CSS and HTML documents do to beginners. Namely, it can be a bit daunting initially. There are numerous resources for jQuery now, being as popular as it is on the Web, but I really like the video walk-throughs that Remy Sharp does on his website jQuery for Designers (http://jqueryfordesigners.com/).

If you prefer to sit down with a good book (and I'm guessing you're quite comfortable with that approach!), SitePoint have a great jQuery book called *jQuery: Novice to Ninja* (http://www.sitepoint.com/books/jquery1/). As the title suggests, it's perfect for JavaScript beginners like your good self.

---

[10] All SitePoint's JavaScript articles are listed at http://www.sitepoint.com/subcat/javascript.

[11] http://www.sitepoint.com/launch/javascriptforum/

[12] http://www.sitepoint.com/books/javascript1/

Improving Website Performance

With all the HTML, CSS, and JavaScript that you've picked up, there's another area that you can learn which really brings it all together; if you can come to grips with it, it will elevate you from mere web developer to front-end engineer. Sounds impressive, right? If you like the idea of calling yourself that, you'll need to get stuck into the details.

Improving website performance is about the following topics:

- making sure content is delivered to the client's computer as quickly as possible

- using the best techniques for displaying images (correct choice of image types, better use of caching)

- configuring the server (assuming you have that level of access) for best results

- creating the perception of speedier pages by making content render quickly on the screen, even if there's still content remaining to be downloaded

Steve Souders wrote two books on the topic of website optimization (for which I'm very thankful), but you can read the bulk of the rules for free on the Yahoo Developer Network article "Best Practices for Speeding Up Your Website."[13] Some of the rules you'll already be following from reading this book (for example, placing scripts at the end of the web page), while others will be new and (I hope) intriguing.

I strongly recommend that you look at the use of CSS sprites, which are in the section called Minimize HTTP Requests, if nothing else.[14]

Learning Server-side Programming

The final part of this road map to becoming an all-round web designer and developer involves server-side programming (or server-side scripting). While JavaScript is downloaded to the client computer and executed there, server-side scripts are executed on the server before the resulting web page is sent to the client. We use these types of scripting in different ways but, generally, you can assume the following:

---

[13] http://developer.yahoo.com/performance/rules.html
[14] http://developer.yahoo.com/performance/rules.html#num_http

- JavaScript is best used to change the display or behavior of elements on the screen in front of you. Depending on what the script does, even if you disconnected your internet connection, the JavaScript may quite happily continue to function, as it's running locally on your computer within a page that's already downloaded to your hard drive.

- Server-side programming is best used to retrieve or update information stored in a database, and to generate a web page based on that information. With server-side programming, a site user's action might be intended to change a record in your database. Thus, a server-side language is essential for tasks such as checking stock levels on an ecommerce site, and adjusting them if an order is placed. JavaScript alone could not achieve this.

Of course, you could use both; for example, a dynamically generated web page based on certain search criteria. A search on an ecommerce website—such as Amazon—that displayed a selection of toasters would use server-side scripting to build the search results page, which would be sent for display on the client computer. JavaScript could then be used on the client computer to manipulate that web page in some way, perhaps allowing the user to drag and drop items into a shopping cart.[15]

In fact, the lines between client-side and server-side scripting are being increasingly blurred, thanks largely to **Ajax**. No, it's not a cleaning product (well, not here), but a fancy buzzword for a collection of techniques that make use of the aforementioned scripting to create dynamic changes to the page. Using Ajax, it's possible to let JavaScript manipulate sections on a page and ask the server to process small parts of code; then update the page without forcing a complete page reload. It's difficult to explain, so at this point I usually refer to Google Maps. It may not surprise you to know that when you load Google Maps, it doesn't load all of the country's maps in one go! It loads the content for the current window and some surrounding areas; then, as you click and drag on the map, JavaScript sends a request to the server to fetch the next parts of the map before you need them. It updates the page without you realizing, so it's unnecessary to reload the whole page. That's a great example of Ajax in action right there.

---

[15] There's a great example of this kind of drag-and-drop behavior on Panic's website [http://www.panic.com/].

Scripting Languages in Brief

Your options for server-side programming are many. All the languages below could be used to create dynamic web pages and retrieve information from databases:

- PHP
- ASP/ASP.NET
- ColdFusion
- Perl
- Python
- Ruby/Ruby on Rails

There are many more in addition to this short list, believe me! Which one's right for you, though? This is where we start to veer into dangerous territory! The proponents of each language will swear blind that their language is the best tool for the job. In reality, each has its pros and cons, and some do a better job in certain circumstances than others. I can't list the strengths and weaknesses of all of them here—it would take far too long, and only confuse matters at this stage.

My advice would be to find out which languages your hosting company supports. That will refine your options quite quickly—there's little point in learning a scripting language only to find out that it won't work with your current hosting provider. If you're unsure which way to go next, you can always post questions to SitePoint's Program Your Site forum.[16] Explain your requirements and your level of expertise, and you can expect to receive sound advice on which language is best suited to your needs, and why.

Learning PHP

Of those languages listed above, I would recommend that you make PHP your first server-side language, because it's:

- intuitive and fairly easy to learn
- highly configurable and flexible
- a great companion language for MySQL (a free, full-featured database software)
- very widely supported by hosting providers (cheap PHP hosting is easy to find)

---

[16] Actually, http://www.sitepoint.com/launch/programsiteforum/ is a collection of SitePoint's subforums that deal with specific languages—it's your best starting point for this kind of query.

■ portable—PHP can be run on Windows, Mac OS, and Linux, so if you switch platforms it won't be an issue (unlike ASP/ASP.NET)

Where Can You Learn PHP?

It's beyond the scope of this book for me to teach you how to create a site in PHP—or any other language, for that matter—but there are many books that do exactly that. Once again, SitePoint has covered this for you: Kevin Yank, an acknowledged PHP expert, is the author of *Build Your Own Database Driven Website Using PHP & MySQL.*[17] If you want to build on the knowledge you've gained in this book to create dynamic websites, Kevin's book is the next logical step.

If, having done some research, you decide to build your site using Microsoft's .NET Framework,[18] SitePoint can help you with this, too: *Build Your Own ASP.NET 3.5 Website Using C# & VB.NET,*[19] by Cristian Darie and Wyatt Barnett, will tell you how to build a dynamic website using this technology.

Summary

In this chapter, I've provided some pointers as to how you can take your web skills to the next level. I've suggested resources that will help you refine your HTML and CSS skills to perfection, highlighted JavaScript as a very practical addition to your virtual toolbox, and promoted scripting languages as a means to creating killer websites. However, the path you choose from this point on is entirely up to you. All I hope is that you've enjoyed the steps you've taken to reach this point, and that I've set you up well for the journey ahead. Happy coding!

---

[17] http://www.sitepoint.com/books/phpmysql1/
[18] http://en.wikipedia.org/wiki/.NET
[19] http://www.sitepoint.com/books/aspnet3/

Index

Symbols

& (ampersand)
   entity for, 42
   preceding entities, 41
<> (angle brackets), enclosing tags, 26
© (copyright), entity for, 42
{} (curly braces), 79
! (exclamation point), preceding doctype,
   25
!— (exclamation point, double dashes),
   preceding comments, 39
> (greater than), entity for, 42
< (less than), entity for, 42
(number sign), preceding contextual
   selectors, 101–102
. (period), preceding class selectors, 111
£ (pound), entity for, 42
/* */ (slash asterisk), enclosing comments in CSS, 81
™ (trademark), entity for, 42

A

a (anchor) element, 49, 64–68, 106
   (*see also* links)
A List Apart (ALA), 488
absolute positioning, 151–161, 162–164
accessibility, 178–181, 223, 228–231,
   240–241, 361
actions, jQuery, 418
active state of links, 107
AddFreeStats, 460
Adobe Fireworks, 11
Adobe Photoshop, 10, 203

Adobe Photoshop Express, 15
ALA (A List Apart), 488
&amp entity, 42
ampersand (&)
   entity for, 42
   preceding entities, 41
angle brackets (<>), enclosing tags, 26
API (Application Programming Interface), 332
article element, 382–383
aside element, 379–380
attribute selectors, 408
attributes of an element, 26, 27

B

b (bold) element, 99
background images, 207–217
   multiple, 408
   nonrepeating, 211
   repeated, 207–210
   for table cells, 237
background property (shorthand), 212
background-color property, 90, 94, 208
background-image property, 207–211
background-position property, 211
background-repeat property, 208–210
bandwidth, 337, 345
"Best Practices for Speeding Up Your
   Website", 496
block-level elements, 120–122
   borders for, 130–137
   display as, 273, 375
   nesting, 124
   sizing, 126–130

504

Hey ...

Thanks for buying this book. We really appreciate your support!

We'd like to think that you're now a "Friend of SitePoint," and so would like to invite you to our special "Friends of SitePoint" page.

Here you can SAVE up to 43% on a range of other super-cool SitePoint products.

Save over 40% with this link:

Link: 🌐 sitepoint.com/friends

Password: friends